Christianity's Unknown Gospel

Paul G. Bretscher

Requests for information should be addressed to the publisher:
Dove Group, Inc.
P.O. Box 1035
Valparaiso, IN 46384-1035

Scripture quotations are from the Revised Standard Version, copyright © 1952, 1957, 1972, but freely modified by the author.

ISBN 0-9705149-0-5

Bretscher, Paul G.
Christianity's Unknown Gospel / Paul G. Bretscher

1. Religion—Christianity

Printed in the United States of America

10   9   8   7   6   5   4   3   2   1

Christianity's Unknown Gospel

Paul G. Bretscher

OTHER BOOKS BY PAUL G. BRETSCHER

Christianity's Unknown Gospel

TABLE OF CONTENTS

PART ONE
▉ Believing the Gospel

PART FOUR

Deciphering the Conflict

PART SIX
▪ Choosing Life

PART SEVEN

Raising the Dead

Foreword

"Christianity's unknown gospel," *as message*, is "the gospel from God" (Mark 1:11), which Jesus heard from the scriptures, believed firmly, proclaimed faithfully, lived out obediently, and died for willingly in the hope of the resurrection. "Christianity's Unknown Gospel," *as book*, is the only work of our time which searches out the gospel Jesus actually proclaimed and why hearts are warmed by it. It is the only work which sees his gospel as prior to and distinct from Christianity's humanly conceived and formulated doctrines.

If you desire to know the gospel of the kingdom of God as Jesus knew it, this book is for you. If you see how church dogma has created conflict and division, and you have a heart for peace and unity, this book is for you. If you are not able to believe what has been imposed on you, because it does not make sense, this book is for you. If you sense that Christianity must be missing something it once had, this book is for you. If you are outside Christianity, and you are feeling an inner emptiness that is not being filled, this book is for you.

You will discover how early Christianity went astray, and why, and thus have more patience and hope for it. You will see why, if the original gospel had prevailed unobscured, Christianity would not have separated from Judaism *or* from Mohammed. You will learn to distinguish between the revelation from above and the humanly conceived convictions which Christianity shares with many ancient religions. You will find yourself engaging in hard and fruitful thinking on a new frontier. Insights gained from this book will enable the church to explore the rest of the New Testament in depths that have not been known.

I graduated from the seminary in 1963, committed to preaching the promises of God. As I subsequently indoctrinated church members in catechetical instruction, I assumed that the gospel and the doctrines of the church were the same. Gradually, I began to sense an incongruity. I began to notice how our doctrines gave my church body a sense of superiority, separated it from others, created controversy within and obscured the gospel I was proclaiming.

Very early I encountered Paul Bretscher's writings, which I found fresh, imaginative and insightful in their focus on the gospel. In 1995, Paul informed me that he had completed his life-long project of writing a book on Jesus and the four Gospels. I read the manuscript and began an exchange with Paul, which has continued ever since. It has led me out of bondage into the freedom of the sons of God.

Reading this book was like drinking from a fire hydrant. I learned to take it a sip at a time. Through perseverance, my thirst was quenched by the living water of life. Like the fragments of memory preserved in the Gospels but originally proclaimed orally, this book is written compactly — no words wasted. It is not for speed-reading. The amount and range of insightful discoveries are enormous. Be prepared to ponder frequently and at length over some new treasure. Be prepared also for earth-shaking and church-shaking discoveries.

This book, though it has a natural order, does not have to be read in sequence. Reading the prefaces to its seven parts first will give you a helpful overview. The Glossary, by simply defining terms, conveys the impact of the book and highlights the gospel's conflict within Christianity's dogma.

The beginning chapters describe a process that is new to the church and biblical scholarship. This calls for much thinking, but it can be done. The actual history begins with John the Baptist in Chapter 7. Part Six tells the drama which culminates in Jesus' passion. Meanwhile, any text can be sought in the index.

I cannot describe how earth-shaking this book was for me — how excited I was by insights which struck me not only as fresh, but authentic. Brought up in the tradition of biblical authority, it was shaking to detect "weeds" which the biblical record did not recognize as such or sort out from the wheat. Yet once I saw this, the wheat of the covenant-gospel stood out in sharp contrast.

Brought up with a literalistic understanding of the scriptures, it was a major breakthrough for me to discover that many stories, which make little or no sense for preaching when taken literally, were actually intended as metaphor. Now they make sense, revealing not only the gospel but the history which gave rise to the good news!

The discovery that the name "son of God" was spoken to Jesus in his baptism in the same sense as to Israel in Egypt, then also to me in my baptism, gave me an honor I had not known! I now see Jesus as one with us in every way, one who can be known and followed.

The discovery that our heavenly Father is merciful and forgiving by self-definition, that he does not need or require an atoning sacrifice to appease his wrath, enabled me to focus on Jesus' own life and temptations, rather than on dogmas about him. Now I can walk his way of righteousness in the obedience of faith with joy and peace in response to his call, "Follow me."

In the midst of such excitement, I also experienced fear as to how this would affect my vocation as a pastor in my church body. I was concerned about disturbing the peace of my congregation. It troubled me that some would think their saving faith was being undermined.

As I heard and proclaimed the glad tidings ever more clearly, however, my fears gradually faded. When conflict did erupt around me in 1998, I possessed a peace which was beyond my understanding.

You too may be caught between excitement over your discovery of the covenant-gospel, and fear of its implications and possible consequences as well. But press on. Any shaking you experience is necessary and will not be wasted. This passage from bondage to freedom has taken years for me. It goes on still. Be assured that God's promise will not fail you along the way. One in particular has sustained me: "'For the mountains shall depart and the hills be removed, but my steadfast love will not depart from you, and *my covenant of peace* shall not be removed,' says the LORD, who has compassion on you" (Isaiah 54:10).

This "covenant of peace" is Christianity's unknown gospel. It need not remain unknown.

Theodore N. Strelow
Gibsonville, North Carolina

Prologue

This book is impossible, yet it happened. Can it be that Christianity for ages has not known its own gospel? Not even known that it does not know? Yes. Crowds who heard Jesus believed him spontaneously. His gospel satisfied their hunger and thirst for righteousness, healed them, set them free. When he pictured it as light, good seed, leaven, pearl, children's bread, they knew what he meant. Christianity does not know. Its supposed gospel consists in doctrines *about* Jesus, which it must forever explain, justify, and enforce.

That is the issue of this book. It began by a prayer of its preacher-author to hear from his text a word of God that could mean something to his people. At once the voice that named Jesus "my beloved son" at his baptism spoke this name equally to him! Thrilled to hear this, he preached it eagerly that Sunday (Epiphany 1957) and ever after. "My beloved son" or "son of God" proved to be covenant-language from Moses and the prophets. Parallel terms are chosen, saints, my people, my sheep, also Johwah as Father or Shepherd. The Lord's Prayer responds in trusting oneness. So does the Shepherd Psalm.

A need for identity and self-worth characterizes all human self-awareness. When this is not secure as purely given, it must be pursued by competitive strategies of sight and reason, desire and fear, self-assertion and self-defense. Its image is of a snake, which cannot walk straight and upright but only slither in the dirt.

Jesus' gospel, symbolized by a descending dove, confers self-worth and dignity, hope and purpose as pure gift from the very beginning, on any who simply hear it. It begets a free and noble uprightness that honors diverse gifts and callings without partiality, repressing none. All who know God and themselves by this covenant-name walk side by side in mutual thanksgiving, hope and love. Each is given a unique place and opportunity of servanthood in relation to every other. Each has gifts and energy to invest day by day, trusting tomorrow and life itself to the Giver-Creator-Father.

Covenant-sonship was the heritage and calling of Israel as God's people. Yet Judeans in Jesus' day had long been seduced by a weed-illusion—that being named God's chosen implied a favoritism on his part, ranking them above other peoples, a special worth which they must show and maintain by laws, however.

Christianity fell victim very early to another weed. Scholars of Greek culture, not knowing covenant-sonship, took "son of God" for Jesus in their sacred documents to mean incarnate-deity. Miracle stories seemed to confirm it. From this they crafted a theologic *about* Jesus. He was God-incarnate, second person of a Trinity, his death God's atoning sacrifice for the sin of the world, his resurrection the bodily proof of it all. To believe this for salvation requires the humility of not thinking, not asking, yet constantly repenting.

Jesus pictured his sonship-gospel as a narrow gate through a blocking wall, leading into a new life. To enter the kingdom by it required leaving every fallacious baggage behind. What will Christians do when they hear this? Some, relieved of that burden, will enter freely. Some will peek in, recoil in horror, slam the gate shut, attack the messenger. Some, seeing their (mistaken) "faith" undermined, will be distressed, unable to even think it. Some, who gave up on Christianity long ago, will not care. Some will indeed care.

The narrow gate opens into a scenery unknown. It reveals how the Gospels were formed independently and early from written fragments of a literacy once oral. Every preserved testimony derived from the climate of Jesus' own gospel and will make sense by it. Parables and miracle stories tell history by way of memorizable metaphor, a common device in oral literacy. Direct memories across all four Gospels show in detail how Jesus' death came about, even how his illicit burial in a holy tomb was reversed that sabbath night by guards instructed to rebury him in the cursed valley of Hinnom (his descent into hell). This set the scene for his and the gospel's resurrection on the third day, revealing him as the only son of the Father, full of grace and truth, who actually chose to put himself between. Titles like Christ, Lord, and Savior take meaning from the event itself, likewise the witness of the apostles to his glory.

The transfiguration announces the supreme verdict, "This is my son, my chosen. Listen to him." Listen to the gospel Jesus believed, taught and embodied. By his love and obedience to the finish, the living God and Father cut off the failed old and started his covenant-people over new. The birth narratives invoke prophetic metaphor to celebrate this and to gather the nations.

Jesus' unknown gospel is the good seed. Christianity has nothing to fear from its sowing.

PART ONE

Believing the Gospel

Revelation

The "gospel" of this book "is not man's gospel," I must say with Paul. Gal 1:11 I did not get it from human philosophy and scholarship any more than he did; neither did I invent it. It is not the doctrinal system I learned at the seminary. It came as by a *revelation.*

A subliminal impression from childhood may have readied the soil. We six children, I the second, were born, baptized, and brought up in the split of Christianity called Western, sub-split Lutheran, sub-sub Missouri Synod. Our father taught at Concordia Teachers College, River Forest, Illinois. Our pastor, O.A. Geiseman, was a seminary classmate and close friend of his. On a wall of our church, Grace Lutheran, a motto was painted as on a broad ribbon scrolled at the ends. On the left it said, "Our aim, save souls," on the right "Our means, the gospel." In the middle it pictured an open Bible. When I was ten, Grace moved into a splendid stone church, but that vision remained fixed. "No one can understand the Bible rightly except by faith in the gospel," Pastor Geiseman would say in confirmation class, and I believed him.

Still, a time of wondering gripped me early. *What does "the gospel" say? How does it "save souls"? Why would anyone "believe" it?* In my teens, a haunting dismay struck me hard: *"If the earliest Christians had known Jesus as little as I know him, there never would have been any church!"* I told nobody, but the thought never left. I see it now as a prayer. I looked to the seminary for an answer, but found at best a blur. When I became a pastor, I preached mostly on texts from the Gospels, searching to know and tell my people "the gospel."

In 1957, my ninth year as pastor of Redeemer Lutheran Church in New Orleans, Epiphany (January 6) fell on a Sunday. I would preach on Jesus' baptism. Mt 3:13-17 I knew the text from childhood, also from my own Bible reading. But my sermon was getting nowhere. So I cried to God, as I often did, "Lord, if this text has no more to say to me than I am seeing now, I don't want to preach it!" An answer broke in. Somehow I heard the voice-from-heaven say *to me* what it said to Jesus: "Paul! Paul! *You* are my beloved son; with *you* I am well pleased!" It was astounding! I could never have inferred this by scholarship or dreamed it out of my own psyche!

This was not the deity-understanding of "my beloved son," however, which I had been taught from childhood. That Christianity mistook the name "son of God" for Jesus to mean deity is understandable. The words *sound* that way. I recall explaining dramatically in a sermon, "The son of a cat is a cat, the son of a dog is a dog, the son of a man is a man, and the Son of God is God!" Let "humble child-like faith" simply *believe* this mystery—no need to understand it!

"Jesus is God," we children agreed piously. "He didn't have to *believe*, he just *knew*!" "Jesus is God, I am only human." "Jesus didn't really have to be baptized, he only did it for us." Every picture-book of Jesus signaled his deity in some way. Every miracle story confirmed it.

Yet now I was hearing this sonship-word for *me myself*. "Paul! *You* are my beloved son!" I walked into the church, trembling. "Wow! Wow!" Never was I more eager to preach, to tell my people, "Put *your* name there! Hear God from heaven say to *you* on earth, '*You* are my beloved son (person-language, pre-gender), with whom I am well pleased!' You don't have to make a name for yourself, or compare yourself with anybody, or prove anything about yourself, or live in fear of put-down or judgment. You have your name and honor from God, in full from the beginning, no less than Jesus himself did! Nobody can take it from you! Just build on it!"

That *revealed-gospel* is the founding principle of this book. All else flows from it.

"*You Are My Beloved Son*"

CHAPTER ONE

■ "My Beloved Son"

"This is my beloved son, with whom I am well pleased."
                                                    Matthew 3:17

I began to know Jesus as his own generation once knew him. He must have heard that revelatory declaration, "my beloved son" and "well pleased," with a thrilled "Wow!" quite like my own! He must have *believed* it for himself just as I *believed* it for myself! He must have told it afterward of himself, just as I need to tell it here of myself! Who else than he could have pictured "the heavens opened," and how "he saw the Spirit descending like a dove and alighting on him"? Everything Jesus taught and did made sense now by this sonship-word—his praying, his temptations, his love and faithfulness even to death.

An early capsule of his preaching reads, "Repent, and believe the gospel." Mk 1:14-15 What *gospel?* It had to be of a *sonship*, intended by God for all his people. "Repent" means "turn from" any falsified "believing." The common folk did so! "They were astonished at his teaching, for he taught them as one who had authority and *not like the scribes*." "They heard him gladly." Mk 1:22; 12:37 The authorities of the temple did not "turn," however. They resisted Jesus' sonship-gospel, called it "blasphemy," sought to silence it by condemning him to death. Yet it revived in his resurrection, raised up the young church, and broke through to the nations.

By that *gospel* I began to understand *believing,* too. I had *believed* the word I heard, joyfully and spontaneously, without even thinking about my *believing!* I had not needed explanations as to *how* this word to me was true and why I *ought to* believe it. It had not occurred to me to *analyze, argue, pray,* make a *decision,* or *examine myself* to be sure that I believed rightly and sincerely, and not like a hypocrite. I had "believed" that voice-from-heaven word simply by what it *said*. That's what "believing" is and has to be! Genuine glad news works its own believing and joy—like a report that says "benign," or news of a grandchild safely born. "I cannot by my own understanding or effort believe in Jesus Christ my Lord or come to him, but the Holy Spirit has called me by the gospel," I had memorized from Luther. That was it! The *sonship-word* I had heard was the Holy Spirit's glad-news *gospel*.

It also opened the scriptures to me! I began to notice what I would otherwise have lightly passed by—like the formative experience Jeremiah recalled in a time of stress. "Your words were found and I ate them," he said, "and your words became to me a joy and the delight of my heart; for *I am called by your name*, O LORD, God of hosts." Jer 15:16 The *revelation* had come to him by "words." "Called by your name" suggests that the words he "found" personalized for him the kind of "name" Jesus had heard from God at his baptism, and I with him. "Jeremiah! *You* are my beloved son!" the LORD had told him. Whatever their specific form, the words Jeremiah heard fed the secret hunger of his heart. "I *ate* them!" he pictured his believing. The words were a "joy and delight" to him. They made him a servant, a prophet of God to his people.

I understood Jeremiah! I could answer as he did, "*Your words* were found and I ate them," and "your words became a joy and the delight *of my heart*." I had been looking self-consciously *inward*—concerned about my name, my worth, my achievements or failures, my desires and my fears, my believing, what people might think of me, what God might think of me, what I might think of me. Those "words" from heaven turned my awareness *outward* to the speaker who named me "my beloved son," who was "well pleased" with me before I *did* anything! The view opened large. I saw my "self" now as though from outside of me, in a way I had never imagined. I was not, did not have to be, my own creator, my own justifier, my own savior. The Father, who made me, valued me as his beloved child! I belonged to him and he to me. He even took the initiative to tell me so! No longer fearful and stifled, but breathing freely, I wanted nothing more of life than to belong to him and serve him.

The Heart

I wondered next about my "heart." Thinking about the sonship-word I heard and my reaction to it, I came to realize how it had pierced straight through every outward layer of me. It had not addressed my behaviors and achievements (as with compliments or criticisms). It had not spoken to my bodily life (as with food or medicine). It had not challenged my intellect (as with evidence or argument). It had not imposed itself on my will (as with commandments or prohibitions). It had not addressed my feelings or emotions (as with pleasure or pain). It had simply made me aware of my God-given nobility and freedom as a human person, prior to anything I did, in a way I could never have known. I had heard and believed this definition of me spontaneously in my inmost, personal selfhood! This was my "heart"!

But it had not stopped there! Like a stone fallen into a quiet pond, that word of honor, "my beloved son," had rippled out into the whole of me. It had created an *emotion* of thrill, then a *will* to get up from my desk, then a *mind* to consider in wonder what I could now preach, then a *body* that trembled as I walked into the church, then a *voice* that exclaimed "Wow!"

The biblical understanding of "heart" intrigued me powerfully now. The heart as a pump to circulate blood was discovered in our era of science by William Harvey (1578-1657). People were aware of it ages earlier, however. A beating at the bosom-center of the body, pulsing to neck, head, and limbs, signaled life. The cessation of that beat signaled death. This "heart" was perceived not physiologically, but as the controlling center of human personhood. "Man looks on the outward appearance, but the LORD looks on the heart." 1 Sam 16:7 "Create in me a clean heart," David prayed. Ps 51:10

The naming that delighted my heart had broken through to a self-awareness which I now perceive as common to every person ever born, regardless of diversities. It distinguishes humans from animals. I observed symptoms of it in my children—a hunger to be right, significant, noticed, approved, have meaning, escape judgment. Jesus knew this hunger and how his gospel could feed it. "Blessed are those who hunger and thirst for righteousness, for they shall be satisfied," he said. Mt 5:6

If this hunger of heart is not satisfied by his gospel, it must be fed in some other way. The burden falls then on each individual. Self-awareness turned inward is self-consciousness, a sense of being under judgment. The heart-hunger for worth and to escape judgment becomes a driving force. Its devices are assertion and aggression, its defenses deception and accusation. The heart seeks satisfaction in visible status, good looks, rankings in comparison with others, achievements, recognition, applause—also, lies and cover-up. The effect, whether success or failure, ripples out from the heart through the entire person—emotions, will, mind, body, and behavior.

Here is a psyche uniquely biblical. "The heart is deceitful above all things, and desperately corrupt; who can know it?" Jer 17:9 "Out of the heart proceed evil thoughts, murder, adultery, fornication, theft, false witness, blasphemy," Jesus said. Mt 15:19 "He knew what was in man," a perceptive memoir of John testifies. Jn 2:25

I could identify further with Jesus and his history. The word of sonship he heard from heaven conferred on him an integrity of selfhood which nothing could diminish or negate—not slander, not cross, not death. I could appreciate the testings he endured. To know Jesus in this way required me to "repent" and give up the supposition I had been taught—that he *had no* such hunger, that his heart did not *need* to be fed by that voice-from-heaven word. As for the authorities who opposed Jesus, I saw that they too were driven by a hunger —not to know the truth, but to preserve a rightness and superiority they had inherited or self-consciously achieved.

Covenant Roots

My heart-knowledge engaged my mind further. The gospel of sonship had spoken to me from a text. Mt 3:17 I inferred that the voice Jesus heard at his baptism must have been rooted in a text he knew. The church of his generation must have known what it was and what it meant.

A quest for Jesus' text occupied me in the early 1960s, when I was teaching Life of Christ and other courses at Valparaiso University.[1] Most commentators linked "my beloved son" and the spirit to a saying from Isaiah quoted in Matthew: "Behold, my servant whom I uphold, my chosen, in whom my soul delights; I have put my spirit upon him." Is 42:1; Mt 12:18 I sensed, however, as others did too, that Isaiah must have said this by reference to some prior word. A related verse from Hosea, quoted in Matthew, was likewise perceived to have had an earlier root: "When Israel was a child *I loved him*, and out of Egypt I called *my son*." Hos 11:1; Mt 2:15 Some called attention to a Psalm verse, which found its way into an early manuscript of Luke: "You are my son, this day have I begotten you." Ps 2:7; Lk 3:22 This seemed even further removed

---

[1] This inquiry was the subject of my dissertation for the degree of Master of Sacred Theology, granted by Concordia Seminary, St. Louis, in 1964. A digest of my findings was published in Journal of Biblical Literature LXXXVII 1968 III:301-311 under the title "Exod 4:22-23 and the Voice from Heaven." "Beloved" occurs in the old testament scriptures as a paraphrase for "first-born," Ps 60:5; Jer 11:15; 12:17; similarly Rom 11:28. "Only" is a variation in Zech 12:10; Gen 22:2. Yet the designation "first-born" for Israel recurs in Ps 89:27; Jer 31:9. Paul remembers Jesus as God's "first-born" in Rom 8:29; Col 1:15,18. John has him as God's "only" son, Jn 1:14,18; 3:16. Luke twice supplants "beloved" with "chosen," Lk 9:35; 23:35. Except for "only," these names carried over also into the church: "beloved," Rom 1:7; Jas 1:16; "first-born," Heb 12:12; "chosen" or "elect," Rom 8:33; Eph 1:4; Col 3:12; 1 Pet 2:9.

from the baptismal word, however. A striking verbal parallel, "your son, your only son, whom you love," had Abraham as Isaac's father, not God. Gen 22:2,16

My Bible reading drew me to a version of Moses' call, patched into the record of his return from the wilderness to Egypt. The LORD commanded him: "You shall say to Pharaoh, 'Thus says the LORD, Israel is *my first-born son*, and I say to you, Let *my son* go that he may serve me; if you refuse to let him go, I will *slay your first-born son.*'" Ex 4:22-23 The key clause was, "Israel is my first-born son." I laid out the Hebrew of this against seven occurrences in Greek — three from the baptism narrative and four from the transfiguration. One proved to be structurally a perfect match. Reproduced word-for-word in English the texts read:

Exodus 4:22 "my son   my first-born   Israel (is)"
2 Peter 1:17 "my son   my beloved   this is"

Here was the root I had been seeking. The voice that said, "My son, my beloved, this is," conferred on Jesus a covenant-name God had spoken on his people when he brought them out of Egypt! "Beloved" proved to be simply a variation of "first-born." Hos 11:1 This was covenant-language! Jesus must have heard it so! In that case, it cannot have meant "deity"!

The clause, "with whom I am well pleased," is likewise covenant-language. "If the Lord delights in us, he will bring us into this land," Joshua pleaded. Num 14:8 "He delivered me because he delighted in me," David marveled. 2 Sam 22:20; Ps 18:19 "He committed himself to the Lord; let him deliver him, let him rescue him now, if he desires him," mockers taunted. Ps 22:8; Mt 27:43 Thus also the text from Isaiah, "Behold, *my servant* whom I uphold, *my chosen, in whom my soul delights.*" Is 42:1 "On earth peace among men *with whom he is well pleased,*" angels sang. Lk 2:14

The term "covenant" depicts the revelatory declaration from God to his people. It draws them as honest and humble *receivers* to himself as *Giver*. The circle of this relationship is closed by a spontaneous "Yes" of joyful participation. This "faith" is not forced but free. It transforms lives from the heart out. "Keeping the covenant" is the very life of those who belong. God will never break the covenant from his side. His people, however, diverted under testings by self-centered desire or fear, may cease to remember his covenant-word or subtly alter its terms.

The "gospel" of the young church was rooted in the covenant-revelation which God had spoken to Israel by Moses and the prophets. To keep this link to Israel's covenant clear, I use terms like "the covenant-gospel" or "the covenant-word." When it is called "the gospel of Christ," this means the gospel

Jesus himself possessed and believed, preached and lived by, died for and was raised. Mk 1:1; Gal 1:7 It does not mean a gospel which Christianity crafted about him.

Peter's Witness

That the wording from 2 Peter at Jesus' baptism, "My son, my beloved, this is," matches so closely the wording "My son, my first-born, Israel (is)" in Exodus, suggests that Peter's fragment-witness is very early. I examined it whole. 2 Pet 1:16-21 What Peter and other disciples told regarding Jesus' "power and coming" in his resurrection was not a "clever myth" of their own devising. They had been "with him on the holy mountain"—as the seventy elders had been with Moses. Ex 24:9 It was awesome *revelation!* "We were eyewitnesses of his majesty, for when he received honor and glory from God the Father, and the voice was borne to him by the Majestic Glory, 'This is my son, my beloved, with whom I am well pleased,' we *heard* this voice borne from heaven." God's verdict had overturned the council's charge of blasphemy against Jesus. Clearly, Jesus had not taken the honor of his sonship-name on himself. He had heard it from the God of Israel. The law of "two or three witnesses" had also been satisfied.

But if critics of Jesus' gospel continued to dismiss this testimony as a "myth" devised by the young church, Peter goes on, let them look to evidences they cannot dismiss: "the prophetic word." The covenant-sonship declared to Jesus was not a new invention. It was what the LORD had declared originally of Israel by Moses to Pharaoh. "You do well to give attention to it." Look it up! Ponder it! "Let his word of covenant-sonship illumine you like a lamp shining in the darkness, until the dawn breaks and the morning star arises *in your hearts,*" as in ours.

"Understand this first," Peter went on, "that no prophecy of scripture is subject to anyone's private interpretation (not yours, not ours either), because no prophecy ever came by the impulse of man." This is *revelation!* "Holy men of God spoke as they were moved by the Holy Spirit." The "Holy Spirit" filled and "moved" Jesus too, and the young church after him.

The "gospel" I tell here and develop throughout this book is no "cleverly devised myth," either. My experience of hearing that voice was no more self-generated than Peter's was. What matters is "the glad news" that created the experience and the texts in which it is rooted. It was *revelation* for Moses at the bush, for Isaiah in the temple, for Jesus at his baptism, for the women at the tomb. Every resurrection-appearance of Jesus was likewise *revelation*, including Paul's. To hear this gospel is to be enlightened from an unrealized darkness. It is to be liberated from an unrealized slavery, raised from an unrealized death, found from an unrealized lostness.

The name, "my beloved son," epitomizes the covenant-wisdom of the scriptures throughout. Paul calls it "the whole counsel of God," Hebrews "the eternal covenant," Revelation "the eternal gospel." Acts 20:27; Heb 13:20; Rev 14:6 Textual evidences in "the Gospels" make coherent sense by this "gospel." By it Jesus becomes known.

The Unknown

When I looked expectantly for a prior root of the sonship-word Jesus heard at his baptism, not one scholar I researched directed me to this fragment concerning Moses' commission to Pharaoh! Ex 4:21-23 The far more dramatic written record has almost swallowed it up! Yet for me, this obscure piece opened the whole! That it could have been so smothered raises the issue of the literature, how it preserved this little item and yet almost lost it. In Part Two, I pursue such questions regarding the Gospels, but my findings there apply here as well.

This concise fragment is actually the pre-literary origin of the whole record! Moses framed it to be memorized, so that messengers could pass it on to his enslaved people in Egypt wherever any of them might be. Hearers would master the message until they too could recite it word-for-word, thus pass its story on even to next generations. Since it was conveyed person-to-person, explanations were a part of the process. These too were remembered and continually retold.

This fragment was Moses' means of conveying to Israel what he had told the new Pharaoh. By it they learned the name "the LORD." They heard that the LORD would lead them out of Egypt to the land of their fathers, to serve him there. They heard also the "signs" Moses should do.

When this treasure, communicated orally for generations, was written down, however, only the literal wording remained. Person-to-person explanations were lost. Writing did not need to be concise. Scribes could embellish texts they had in hand by their own imaginations. They preserved original texts faithfully, but what they added could readily corrupt meanings.

My sense of the covenant in relation to "the gospel" helps me sort this fragment out. Embellishments portray Moses' "signs" as acts of divine power, competitive with the magicians of Egypt. Ex 4:1-9; 7:8-14 This violates the covenant-meaning. I attribute it to scribal imagination. The predicted outcome, that the LORD would harden Pharaoh's heart (this before he had even heard Moses) also conflicts with the covenant-meaning. This too must be a later embellishment.

The oral recitation would have said something like this: "The LORD said to Moses, 'When you go back to Egypt, see that you do the signs before Pharaoh. And you shall say to him, 'Thus says the LORD, Israel is my son, my first-born; and I say to you, let my son go that he may serve me. If you will not let him go, I will slay your first-born son.'" That was all. When this was first told to Moses' people, Pharaoh's reaction was not yet known.

Much story can be deduced from this and related evidences. The newly enthroned Pharaoh and Moses had grown up together. He was aware that Moses was born of the slave people Israel. Moses, on returning from exile, would have shared everything he learned with the cousin he had known so well—above all, the name and honor, truth and freedom of "the LORD." This would have been humbling for Pharaoh, yet exalting. He held the throne by right of a "first-born son" in Egypt. This was not his own doing, however, but a gift and calling to him from the Giver-Creator-God. His authentic worth and wisdom and freedom lay in the LORD, therefore, not in his visible rank or in the admiration of his people.

The LORD of heaven and earth now summoned Pharaoh to do him a service. "Israel is *my son, my first-born*." The point of "first-born" was not to make Israel superior, but that they and their fathers were the first to hear this covenant-word. Outwardly they rank as slaves, yet in person and worth before the LORD, they are Pharaoh's equal. Let Pharaoh humble himself and give thanks. Let him receive his rule from the LORD and fulfill it as a trusting servant!

The signs illustrated Pharaoh's choice. Ex 4:1-9 He could be a staff in the LORD's hand, strong and upright, serving him and doing his will, a source of blessing to his people. Or he could break free, assert his proud independence, fall to the earth, slither like a snake, grab whatever might look good and evade whatever threatened evil. Pharaoh could put his hand into his bosom over his heart, draw it out leprous, thus corrupt everything and make his whole land leprous. Or he could draw his hand out whole and clean, put it into the LORD's service, be a source of blessing to his whole land. Pharaoh could celebrate the Nile humbly as a wondrous gift from the LORD. He and his people could receive and use its waters with praise and thanksgiving. Or he could draw from that mighty river a little bucket of proud power, pour it out as though both water and ground were his own, and by such arrogance turn his whole land into blood, tyranny and death.

With that came the LORD's challenge: "I say to you, 'Let my son go, that he may serve me.'" Would Pharaoh, in the honor and freedom of the LORD, summon his God-given authority over Egypt to do the unimaginable—let this long-enslaved people go home to the land of their fathers, if they wish, so that they might serve the LORD there? It would not be easy. Nobles and princes might think him mad. Egyptians who depended on slave labor in home and field would not like it. Will Pharaoh nevertheless invoke his authority to free Israel for the LORD's sake? If so, the LORD will turn this into blessing not just for Israel, but for Pharaoh himself and all Egypt.

"But if you refuse to let him go, I will kill your first-born son," the LORD said. If Pharaoh weighs advantage against disadvantage by his own wisdom in his own interest, his authority and power will not save him. He will bring judgment not only on himself and his next-generation first-born, but on Egypt, too. Defy the LORD once, and he will persist until his decision destroys him. In covenant-language, "Pharaoh hardened his heart," or (since even his heart was not really his own), "The LORD hardened Pharaoh's heart." Ex 8:32; 10:27; 11:10

This was the crux of Israel's covenant throughout the history. When prophets spoke the word of the LORD to kings of his people, would they heed his call? Would they lead their people to serve him only, trusting him to bless them and to deliver them from any evil? Or would they stake their future on their own visible wisdom, strategy, and power? It was so in Jesus' day, too. Rulers of synagogue and temple, secure in their tradition and authority, could not yield to the honor of covenant-sonship and free servanthood Jesus taught, any more than Pharaoh could.

Creedal Christianity faces a similar crux. "The way is hard that leads to life, and those who find it are few," Jesus said. Mt 7:14 The narrow way of covenant-sonship is expressed in his Prayer. The broad and easy way is of long tradition and conviction. If it persists in the misbelief that the name "son of God" for Jesus means "deity," it will read this into every text. Hearts that defend the *rightness* of creedal formulations against the *righteousness* of covenant-sonship from heaven may harness majority power once again to enforce the falsity and keep God's people enslaved. If so, they will no more escape judgment than Pharaoh did.

The beginning problem is not hardness of heart, however, but the "unknown." "I received mercy because I had acted *ignorantly* in unbelief," Paul confessed. 1 Tim 1:13 The "unknown" of Christianity is understandable. How could anyone *know* that formulations long sacred are contrary to its own Prayer? Or that the creeds are not the gospel Jesus himself heard and believed and taught and died for? Or that creedal doctrine does not feed hearts hungry for righteousness, but only dictates what Christians must believe if they want to belong and be saved?

The LORD commissioned Jeremiah "to pluck up and break down," then "build and plant." Jer 1:10 The "gospel" Jesus taught has power to do just that. It can "pluck up and break down" what must be "repented" and left behind, so as to "build and plant" a joy and freedom unknown.

As for me, my course was set. "No one who puts his hand to the plow and looks back is fit for the kingdom of God," Jesus said. Lk 9:62 There could be no turning back.

CHAPTER TWO

The Covenant Enemy

"If you are God's son..." Matthew 4:3

The narrative of Jesus' temptations became a first test for me of the meaning of his name, "my beloved son." Mt 4:1-10; Mk 1:12-13; Lk 4:1-13 Since I cherished that name for myself, I expected to understand my temptations by his and his by mine.[2] The lack of a "the" in Greek seemed to confirm "God's son" as covenant-language for the whole of Israel. The writer of Hebrews implies this: "He (Jesus) had to be made *like his brothers* in every respect," and "He was tempted in every respect *as we are*, yet without sinning." Heb 2:17-18; 4:15 That Jesus did not give up this name but served and trusted his Father by it, regardless of cost, marked the victory of the sonship-gospel in him.

Early Christian fathers missed this. Their assumption that the name "son of God" for Jesus meant deity yielded the inference that he, being God, knew everything and could not have sinned. It followed that the temptations did not test *Jesus* really, but the *devil*. Satan wanted to find out whether Jesus was actually God's son (deity) or not, but Jesus thwarted him. He could have turned stones into bread, but did not. He had power to capture all the kingdoms of the world without Satan's help, but did not. He could have leaped from the pinnacle and been caught spectacularly by angels, but did not. Later interpreters had to decide whether "son of God" meant deity or messiahship or both. Since *we* are neither, Jesus was not really "tempted as *we* are." Among the commentators I searched, not one noticed that the name "my beloved

---

[2] This became the pursuit of my doctoral dissertation, *The Temptation of Jesus in Matthew* (Concordia Seminary, St. Louis, May 1966). For my survey of interpretation from the ancient fathers to Luther, I drew on M. Steiner, *La Tentation de Jesus dans L'Interpretation Patristique de Saint Justin a Origene* (Paris: J. Gabalda, 1962), and Klaus-Peter Koeppen, *Die Auslegung der Versuchungsgeschichte unter besonderer Beruecksichtigung der Alten Kirche* (Tuebingen: J.C.B. Mohr, 1961).

son" for Jesus was rooted in Israel's exodus history, thereby making Jesus "like his brothers."

My finding was that the temptations are taunts. The devil's "if you are God's son" mocks his noble name as meaningless, ridicules the promises implicit in it, and portrays God's call to "serve me" as fruitless and self-destructive folly. The episodes are packaged as a literary unit, but recall three distinct crises in Jesus' life—different not only in place, as the preserved narrative indicates, but also in time. The clue to their meaning lies in Jesus' responses, drawn in each case from covenant-words of Moses to Israel in Deuteronomy.

The Wilderness

By my reconstruction, the first temptation occurred while Jesus was still with John. After his baptism he was "led" or "driven" by the Spirit into the wilderness to be tested by the devil. The memory views this testing as intended by God himself. The devil is an instrument of God. He speaks an inviting alternative to the voice-from-heaven word Jesus heard and trusted. This accords with the pattern of Eden (the snake), of Israel in the wilderness (where no devil or alternative voice is mentioned), and of Job. Testings serve a divine purpose.

Jesus went into the wilderness as John had done before him. Lk 1:80 The Spirit led him there (Mark has "drove him"). Mk 1:12 The testings imply the "wilderness" where God's "first-born son" out of Egypt had wandered prior to entering the land. Jesus' forty days and forty nights link him to Israel's forty years there. He had heard the voice from heaven speak Israel's sonship specifically to himself. The spirit or "breath" of God had descended also on him. That name and breath would be his authentic "life." In the wilderness, however, it became the crux of the testing.

He went with an exhilaration like Israel's out of Egypt, to meet God where Israel had met him. But nothing happened. Day after day, even week after week, he was alone, abandoned. The hunger he began to experience was not what his noble name, "my beloved son," might lead him to expect from a caring Father. Surely God had not named him this for nothing, had not brought him here for nothing! Yet the wilderness was as inhospitable to him as it had been to Israel out of Egypt. The only companionship it offered was of the "wild beasts" mentioned in Mark, like serpents and scorpions. As the memory of soup pots and leeks had haunted the fathers out of Egypt, so Jesus' hunger yielded memories of Galilee's abundance—bread, fish, eggs. He recalled it later: "What man of you, if his son asks for bread, will give him a stone? Or if he asks for a fish, will give him a serpent?" Mt 7:9-10 "If he asks for an egg, will he give him a scorpion?" Luke adds. Lk 11:11-12 Yet until God showed himself in some way, Jesus could not think to leave.

What he met finally in this long and arid wilderness was not his God and Father, but temptation. The alternative wisdom of a taunting devil mocked the name that had so honored him. "What good is it? You can't eat it! How long will you wait for a God who does not come? 'My beloved son,' he calls you. 'Father,' he calls himself. 'I have delighted in you,' he says. Admit it, Jesus! It is all a mistake! What does this God of yours expect you to eat? Stones? Snakes? Scorpions? Where is he when you need him?

"Open your eyes, come to your senses! Give it up before it's too late! There is no Father-God! Religion is fine as far as it goes, but have the good sense to get back to Galilee where you belong! Galilee is the promised land! That's where you will find God, not in this dry wilderness. Don't be a fanatic! Be pious the way your people there are pious. To stay here, waiting forever and for nothing, is madness! You'll end up dead. The vultures will eat you, and that will be the end. All right then, son of God, pick up that stone at your feet. Bite it! Tell it to be bread! See if it obeys you! But do something! Don't die here waiting for a God who will never come!"

With that temptation I can identify. The alternative voice attacks my name, too, and the God who spoke it on me, "my beloved son." I know its "Wow!" but I have also known its "wilderness"—when God is far off and all expectations of his presence and help fail. Prayers are not answered. Hopes are crushed. Faith dries out and becomes empty. Worship seems forced. The way of the Lord looks like a hopeless dead-end. Common sense points invitingly to a God who does not control me but whom I control, a God who does what I want of him.

I stand in awe of Jesus then. I would not have remembered the God who said to me, "Paul, I have called you by name, you are mine!" Is 43:1 I would have fallen before I so much as realized I was being tested. I stand in awe also of his answer. Another word from Moses spoke as from heaven to his heart, to be hurled back against the tempter, "It is written, man does not live by bread alone, but man lives by every word that proceeds out of the mouth of the LORD." Dt 8:3 This covenant-word, Moses had said, is what his people needed to learn, what their forty years of wilderness testing had been about. By this word God met his beloved son in that crisis, delivered him, fed his heart on a food far beyond bodily comfort and survival.

This classic text, I assume, was among those selected for reading in synagogues throughout Israel on a particular sabbath each year. Acts 13:27 Jesus would have known it, even memorized it, from childhood. But now its meaning broke through in full power. Added to Israel's elect name, "my first-born son" and God's name as "Father," this "not by bread alone" word lies at the heart of his life and preaching. "Life is more than food, and the body more than clothing!" Mt 6:25 "A man's life does not consist in the abundance of things he possesses." Lk 12:15 Without "life" by the word of God, bodily aliveness is no life at all! "Do not labor for the food that perishes, but for the food which endures to eternal life." Jn 6:27 "Your fathers ate manna in the wilderness and they died. This is the bread which comes down from heaven, that a man may eat of it and not die!" Jn 6:49-50

Thus Jesus met God in the wilderness, heard his word, learned what he needed to know, and emerged, strengthened. Our testings are like his. If we fail, as Israel failed, God is there to pick us up again. As we perceive what this and every testing is about, we learn not to be diverted so lightly from God's way but to stay our sufferings through, walk with God and serve him still, regardless of cost, be raised with Jesus even from the dead!

The Mountain

Matthew's version puts the mountain temptation last. "Begone, Satan!" seemed a fitting close to the literary unit as a whole. Luke seems to preserve the time sequence.

The wilderness temptation attacked Jesus' name, that of the mountain his hope. The covenant-name, "my beloved son," implies an inheritance. Israel's inheritance out of Egypt was the land. Jesus rested his hope in his Father's promise of life, care, and kingdom. Walk straight and true with your God and do his commandments, Moses said, "that you may live and that it may go well with you." Dt 5:33 Exactly what this promise means or how things will turn out is not given us to know. The call is clear, however. Trust God in steadfast hope and serve him only.

Testings hit when the promises seem to fail. I associate the temptation on the mountain, therefore, with a low turning point at the middle of Jesus' ministry—the death of John the Baptist, followed by Jesus' determination to go to Jerusalem.

It appears that John was being held at Herod Antipas' Galilean capital, Tiberias on the lake—not (or no longer) at Machaerus, the Perean fortress at its southern border, mentioned by Josephus.[3] Disciples of John could communicate between him and Jesus. Now they came to tell how their master had been suddenly and brutally executed on the occasion of Herod's birthday party. Mt 14:1-12; Mk 6:14-29 It was shockingly hard to believe. Herod had respected John and seemed to enjoy talking with him. His disciples were beginning to hope even that he might be released! But now, by a stupid oath, he was dead! Herod had given them the body for burial.

The memory indicates that Jesus, on hearing this, withdrew by boat, needing to be alone. Mt 14:13 The mountain temptation visualizes his testing. What of God's promises? John had been a faithful, devoted preacher of the kingdom of God. He had trusted the God, whose word he proclaimed, to overrule the kingdoms of men. How could the living and reigning God stand back then and do nothing? How could the petty tyrant Herod, cowed by a domineering wife Herodias, lust stirred by her daughter's dancing, command John's head to be chopped off and brought up into the party on a platter? Where was God when his faithful prophet needed him?

If God had failed John, could Jesus expect anything different? John's death portended his own. The kings of the earth ruled still. Rulers of synagogues had been summoning delegations from Jerusalem to spy out and accuse him, spreading rumors that he was possessed by the devil. These critics heard what they wanted to hear, saw what they wanted to see. The time was opportune for the devil to contradict the word and promises of God. Mt 4:7-10; Lk 4:5-8

No mountain exists from which one can literally see "all the kingdoms of this world and the glory of them" and "in a moment of time." To depict God's promises by a mountain vision is natural, however. From a mountaintop, God had granted Moses to see the whole land his people would possess. Dt 34:1 "All the kingdoms of the world and their glory," recalls Daniel's vision of "the saints of the Most High" as "one like a son of man coming with the clouds of heaven" (in contrast to beasts from the sea), and given "dominion and glory and kingdom, that all peoples, nations, and languages should serve him" in a kingdom "that shall not pass away" or "be destroyed." Dan 7:3,13-14,18 John had preached this hope too, "the Mightier One" coming, the Lord himself, who would brook no argument and before whom every knee must bow.[4]

---

[3] Antiquities 18:5:2. "He was sent a prisoner, out of Herod's suspicious temper, to Machaerus, the castle I before mentioned, and was there put to death."

[4] See my study, "'Whose Sandals?' (Matt 3:11)", Journal of Biblical Literature, LXXXVI,1967,81-87.

But the promise had failed. God had not saved John at all. A contemptible Herod, symbol of ungodly kingdoms in this very event, had by arbitrary command wiped out the life of God's prophet. The devil's taunt set the experienced reality against the promises.

"Come to your senses, Jesus! Give up this kingdom and hope you talk of! John believed and preached it too, but look what happened to him! It will never work. If you want a kingdom, be realistic. Trust me and do it my way. I know how to manage these things. You have great gifts and possibilities! People are looking for you to just say the word. A little strategy, a little weaponry, a little compromise to get the authorities on your side—that's all it will take. Get real! Use the common sense God gave you. Work with me. Nothing will stand in your way!" The account in Matthew links the devil's appeal to the memory of Nebuchadnezzar's golden image: "Fall down and worship me." Dan 3:5

I know this temptation well enough, as does the church. Give up on a kingdom that comes by the word of God and faith. Invoke God's name on visible goals, on organized strength and strategies, on partisan alliances and institutional authority, on psychological motivations and rewards. Overcome the opposition. By pressure and conspiracy and efficient organization, accomplish what the word of God is unable to accomplish.

Jesus was not deceived. A word from heaven came to him again out of scriptures he had heard from childhood, "It is written, You shall worship the LORD your God and him only shall you serve." "Son" and "servant" are one, as the LORD declared by Moses to Pharaoh, "Let my son go, that he may serve me." Ex 4:23 Jesus drew on the commandment, too, "I am the LORD your God.... You shall have no other gods over my face." Dt 5:6-7 "You shall not turn aside to the right hand or to the left. You shall walk in all the way which the LORD your God has commanded you, that you may live and that it may go well with you...." Dt 5:32-33 "You shall love the LORD your God with all your heart...." Dt 6:4 "You shall fear the LORD your God; you shall serve him, and swear by his name." Dt 6:13 No complaint in Jesus about a failed hope! He would walk his way straight and steadfast, refusing to be bluffed, trusting the outcome to his Father as John had done. That is how to defeat Satan, the real enemy. That is how the Father's kingdom comes.

The drama heightened when Jesus told his disciples he must go to Jerusalem, something John had not done. Mt 16:21-23 He would preach his message to the authorities on their own ground. Chief priests and elders of the temple would hear him face-to-face. Jesus did not expect them to receive his word.

He would suffer and be killed, too—but not by Herod. The leaders would have to do it themselves. Yet he would not lose, any more than John had lost! "That it may go well with you," the LORD had promised his "son," who served him to the end. "After two days he will revive us, on the third day he will raise us up, that we may live before him." Hos 6:2

Simon Peter, looking for the devil's kind of kingdom, could not accept this. "God forbid, Lord! This will never happen to you!" he protested, defending his own hope and countering Jesus' evident pessimism. Jesus' reply, "Begone, Satan" overlays his rebuke of the devil in the temptation on the mountain. Mt 16:23; 4:10

Once again I stand amazed. The devil's tough alternative is ever so reasonable! "Don't let them do that to you! Devise a strategy! Get people on your side! Work with any available weaponry and authority structure! Take matters into your own hands!" I would not have realized, had I been there, how the devil's very testing would challenge me to defy fear and serve my Father in heaven—to experience how mountains would move out of the way for me by God's holy name. Jesus understood this in full and without compromise. He did not reduce himself to slithering in the dirt like a snake (or like Herod) so as to save himself. He stood tall and walked straight through, willingly, all alone, even into death. Thus he crushed the head of the serpent, whose venom could reach no higher than his heel. Gen 3:15

The Pinnacle

One of my surprises on visiting the Holy Land was to learn that "the pinnacle of the temple" (*hieros* in Greek) was not the top of the hundred-cubit-high porch leading into the inner sanctuary (*naos*), as I had long assumed.[5] *Hieros* referred to the entire compound with all its courts, closed in by an outer wall. *Pterygion* or "pinnacle" (a diminutive of "wing") was the southeast corner of that wall, built by Herod the Great, rising a hundred feet from its base in the hillside, whose long and rock-pocked slope descended steeply to the floor of the Kidron Valley.

I could imagine how this corner of the temple came to be called the "little wing." "Let me dwell in your tent forever! Oh to be safe under the shelter of your wings," the people sang, a familiar theme in the Psalms. Ps 61:4; 17:8; 36:7; 57:1; 63:7; 91:4 Devotional piety could view God as a dove—its body the

---

[5] John Wilkinson, *Jerusalem as Jesus Knew It* (London: Thames and Hudson, Ltd, 1978), p. 92, was misled, just as I was, by the notion of "pinnacle" in English as meaning "highest point."

sanctuary facing east, its wings stretching out over temple courts. The southeast corner would be its right wing-tip.

The setting for this temptation (third in the Lucan sequence) is the holy city and temple. It makes graphic Jesus' crucial testing in Gethsemane. From the "olive-press" garden on the lower slope of the Mount of Olives, under the full moon of Passover, the temple wall across the Kidron Valley and its pinnacle corner would stand out against the night sky.

Jesus knew the mind and strategy of the ruling council, and of Judas, too. His arrest would happen here this night, at the place where he and his disciples had encamped. The council would condemn him for blasphemy, then deliver him to the Roman governor to be crucified as an insurrectionist. It would be done expeditiously, before the next sunset when the Passover-sabbath would begin. The death Jesus anticipated when he left Galilee was no longer weeks away, not even days, but now. This was his last chance to escape, over the mountain and in the night. The council would not mind if he fled, they had even hoped for it. Jn 7:35 The crisis they saw in him would be over. They would no longer have to deal with him.

The preserved memory tells how Jesus cried to his Father for some other way, but then his final choice: "Abba, Father, all things are possible to you; remove this cup from me; yet not what I will, but what you will." Mt 26:36-46; Mk 14:32-42; Lk 22:39-46 He was not forced to do his Father's will but he chose it freely, straight through to the finish, even when faced by that awful death. He would do to the end what his Father gave him to do, trusting God's promise of resurrection and life, even though he could "see" this no more than I can. "Let my son go, that he may serve me" was his covenant-calling, and he would do it. Only so could he love his people to the finish, imaging his Father's love for them. The steadfast nobility of his walk through arrest, trial, condemnation, and crucifixion, pictured in all four Gospels, derived from that struggle and prayer.

The pinnacle episode makes this crisis even more vivid. As the wilderness temptation mocked his name, "my beloved son," as the mountain temptation mocked God's promises, this temptation mocks Jesus' servanthood as not only empty and meaningless, but an impossible madness. The devil took him up to that pinnacle, visible to Jesus from where he prayed. Standing on its height, he could look down into the deepest and darkest pit. The devil's taunt mimicked the Father's call. "Do you see what this Father of yours is asking of you, his beloved son? 'Cast yourself down,' he says. Oh yes, he promises that angels will bear you up, save you from getting hurt! So go ahead, jump if you want!

But I tell you straight and you know it—there won't be any angels! Once you take that plunge, once you deliver yourself up to those who arrest you, it will be too late to change your mind. It will be death to you, complete and certain—a death far more horrible and prolonged than John's. This 'Father,' whom you so love and trust, will not save you at all! Is that fair, Jesus? Haven't you done enough? How can he ask that? It's too much!

"Maybe it's all a mistake anyway. You must be misunderstanding him! If you are his 'beloved,' he cannot really mean this! If he truly delights in you, as he claims to do, he cannot really be asking this of you! Why do you even think about doing it, Jesus? Are you in so deep that you cannot back out? You were stupid to have let it come to this! Have you no mind of your own? All right, take the leap if you must! See where it gets you, fool!"

Jesus answered by yet another synagogue reading from Moses. "It is written" invites anyone who can read to unroll the scroll and see for himself. "You shall not put the LORD your God to the test." Dt 6:16 Your God puts *you* to the test, not you *him*! You shall not exalt yourself as judge over the LORD your God. You shall not pronounce him a failure. No matter what happens, no matter what lies before you, you shall not infer that he does not love you, or that he is not fair, or that he has abandoned you, or that his promises are empty, or that he does not even exist. You shall not forsake the LORD your God for a god whom you can hire to serve you. Your calling is to do your Father's work on earth, trusting his word and promise, his love and faithfulness. Whatever the trials may be through which he leads you, you shall follow him straight and upright, fearing him alone, setting your hope in him, regardless of cost. That is how you glorify his name. That is how your name is glorified in his. That is how his kingdom comes.

Gethsemane and the pinnacle tell the same temptation. The one remembers the history, the other pictures it by cartoon-like metaphor. In the garden the name for God is "Father"; on the pinnacle it is "the LORD." The garden response is positive, "Your will be done." The pinnacle response states the negative, "You shall not put the LORD your God to the test."

Jesus asked nothing less than this of his disciples and church: "If any man would come after me, let him deny himself and take up his cross and follow me. Whoever would save his life will lose it, and whoever loses his life for my sake will find it." Mt 16:24-25 "In every respect he has been tempted as we are," the difference only that, whereas we readily fall, he did not. Heb 4:15 There lies our noble authority as "beloved sons" of the God who is our Father, too.

Thus the covenant-word to Israel by Moses provided the principle of coherence I needed toward knowing Jesus—first his name from heaven, "my beloved son," then its testing by an alternative voice and wisdom. The temptation episodes are preserved from the memory of people who knew him in his own generation. They provide a time-frame for the whole of his ministry. Abundant evidences still to be considered derive from, amplify, and conform to this pattern.

But who is the enemy? Is it God, who puts his son through such trials? No. Is it the devil, whose assignment is to tempt by ridiculing God and giving voice to every enticing advantage or escape? Not really. The devil can force nothing, either. Are people the enemy, who turn against one another in violence and conspiracy for the sake of their own petty kingdoms? No. None of these had power to destroy Jesus or rob him of his name and heritage. The enemy is any human heart which, offered both possibilities, rejects the word of God and chooses, in remarkable freedom, to believe and live the lie.

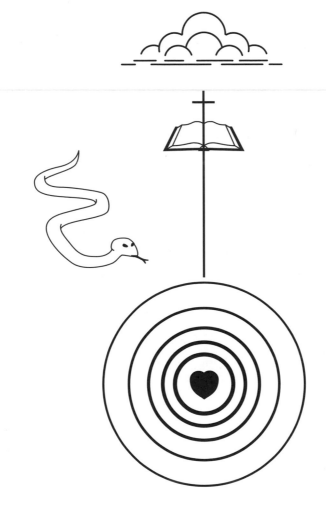

"Your Eyes Will Be Opened"

CHAPTER THREE

The Ultimate Choice

*"See, I have set before you this day life and good,
death and evil ... life and death, blessing and curse;
therefore choose life."*   *Deuteronomy 30:15-20*

In the fall of 1966, following my study of Jesus' temptations, I offered a
course on "Temptation" for religion majors at Valparaiso University, using
Dietrich Bonhoeffer's compact *Temptation and Fall* as a text.[6] My procedure
was to assign a brief section to a student, challenging him or her to make sense
of it for the class. When we came to "the tree of the knowledge of good and
evil" in the garden of Eden, two paraphrases for "good and evil" in Bonhoeffer
struck me—"pleasure and pain," then "passion and hate." Gen 2:9,17; 3:1-6

What is it to "know good"? See something that looks *pleasurable* and
pursue it with *passion*! What is it to "know evil"? See something that threatens
pain and reject it with *hate*! Who decides this? Each person for himself alone.
What about other people? Those who may help you are "good"; ally yourself
with them. Those who might hurt you are "evil"; avoid or attack them. This
is a psyche of self-determinism—manipulative, competitive, aggressive, defensive, self-contained. It is what Moses set before his people as "death and
evil."

It made sense! "Sins" are not accidental or isolated, then. They do not
happen because the doer "did not know any better" or "was not taught right."
They are not preventable by education, moralistic pressure or punishments.
"Sins" are driven by the psyche of individualistic determinism! Jesus' tempta-

---

[6] *Schoepfung und Fall*, Munich: Chr. Kaiser Verlag, 1937. Translated by John C. Fletcher, *Creation
and Fall*, London: SCM Press Ltd., 1959.

tions were not about doing right or wrong, but about adopting that psyche as his own! Why did he refuse? Because his name from heaven, "my beloved son," was of the psyche called "life and good"! Knowing the difference, he chose life!

The Two Psyches

"See, I have set before you this day life and good, death and evil," Moses said. His people, chosen by God, were in the *psyche* of "life and good." To love the LORD their God with all their heart, cleave to him, trust and serve him in joy and freedom, was their very character. They were capable of the other *psyche* too, however—"death and evil." Throughout this wilderness era, Moses had been setting both possibilities before them, even through their failures. Nearing the end he made it his last bequest, as it were. "Therefore choose life," he pleaded.

He could *teach* the choice, but he could not make it for them. They would make it individually in any moment of temptation. This would not be a passing decision, like a menu or a career. Their very personhood was at stake, the inner psyche that would determine and control the outer life of their mind and body. No animal could have such a choice, only they. Let them not fear or regret it! To be trusted so was honor and freedom! The LORD their God, who had made and called them, was willing to risk their choosing *against* him! If they did choose *for* him then, they would love and serve him freely as full and independent persons, not as puppets.

All this was *revelation* to me, like the dawning of a great unknown. I began to wonder about Moses himself. Where did he get his amazing insight? Surely not from the wisdom of Egypt! Not from the heritage of his own people, either! The name "the LORD" subsumes it, yet a fragment of direct memory declares explicitly: "God said to Moses, 'I am the LORD. I appeared to Abraham, to Isaac, and to Jacob, as God Almighty, but by my name the LORD I did not make myself known to them.'" Ex 6:2-3 By this name God revealed himself to Moses at the bush. Ex 3:13-15 By this name Moses addressed Pharaoh and Israel. Ex 4:22-23

What was in that name? The Eden story! Gen 2-3 The name "the LORD God" dominates it! Its two special trees, one of life and the other of death, define the very choice which Moses set before his people. It is the root text of the Mosaic covenant! There is none like it anywhere! But where did Moses get it? I infer, from the family of the Midianite shepherd-priest Jethro, his father-in-law! Ex 3:1 Midian was a son of Abraham by Keturah. He married her after Sarah died. Gen 25:1-4 Sometime, even generations earlier, the LORD had granted someone of that Midianite family this insight into the conflicting psyches of humanness, and the art of framing this "choice" in the form of story for the sake of memorizing! It had been learned and passed on orally to children and children's children. When Moses heard it, it struck him as *revelation* from the LORD! Its truth and realism filled the covenant of his fathers, Abraham and Isaac and Jacob, with a depth of meaning he had never known!

That story speaks also to me. It tells me about *my* humanness, the "breath of life" which LORD God breathes into my bodily life. By it I know myself as a pure receiver of gifts that come from him. He honors me, reveals to me what I am, who I am, where I am, to whom I belong, what those two trees are, and my calling and freedom to choose. He liberates and challenges my natural creativity toward the earth and everything in it as a meaningful servanthood to him. The LORD God put the man he had made (meaning *me)* into his garden "to till and keep it." He blessed him with freedom also to "eat of every tree of the garden." He binds me in love and mutual honor to people around me, beginning with marriage and home.

The story in Genesis 1 does not say the name "the LORD," but it is in many ways parallel. It too makes us pure receivers from God, the Giver-Creator. Gen 1:1-31 It heralds our "male and female" humanity as made "in his image." It puts us in charge of everything God created—earth, plants and animals. It summons us to apply our God-given imagination toward knowing, using and enjoying the earth he gives us. Our creativity continues and extends God's own. We do not threaten or diminish the earth and its life when we stretch its possibilities this way, but honor and enhance what God has made. The science and technology, manufacturing and commerce in which we engage are *good.* The common sense to clean up after ourselves, also to anticipate and overcome any backlash of disadvantage, is likewise *good.* Passing all this on to our children, encouraging them to discover and enjoy their own creativity on any level and to any degree, is *good.* Serving God, ourselves, and one another by our individual freedom is *good.* Trusting God to lead us on, fit it together, enjoy our achievements with us and make good our failures, is *good!*

The "choice" Moses set before his people did not derive from Genesis 1, however. It is rooted in the name "the LORD" and the drama of Eden.

Snake Stories

The L ORD made Moses' rod a sign to his people and to Pharaoh. Held upright in his hand in service to him, it signaled "life and good." Cast down by itself, flat on the ground like a snake, it signaled "death and evil." Ex 4:2-5 The snake Moses raised on the pole is yet another sign, to which I shall return in a moment. These signs are rooted, however, in the snake of Eden.

The Snake of Eden. Gen 3:1-6 The Eden story portrays the psyche of "death and evil" by a snake. Snakes slither in the dirt. They cannot stand upright or walk straight. Lacking horizons, they see only what lies immediately before them. For them this is natural, but for humans it is deadly. A snake can never become human. Humans, however, descend readily to snakehood.

The woman listened to the snake and took on its image. "You will not die," it said, contradicting the L ORD God. "Your eyes will be opened and you will be like God. You will be wise! You will know good and evil on your own. Decide for yourself! Does it look *pleasurable?* Then it is *good!* Pursue it with *passion!*" The wisdom of the snake sounds *good.* The choice it offers, however, is individualistic and immediate, self-gratifying and self-determined.

As always in temptation, the woman was alone. Her husband was not in on it. She *"saw* that the tree was *good* for food, and a *delight to the eyes,* and that the tree was to be *desired* to make one wise." She decided for herself. Action followed. "She *took* of its fruit and *ate* it."

I began to see this progression elsewhere in the scriptures. David *"saw* a woman bathing ... and the woman was *very good to look at* ... so he *took* her." 2 Sam 11:2-4 The commandment, "You shall not covet," became powerfully meaningful to me. "I am the L ORD your God.... You shall not covet your neighbor's house... your neighbor's wife...or anything that is your neighbor's." Ex 20:17 You shall *not desire* anything that *looks good* to you, but which I, the L ORD your God, do not give you. "Take heed and beware of all covetousness," Jesus warned, "for a man's life does not consist in the abundance of his possessions." Lk 12:15 "Every one who *looks* at a woman to *lust* for her...," he said. Mt 5:28 Adultery begins in the heart. James said it, too: "Each person is tempted when he is lured and enticed by his own *desire.* Then desire, when it has conceived, gives birth to sin; and sin, when it is full-grown, brings forth death." Jas 1:14-15

The backlash was immediate. The woman's eyes were opened in a way she had not anticipated. She knew *evil* or "pain," the obverse of knowing *good.* She was guilty! How could she confront her as-yet innocent husband without feeling judged? She did not tell him what she had done, but adopted the psyche of the snake. Pretending *evil* was *good*, "she gave some also to her husband, and he ate." Might he have saved her by refusing? He did not.

Earlier the story pictured "the man and his wife" as "both naked and were not ashamed." Gen 2:25 This was "life and good." They were aware of God the Giver, of themselves, and of each other, but were not self-conscious, not fearful of judgment. When they chose "death and evil," however, "the eyes of them both were opened" to see their *evil*. Gen 3:6-24 Self-conscious shame took over. "They knew that they were naked." Fearing it, hating it, desperate still for self-worth, they slithered to save themselves. They tried the laughable device of "sewing fig leaves together" as a cover-up. It did not work. They conspired to hide from God. It did not work. The psyche of sin betrays itself. "Who told you that you were naked? Have you eaten of the tree of which I commanded you not to eat?" the LORD God asked the man. The next tactic was to divert the blame. Jesus understood all this. "He knew what was in man," John's memoir comments. Jn 2:25 His slithering disciples did not deceive him, neither did the plottings of a self-saving priesthood.

The story of David's pathetic cover-up, even the secretive murder of Uriah, illustrates this backlash dramatically. 2 Sam 11:6-27 So does his son Amnon's tragic rape of Absalom's sister, Tamar. "Then Amnon hated her with very great hatred, so that the hatred with which he hated her was greater than the love with which he had loved her." 2 Sam 13:15

"The day you eat of it you shall die," the LORD had warned. Gen 2:17 Those who fall prey to the deceitful wisdom of the snake are doomed to a futility sealed by death. Their sweat and labor cannot rescue them. "Till you return to the ground," the judgment said, "for out of it you were taken; for *dirt is what you are* and to dirt you will return." Gen 3:19 The human hunger to be important is urgent, but it will go unfed. If my origin is nothing but "dirt," and I am destined to be nothing but "dirt" at the end, what fantasy it is to imagine that monuments I build to myself can make me more than dirt in between! Yet, since bodily aliveness is the only "life" people know, and the only arena to achieve the worth they crave, they will look to whatever illusory "tree of life" they can imagine to save themselves from death and to "live forever." Gen 3:22

Is it possible for one who has chosen "death and evil," then tasted the disaster, to be granted that choice once again and to start over? Yes, says the ancient story. The woman broke down and confessed that the snake had "beguiled" her. Through her and her child-bearing, the LORD God renewed the warfare. "I will put enmity between you and the woman," he said to the snake, "and between your seed and her seed." Her seed, walking nobly upright, would bruise the head of the snake. It, in turn, could bruise only his heel. Gen 3:13-15

The tree of life remained. "The LORD God... drove out the man; and at the east of the garden of Eden (east the direction of origins) he placed the cherubim, and a flaming sword which turned every way, to guard the way to the tree of life." Gen 3:24 A return can indeed happen—yet only by the hot shame of "repenting" the wisdom of "eyes-opened" lust and fear. Start over! Go in through that east entrance. However *evil* that flaming sword may look, face it through! It will kill only what needs to be killed. Then you will *live*!

Is there hope for covenant "sons" who have listened to the snake and fallen back into slavery? Yes. The story of David's return is classic. 2 Sam 12:1-15 "Hide your face from my sins, and blot out all my iniquities," he could pray. "Create in me a clean heart, O God, and put a new and right spirit within me." Ps 51:9-10 "Everyone who commits sin is a slave to sin," Jesus said. "If the son makes you free, you will be free indeed." Jn 8:34-36

"I call heaven and earth to witness against you this day," Moses said, "that I have set before you life and death, blessing and curse; therefore *choose life*, loving the LORD your God, obeying his voice, and cleaving to him; for that means *life* to you." Dt 30:19-20

The Snake on the Pole. Num 21:4-9 Israel's testing in the wilderness was like that of Eden. How shall they respond in a situation of prolonged hardship without visible hope? "Life and good" would mean entrusting "the knowledge of good and evil" to the LORD their God. By his own initiative, he had brought them out of slavery in Egypt. He was taking them now to the land he had promised to give their fathers. The way, though hard, was not impossible. The LORD was sustaining them with manna day by day. Their call was to thank, praise, and trust him even in hard circumstances, follow his leading still, bear the burden in patient hope, do his will with noble cheer, also love and care for one another. He would see them through and make it *good* by a wisdom beyond their own. They would be a light of hope and blessing even to the nations.

The people listened to the snake, however. "They became impatient on the way. And they spoke against God and against Moses, 'Why have you brought us up out of Egypt to die in the wilderness? For there is no food and no water, and we loathe this worthless food.'" This was to "know good and evil" by their opened eyes. Egypt was *good* for foods they ate there, life in the wilderness was *evil*. They had not expected this when they came out. Self-pity and complaint swept over them. A conspiracy of protest and demand took form and grew. Moses and his God were the enemy. "You got us into this mess, you get us out!"

"Then the LORD sent fiery snakes among the people, and they bit the people, so that many people of Israel died." Let them learn by experience what was really killing them! "The people came to Moses, and said, 'We have sinned; for we have spoken against the LORD and against you; pray to the LORD, that he may take away the snakes from us.'" Moses prayed. The LORD said to him, "Make a fiery snake and set it on a pole; and every one who is bitten, when he sees it, shall live." Moses did so. "Look at the snake on the pole!" he said. "See how its lies have turned you from trusting and serving the LORD your God! Turn from it and live!"

Thus Moses taught his people their choice—"life and good" or "death and evil." To see the snake on the pole was to see the psyche of "death and evil." By seeing it in truth, they would see and return to the psyche of "life and good," of patient hope in the LORD their God.

The Tree of Life

A common-sense "knowledge of good and evil" belonged to the creative intelligence of the Israel whom the LORD God named "my son" and "my people." To use it well was to serve the God who gave it. They would leave the ultimate knowledge of good and evil to him, however. They would not judge him by what their "opened eyes" could see, or try to control what he had not given them to control. If hard trials befell them, they would trust God still. The story was not over. His promise of life and blessing stood firm. To wait for and serve the LORD in patient hope still was their very *life*.

I began to see such understanding throughout the scriptures. "The Rock, his work is perfect; for all his ways are justice," Moses sang of the LORD. "See now that I, even I, am he, and there is no god beside me. I kill and I make alive, I wound and I heal; and there is none that can deliver out of my hand." Dt 32:4,39 No matter what troubles his people might experience from their God, there was no other Rock to whom they could turn. Let their trust not fail. Job's confidence was similar: "Shall we receive good at the hand of God, and shall we not receive evil?" Job 2:10 Amos understood it: "Does evil befall a city, unless the LORD has done it?" Amos 3:6 So did Isaiah: "Is there a God besides me? There is no Rock; I know not any." Is 44:8 "I am the LORD and there is no other. I form light and create darkness, I make weal and create woe,

I am the LORD, who do all these things." Is 45:6-7

The LORD God himself is our *good!* "I have no *good* apart from you." Ps 16:2 "O give thanks to the LORD, for he is *good.*" Ps 118:1 "But for me it is *good* to be near God." Ps 73:28 The LORD as "my shepherd" leads me to green pastures and still waters (which look *good*), but also into the valley of the shadow of death (which looks *evil*). I follow "in the paths of righteousness for his name's sake" regardless. "Surely goodness and mercy will follow me all the days of my life and I will dwell in the house of the LORD forever." Ps 23

I watched for the language of "good and evil" in Jesus. A rich youth called him "*good* teacher." "Why do you call me good?" he replied. "No one is good but God alone." Mk 10:17-18 Would this youth choose the *good* that is God alone, or the *good* of his many possessions?

In his parable of the laborers, those named to the vineyard from the beginning judged their master to be "not good" for the way he gave wages. Mt 20:1-16 "These last worked only one hour, and you have made them equal to us, who have borne the burden of the day!" they grumbled. "Take what is yours and go," the master replied. "Is *your eye evil* because I am *good?*"

Guests invited to the wedding were disappointed in the kingdom of servanthood Jesus offered. Mt 22:2-10 The *good* they saw lay in what they controlled. The servants were sent then to invite anyone they might find, "both *evil and good.*" Mt 22:10 Such was the non-partiality of God!

"Son, remember that you in your lifetime received your *good* things, and Lazarus in like manner *evil* things," Abraham reminded the rich man, now in Hades. Lk 16:25 That vast disparity was not a measure of worth. Their true *good* was to be sons of Abraham together, brothers side by side. This is Moses and the prophets! Let the brothers still living "hear them"! Lk 16:29-31

The Name

Moses saw in the account of the two trees the ultimate human choice between "life and good" or "death and evil." Priestly scribes, in charge of the sacred documents, lost this at some point. Assuming "Adam and Eve" to be the physiological progenitors of the human race, they added to the account of Eden and the two trees a "book of the descendants of Adam." Gen 5

The loss was fearful. The history of kings after David, and the protests of the prophets, testify that the *psyche* of noble trust was not even known. A *psyche* of self-pity and complaint took over, as in the story of the snake on the pole. Things were not going as "God's chosen people" might expect. Foreigners dominated them. "Eyes opened to know good and evil" saw *people* as the enemy—not the snake. God ought to reverse things, give his people dominance, reveal his kingdom and glory. When he did not, the priesthood inferred that he must be angry. "Do sacrifices to appease him, to get him on our side," they prescribed. Priestly scribes, descendants of Aaron, wrote detailed laws of sacrifice, as from the LORD, into documents they attributed to Moses. A bronze snake, presented as that which Moses had fashioned and put on the pole, was raised as an object of worship, in hope of deliverance. Num 21:9; 2 Kgs 18:4

It seemed right for the chosen people to exalt their God above the heavens and to humble themselves before him on the earth. Earlier names like "Most High" and "Almighty" were more appropriate. Gen 14:18-20; 17:1; Ps 91:1-2,9; Dan 4:2,25 "The Blessed" was another diversion. Mk 14:61 Rather than say the name Moses taught them, they spoke a reverent "the LORD." Such concealment testifies that the covenant-meaning, epitomized in the Eden story, was lost and unknown. The Septuagint, Greek translation of the Hebrew scriptures from the third century B.C., exhibits this falsified modesty. The King James Version of the Bible (KJV, 1611) adopted it in English.

But if the *covenant* which that name epitomizes is known again, let its authentic *sound* be known, too. Hebrew has it as four consonants, JHWH. The KJV renders it "Jehovah" in a few places. The Jerusalem Bible of 1966 adopted the pronunciation "Yahweh"—proposed in the mid-1940s as "more accurate" than "Jehovah." I recall being skeptical of this nondescript sound, when it was first proposed in the mid-1940s. Recently a passing remark of Hershel Shanks, Jewish scholar of the Dead Sea Scrolls, caught my eye: "In the Isaiah scroll four dots appear where we would expect to find the Tetragrammaton, the four-letter Hebrew name for God, *often pronounced Yahweh* (my emphasis), which the scribe did not want to write—it was too holy."[7] "*Often pronounced Yahweh*"? Shanks' honesty seems to have gotten the better of him. He knew all along that "Yahweh" is *not* the true pronunciation. Why then did scholars foist this known falsity on English-speaking Christianity? I suppose they felt it necessary still, in deference to Jewish piety, to guard the sacred name from being properly known and spoken!

Two forms of abbreviation in proper names suggest that it was pronounced

---

[7] *The Dead Sea Scrolls after Forty Years*, Washington, D.C.: Biblical Archaeological Society, 1991, p. 4. Shanks is the editor of *Biblical Archaeological Review* and *Bible Review*.

in long vowels. At the beginning of a name it appears as JO-el or JO-chanan (John). The sound of the first syllable must have been a long JO. Its abbreviation at the end of a name, like Eli-JaH, Hezek-JaH, also hallelu-JaH, uses the first letter and the last but elides the middle: J(HW)AH — a long "AH." The two syllables together would have sounded something like "JOH-WAH."

John the Baptist revived the suppressed name in its covenant-meaning. That his own name, JO-chanan, meaning "Johwah is gracious," is highlighted in his birth narrative testifies to this. Lk 1:13,60-64 For the priest Zechar-JaH to write his son's name on the tablet indicates the recovery of its heart-meaning! With that his mouth was opened and his tongue loosed to bless his people as Johwah himself had commissioned him. "Say to Aaron and his sons, Thus you shall bless the people of Israel: you shall say to them, Johwah bless you and keep you; Johwah make his face to shine upon you and be gracious to you; Johwah lift up his countenance (smile) upon you, and give you peace. So shall they put my name upon the people of Israel, and I will bless them." Num 6:22-27 Zechariah's song indicates this recovery, too: "You, child... will go before Johwah to prepare his ways, to give knowledge of salvation to his people in the forgiveness of their sins, through the tender mercies of our God, when the day shall dawn upon us from on high, to give light to those who sit in darkness, to guide our feet into the way of peace." Lk 1:76-79

But how can Johwah be "a God merciful and gracious" to a people who silence the name he has given them to know him by? How can he forgive a people who want him to be something else than a God who "forgives iniquity and transgression and sin"? The rulers rejected the name "my beloved son," which Jesus held so precious. They even called him a blasphemer for claiming it for himself. He in turn called their defense of a misled piety a "blasphemy against the Holy Spirit." Mt 12:31-32 How could Johwah forgive them if they suppressed his grace and forgiveness, if they chose instead a God they could impress or appease by sacrifices?

Jesus exposed such snake-like dishonesty in his saying concerning oaths. Mt 5:33-37; 23:16-22 The commandment said, "You shall fear *Johwah* your God, and serve him, and *swear by his name*!" Dt 6:13 Yet his people assured themselves that the way to be safe from "taking his name in vain" was to not utter it at all. Ex 20:7 They swore "by heaven," or "by the earth" (a humble opposite of "heaven"), or "by Jerusalem," or "by my head" (a humble opposite of God's "head"), or "by the temple," or "by the gold of the temple," or "by the altar," or "by the gift on the altar." Jesus saw the guile. To strip God's name of meaning and authority was to convert oath-taking into a game under their own control. "I say to you (if you cannot say 'Johwah'), do not swear at all. Let your 'Yes' mean yes and your 'No' no. Anything more than these comes from the *evil*"—the *psyche* of "evil," as God knows "good and evil."

"Father" and "Son of Man"

Knowing Moses and the psyche of the silenced name is critical toward knowing Jesus by the Gospels and the Gospels by him. He did not force the sound "Johwah" on his people, but conveyed its meaning by calling God "Father." Moses' word to Pharaoh, "Thus says Johwah, Israel is *my son, my first-born,*"implied this obverse. Ex 4:22-23 His song made it explicit: "Johwah,... is he not your *father* who created you?" Dt 32:6 Prophets had it, too. "You, Johwah, are our *father*, our redeemer from of old is your name," Isaiah confessed. Is 63:16 "Father" for God and "son" for God's people occurs in the intertestamental "Wisdom" of Sirach and of Solomon.[8] A memory in John cites Jesus' critics as being at least aware of it. "We have one father, even God," they claimed. Jn 8:41 Self-conscious humility avoided such language but did not directly prohibit it. The *Mishnah* of rabbinic tradition has God as Israel's "father," and Israel as "sons of God" in its oldest document, the *Pirke Aboth*, "Sayings of the Fathers," but nowhere else. The lack is likely a reaction to the bold use of those names by Jesus and the young church.[9]

A people whose piety considered it impious to utter the name Johwah, who hesitated likewise to call God "Father," could hardly call themselves God's "first-born" or "beloved son," either. For Jesus the covenant-sonship was the rock foundation; yet in ordinary circumstances, he deferred to the prevailing piety by calling himself "the son of man," humble opposite of "son of God." It had precedent. "One like a son of man" in Daniel stood for Israel as "son of

---

[8] Sirach 4:10; 23:1,4; 36:12; 51:10. Wisdom of Solomon 2:16,18; 5:5; 14:3; 16:26; 18:13. Sirach, written originally in Hebrew, is dated about 180 B.C. Wisdom of Solomon, from Alexandria and written in Greek, is generally dated about 100 B.C.

[9] "Rabbi Judah ben Tema said: Be bold as a leopard, and light as an eagle, and swift as a gazelle, and strong as a lion, to do the will of thy Father which is in heaven." *Pirke Aboth* 5:23. R.H. Charles, *The Apocrypha and Pseudepigrapha of the Old Testament*, in English. II. Oxford: At the Clarendon Press, 1913, 1963, p. 710. Also, Herbert Danby, *The Mishnah*. Oxford University Press, 1933, 1963, p. 458. *Pirke Aboth* has also a reference (3:19) to Israel as God's beloved son: "Beloved are Israel, that they are called sons of God.... As it is said, Sons are ye to the Lord your God." Dt 14:1 Charles, p. 702.

[10] The definitive study in my mind is Josephine Massyingberde Ford of Notre Dame, "The Son of Man": A Euphemism?" (*Journal of Biblical Literature* 1968) pp. 257-266.

God"—identified as "the saints of the Most High." Dan 7:13,18,27 Luke's account of Jesus' trial reveals the equivalence. "From now on *the son of man* shall be seated at the right hand of God," Jesus testified, to which Caiaphas responded, "Are you *the son of God* then?" Lk 22:69-70 "Son of man" did not obscure the covenant-meaning but even called attention to it.[10]

Jesus could refer to God as "the Father" of "the son of man." "The son of man is to come ... in the glory of his Father." Mt 16:27 "The hour has come for the son of man to be glorified.... Father, glorify your name." Jn 12:23,28

Apart from the confession of Stephen in Acts, the name "the son of man" for Jesus occurs only in the Gospels, and on his lips alone. Acts 7:56[11] The name "son of God" became the crucial issue. It epitomized the covenant-gospel of Moses and all the scriptures. By it the young church confessed Jesus boldly to authorities who persisted still in accusing and denying him.

Christianity knows nothing of this, however. Its piety has assumed that, as the name "son of God" for Jesus implied his deity, so his name "the son of man" implied his humanity. Modern theologians separate these names accordingly under the category "Christology."[12]

"One Johwah"

The covenant drama of Eden's two trees, and of Moses' ultimate choice, carries through in the prohibition of idolatry. "Hear, O Israel, Johwah our God is one Johwah; and you shall love Johwah your God with all your heart and with all your soul and with all your might." Dt 6:4-5 "I am Johwah your God, who brought you out of the land of Egypt, out of the house of bondage. You shall have no other gods over my face. You shall not make yourself a graven image." Ex 20:2-4 "I am Johwah, that is my name; my glory I give to no other, nor my praise to graven images." Is 42:8

"One Johwah" excludes the dualism of an "*evil* God" (like the devil) who inflicts trouble and sufferings, offset by the "*good* God" (supposedly Johwah),

---

[11] Two references in Revelation derive from its occurrence in Daniel: Dan 7:13; Rev 1:13; 14:14.

[12] Oscar Cullmann, *The Christology of the New Testament* (translated by Shirley G. Guthrie and Charles M. Hall. Philadelphia: The Westminster Press, 1959). Wolfhart Pannenberg, *Jesus—God and Man* (translated by Lewis L. Wilkins and Duane A. Priebe, Philadelphia: The Westminster Press, 1968). The tendency has been to sort out the name, "the Son of man," in three accents: sayings in which Jesus refers to his present ministry, sayings in which he speaks of his passion, and sayings which point to his future coming. All such studies presuppose still, that the name "the Son of God" means Jesus' deity.

who gives good and blessings. The snake in the garden, the voiceless testings of Israel in the wilderness, the Satan of Job, and the devil who tempted Jesus—all serve Johwah. People who yield to such lies cannot say, "The devil made me do it." The devil has no such power. The choosing is their own.

Idolatry has no concept of servanthood. It is a device of the self-assertive human psyche to harness the supernatural toward attaining what looks *good*, escaping what looks *evil*, or controlling what looks to be out of control. Worship arouses a *good god* to come through with the *good*, or induces an *evil god* to hold off some impending *evil*. Ahab's complaint against Micaiah illustrates the principle. "I hate him, for he never prophesies *good* concerning me but *evil*." 1 Kgs 22:8 He chose to believe four hundred prophets of a god who would do him *good*.

"One Johwah" is the wisdom of a trusting heart. "I believe that I shall see the *goodness* of Johwah in the land of the living. Wait for Johwah, be strong and let your heart take courage; yes, wait for Johwah." Ps 27:13-14 People who have not heard their sonship-name and calling do not know this choice, however. They can only improvise a religion or anti-religion of their own.

Lest the name Johwah become more a distraction than a help, I shall revert now, with rare exceptions, to the custom of concealing it under the familiar form, "the LORD." Readers will be aware of its covenant-meaning.

PART TWO

Solving the Gospels

The Question

I came to the religion faculty of Valparaiso University in the fall of 1958 and taught courses on the Gospels and the life of Christ. The "Wow!" of knowing myself as God's "beloved son" by "the gospel" Jesus himself believed opened texts for me and became the heart of my teaching. It was not the way of my tradition, but conflict did not arise until much later.

My immediate trouble was over biblical authority. A discipline of joint study with colleagues forced questions on me which I had never known to ask. I defended the Bible valiantly, determined to save it from rationalistic methodologies into which I felt they had fallen. The task became increasingly agonizing. It also diverted me from the real interest of my heart. One day, walking down a hallway in deep distress, I found myself praying helplessly, "Lord, it's your book. You are going to have to take care of it, I can't!" A voice answered dryly as from heaven, "I was wondering how long it would take you to catch on!" With that I was free. The word of God saved me; it did not need me to save it. I could ask the Bible any question now without fear of loss. For every question there must be an answer.

The sonship-gospel by which I lived had created Israel as God's people in the era of Moses. It had created Jesus too, and the young church. It had created the climate of understanding out of which every story and saying preserved in the Gospels was first told. My childhood pastor had it right: "No one can understand the Bible except by faith in the gospel." My first question of any text became "How does this flow from the gospel?" and "Why was this said the way it is said?" Answers that broke in were convincing and coherent in ways I could not have imagined. Doors opened to next questions which I would never have thought to ask.

My new world was exciting but lonely. The tradition of biblical authority in which I had been brought up could ask only "Is this true?" or "Did it really happen?" Any answer short of "Yes" would be rationalistic unbelief. As for contemporary biblical scholarship, this was not its world, either. Insights dependent on "revelation" or "gospel" or "faith" were beyond its province.

My decade at the University offered time and challenge for much searching. I joined the Society of Biblical Literature in 1959, read its *Journal*, respected its methods and its findings, even contributed articles. I searched resources beyond the Gospels—Qumran scrolls, Mishnah, Apocrypha and Pseudepigrapha, other Gospels like Thomas, and the first-century Jewish historian Flavius Josephus.

I read Albert Schweitzer's classic, *The Quest of the Historical Jesus* (1906). He surveyed numerous nineteenth-century efforts to write a life of Christ, then perceived that every writer tended to form Jesus in his own likeness. "There is nothing more negative than the result of the critical study of the Life of Jesus," he said.[1] Schweitzer saw Jesus as caught up in futurist eschatological expectations, which, he concluded, render him unknowable to our time.

One work Schweitzer reviewed intrigued me enough to investigate it further—David Friedrich Strauss' *Leben Jesu* (1835-36), in English *The Life of Jesus Critically Examined*.[2] Strauss impressed me not for his conclusions, but for noticing troublesome minute questions, especially in the birth narratives. His questions were honest! I felt the church ought to welcome them, be willingly tormented by them, not fear or suppress them! Yet the church of his day, trusting and reasserting its "scripture principle," could only denounce him.

Scholars had invested enormous effort in analyzing the "synoptic" or "lookalike" Gospels (Matthew, Mark, and Luke) and imagining how they came to be. A theory emerged which prevails to this day. Martin Dibelius in 1919 called it The Theory of Two Sources, "a relatively sure result," he thought. "This theory holds that Matthew and Luke are both dependent upon Mark and, in addition, upon a source which can be reconstructed out of the text of Matthew and Luke as the postulated collection known as Q."[3] Materials unique

---

[1] From the German, *Von Reimarus zu Wrede*. Translated by W. Montgomery. London: A. & C. Black, LTD, 1931. New York: McMillan, 1961, p. 398.

[2] Philadelphia: Fortress Press, 1972. In Schweitzer, chapters VII to IX, pp. 68-120.

[3] *From Tradition to Gospel*, translated by Bertram Lee Woolf. New York: Charles Scribner's Sons, p. 9. "Q" is from the German "Quelle," meaning source. The Research and Publications Division of the Society of Biblical Literature, with the Institute for Antiquity and Christianity in Claremont, CA, by its "International Q Project," is reconstructing out of Matthew and Luke what the lost "Q" might have looked like.

to Matthew (M) and to Luke (L) were further sources. The theory assumes that the four evangelists were theologian-authors and that the Gospels took form relatively late—Mark about 70 A.D., Matthew and Luke later still, and John toward the end of the century.

Recovering "the historical Jesus" from the Gospels seemed impossible. B.H. Streeter's metaphor of John could apply to any of them: "As well hope to start out with a string of sausages and reconstruct the pig."[4] Rudolf Bultmann searched the Gospels so, then concluded after long struggle, "I do indeed think that we can now know almost nothing concerning the life and personality of Jesus, since the early Christian sources show no interest in either, are moreover fragmentary and often legendary; and other sources about Jesus do not exist."[5]

The longing to know Jesus revived, however. Bultmann's student, Ernst Kaesemann in 1953, and his English counterpart James M. Robinson (1959), envisioned a "new quest of the historical Jesus."[6] Books or movies on Jesus continue to appear—some out of the church's piety, some simply travelogues, some out of critical scholarship, some pursuing limited questions, some speculative or even sensational. Recent scholarship has sought to reconstruct the distinctive "theology" of each Gospel on the assumption that the evangelists were editor-author-theologians.

But the quest to know Jesus continued. A well-advertised device of the "Jesus Seminar," founded by Robert W. Funk in 1985, subjected sayings of Jesus item by item over several years to the considered judgment of a group of scholars by way of a weighted vote, on the theory that sayings authentically Jesus' own would be a sound base toward knowing him historically. It has published an edition of Mark, in which the degree of consensus regarding the authenticity of various words this Gospel ascribes to Jesus, is color-coded.[7]

---

[4] *The Four Gospels*. London: Macmillan and Co., Limited. Fifth impression, 1936, p. 377.

[5] *Jesus*. Tuebingen: J.C.B. Mohr (Paul Siebeck), 1926. Translated as *Jesus and the Word*, by Louise Pettibone Smith and Ermine Huntress Lantero. New York: Charles Scribner's Sons, 1958, p. 8.

[6] Ernst Kaesemann, "The Problem of the Historical Jesus," in *Essays on New Testament Themes*. Translated by W.J. Montague. London: SCM Press Ltd, 1964. James M. Robinson, *A New Quest of the Historical Jesus*. London: SCM Press, 1959. The continuing interest is testified in a valuable collection of essays on specific points by notable scholars, edited by Harvey K. McArthur, *In Search of the Historical Jesus*. New York: Charles Scribner's Sons, 1969. Also essays by students in honor of Ernest Cadman Colwell, edited by F. Thomas Trotter, *Jesus and the Historian*. Philadelphia: The Westminster Press, 1968.

[7] Robert E. Funk, Roy W. Hoover, and the Jesus Seminar, *The Five Gospels: The Search for the Authentic Words of Jesus*. New York: Macmillan, 1993.

In a subsequent book, Funk surveys two centuries of effort to know the historical Jesus.[8] Scholarly theory has always assumed that in the actual history Jesus was not deity (which is true). It agrees with Christianity, however, that the name "son of God" for him implies deity (which it does not). How did the idea of Jesus' deity-sonship originate then? Paul did it. How did it get into the Gospels? Pauline theology influenced theologian-author Mark to write it into his Gospel. Mark had to be after Paul then, thus relatively late, 70 A.D. Matthew and Luke got it from Mark. The Gospel of John culminated the deification process. Funk is in this stream. He views his dispassionate method as initiating a "renewed quest." A final chapter, "Jesus for a New Age," proposes twenty-one rules to govern such inquiry. But it is a dead-end. "Son of God" for Jesus in Paul as well as in the Gospels is a language of covenant, *not* of deity.

In 1969 I left Valparaiso University to become pastor of Immanuel Lutheran Church, to which my family had belonged for a decade. My texts for preaching were usually Gospel readings designated for each Sunday of the church year. In 1970 we adopted a three-year cycle of lections, fruit of the Second Vatican Council. This tripled my texts! Readings from the Old Testament were added and the chanting of Psalms initiated. During the 1980s I had opportunity on three occasions to visit the Holy Land—walk where Jesus walked, see landscapes he saw, visit archaeological sites, understand details like "the pinnacle" and the technique of crucifixion.

Certain convictions have crystallized for me. The four Gospels remain our only real source toward knowing the young church and its Lord. Every preserved text is a testimony from the young church. The number of such testimonies is actually enormous. The peculiar heartbeat of my own self as God's "beloved son," parallel with Jesus, is the faith-climate from which these testimonies came and by which they make sense. The scriptures (Old Testament), as Jesus understood them, are *crucial* toward grasping the young church's thinking as well as his own.

As meanings of texts broke through for preaching and teaching, I began to sense how the four Gospels must have originated, what kind of literature they are, thus how they are to be read. That story follows. It departs from "the scripture principle" of my tradition. It departs also from the suppositions of biblical scholarship. Caught in its misconception of Jesus' sonship and of the origin of the Gospels, such scholarship dismisses concepts like revelation,

---

[8] *Honest to Jesus.* A Polebridge Press Book, Harper San Francisco, 1996, p. 240.

covenant, gospel, and faith as subjective and intangible. Yet the substantive content of these (like what Jesus himself believed), is not only accessible and comprehensible, but valid and crucial as evidence toward knowing him historically.

It will not be given me to study the rest of the New Testament with the intensity I have brought to texts of the Gospels these many years. My principle of coherence would lead me to assume, however, that the climate out of which the Epistles, Acts, and Revelation arose was likewise of the young church, namely Jesus' revelatory gospel and the history that grew from it. If the coherence I anticipate seems to fail at some point, there must be an explanation.

CHAPTER FOUR

From Old Testament to New

"Every scribe who has been trained for the kingdom of heaven is like a householder who brings out of his treasure what is new and what is old."

Matthew 13:52

Understanding the Gospels and recovering the history they preserve requires interweaving a second principle with that of the covenant-gospel, my principle of coherence. Texts need to be viewed stereoscopically in a kind of depth-perspective. The near level to be searched is the text as such, how it came to exist, why it says what it says the way it says it. Beneath and preceding this is the idea or event which the text remembers and wants to tell.

Detecting these levels is not easy. The tradition of inspiration as the ground of biblical authority cannot tolerate this notion. It reads everything flat. Truth lies in the first-impression sense of a text, for "the Spirit would not deceive." Such believing is called "childlike faith." When the sonship-gospel exposes this "faith" as a fallacy and breaks its tyranny, another difficulty looms. Reading texts in depth-perspective requires close study and clear thinking. Readers may follow my reasoning as this book proceeds and trust it somewhat, but few will undertake such work themselves. To test (perhaps correct or modify) a finding I propose, by entering the thought-process that yielded it, is not easy. To carry on into areas like the Epistles (which I do not touch), though not impossible, is harder work still. For those who venture it, the potential is unlimited. Insights will emerge which prove enriching, intelligible, discussible, convincing.

To illustrate, consider the word "testament." Greek Christianity, not knowing the root-meaning of "covenant," took "Testament" (Old and New) as title for two parts of its sacred Bible. Since Matthew, first book in the "New," began with a genealogy of Jesus and a birth narrative, the turning of "old" to "new" seemed to be Jesus' birthday. That was the view of Dionysius Exiguus (Dennis the Little), monk of Rome, originator of a universal calendar in 532 A.D. (in itself a brilliant concept). From it he counted backward ("before Christ") and forward ("Anno Domini," the year of our Lord).

At its root level, however, "covenant" means the revelatory word by which the LORD God binds himself to his people and his people to himself. When an enslaved Israel heard this word through Moses in Egypt, they "believed" the LORD's noble calling and were ready to follow. Thereby they entered a life of oneness with the God who spoke it. On God's side the covenant word stands firm and forever. He forgives and gladly receives home his children who fail him, if they will only return. It is his people who defect and fail.

The defection of Israel was long and sad: "My covenant which they broke, though I was their husband," the LORD grieved by Jeremiah of the Israel he once "took by the hand" and brought out of Egypt. Jer 31:31-34 He promised a "new covenant"—new not in substantive content but in the way it would get through to his people. "I will put my torah (synonym of covenant) within them, and I will write it upon their hearts; and I will be their God and they shall be my people.... They shall all know me, from the least to the greatest, says the LORD; for I will forgive their iniquity and I will remember their sins no more."

In the history itself, the turning point from old to new was Jesus' blood or death. "This cup is the new covenant in my blood," Jesus says in Paul's version of the supper. 1 Cor 11:25 By his blood, Jesus is "the mediator of the new covenant," Hebrews has it. Heb 9:14-15 Recognizing that his death-date was the turning point cannot affect a calendar that turns on his birth-date, but has rich significance toward reading the Gospels in depth-perspective, or stereo-scopically.

Jesus' entire ministry, John the Baptist's too, lay on the "old testament" side of his dying. The need is then to distinguish pre-death memories of Jesus preserved in the Gospels, from memories which, though randomly mixed with these, view the event of his cross and resurrection as completed. Such sorting is the work of the "scribe trained for the kingdom of heaven," who, as Jesus put it, "brings out of his treasure what is new and what is old." Mt 13:52 "His treasure" is the covenant revelation. It does not change. The distinction between new and old pertains to what happened in the history. It was new to proclaim without compromise the tragic distortions which had caused the deaths of both John and Jesus. The "treasure" of a scribe "trained for the kingdom of heaven" will continue to expose that grief even now.

The covenant-gospel (epitomized in the name "son of God") is my principle of coherence toward recovering what any preserved saying or story means, every sentence and word of it. Asking "why this was said the way it is said" reveals also levels of the history. For example, I showed in Chapter 2 how Jesus' covenant-sonship opened the temptation narrative for me. This treasure enabled me to understand each episode in its own right. I could then see that these episodes, though preserved as a literary package, mark three distinct points in Jesus' ministry—beginning (wilderness), middle (mountain) and end (pinnacle). All three make sense on the "old testament" side of Jesus' death. They are evidence therefore toward knowing him historically.

"New Testament Overlay"

"New Testament overlay" is my term for memories which, though mixed into the Gospels, could not have made sense or been told until after and in view of Jesus' death and resurrection. Such material must be held in reserve toward reconstructing the post-resurrection history of the young church, source of all preserved testimonies. This distinction yielded also a preliminary operating principle. Anything told in the Gospels that *can* be understood on the "old testament" side *shall* be so understood.

An early puzzle was Jesus' call to "take up *the cross* and follow me." Mt 16:24 "Follow me" could express a pre-death memory of Jesus. The drastic imagery, "take up the cross," however, could not have made sense to Jesus' disciples until they had seen him both crucified and victorious. Thus it is "New Testament overlay."

The opening verse of Mark says, "The beginning of the gospel of *Jesus Christ, the son of God.*" Three names for him are gathered here as in a set. Each of these flowed from "the gospel" which Jesus himself believed, lived by, and preached on the old testament side. Together, however, they express the young church's full-blown confession on the "new testament" side. Mark's scroll will tell how the "gospel" that yielded this confession began.

Another testimony in Mark summons the term "gospel" as a title for Jesus' message at the very beginning of his ministry. "Jesus came into Galilee *preaching the gospel of God*, and saying 'The time is fulfilled and the kingdom of God is at hand; *repent and believe the gospel.*'" Mk 1:14-15 I suggested earlier that "glad news" as a title for the covenant-message entered the vocabulary of the young church from Isaiah. Luke 4:18; Is 61:1; 52:7 Old testament or new, that "glad news" in itself has not changed. Whether spoken by Moses to Israel in the exodus history, or to Jesus at his baptism, or to the disciples out of Jesus' death and resurrection, it is always his revelatory covenant-word from heaven, unknown and unknowable except by his saying it. "Repent" means let go any "believing" which would inhibit a hearer from believing this.

Some meanings change, however, as words pass from the old testament side to the new, and this must be detected. When John introduced Jesus to two of his disciples as "the lamb of God," this was familiar old testament language. Jn 1:35-36; Is 40:11 Jesus as "the lamb of God *who takes away the sin of the world,*" heralds the completed event, however. Jn 1:29 As a post-resurrection amplification, it contributes to the history of the young church and its witness.

On the old testament side, the name "son of God," which Jesus treasured for himself and lived out to the end, was embattled—not only in his temptations but by the authorities of temple and synagogue. This core-truth of everything Jesus taught revealed the aberration of their own tradition. It called them to "repent" of it, thus imposed his authority over theirs. They charged Jesus with arrogance and blasphemy for taking this name for himself and teaching his people so. In Caiaphas' court, that charge became the ground for condemning him to death. On the new testament, post-resurrection side, the dispute is settled. The voice of Majestic Glory from heaven has vindicated that name, pronounced it on Jesus again in the presence of witnesses with unarguable finality, "This is my son, my beloved, with whom I am well pleased." 2 Pet 1:17 To resist this verdict is to defy the word of the living God.

The name "Jesus," as English Christianity speaks it, transliterates the Greek. In Hebrew it is "Joshua," a common hero name at the time, meaning "savior." The amplification, "he will *save* his people *from their sins,*" fills Jesus' name with a content learned from the event of his death and resurrection. Mt 1:23 This meaning is a witness of the young church, knowable only on the "new testament" side. To read the Joseph-story in Matthew at this level, thus in depth-perspective, is to recognize that it is a post-resurrection witness and needs to be understood so.

A major shift occurred with respect to "christ" or "messiah." On the old testament side, popular expectation attached that name to its hope for a leader who would inaugurate Israel's long-promised kingdom and glory. Peter had this ambition in mind when he broke down under pressure and confessed of

Jesus, "You are the christ." Mk 8:29 The amplification of this confession in Matthew, however, abandons that illusion and redefines "christ" by the insight of the young church—a manner of messiahship which nobody would have imagined. "You are the christ, *the son of the living God.*" Mt 16:16 Nathanael's confession is likewise full-blown new testament: "Rabbi, you are *the son of God*, you are *the king of Israel.*" So is Jesus' reference to himself in that context as the Jacob upon whom "the angels of God ascend and descend." By him Israel's God will accomplish what he promised and intended all along, break through to bless not only his people but the nations. Jn 1:49-51; Gen 28:12-14

The name "Lord" for Jesus underwent similar transformation. His disciples and people had called him this respectfully as their teacher and leader. "You call me teacher and lord; and you are right, for so I am,"Jesus said. Jn 13:13 "A disciple is not above his master, or a servant above his lord." Mt 10:24 After the resurrection, however, "Lord" testifies to Jesus at the right hand of God, as in the psalm, "The LORD said to my lord, Sit at my right hand, till I make your enemies your footstool." Ps 110:1; Mt 22:44 Other sayings in the Gospels have him as "Lord" in this post-resurrection sense, too. "Not every one who says to me, '*Lord, Lord,*' will enter the kingdom of heaven." Mt 7:21-23 "'*Lord, Lord,* open to us!'" Mt 25:11 Depth-perspective insight will infer from such usage that the entire text in which it occurs is a post-resurrection witness of the young church—speaking not in its own name, however, but in his.

Even ambiguities can yield profit. Consider Jesus' word from the cross, "Father, forgive them, for they know not what they do." Lk 23:34 This saying images the character of his Father who "forgives iniquities and transgressions and sins," also of a Moses who interceded for his people in just this way. Ex 34:6-7; Ex 32:32 It lives out Jesus' call to "love as yourself" not only those who love you, but even persecutors who appear to be "enemies." Mt 5:44 Surely this was Jesus' mind in the pre-death history, as the young church knew him.

Yet the question is in order: Did Jesus actually utter this aloud on the cross, so that a witness heard and reported it? Or might some witness, in his own telling of the passion history, have had reason to put this saying into his mouth? Assuming the latter, a subsequent level of the history needs to be imagined. Why might someone, in telling Jesus' passion, have wanted to report Jesus as saying this? Perhaps a shamed disciple perceived himself among those who did "not know what they were doing," yet came to know how Jesus loved and forgave him in the dark hour of his dying. How could he testify to this briefly and yet unmistakably, so that others who "did not know what they were doing" might hear Jesus' love and forgiveness for their comfort, too? He did so by putting into Jesus' mouth words which reflected his heart. No one else than he could ever pray like this—the son who died at his Father's call for the sake of just such love. A depth-perspective question of this sort opens the event on both sides—the mind and heart of Jesus in his dying, but also the young church testifying to his unimaginable love.

Such questioning may illuminate the "pinnacle of the temple" narrative. Its association with Jesus' temptation in Gethsemane puts it on the old testament side of his death. Yet Jesus could hardly have told this of himself. Some witness in the young church must have dramatized by it what was at stake in Jesus' climactic prayer. Temptation narratives Jesus told show the devil mocking the word of God. This one does the same. But how might an imagery as drastic as "Cast yourself down" from the pinnacle have even occurred to the one who told it so?

In 1982 I walked the Kidron Valley road northward from Hinnom and the pool of Siloam. As it curved, I saw the dramatic southeast "pinnacle" corner of the temple wall come into view. The modern Ha Ofel road around its base was obscured. The pinnacle rose high from the slope of the temple mountain, which descended steeply then to the valley floor. Judas' suicide came to my mind as in Acts: "Falling headlong he burst open in the middle and all his bowels gushed out. And it became known to all the inhabitants of Jerusalem." Acts 1:18 Judas must have leaped from that wing-tip corner! His body, plunging unrestrained down the ruthless hillside, had been torn apart by protruding rocks until it hit bottom and came to gory rest! Subsequently I found the translation "hanged himself" in Matthew's account to be excessive. Mt 27:5 The term means literally, "cut off his own breath of life." Any self-inflicted death could be depicted so.

The pinnacle was in full view from Gethsemane. I imagined how one of the disciples, sensing now the horror Jesus faced when he prayed to do his Father's will, might juxtapose that horror with the horror of Judas' suicide. Judas had "cast himself down" from the pinnacle in despair of his unbearable evil. The devil's taunt, "Cast yourself down," mocked the Father's will as impossible, unreal, insane. It made graphic the horror of Jesus' willing "Yes" to crucifixion, a plunge more vividly awful than Judas'. How could God's "beloved son" even think of doing this? Why should he? But Jesus did it! He did not question his Father's love or sanity. "You shall not put the LORD your God to the test," he quoted Moses. Dt 6:16 He did not slither right or left like a snake, but clung to promises like, "that you may live and that it may go well with you," or "on the third day I will raise you up, that you may live before me." Dt 5:33; Hos 6:2

Jesus knew what he was doing. By the wisdom and faithfulness of his Father's covenant-word, he lived his sonship-servanthood to the finish. Thereby he exposed, all alone, the perversity that had corrupted his people for so long and forced it to its inevitable end. Imaging the love of the Father in his own body, he did not give up on his people or his wayward disciples, but swallowed up their guilt even to death. He trusted the outcome to the Father who sent him.

This was the turning-point of the new covenant. It had not happened before. It would not happen again.

CHAPTER FIVE

From Oral Literacy to Written

"Preach as you go, saying, 'The kingdom of heaven is at hand.'"   Matthew 10:7

It was on the new testament side of his death and resurrection that Jesus commissioned his apostles to preach the Gospel to all nations. Mt 28:19 "As the Father has sent me, even so I send you," he said. Then he "breathed on" them and added, "Receive the Holy Spirit." Jn 20:21-22 The church knows this sending as its call to mission and evangelism.

An earlier "sending" belongs to his ministry on the old testament side. Mt 10:1-15; Mk 6:7-13; Lk 9:1-6; 10:1-12 It appears that Jesus would send his disciples on assigned routes to all the towns of Galilee. Of the message he gave them only a headline is preserved: "Preach as you go, saying, 'The kingdom of heaven is at hand.'" Mt 10:7 A memory in Matthew has John the Baptist preaching this, too. Mt 3:2; 4:17

Oral Literacy: Memorizing

Reading and writing was a scholarly specialty in Jesus' day. Ordinary communication continued to be word-of-mouth. The prophet received a word from God in response to some need, then compacted it mentally into a form which he himself mastered. When an occasion to preach came, he would drill this "text" into his audience until they had memorized it and could recite it back to him. He would then teach what it meant. If the message were one which the whole land should hear, disciples were his instrument.

They were young men, teen-agers, whose families released them for this service. Others in the prophet's audience would come and go, but these youth stayed and mastered everything he taught. Preparation for a mission was especially intense. Every word was important. Explanation and context needed to be fully understood. When the disciples had mastered the words and their meaning, the prophet would send them out on assigned routes to every town in the land. They would drill the message into local youths, who would spread this "word of the LORD" in turn throughout their community. In the days of Elijah and Elisha, young men who served this function were called "sons of the prophets." 2 Kgs 2:3; 6:1; Amos 7:14 In Isaiah, as in our Gospels, they were called "disciples." Is 8:14

The system of communication was efficient. Prophets were a threat to kings and priests because their message was never private. "All Israel from Dan to Beersheba knew that Samuel was established as a prophet of the LORD," a memory says, and "the word of Samuel came to all Israel." 1 Sam 3:20; 4:1 By youthful voices Samuel could "call the people together to the LORD," as at Mizpah, so that all Israel would know how the LORD by Samuel had anointed Saul to be king. 1 Sam 10:17 When Saul's kingship failed, all Israel learned Samuel's rhythmic oracle of judgment against him and its occasion. This saying is among the few preserved in writing: "Behold, to obey is better than sacrifice.... Because you have rejected the word of the LORD, he has also rejected you from being king." 1 Sam 15:22-23 All Israel heard Amos' judgment against Jeroboam and Amaziah, priest at Bethel, who complained, "The land is not able to bear all his words." Amos 7:10-17 John the Baptist spread his word by disciples, too. The authorities resisted him, but "the people all held that John was a real prophet." Mt 21:31-32; Mk 11:32

The oracle would be framed concisely in a form readily memorized—rhythmic or song, metaphor-story or parable, vision or proverb. Symbolic enactments could be verbalized, too, as in the ministry of Ezekiel. Isaiah embodied a summary judgment in the startling names he was commanded to give his children—Shearjashub, "a remnant shall return," or Mahershalal-hashbaz, "the spoil speeds, the prey hastes." Is 7:3; 8:1-5 His testimonies and the names of his children were written down and sealed among his disciples, so that what the authorities rejected would be heard even when those who had memorized it died away. Is 8:16-18

The capacity to memorize, retain, and recite was a noble art. Hints of the discipline are preserved in Isaiah, in part where words well-known were being recited with little awareness of meanings. "For it is precept upon precept, line upon line, here a little, there a little." Is 28:10-13 "Their fear of me is a commandment of men learned by rote," Isaiah grieved. Is 29:13

Prophets were "disciples" themselves first. Since God was the originator of their word, they needed to learn humbly from him what they would
then pass on. Thus Isaiah says of himself, "The Lord GOD has given me *the
tongue of those who are taught,* that I may know how to sustain with a word
him that is weary. *Morning by morning he awakens my ear to hear as those
who are taught.* The Lord GOD has opened my ear, and I was not rebellious,
I turned not backward... I hid not my face from shame and spitting. For
the Lord GOD helps me...." Is 50:4-7

The accumulating tradition was passed similarly from parents to children, beginning when a child could eat at the family table. "To whom will he
teach knowledge, and to whom will he explain the message? Those who are
weaned from the milk, those taken from the breast." Is 28:9 Words were repeated, sacred stories told, psalms sung. Explanations could come as the child
grew, but the words needed to be mastered first. "Things that we have heard
and known, that our fathers have told us, we will not hide from their children,
but tell to the coming generations the glorious deeds of the LORD, and his
might, and the wonders he has wrought. He established a testimony in Jacob
and appointed a law in Israel, which he commanded our fathers to teach to
their children, that the next generation might know them, the children yet
unborn, and grow up and tell them to their children, so that they should set
their hope in God, and not forget the works of God, but keep his commandments." Ps 78:3-7

"These words which I command you this day shall be upon your heart,
and you shall teach them diligently to your children," Moses said. Dt 6:6-7;
11:18-19 Another context summoned adults to remember and recite again what
they had learned by heart from their parents: "The word is very near you; it is
in your mouth and in your heart, so that you can do it." Dt 30:14 Disciplined
accuracy was demanded: "You shall not add to the word which I command
you, nor take from it," meaning "the statutes and ordinances which I teach
you." Dt 4:2; 12:32

"Writing and sealing," as in Isaiah, illustrates how "oral literacy" (as I call
it) became written. Is 8:16 Of Elijah's prophetic words few are preserved, of
Elisha's next to none. Sayings of Hosea and Amos were at some point gathered
from the memory of their disciples, written down, and arranged on manuscript by some scribe who cherished them. Preservation became purposeful
and common. A large array of what began as oral, including psalms, was gathered, arranged, written down on scrolls, and thus preserved. Much of our

scriptures originated in this way.

Prophetic communication remained oral, however. In Judaism, the sayings of revered teachers were conveyed to a next generation of teachers by recitation and memorization. It appears to me that the New Testament "letter" labeled "James" was formed by laying randomly, end to end, a collection of his carefully crafted sermon-starters, all once memorized.

The virtue of writing was preservation. But there was risk. Oral literacy was by nature person-to-person. Explanations were added out of the covenant-memory and faith which had originally produced it. Written literacy was an object, impersonal, subject to interpretation by the culture and private mind of any scholar who read or researched it. Original and thus authentic meanings readily gave way to mere impressions of meaning.

Disciples

In Jesus' day, not only the temple but every synagogue had its library of biblical scrolls and related literature, hand-copied on durable sheep or goat leather, or on papyrus from Egypt. Lessons appointed for each sabbath were read in worship throughout the year. Acts 13:27 One preserved memory has Jesus do a reading from Isaiah in his home synagogue and preach on it. Lk 4:16-22 John in Judea and Jesus in Galilee grew up hearing and learning to recite the same sacred readings, also singing the same appointed psalms. Synagogue schools taught boys to read. Those who wished to read further were granted access to the sacred library. The language of community and commerce was the widely prevalent Aramaic, but Hebrew remained the language of the scriptures and psalms.

Such fragments of John's preaching, as are preserved in our Gospels, had been taught throughout Judea by his disciples. That dissemination made John troublesome to the priestly authorities in Jerusalem, even though he himself remained across the Jordan in Herod Antipas' Perea, the last edge of Israel's "wilderness" wanderings.

Jesus' disciples had learned basic passages of the scriptures from synagogue readings in their growing-up years, as he himself had, but he taught them further. The time for such discipline was early morning, as Isaiah said of himself, "Morning by morning he awakens my ear." When Jesus had a message he wanted them to convey, he may have framed this first for a sermon. It could take the form of a dialogue with critics, or a decisive "either-or" in parable. It would be drilled unforgettably, context and meaning clear for them to share.

When they were ready, he would send them out on their assigned routes. I take the instructions preserved in the Gospels to have been standard. Mt 10:5-14; Mk 6:7-11; Lk 9:1-4; 10:4-11 The audience Jesus envisioned was "the lost sheep of the house of Israel"—in effect, his whole people. The gospel-truth by which he himself "healed the sick, raised the dead, cleansed lepers, and cast out demons," would have the same effect when spoken out of the disciples' mouths.

"What you received for nothing, pass on for nothing," Jesus said. "Take no staff or weaponry, no money, no food, no extra clothing, no sandals. When you enter a town, state your mission, then wait for someone to invite you in. Don't feel embarrassed to depend on such hospitality. You are givers also to them, and in like freedom. Find youths in each town who will learn the message from you and pass it on further. When you have taught them well, go on to the next town. If you face opposition, or if no one wants to receive you, don't fret. Give that town a public sign though, shake its dust off your feet so as to have no part in it, and go on."

To speak "in Jesus' name" was to extend the range of his voice. His disciples must not add to what he taught them nor subtract from it. When they returned, they would report not only how they were received, but also what they were hearing from the people they served, including questions or criticisms to which Jesus could then respond. Thus he could fairly ask them on one occasion, "Who do the people say that I am?" Mk 8:27

The impact Jesus made on the people was largely positive at first. He was often invited to speak in a synagogue. Being at odds with elements of his own background tradition, however, he became a growing threat.

Remembering

The abundant and widely memorized materials, spread abroad by the disciples from the mouth of Jesus over an extended period, are a prime element of the "oral literacy" preserved in the Gospels.

After the resurrection Jesus' disciples returned to Galilee, as he and angels had directed them. They saw him there alive as he had promised, and their own transformation became full.[9] They revisited towns they had known on their former routes, telling how the death that had seemed a disaster was not so after all, but the ground of forgiveness, resurrection, life, and salvation.

---

[9] The story of the young church in Galilee, strongly hinted in the passion-resurrection contexts of Matthew, Mark, and John, but unknown in Luke and Acts, will be told in Part Seven.

The message struck home. It seeded the young church everywhere. People who only recently had despaired of him, now saw Jesus victorious—not a liar and blasphemer as the priestly authorities had portrayed him, but faithful and true to his Father and theirs.

Out of such celebration, the impulse arose naturally to recall and recite again words learned from Jesus directly or through his disciples long ago.[10] Indications of this are preserved. "*Remember* how he told you, while he was still in Galilee, that the son of man must be delivered into the hands of sinful men, and be crucified, and on the third day rise," the angel told the women. Lk 24:6 Such remembering was not casual. Jesus had formulated his passion-prediction precisely, made his disciples learn it "line upon line" against their own will, then recite it back until they had mastered it. To "remember" meant to replay it not only in mind but by lips and tongue. So repeated, what Jesus had believed and taught began to make awesome and liberating sense.

A promise in John has a broad connotation: "The Holy Spirit will bring to your remembrance all that I have said to you." Jn 14:26 The disciples will systematically recite again everything they had once committed to memory and taught others.

Most specific is the imagery of "baskets" attached to the feeding narrative in all four Gospels. John has it in greatest detail: "Jesus told his disciples, 'Gather the fragments that nothing may be lost.' So they gathered them and filled twelve baskets with fragments from the five barley loaves, left by those who had eaten." Jn 6:12-13 Twelve is the number of the young church after the resurrection. The wilderness feeding was not of body, but of hearts nurtured on and satisfied by the word of God—as when Jesus answered Satan in his own wilderness testing, "It is written, Man shall not live by bread alone, but man lives by every word that proceeds out of the mouth of the LORD." Mt 4:4 The five barley loaves, though a boy's literal lunch, came to depict what

---

[10] This reconstruction and the conclusions drawn from it depart radically from the view of scholars concerning the relatively late origin of the Gospels, as represented in Birger Gerhardsson, *Memory and Manuscript: Oral Tradition and Written Transmission in Rabbinic Judaism and Early Christianity* (Uppsala: C.W.K. Gleerup, 1961). Gerhardsson summarizes his thesis, "There is a good deal of evidence that the majority of Jesus' disciples came, not from some Jewish sect, but from the main stream of Judaism...which looked to the learned Pharisees as its teachers and spiritual leaders.... It is against such a background that we must see the fact that *for several decades* (my emphasis) the tradition concerning Christ appears to have been carried orally. This was normal traditional procedure in this section of Judaism.... But just as the Rabbi's pupils had their own private notes... so they began within the Church to write down parts of the tradition concerning Christ in the same way. With the help of such notes, but naturally on a basis of oral tradition, a beginning was then made to put together more extensive collections in the style of the Gospel of Mark—both oral and written." (pp. 201-202)

Jesus taught during his ministry, which his disciples had learned and distributed. The fragments were every item still recoverable. The baskets were collections of such fragments.

Memories flashed back awesomely to any who were filled now with Jesus' Spirit and life. "Do you remember?" one would ask another, then begin reciting, the other perhaps joining in. Moses had longed for such a day, "Would that all the people were prophets, and that the LORD would put his spirit upon them!" Num 11:29 It was happening—to sons and daughters, old and young, servants too, both male and female! Joel 2:28-29 Excitement grew as familiar words yielded heart-meanings beyond anything their reciters had realized when they first learned them.

Written Memory

By an equally spontaneous impulse, some who had learned a bit of writing as well as reading from synagogue teachers in their youth, though not professional scribes, began to inscribe these recovered sayings and story-contexts on parchment or papyrus, lest they be forgotten. Disciple groups in town upon town developed "libraries" of such fragments, not formally but in homes. The language was Aramaic, except that quotations of the scriptures would preserve the familiar and traditional Hebrew.

Sayings of Jesus once memorized were the catalyst, but items of personal memory and witness began soon to be added. A major impetus was the desire to recover and preserve details of what had happened to Jesus in Jerusalem at his passion. Witnesses told what they had seen and heard. Inside information was sought from any who had been there and might know. The record preserves what are likely names of such sources—Malchus of the temple guard, Chuza of Herod's court. Jn 18:10; Lk 8:3 The centurion of the crucifixion squad, though unnamed, was another. Other memories took precise form, too, like healings Jesus had done as people once told them. Apostolic story-texts of Jesus' glory, graphic metaphor, condensed for memorizing, were treasured, recited and written down. Readings familiar from synagogue worship came alive, "filled full" in Jesus as he had understood them.

Those who could read began to search the scriptures further in their synagogue, but through Jesus' eyes and mind. Exciting findings were eagerly shared. John accounted for Jesus' dramatic interruption of trade in the temple by citing a Psalm, "Zeal for your house has consumed me, and the reproaches of those who reproached you have fallen on me." Jn 2:17; Ps 69:9 Someone perceived in Isaiah a remarkable description of Jesus' character: "Behold my servant, whom I uphold, my chosen, in whom my soul delights; I have put my Spirit upon him ... a bruised reed he will not break, and a smoldering wick he will not quench." Mt 12:18-21; Is 42:1-4 Thus Jesus, to whom the scriptures had made such rich sense, became the more known himself through them.

Sharing and interchange followed with like spontaneity. When one community learned that another was accumulating a similar library of Jesus-memories, the natural impulse was to expand its own resources by exploring and copying from the other. Before long, representatives of Galilean churches came to Judea to search Judean treasures, and Judeans to Galilee. Memory items were preserved as individual fragments, sometimes more than one on a single sheet. As the process of exchange grew, related fragments began to be copied together, so as to fill up valuable writing material. Others would copy this later as a whole. Nevertheless, randomness prevailed for the most part, with no conscious movement toward widespread comprehensiveness or uniformity. Each local library possessed some materials rather commonly known, but others peculiar to itself. As people came to value these libraries and depend on them, "oral literacy" as the means of preserving Jesus-material for a next generation diminished.

This was the era when, to borrow a term from the two-document hypothesis, everything was Q (Quelle, "source") and Q was everywhere. The process began from the first years after the resurrection. It continued into the second decade. "Eyewitnesses," who had participated in one or another aspect of the event, were still alive and available for interview. Lk 1:2

The Four Gospels

Meanwhile, by Paul and others, the gospel of Jesus' sonship, death, and resurrection was reaching colonies of Jews throughout the Greek world, who nevertheless maintained their identity in relation to Jerusalem, law, and temple. The message overflowed freely and warmly to the native populations, the Gentiles. These churches knew something of Jesus' passion and resurrection, as Acts and the letters indicate, but not much else of him. They would gladly know more, if that were possible. Once it was rumored that churches in Judea and Galilee even possessed libraries of written memory concerning Jesus, the urge to find and copy such treasures would be compelling. It would stir spontaneously in many places at much the same time.

In that early era the churches of Judea and Galilee, young and fresh, rich in understanding and freedom, remained within synagogue and temple. Authorities who upheld the tradition considered the Jesus-affair to have been settled by his death. A few stubborn fanatics might testify to Jesus as risen from the dead, but such illusion must soon give way to reality. That did not happen, however. The young church saw Jesus alive, knew him, and cherished the wonder of his truth amd freedom. They believed and lived by his gospel, shared it with their neighbors, waited for the breakthrough when leaders of temple and synagogue would see in Jesus their own authentic heritage and glory.

Once a researcher from some distant Greek church found a treasury of Jesus-fragments in a community of Judea or Galilee and gained access to it, three obvious requirements would govern his work. He would secure a quality scroll on which to transcribe his findings. He would translate each fragment-item from Aramaic into Greek. He would group his materials, lay them out in some organized sequence, then transcribe them. The document he carried home would not look like random fragments laid end to end. It would exhibit the best progression he could manage for the sake of readers—culminating in the passion story. An analogy might be finding a box of old but cherished family photographs, mostly unlabeled, some recognizable, others making little sense, wanting to preserve each of them intact in an album, but arranging them as well as possible in what would appear to be a progressive story.

Some of these Jesus-fragments were found already grouped. A commonly known sequence offered some help—John the Baptist first and then Jesus, Jesus' ministry in Galilee first and then his decision to go to Jerusalem, his ministry and conflicts there, then his cross and death. Many witnesses were still living. They might tell more. Jesus' final days in Jerusalem and his passion would come at the end, followed by the resurrection. Within this basic structure, each album-maker grouped his materials as best he could.

These principles account largely for the phenomenon of the Gospels as we know them. The need and desire to have such material was spontaneous in each instance. The "evangelists," so-called, worked individually, at different places, independent of and unknown to any other, but within a limited time-frame. Where the collections they researched preserved similar resources, portions of these already grouped, they would look somewhat alike or "synoptic." Differing materials in the Gospels reflect the randomness of the collections. Variations between materials basically alike, or a doubling of texts, may have existed already in the library sources, although the literary style of translators could also vary.

Luke, a Gentile to whom tradition has attributed the third Gospel and Acts, explains his process to "Theophilus," whom I take to be any God-loving reader. He identifies his resource as "delivered to us by those who from the beginning were eyewitnesses and ministers of the word." Lk 1:1-3 This suggests access to a library of written fragments. He has looked these over closely for some time, studying how to arrange them into "an orderly account" as a continuing narrative.

As for Mark, I see no reason to doubt that he was of Jerusalem. Acts 12:12 His account of a youth who fled home naked from Jesus' arrest appears to be a signature out of personal memory. Mk 14:51-52 I infer that he and Luke drew their materials from churches in Judea. Luke gives evidence of having known Galilee only by reputation.[11]

I would assume that the source for Matthew was an extensive library of Jesus-fragments, gathered and preserved in Matthew's home town, Capernaum, where he as apostle was prominently known. Since the name "Matthew" displaces "Levi," chief tax collector in that district, and since Levi would have been too old for a place among Jesus' disciples, I take Matthew to have been Levi's son and the entry of Matthew's name a kind of signature to this Gospel. Mt 9:9-10; Mk 2:14; Lk 5:27-29 The Gentile church of Antioch, with which Matthew is traditionally associated, may well have commissioned it.

The Gospel of John fits this reconstruction, too. John reports that Jesus from the cross gave his mother into his care. Jn 19:27 His own mother, wife of his father Zebedee (probably the "Salome" of Mark), was also at the cross. She and John would have taken Mary home with them to Bethsaida. The memory suggests that Mary, rather than return to Nazareth, lived out her life in continuing association with the women who had followed her son to Judea and the cross, among whom she had been a first witness to the resurrection.

I infer that John wrote his basic memoir of the passion very early (specifically John 7-8,10-13,18-20), that he added other memories and commentary later, and that his materials were preserved in Bethsaida, his family home. He may have stayed and served there far longer than the record of Acts would lead us to imagine. Other items may have entered this special collection too, such as memories associated with Nathanael of Cana. Jn 1:45; 21:2 The Bethsaida "library" was of a different order than the usual Jesus-fragments. A researcher from afar came upon it, translated its varied items into Greek, arranged them

---

[11] Hans Conzelmann, *The Theology of Luke*, translated by Geoffrey Busswell (New York: Harper & Brothers, 1960), pp. 69-71.

as best he could, transcribed them on a scroll, and brought this treasure home to his own community.

Other collections than the four Gospels, more limited, were gathered also and in other languages. These four commended themselves to churches of the Greek world, however. By eager copying and exchange, they quickly became a common heritage.

Two considerations dictate an early date for all four. Although the process of exchange yielded an increasing commonality of material, the collections were still randomly diverse, each holding treasures unique to itself. Secondly and strikingly, abundant and widespread as the Jesus-material was for a time, it disappeared early and utterly, not a shred of it preserved. Nothing that looks in any way like what scholars suppose "Q" to be has ever been found.

Why not? Those who began to write such memories, keep them in their homes, then seek out additional materials from neighboring towns, had no reason to keep this secret. As the leaders of synagogues and of the temple sensed that the Jesus-movement was not dying away but growing, that shocking conversions were happening, tensions increased. The Jesus-people came to be viewed as subversive. Rulers faithful to their tradition had reason to become the more aware. Climactically, if they noticed strangers from foreign lands coming in to research and copy materials from what by now had become extended libraries among the Jesus-people, the notion of their importance would begin to dawn.

Someone among these critics would at some point see an opportunity to wipe out every last memory of Jesus. He would consult with others in both Judea and Galilee. They would agree on a day to search out and systematically destroy every shred of these pernicious collections, everywhere and at once, leaving the Jesus-people no chance to hide them away. That action, rigorously pursued, would occasion a widespread and intense persecution. Lashings, excommunications, imprisonments, even death, would await any who tried to hide such treasures or cover up for others. Members of households would be forced in the name of faithfulness to betray father or mother, sister or brother.

A memory of such anguish in Hebrews refers to Judea in particular: "But recall the former days when, after you were enlightened, you endured a hard struggle with sufferings, sometimes being publicly exposed to abuse and affliction, and sometimes being partners with those so treated. For you had compassion on the prisoners, and you joyfully accepted *the plundering of your property*, since you knew that you yourselves had a better possession and an abiding one." Heb 10:32-35 Persecution of this sort would account for the utter loss of "Q." The once-extensive libraries of Jesus-memory would have been wiped out relatively early, to be preserved only in the "Gospels" that had been compiled on behalf of Greek churches and transported to distant lands. True, I am bridging minimal evidences by broad leaps, yet not nearly as broad as the speculations on which the two-document hypothesis rests.

The Gospels must be perceived then as independent collections of random fragments. Each preserved item is to be valued and examined in its own right. The location of a given fragment in a Gospel derives from the logic of the compiler. It does not testify to a known sequence of events. John's account of the cleansing of the temple occurs early in his Gospel, not because it happened early, but because the evangelist-compiler had it as a separate piece and, by a reasoning of his own, wrote it in where it is still found. Jn 2:13-22 Contexts derive from the compilers, not from the history. Transitions of fragment to fragment, by which the album-makers sought to give their materials some flow of continuity, are generally detectable. They do not contribute to meanings.

The compilers did not understand everything that came to their hand; indeed, they misunderstood much. They fitted considerable post-resurrection testimony into their pre-death history. Yet they accomplished their prime purpose, to preserve every fragment accurately as it came to them! We have their material and can examine it to this day. We can recover meanings in depth. We can sort out each piece conceptually as it makes sense to us, without in any way violating the integrity of the original.

I see yet another wonder. In addition to fragments of oral literacy, each Gospel, randomly and independently, preserves certain elements of witness-memory peculiar to itself. Cumulatively, this offers a surprising amount of background. Details blurred in one Gospel may be quite precise in another. John makes it clear that the place of the Baptist's ministry was the far side of the Jordan. Jn 1:28; 10:40 Mark tells how a distinct crowd came to Pilate on its own initiative to appeal for the release of Barabbas. Mk 15:8 Luke has a clear memory that Jesus made his critical journey to Jerusalem through Samaria. Lk 9:52 Matthew, more than any other, cites what the young church discovered of Jesus from the scriptures. Thus a depth-perspective view of the origin of the Gospels reveals their composite value toward getting at the history.

CHAPTER SIX

Copyist Interpolations

"You shall not add to the word which I command you, nor take from it."   Deuteronomy 4:2; 12:32

My suggested time-frame, that the four Gospels came into existence unknown to each other within twenty years of Jesus' death (thus by 50 A.D.), is reasonable. The impulse to put oral memories into writing must have occurred almost immediately, else it would not have happened at all. Persecution set a limit. Meanwhile there is zealotry, a story yet to unfold. Recall the change in meaning of "christ." Crowds escorting Jesus into Jerusalem took it to mean a warrior-leader by whom God would bring in his promised kingdom. Jesus swallowed up that illusion in his dying. The kingdom of God is not futurist but *now*, in his doing the will of his Father even to death, and in our following him. As the young church's witness was suppressed, however, the old zealotry revived. Warnings against false "christs" foresee disaster. Paul anticipates that very rebellion—the restraint of the young church no longer heard, the priesthood overthrown, the son of perdition taking control of the temple of God. 2 Thess 2:3-12 This horror came to fruition in 66 A.D.

Meanwhile, four fragment-libraries from the young church, in the form of scrolls that came to be called "Gospels," were being read in the Greek churches which had sponsored them. As their existence became known elsewhere, the desire for copies grew—cost immaterial.

Envision the publishing industry of that world. Highly trained scribes, some perhaps slaves, sit at specially designed tables, each with a fresh scroll and writing materials. A master-reader positions himself before them, unrolls the text to be copied, and reads professionally what they should write down. This reader would have studied his text in advance, possibly in company with

others. If an editorial comment seemed helpful at some point, he would simply *read it in!* His scribes would not know, neither would subsequent readers.
Copies would be preserved in quantity, more intelligible, reading more
smoothly. The original would be lost!'

Moses' prescription from the era of oral literacy (quoted above) meant in
effect, "You shall memorize my words accurately, pass them on accurately,
adding nothing, leaving out nothing." That principle failed as the Gospels
were produced. Compilers, who arranged the fragment-memories into a progressive story on a scroll, supplied transitions in some cases. It failed also
when copies were made. Interpolations at this level may be casual, but can
also be substantive. They are detectable by the principle of coherence (Jesus'
own sonship-gospel), interwoven with freedom to read the Gospels in depth-
perspective.

Let me illustrate three modes of copyist interpolation—from the relatively harmless to the seriously misleading. Others will appear as this book
unfolds.

Adjusted Sequences

A memoir-fragment in John tells of a conflict between John and Jesus
regarding baptism. Jn 3:22-30 The actual event was post-resurrection, "John"
and "Jesus" standing for their respective disciples in the era of the young church.
The compiler, not realizing this, entered the episode near the beginning of his
scroll. A copyist, knowing from other sources about John's arrest, interpolated
to his scribes that "John had not yet been put in prison." This created a new
problem, for Jesus' ministry was known to have begun only after John had
been imprisoned. It required another clarification later, that "Jesus himself
did not baptize, but only his disciples." Jn 4:2

The next fragment, as the compiler had entered it, told how Jesus and his
disciples passed through Samaria on their way to Jerusalem, and how his glad
reception by the Samaritans yielded his saying that "a prophet has no honor in
his own country." Jn 4:5-45 A master-copyist noticed that the previous episode
had Jesus in Judea already. Inverting the direction of his travel, he read into
his text that Jesus "left Judea and departed again to Galilee," and so "had to
pass through Samaria." Jn 4:3-5 Since his text had Jesus stay with the Samaritans "two days," the master-copyist inserted, "After the two days he departed
to Galilee." Jn 4:40,43 That "the Galileans welcomed him" may have been an
independent fragment of post-resurrection memory, however. Jn 4:45 Other

interpolations likewise assume the sequence of the manuscript to be the actual history. "He came again to Cana in Galilee, where he had made the water wine." Jn 4:46 "After this there was a feast of the Jews, and Jesus went up to Jerusalem." Jn 5:1

The library of John's memoirs in Bethsaida preserved some late conversations between Jesus and his disciples. Jn 14-17 The compiler laid these end to end, then entered them on his scroll as an extension of the supper scene in the upper room. One of these fragments had Judas asking, "Lord, how is it that you will manifest yourself to us and not to the world?"—in my mind, evidence of his ambitious longing. A master-copyist, reasoning by the sequence of his text that Judas had already left the supper, interpolated a parenthetical "not Iscariot." Jn 14:22

Enhancements

A prophecy of Zechariah, quoted in Matthew, has a meek king come, "mounted on an ass, and on a colt, the foal of an ass." Mt 21:2-7; Zech 9:9 In Hebrew this is synonymous parallelism, referring to just one animal. A copyist, not realizing this, amplified Jesus' instruction to read, "You will find an ass tied *and a colt with her; loose them and bring them to me*," whereupon the disciples "brought the ass *and the colt*, and put their garments on *them*, and he sat on *them*."

After the post-resurrection breakfast at the Sea of Galilee, Jesus, in conversation with Simon, contrasts his former self-assertive independence with the child-like dependence and willing servanthood of his old age. Jn 21:18 A copyist, not comprehending this but knowing Peter's martyrdom, interpolated the explanation, "He said this to show by what death he was to glorify God." Jn 21:19

A master-copyist dismissed Peter's proposed "three tents" on the mount of transfiguration by explaining, "he did not know what to say"—thus precluding any curiosity on the part of readers. Mk 9:6 An interpolation in Luke is similar: "not knowing what he said." Lk 9:33

Copyists assumed that their manuscript told events in their historical sequence. Hence they could enter a count. "This, the first of his signs." Jn 2:11 "This was now the *second* sign that Jesus did when he had come from Judea to Galilee." Jn 4:54 The breakfast at the lake "was now the *third* time that Jesus was revealed to his disciples after he was raised from the dead." Jn 21:14

Evidence in John suggests that Jesus was buried with a cloth over his body and a napkin over his face. Jn 20:5-7 John's memoir on the raising of Lazarus says that "the dead man came out" at Jesus' cry. A copyist's experience with tomb burials led him to depict Lazarus as mummified, "hands and feet wound in bandages and his head bound in a cloth," in which case Jesus must add, "Unbind him and let him go." Jn 11:44

Enhancements could distract from, even negate a meaning. The Father to whom we pray, "Forgive us what we owe you, as we forgive those who owe us," does not look to be repaid for his giving and forgiving. Mt 6:12 To be his children is to pass on his love as our very character, without looking for profit or securing ourselves against loss. "When you give a feast, invite the poor, the maimed, the lame, and the blind; you will be blessed *because they cannot repay you*," Jesus taught graphically. A copyist, not grasping this, reinstated the psyche of investment by interpolating the expectation, "You will be repaid at the resurrection of the just." Lk 14:13-14

The original text of Jesus' concern for an erring and even persecuting "brother" proposed two stages, both tenderly personal. Mt 18:15-17 The first was "Go and expose the trap he is in between you and him alone." The second stage, "Take with you one or two more," offered the hope that another witness or two, added to yours, might get through to him. The conclusion followed, "If he will not hear them, let him be to you (*singular*) as a Gentile and a tax collector"—an outsider like those he himself excludes. A copyist interpolated an institutional third stage, however: "tell it to the church; and if he refuses to hear the church." This was quite reasonable, yet of the same psyche as the errant brother's "Tell it to the synagogue."

Copyist deletions were likewise possible. The account of Jesus' arrest in John has Simon Peter follow and with him "another disciple." Jn 18:15-16 This other, "being known to the high priest, entered the courtyard along with Jesus," then returned and got Peter in. After the resurrection Peter confessed many faults freely, including this one, which otherwise could not have become known. He would not have concealed his complicity with Judas. A master-copyist, however, honoring Peter and abhorring Judas, obscured Peter's role in the tragic conspiracy.

Deity Inferences

That Greek thought would take the name "my beloved son" for Jesus at his baptism to mean deity, likewise references to him as "the son of God," is not surprising. It sounded so. Power was the most obvious attribute of deity.

By deity-power, Jesus' miracles made simple sense. Since omniscience is likewise an attribute of God, it made sense also that Jesus would know the future from the beginning. A memoir of John, that "he knew all men and needed no one to bear witness of man; for he himself knew what was in man," referred to his covenant-understanding of hearts captive to desires and fears. Jn 2:25 To Greek minds, however, it sounded like "divine" knowledge.

Jesus' mother recalled and told afterwards how they took Jesus to the Passover in Jerusalem at age twelve and missed him after a day's journey. On their return, they "found him in the temple, sitting among the teachers, *listening to them and asking questions.*" "Didn't you know that I must be about *my Father's business?*" Jesus said. Lk 2:41-52 A master-reader entered all this faithfully. Inferring, however, that Jesus as "deity-son" must already have known more than any of his teachers, he interpolated an inversion: "*And all who heard him were astonished at his understanding and answers.*" The temple teachers became *his* pupils. They questioned *him*. His answers astonished them!

A copyist viewed Judas as a treacherous villain, Simon Peter as a noble hero, and Jesus by his "deity" as having known this all along. John framed his extended memoir on the bread of life to strengthen the young church in a time of severe testing. Jn 6 The copyist assumed from its location on the scroll that Judas was among the disciples at the time Jesus said all this. "The words that I speak to you are spirit and life," would surely not have been meant to include Judas, however! The copyist therefore has Jesus voice an exception: "But there are some of you that do not believe," adding the further comment, "for Jesus knew from the first who those were that did not believe, and who it was that should betray him." The copyist, viewing Judas as a lying pretender throughout, interpolated regarding him also a reference to an earlier saying: "This is why I told you that no one can come to me unless it is granted him by the Father." Jn 6:44,64-65 As the copyist saw it, the Father had not granted Judas to come to Jesus in truth. He had come only in pretense.

John's "bread of life" memoir concluded with a grave testing in the young church: "Out of this many of his disciples drew back and walked no more with him. 'Will you also go away?'" Jesus asked those who remained. Simon Peter responded for them all, "Lord, to whom shall we go? You have the words of eternal life, and we believe and have come to know that you are the Holy One of God." Jn 6:66-69 This is a fitting climax of faith and confession. A copyist ruins it, however. In his mind, the all-knowing Jesus could not have allowed Peter's "we believe" to stand without an exception: "Have I not chosen you twelve, and one of you is a devil?" From the later table scene, the copyist added knowingly that Jesus "spoke of Judas the son of Simon Iscariot, for he, one of the twelve, was to betray him." Jn 13:26; 6:70-71 Another Judas-exception appears in Jesus' prayer: "I have guarded them, and none of them is lost." A copyist felt driven to add, "except the son of perdition." Jn 17:12

Interpolations herald Jesus' divine power even when under arrest. "I am he," Jesus said, and surrendered without resistance. The squad of temple police were not only taken aback at this, but (a copyist felt compelled to add) "fell to the ground." Jn 18:6 When Peter drew his sword and cut Malchus' ear, a still all-powerful Jesus "touched his ear and healed him." Lk 22:51

Such interpolations entered the Gospels at the earliest stages of copying, long before scholarly study of "comparative readings" in extant manuscripts became possible. Further instances will be noted as they come up. Jesus' authentic gospel exposes what cannot have been original. Anything incoherent must be accounted for by another mind at a later level of history.

The Disjunction

The church of Jesus' generation knew him personally. The fragment-libraries derived from its memory. "Christianity" depended on its Gospels. It read them by culturally conditioned understandings. Copyist interpolations are evidence of the disjunction between these.

Newly formed churches in the Greek world discovered that four independent documents about Jesus existed and wanted copies. As long as the apostles lived and labored, covenant-meanings remained strong and could still be heard. When the original fragment-libraries had been destroyed, however, and when the apostolic witness too had died away, only documents remained. That circumstance put scholars who could read and write in charge. They took the Gospels to be sequential histories. They took "son of God" language for Jesus to mean deity, thus interpreted him by divine attributes like omnipotence and omniscience. Copyist interpolations corrupted their documents from the earliest beginning, but who could even know it?

The young church experienced healing by the covenant-word Jesus believed, preached and lived. Greek copyists, and the Christianity which depended on them, attributed healings and other miracles to his deity. The young church titled Jesus' message "the gospel." Christianity titled sacred scrolls "the Gospels." The young church believed and lived the ancient covenant-word, which it saw embodied in Jesus himself. Christianity, in contrast, believed and lived by its documentary-word. In the young church, the Holy Spirit spoke the covenant-sonship as revelation from heaven to hearts. In Christianity, the Holy Spirit spoke documentary-words as revelation from heaven to theological minds.

Christianity had no way to realize any of this. My intent is not to accuse. I rejoice in and gladly nurture whatever authenticity remains for the church in which I was planted—as Jesus did with and for his people. But I long for his covenant-gospel to be become known without fear. Its leaven is truth and life, its potential rich and liberating. If only implanted, it will grow and gather and cleanse and heal, in love and without argument, by its inherent spirit and truth.

PART THREE

Reconstructing the History

Historical Imagination

Intriguing footnotes in my reading during the early 1960s directed me to R.G. Collingwood, *The Idea of History*.[1] His specialty was ancient Greece and Rome. He illustrated by the way his own mind worked a thought process available to any historian. Having decided just what it was he wanted to know toward a coherent history of the Caesars, Collingwood could think himself into the "mind" of varied extant sources, like Suetonius, Livy, Tacitus and Plutarch. How astonishing, I realized, that my Bible should shower me with *four extant sources, each rich but distinct,* toward knowing what my mind wanted to know of Jesus!

Collingwood coined the term "scissors-and-paste" for the age-old method of writing history.[2] Gather whatever sources are available, consider them "authorities" just because they are written, clip useful contributions from each, paste the pieces into a continuous narrative. Modern skepticism yielded a variation which Collingwood labeled "critical history" or "historical criticism."[3] "Authorities" were now "sources," subject to cross-examination for their believability. The skeptic-historian would judge which excerpts were "fit for the scrap-book." Any which failed his test he would consign "to the waste-paper basket." To Collingwood, this was the same old "scissors-and-paste" history in a new guise.

---

[1] New York: Oxford University Press, 1956. The book is a compilation of essays from the 1930s, published posthumously, first in 1946. With an introduction by T. M. Knox.

[2] *Ibid.*, p. 143, 257-266, and *passim*. "The Passion History according to the Four Gospels," which I read in worship for years, was of this sort. See also William F. Beck, *The Christ of the Gospels*, subtitled "The Life and Work of JESUS as told by Matthew, Mark, Luke, and John, Presented as one complete story." St. Louis: Concordia Publishing House, 1959.

[3] Collingwood, *ibid.*, pp. 259-261.

His genius was "scientific history." "The important question about any statement contained in a source is not whether it is true or false, but what it means," he said.[4] Yes! That yielded my own persistent question, "Why is this said the way it is said?"

"The historian must reenact the past in his own mind.... His business is to discover what the past was which left these relics behind it. For example, the relics are certain written words; and in that case he has to discover what the person who wrote those words meant by them. This means discovering the thought which he expressed by them. To discover what this thought was, the historian must think it again for himself."[5] Yes! The working of the human mind is a constant through all ages. I am able indeed to "imagine" how preserved words made sense to the one who first said or wrote them, what he was thinking when he said what he said the way he said it. I can even think accurately what a copyist was thinking when he corrupted a text by dictating a thought of his own into his new manuscript.

"The historian's picture of his subject...thus appears as a web of imaginative construction stretched between certain fixed points provided by the statement of his authorities; and if these points are frequent enough and the threads spun from each to the next are constructed with due care, always by the *a priori* (unprejudiced) imagination and never by merely arbitrary fancy, the whole picture is constantly verified by appeal to these data and runs little risk of losing touch with the reality it represents."[6] Yes! That is how my reconstructing works. It can also be put to the test, for new data will either corroborate it or require its modification.

"The hero of a detective story is thinking exactly like an historian, when, from indications of the most varied kinds, he constructs an imaginary picture of how a crime was committed and by whom."[7] "The historian's picture stands in a peculiar relation to something called evidence.... Everything is evidence which the historian can use as evidence.... And of all the things perceptible to him there is not one which he might not conceivably use as evidence on some question, if he came to it with the right question in mind. The enlargement of historical knowledge comes about mainly through finding how to use as evidence this or that kind of perceived fact which historians have hitherto thought

---

[4] *Ibid.*, p 260.

[5] *Ibid.*, p. 282-283.

[6] *Ibid.*, p. 242.

[7] *Ibid.*, p. 243.

useless to them."[8] Yes! By "evidences" in the Gospels, beginning with the discovery that "my beloved son" for Jesus is covenant-language, I have come to know him as the young church of his own generation knew him.

I recall a relic in the Bethphage chapel on the Mount of Olives—a large stone, plastered into a cube in the Crusader period, from which Jesus, according to medieval piety, mounted the ass for his entrance into Jerusalem. All sides of this cube show remnants of fresco painting, each a facet of the entry event. An artist restored this stone in 1950, replastered it where necessary, then added simple line drawings to suggest what the lost portion of each original painting may have shown. His drawings, though imaginative, are not fiction. They help viewers perceive at least something of the original intent.

My artifacts are preserved words. I examine them closely, am struck by possible links to other evidences, wonder what awareness might have produced the remnants I can still perceive. The "historical imagination" that fills in gaps toward recovering a coherent picture of what produced such "artifacts" is not fanciful or arbitrary, but bound by the need to make sense of what is *there*. A tentative explanation is tested by watching how it may fit or not fit into a tapestry being enriched also by other evidences. Any reconstruction can be tested, corrected, or sharpened by a next scholar who examines the same evidences, perhaps noticing still others. His contribution to the emerging picture will be subject in turn to similar testing by yet another scholar.

The coming chapters apply "historical imagination" toward recovering the historical Jesus from evidences that are actually abundant. They view the scriptures, especially now the Gospels, as a depository of historical evidences. They apply systematically, as a principle of coherence, the prime evidence that the name "my beloved son" and "son of God" for Jesus is a language of covenant, that it does not and cannot mean deity.

---

[8] *Ibid.*, p. 246-247.

CHAPTER SEVEN

The Son of Zechariah

"The word of God came to John, the son of Zechariah, in the wilderness."   Luke 3:2

Three "artifact" recollections of John are preserved in Luke. He was born to the priesthood, Zechariah and Elizabeth being descendants of Aaron. Lk 1:5 Surprisingly, however, "he was in the wilderness until the day of his showing to Israel," not in Judea or Jerusalem. Lk 1:80 Thus "the word of God came to John the son of Zechariah in the wilderness," not in the temple. Lk 3:2

There had to be a time when these residual pillars bore and were spanned by a bridge that made coherent sense. To begin, what impelled young John to abandon his priestly heritage in favor of the wilderness? He must surely have gone there on his own volition.

Given such a question, trusting that my own humanness of heart and mind will correspond to his, I notice fragments of possible evidence. Consider John's metaphor of "wheat" and "chaff." "His fan is in his hand, and he will clear his threshing floor, but the chaff he will burn with unquenchable fire." Mt 3:12; Lk 3:17 "What is chaff to the wheat?" the LORD asked by Jeremiah. Jer 23:28 The wicked are "like chaff which the wind drives away." Ps 1:4

I learned about chaff as a child when visiting an aunt's farm in Wisconsin at wheat harvest. A cousin showed me how to pluck a head of ripened grain, rub it between my hands, loosen the chaff, blow it away, pop the wheat into my mouth, enjoy the wonder of chewing it into a paste and swallowing it down. The chaff was a tiny double-leaflet within which each grain grew to maturity. Once broken loose of its grain, it resumed the exact shape, size, almost color even, of the kernel it had held. But it was empty now, a pretense, weightless, worthless, inedible, even a contaminant. If swept together with other chaff and set afire, it would burn up in a puff before anyone could even think of quenching the flame. That was John's diagnosis of the temple religion—rich in outward forms but empty of the message that had once given it worth and life.

I infer that John in his youth came to know the emptiness, that he looked for what was authentic and did not find it. "From his fullness have we all received" refers to Jesus but also to the ministry of John. Jn 1:14,16 Fullness answers to emptiness. Having known emptiness myself, I could appreciate this imagery. John's priestly studies in the temple school did not fill his hunger. His teachers could detail from the scriptures the priestly task, privilege, and authority—also genealogy, history, worship, liturgy, feasts, sacrifices, tithes, temple architecture and artistry, and vestments. Yet none of this fed the longing of John's heart—to know God and the core of truth and life which, like that grain of wheat, had given rise to these forms. When John asked such things, his teachers were at a loss, not even comprehending his questions.

Young John heard whatever scriptures were read in worship, learned them with a child's aptitude for memorizing, had access to the sacred scrolls and searched them himself, was free to copy portions for his own use, as his father had likely done before him. The "word of God" that "came to John in the wilderness" was not new in the sense that he had never heard the words. It turned out to be what Moses, prophets, and psalmists of the scriptures had heard from the LORD long ago, even as the voice-from-heaven word Jesus heard was a heritage from Moses. The exodus and wilderness history of Israel must have intrigued John, also references to it in the prophets. A word from Isaiah became central to his preaching: "A voice cries in the wilderness, Prepare the way of the LORD, make straight in the desert a highway for our God." Is 40:3; Lk 3:4 "The people found grace in the wilderness," Jeremiah said. Jer 31:2 "Grace" (Hebrew: chen) belonged to John's very name, "Jo-chanan." He yearned to find a "fullness of grace and truth" for himself, but was not finding it in the temple. The place to seek it was "the wilderness"—not just any desert country, but the place where ancient Israel had known it.

John's Wilderness

Thus a day came when John bade farewell to parents and classmates and set out on a quest none of them could comprehend. I detect recollections of him in Jesus. To a prospective disciple who felt he could not follow Jesus until his father died and he had fulfilled the duty of burying him, Jesus said, "Let the dead bury their own dead." Lk 9:60; Mt 8:21-22 It weighed on John that he, an only son, would not be home to do his parents that last honor, yet his quest had to take primacy. Others, still "dead," would reverently bury one of their own.

"The kingdom of heaven is like a treasure hidden in a field, which a man found and covered up; then in his joy he goes and sells all that he has and buys that field," Jesus taught. Mt 13:44 I sense John in this saying, too. He had joyfully "sold everything," the whole honor and security his priestly heritage offered him. But it was worth the cost. In this "field," the wilderness, he was confident of finding the treasure he longed for, which had been hidden from him.

The road to that wilderness may be walked still. It passes from Jerusalem over the Mount of Olives through the hill country of Judea to Jericho and the Jordan. Engineered to be as straight and level as possible, it curves gently along the higher levels of hillsides, one hill linked to the next by a plateau area, looking down into deep valleys but never descending to them. John, like Isaiah before him, visualized by it the straight and level "way of the LORD." Is 40:3-5; Lk 3:4-6

The Jordan marked the boundary between "the land" and the wilderness of Israel's wanderings, as the Red Sea was the boundary when the LORD brought Israel out of Egypt. By passing through that sea, the people ceased to be slaves of Pharaoh and were marked as children and servants of God alone. For John, the land itself, once so full of promise, had become under its priesthood as oppressive as Egypt had been to the fathers of old—void of the grace and glory of the LORD, demanding in its law, not feeding or uplifting at all. Whatever treasure all this had once held had long been lost. Old Israel might seem to have come out of Egypt into the wilderness empty. They had no priesthood as yet, no temple, no calendar of worship or feasts, not even their law. What they did have was the covenant-word the LORD spoke to them by Moses.

When John returned years later, his clothing was not the fine linen of the priesthood but a garment of camel's hair with a leather belt. Mt 3:4; Mk 1:6 This was not a self-conscious imitation of Elijah—like prophets who "put on a hairy mantle in order to deceive." 2 Kgs 1:8; Zech 13:4 John must have belonged to and served a camel-herding Bedouin household, as Moses had once been joined to the shepherding household of Reuel (or Jethro), priest of Midian. Ex 2:21; 18:1 John had somehow stumbled on them or they on him. Perhaps a suspicious circling of vultures had directed a rescuer to him, as in a wilderness lore Jesus quoted. Mt 24:28 A woman of that household had brushed out the camel's hair in season, spun it into yarn and woven it into a garment for him, crafting also the belt of camel leather. John had learned the wilderness art of finding and eating locusts, and of following the desert bee to its cache of honey. Israel's wilderness era, with which John identified, had long preceded laws of cleanness. Lev 11:4; Mt 23:24 He freely ate the otherwise-prohibited camel meat with his host family on festive occasions, and drank camel's milk.

Jesus' saying regarding "eunuchs who have made themselves eunuchs for the sake of the kingdom of heaven" may likewise reflect a memory of John. Mt 19:12 It suggests that John had opportunity to marry a woman in that Bedouin household, perhaps even desired her. Did not Moses marry Zipporah, daughter of the Midianite priest? Ex 2:21 Were not the two sons she bore him full members of God's Israel out of Egypt too, as well as a "mixed multitude" of enslaved peoples who came out with them? Ex 12:38; 18:6 Had not Moses subsequently married a Cushite woman and been defended by the LORD against the complaint of Miriam and Aaron? Num 12:1-9 Why then should John not marry this woman? This possibility had long preceded laws against such inter-marriage, which the priesthood rigorously enforced. John's wrestling with God in desire and need for her could have been powerful indeed, yet he under-stood why it could not be. If he expected to return to his people, he must submit to the law of racial integrity that had bound priesthood and people for many generations. Lev 21:14-15; Dt 7:3 The offense of intermarriage could dis-miss his voice out of hand. Thus John had actually chosen what Jesus' saying recalled, "made himself a eunuch for the sake of the kingdom of heaven."

The most significant pillar of memory, however, is that which made John a prophet: "The word of God came to John the son of Zechariah in the wil-derness." Lk 3:2 Jeremiah had said this similarly and repeatedly, "The word of the LORD came to me...." Jer 1:2,4,11,13 What was this "word of God" then? Not sacred scrolls. The temple had these in abundance. Not some long-lost document either, found in sand or cave, such as would thrill archaeologists today.

"Blessed are those who hunger and thirst for righteousness," Jesus said, "for they shall be satisfied." Mt 5:6 It had happened so to John. The word that fed his hunger and quenched his thirst for righteousness was a substantive message from outside himself, a covenant-word of honor and chosenness like that which spoke later to Jesus—significantly, while he was with John. "Say to Pharaoh, Thus says the LORD, Israel is my son, my first-born...; let my son go that he may serve me." The LORD had sealed this word by bringing his people out of Egypt through the sea. Ex 4:22-23 Having thrilled to hear it myself, I suspect it thrilled John, too. It opened the scriptures. It uttered the name which priestly authority declared must not be uttered: "Thus says Johwah...!"

"Johwah, Johwah, a God merciful and gracious... forgiving iniquity and transgression and sin." Ex 34:6-7 That word was found in John's very name, Jochanan, "Johwah is gracious." Lk 1:63 "Prepare the way of Johwah," it said, straight and level. Is 40:3 That word filled John's emptiness. It revived Moses' "life and good" against what had become "death and evil."

John's Ministry

One day John returned in his wilderness garb to the shallow ford of Jordan. Pilgrims, merchants and officials of government passed through the river here on their way to and from Jerusalem. John did not cross back into Judea, however. He stayed on the "wilderness" side of old Israel's wanderings. The Gospel of John mentions a town here, Bethany. Jn 1:28 The Bethany crossing was a natural stop-over, Jerusalem a day's journey away. Travelers might lodge for the night in an open area or find shelter in homes. It appears that some family opened its home to Jesus during his stay with John. Jn 1:39 Quite likely, John stayed with some family as well.

This territory was Perea. When the Romans in 6 A.D. banished Archelaus, first heir of Herod, and divided his kingdom into four quarters, they assigned it and Galilee to the rule of Antipas, a son of Herod the Great. The title "tetrarch" or "quarter-ruler" implied a petty king, hardly complimentary. As for Judea, Rome chose to rule it directly through governors and a visible military presence, though charging the high priest and council to maintain order.

Thus John did not consult with priests he had known, or try to explain himself to them, or seek their approval for what he would do. He spoke to the common folk, trusting his covenant-word to reach the authorities through them. Nothing about him conveyed the authority of the priesthood from which he had sprung. People perceived him as a man of the wilderness, like Moses and Elijah of old. His appearance and location were "signs," to which his preaching gave meaning. He invited his listeners to know God out of Israel's root beginnings, to know chaff by cherishing the wheat, to leave behind the emptiness that had crept into their tradition and start over new. Turning back and starting over was the "repentance" to which he summoned them—a knowledge of God and a freedom of servanthood from the heart out.

The very act of coming to John through the Jordan, routine as it might seem, now signaled "repentance," that is, leaving the old behind and starting over new. John proclaimed it as reliving old Israel's passing out of Egypt through the sea. He had made that passage himself, when he left the priesthood behind to go into the wilderness. It came to be called "John's baptism" — not just an external washing as in Judean piety but with "authority from heaven." Mt 21:25 This was Paul's understanding when he retrojected John's term "baptize" onto Israel's exodus crossing, an unprecedented usage: "Our fathers ... all passed through the sea, and were all baptized into Moses in the cloud and in the sea." 1 Cor 10:2

John preached a "word of God" which the law-tradition of temple and synagogue had smothered. He conferred on those who passed through the Jordan the noble name, promise, and calling which the LORD had spoken to Israel out of Egypt. Covenant-names like "my people," "my chosen," "my first-born son" came to life. As God had sustained their fathers along their wilderness way, brought them to the land he promised, and given it to them, so also now! They would not attain the kingdom the LORD had in store by right of genealogy, or by doing their separatist law, or by power and aggressive ambition, but by his gracious will alone. To trust the God who had called them, follow him and do his will, was their free and noble privilege. The song of Zechariah reflects this, "that we, being delivered from the hand of our enemies, might serve him without fear, in holiness and righteousness all the days of our life." Lk 1:74-75 Amen! That is how the kingdom of God comes! Here was fullness indeed, wheat and not chaff.

All four Gospels cite John's theme from Isaiah, mentioned earlier. "A voice cries in the wilderness, Prepare the way of the LORD, make straight in the desert a highway for our God. Every valley shall be lifted up, and every mountain and hill be made low; the uneven ground shall become level, and the rough places a plain. And the glory of the LORD shall be revealed, and all flesh shall see it together, for the mouth of the LORD has spoken." Is 40:3-5 The LORD raises valley people and lowers mountain people. Visible diversities do not negate the honor which God confers on every child of his equally. He calls his people to walk side by side with him on one straight and level way—no one ranked superior or inferior, no one above or below any other.

Travelers who stopped at Bethany heard John gladly, then talked about his message when they arrived where they were going. A fragment in Luke preserves some significant questions and John's responses. Lk 3:10-14 To those who asked, "What then shall we do?" he prescribed a servanthood of love, honor, and practical generosity toward any neighbor—not religious observances, sacrifices or offerings. John did not regard tax collectors as agents of Israel's enemy. "Collect no more than is appointed you," he said, thus serve God by doing your assigned work honorably and without greed. Military service to Herod and Caesar did not compromise God's holy identity for soldiers, either. Let them serve their human authorities as they serve the God to whom they ultimately belong. Then they will not turn their little authority to personal advantage by oppressing others, or take forcibly what God has not given them, or accuse anyone falsely. "Be content with your wages," John added. Servants who trust their God are not covetous.

John gathered young men to be his disciples, some from Perean Bethany perhaps, some from Judea. Two were of fisherman families from Bethsaida in Galilee. They were Andrew, younger brother of Simon, and John (younger brother of James). Jn 1:40-42 John, author of this memoir, does not name himself. Both became disciples of Jesus later, their brothers, too. They would likely have met the wilderness prophet while on a pilgrimage to Jerusalem with their families. John asked for the younger brothers, knowing that the older were needed at home.

John would have his disciples memorize many scriptures he himself cherished, but also carefully worded condensations of his preaching. Like prophets before him, he extended his voice through them, sending them out on assigned routes to towns throughout Judea. Touched by the message and wanting to hear more, people began to come out to John in great numbers, also from Jerusalem. Their religion and worship took on coherent meaning, full of honor and hope, purpose and freedom, such as they had not known.

Conflict

A memory in Matthew attributes to John a theme basic also to Jesus: "Repent, for the kingdom of heaven is at hand." Mt 3:2; 4:17 Give up your fantasy of a day when God will intervene to exalt you over the nations. His kingdom is here, ready for you to enter and serve him joyfully now! Prophets like Amos had spoken so. "Woe to you who desire the day of the LORD.... It is darkness and not light.... But let justice roll down like waters, and righteousness like an everflowing stream." Amos 5:18,24 Thus John preached, "Who warned you to flee from the wrath to come? Bear fruits that befit repentance!" Lk 3:8; Mt 3:7-8 The futurist kingdom you lust for will bring wrath, not glory! The true kingdom and glory of God is in the servanthood you give him now, the fruits you bear for him now.

Such repentance did not come easily. The expectation of a futurist kingdom, when God would intervene to exalt his people over the nations once and forever, was deeply rooted. Speculations stirred. Many heard from John what they wanted to hear. "The kingdom of heaven is at hand," could mean that the day was imminent. John's wheat, in contrast to the temple's well-administered but empty chaff, encouraged broad suspicions of a self-serving priesthood. Priestly authority subservient to Rome could never bring in the kingdom of God.

A judgment from Malachi is cited in Matthew and Mark: "Behold, I send my messenger to prepare my way before me, and the Lord whom you seek will suddenly come to his temple; the messenger of the covenant, in whom you delight, behold, he is coming, says the LORD of hosts... and he will purify the sons of Levi." Mal 3:1-3; Mt 11:10; Mk 1:2 Could John be this "messenger," this "purifier"? He was of priestly descent, yet had left all that behind. He had appeared across the Jordan as out of nowhere. People were flocking to him in great numbers. The prophet Zechariah envisioned Zerubbabel of the house of David, and Joshua, high priest of the returned exiles, as "the two anointed who stand by the LORD of the whole earth." Zech 4:6,14 If John as God's "anointed-christ" were to take over the priesthood and purify it, enthusiasts would rally to help!

Speculation of this sort shifted attention from John's message to his person. A memory in Luke reports that "the people were in expectation, and all men questioned in their hearts concerning John, whether perhaps he were the christ." Lk 3:15 A parallel in John recalls how "priests and Levites from Jerusalem" were sent to ask, "Who are you?" "I am not the christ," John replied. They pressed him further: "Let us have an answer for those who sent us. What do you say about yourself?" He returned them to his message: "I am the voice of one crying in the wilderness, 'Make straight the way of the Lord,' as the prophet Isaiah said." Jn 1:19-23; Is 40:3

Common piety looked for the promised kingdom to come by war. "From the days of John the Baptist until now the kingdom of heaven has suffered violence, and men of violence take it by force," Jesus said. Mt 11:12 Flavius Josephus, Jewish historian of the first century, attributes John's arrest and death to this looming threat. "Herod, who feared lest the great influence John had over the people might put it into his power and inclination to raise rebellion (for they seemed ready to do anything he should advise), thought it best, by putting him to death, to prevent any mischief he might cause."[9]

Priesthood and council, of course, had reasons of their own to be concerned. John had not consulted them, yet was making himself the talk of the

---

[9] Antiquities 18:5:2

land. His preaching threatened their tradition and authority. Memorized messages spread by his disciples kept the conversation going. People in great numbers, from Jerusalem and all Judea, were making the hard journey to see and hear him personally. If the "starting over" John taught, like Israel fresh out of Egypt, were pressed to its end, what would become of the subsequent law and tradition, the calendar of feasts, and respect for priesthood and temple? The possibility of actually hearing John, of learning how his word might refill their outward forms with truth, vitality, and freedom in the knowledge of God, seems not to have occurred to these anxious critics.

Delegates sent to investigate John would likely have included classmates or teachers from his student days. The authority of priests was rooted in Aaron, from whom they were descended. Ex 4:14-16; 28:1; Num 6:22-27 John had been born into such authority but had turned his back on it. By what authority did he teach that coming to him through the Jordan was like going back to Egypt and starting over? Did he expect priesthood and temple and law to start over again, too? When they asked Jesus later, "By what authority are you doing these things, and who gave you this authority?" he appealed to John: "The baptism of John, whence was it? From heaven or from men?" Mt 21:23-25 John's arrest had rendered that question moot, but it had never been resolved.

I assume that John understood and loved his fellow priests and the Pharisees who came out of the land through the Jordan to investigate him. He yearned to fill their emptiness as he himself had been filled and as many others were being filled. Yet he could not compromise his word or allow it to be dismissed or diminished. His words were surely familiar to them, for they knew the scriptures even as he did. Yet the specific "covenant-word" which fed John's heart had not fed theirs. That made it difficult. "Of course!" they could reply, "We know all that, but...." Always a "but," always a reversion to the law, tradition and authority on which they relied.

John's "Ax and Fire" Sermon

The digest of a memorable sermon is preserved. Mt 3:7-12; Lk 3:7-9,16-17 Critics were among the crowd to whom John preached it. In its tightly condensed form, as his disciples once memorized and taught it through the land, it leaves an impression of anger and accusation. Let me reconstruct it by the positive appeal of John's preaching, however. I take the liberty of adding his saying regarding "the mightier one," and of incorporating a dramatic theme from Jesus' later testimony to John, which I suspect he recalled from John's own preaching: "What did you go out into the wilderness to see?" and "Why did you go out?" Mt 11:7-9

"Let me tell you the word of the LORD!" John began. "You who are of the priests and Pharisees, take it to heart for your own sakes, and then take it home to those who sent you. You came to me through the Jordan, as our fathers passed through the sea out of Egypt and into the wilderness. But why? Did you come out, as they did, to belong to and hear and serve your God? Ex 3:12 'Israel is my first-born son, let my son go that he may serve me,' the LORD said to Pharaoh by Moses that day. He says it to you even now! So did you come out to leave your slavery behind for the honor of knowing and serving your God in his grace and truth? I rejoice with you! The glory of the LORD your God is your glory even now!

"Then bring forth the fruits of it! Give up any illusion of superiority. Don't fear losing your authority. Find your delight in simply filling full what the steadfast grace of the LORD is calling you, his sons, to be! Pay attention to the nobility of valley people and lift them up to honor as children of God with you. Free them from voices that disparage them as inferior. Join me in gathering sinners and outsiders whose bloodlines are not as pure as yours. Walk the level way of the LORD—so that you are not above anyone and no one is above you. Walk side by side with me and your people, freely and joyfully, in the one straight way which is our wisdom and life as the people of God. By this the glory of the LORD will be revealed, so that all nations see it together and come eagerly to his light and truth. So I ask, is this why you have come?

"But if not, what reason might you have for coming to me? Are you uneasy? Have you been hearing voices of threat and fear, perhaps? You know how angels from the LORD visited Lot in Sodom. Have they perhaps visited you, too, shown you what is amiss, warned you to flee from the wrath that is coming? Gen 19:13 If so, rejoice to be so warned and do not resist it! If the LORD must consume his holy city and temple with fire from heaven, as he consumed Sodom, be sure that he will not cease to love and care for you who are his own! He delivered Lot in spite of his sins. He upheld our fathers through the destruction of Jerusalem and their exile from the land. He gathered them home and restored them. What he did for them he is eager to do for you, too. So is it for fear of his wrath that you have come out to me? Then know your God, the LORD of pure mercy! Fill full your own glory as his sons and servants. Be his light to the nations! You have no higher calling than that, no higher freedom than that!

"But if you have not come out to meet your God, then whom else do you expect to meet in this wilderness? Snakes, perhaps? Vipers? No, that cannot be! Surely you are not more comfortable with slithering snakes than with the spirit of the living God! Still, as you well know, the world is full of the serpent's offspring. Nations who do not know God have no other wisdom. It is not given snakes to stand upright and walk straight, as you and I do. Ah, but we, the noble children of God, we can so easily descend to them! I have watched snakes in this wilderness. They slither right and left on their belly, then slip lightly into the tiniest hole. From the day when the serpent in the garden contradicted the word of the LORD God, he made snakes the very sign of deviousness. Do not deceive yourselves, the snake is not only in the wilderness but in your garden, too! His voice is still heard! If you do not hear and remember and believe the voice of your God, no voice will be left for you except the snake's. Either you hear and cherish the straight way of the LORD, or you hear and succumb to the seduction of the slithering snake!

"So I ask again, Why have you come out to this wilderness? To be sons of the living God with me, and to walk true and upright as his servants? Or to be a brood of snakes, the offspring of vipers—slithering on their belly, eyes in the dirt, unable to see beyond the desire of the moment, the fear of the moment? Is that why you have come here this day? No, that cannot be!

"But then, why did you come out to me? To investigate me? Good! At least you are hearing me. I shall hide nothing from you. Still, maybe you are not hearing me at all! Maybe you cannot hear! You are confident that you are full, that all is well with you, that there is nothing you need to receive and learn through me. Can that be? So you set yourselves above me. You judge me by what you know or think you know. What is this superiority on which you rely? Is it your ancestry, the purity of your descent—not from serpents, of course, not even from God as his sons, of course—but from Abraham? Is it your pride of Abraham that blocks your hearing? If so, I am troubled for you. Do you not remember? The LORD of this wilderness knows no rankings of superior over inferior. He is a God without partiality, who takes no bribe. Dt 10:17 Don't deceive yourselves! You may impress people by the purity of your genealogy, by your show of rightness and worth, by your status of authority. You may succeed in making ordinary folk look up to you. But your God is not impressed!

"Know this! You are the sons of the living God this day, that is true. But how? Not by your descent from Abraham, not by the purity of your bloodlines, not by the righteousness of your obedience. You are sons of the living God by his steadfast love and patience alone! He holds you as his own this day in spite of your sins. On the day when the LORD your God brought our fathers through the sea out of Egypt, he made sons of Abraham out of a mixed lot of enslaved people who came out with them, did he not? Ex 12:38 He has made sons of Abraham out of alien Itureans and Idumeans and Galileans—even tax collectors and harlots, has he not? Why, the LORD your God can make sons of Abraham even out of these stones!

"Truly, I wish I knew why you have come. As it is, I am afraid for you! You may think you are dealing with just me, one single and very frail man. 'Who is this John, that we need to listen to him?' you tell yourselves. 'The responsibility is ours. We have authority from God to judge him and decide what to do about him!' you tell yourselves. Do you honestly believe that? If even a small doubt or fear is stirring within you, thank God for it! Let your doubt warn your heart that it is not with me you are really dealing. I am only a voice in this wilderness, after all. Do with me as you will, judge me as you will, but know this! You are dealing with the living God! You have no authority to judge him! It is he who judges you!

"And his judgment is not far off. Say to those who sent you, the day of his kingdom and glory is here and now. The LORD your God is weary of trees he planted in hope, but which refuse to delight him with their fruit! He does not know his orchard only, but every tree in it. Lies and pretenses will not deceive him. Look, he has picked up his ax! It is in his hand. He is coming to cut down every fruitless tree at its roots and cast it into the fire. The determination to start over and plant anew is his, not mine! He will not be denied! So, if you cannot hear your God when he speaks to you, if you cannot love him and trust him when he speaks to you, will you not at least fear him?

"Go on with it, if you must! Seal yourselves in the pride of your rightness, if you must. Hold me and this water crossing in contempt, if you must. Find some way to silence me and the word of your God, if you must. But know this! There is one coming after me who is mightier than I. What will you do when you face him? The LORD your God commanded Moses at the bush, 'Put off your shoes from your feet, for the place on which you are standing is holy ground.' Ex 3:5 I tell you, this place where I am standing and you with me, this too is holy ground, holy because the word of God speaks here. I myself am not worthy to wear shoes in his presence—not worthy even to stoop and untie my sandals and take them off before him.[10] Mt 3:11; Acts 13:25 What is this worthiness of yours, that you stand so secure and do not tremble?

---

[10] Paul G. Bretscher, "'Whose Sandals?' (Matt 3:11)." *Journal of Biblical Literature*, LXXXVII, 1967, pp. 81-90.

"This Jordan crossing into the wilderness is only a beginning sign. Its ending will be a baptism the LORD alone can accomplish. What will you do when his Holy Breath and fire fills the ordinary folk who actually believe the word of their sonship and honor and freedom in this water-crossing, as their fathers believed it of old? Will you deny it to them? Shame it? Crush it? Or will you hear and rejoice in it yourselves? I tell you, the LORD himself will be your 'Joshua.' As Joshua led your fathers through this Jordan into the land, so he will bring you out of the old and empty into his own presence and kingdom. His Spirit has power to drive out every last poison of unclean spirits that still infects you. But how will you be heirs of his kingdom and Spirit then, if you refuse for yourselves and deny others the honor of his sons and servants here and now?

"Is it too much for you to take off your shoes before your God? Will you present yourselves before him like mountain people? Will you expect God to exalt you over those you judge to be inferior? I tell you, the wrath of his coming will crush you! His fire will consume your city, your temple too, and the worship in which you glory. It will consume the archives and the genealogies you so love. Can you not hear? The harvest is ripe, the day of threshing has come. Your God knows empty chaff from fullness of wheat. See! He has taken his fan in hand! He is coming to clear his threshing floor. He will blow the chaff away and consume it with a puff of unquenchable fire!

"Listen! You passed through the Jordan to come to me in the wilderness this day. Don't despise it! Let your crossing that boundary yield a new heart and a new spirit in you, like the sprinkling and cleansing God promised by Ezekiel, 'A new heart I will give you, and a new spirit I will put within you; and I will take out of your flesh the heart of stone and give you a heart of flesh. And I will put my spirit within you, and cause you to walk in my statutes. And you shall be my people and I will be your God!' Ezek 36:26-28 Turn from the serpent who deceives you. Turn from emptiness and live! Look up! Hear the LORD name you his own 'beloved son' by this water-crossing. He does not want to shame you but to start you over new and free. Let him seal you by it in the grace of his promises. What greater honor can you have than that?

"Think what steadfast patience he has had with us, his people! For all our sins he has not given up on us, or turned against us in hate, or forgotten the name by which he named us, or put us out of his house. He longs for you to know and love him, so that you belong to him and are formed in his likeness and serve him in freedom. Therefore hear him this day! Let the voice of the LORD rebuke every voice that rises to seduce or accuse or frighten you. Breathe his breath, for he is your true life and glory. Receive what he so longs to give you, and return to him your love and trust. Don't be weightless and futile chaff, which his fan blows away! Be his wheat, the fruit of his gracious planting, so that he may gather you joyfully into the glory of his garner!"

John's sermon did not remain on the wilderness side of the Jordan. By his disciples and a memorizable condensation still preserved, it was heard in Jerusalem and through all Judea.

John and Jesus

At some point Jesus heard of John, left his carpentering in Nazareth of Galilee, came to him, and stayed a good while. Mt 3:13; Mk 1:9; 6:2 The road he walked led eastward, crossed the Jordan below the Sea of Galilee, then turned south. A memory is preserved that Jesus and John were the same age, John only six months older. Lk 1:36

Though Jesus was a Galilean and John a Judean of the priesthood, they shared a common treasure. Sabbath upon sabbath and year after year they had worshiped with their families in the synagogue. Both had heard the appointed selections from the law and the prophets, as these were read from "Moses' seat" by a designated scribe or Pharisee.[11] Acts tells how Paul was invited to speak in the synagogue of Antioch in Pisidia after "the law and the prophets" had been read. Paul told how the people of Jerusalem and their rulers "did not understand the utterances of the prophets which are read every sabbath." Acts 13:15,27 Lections and chanted psalms belonged to the oral literacy of God's people everywhere. For John and Jesus, despite the disparity of their backgrounds otherwise, these were a common resource.

It appears that Jesus heard John with deep appreciation, and that they were drawn to each other from the outset. John could tell Jesus questions which his teachers and fellow-priests could never grasp—how these exposed the emptiness of temple religion and drove him to seek answers in the wilderness. That Jesus was a questioner, too, is indicated in encouragements which have liberated my own searching. "Ask and it will be given you, seek and you will find, knock and it will be opened to you!" Mt 7:7 "Ask and you will receive, that your joy may be full." Jn 16:24 "Search the scriptures" for "eternal life," he urged his critics, for "they testify about me," and "Moses wrote of me." Jn 5:39,46 "The word of the LORD" which "came to John in the wilder-

---

[11] On "Moses' seat," see Mark Allan Powell, "Do and Keep What Moses Says" (Matthew 23:2-7). *Journal of Biblical Literature*, 114/3 (1995) pp. 419-435.

ness" fed Jesus' hunger, too, and made sense to the minds of both. They had much to talk about. Jesus stayed until John was arrested, which may have been a good while.

A fragment of direct memory recalls the occasion when Andrew and John first met Jesus, their fellow Galilean. Jn 1:35-40 Their teacher saw Jesus walk by and pointed him out: "Look, the lamb of God!" Whatever else John may have told them, that phrase was startling and memorable. It occurs in the context of the Baptist's familiar text from Isaiah: "Prepare the way of the LORD." "Behold, the Lord GOD comes with might... He will feed his flock like a shepherd, he will gather the lambs in his arms, he will carry them in his bosom." Is 40:10-11 "Bosom" is of the heart. Being held in the "bosom" suggests belonging and rest, oneness and trust. A parallel imagery, "the only son, who is in the bosom of the Father," occurs in the prologue of John's Gospel. Jn 1:18 Shepherd and lamb, Father and son, the covenant-implication is the same.

"It was about the tenth hour," John's memoir remembers. Counting from sunrise that would be about four o'clock. John and Andrew ran to catch up with Jesus. He heard them coming and asked what they wanted. What they talked about then is not told, only that they asked, "Rabbi, where are you staying?" "Come and see," he invited them. They went with him, then stayed the rest of that day—presumably in a home of Bethany that was hosting him. That they called him "Rabbi" or "Teacher" could reflect their later relationship to him, though they may have acknowledged him a teacher already then.

A passing memory like this may seem trivial, but it proves significant toward reconstructing the history. Andrew and John were a link between Jesus and the disciples of John, while Herod held John prisoner in Tiberias. In the era of the young church, they contributed toward resolving a deep stress and unifying the two companies into one church—a story to be told later.

Andrew is the likely source of a memory concerning Jesus' desire to be baptized, this one preserved in Matthew. Mt 3:13-15 "John would have prevented him," he recalls. Why the hesitation? A copyist answered by interpolating John's humble inferiority before Jesus' presumed deity. "I need to be baptized by you, and do you come to me?" Similar concern to rank Jesus above the Baptist corrupts the prologue of John's Gospel. Jn 1:8,15 I suspect that Andrew was not interested in John's hesitation so much as in Jesus' response. As for the hesitation, there could be a simple and practical reason. Jesus had come from Galilee by the usual route on the wilderness side of the Jordan, rather than through Samaria. Judeans who came to John needed to cross the Jordan, but Jesus was already here. To be "baptized" like them, he would need to cross into Judea first, then back to the wilderness side. Why should he do that? Surely he already knew every covenant-promise this "baptism" could give him!

But Jesus answered, "Let it be so now, for thus it is fitting for us to fill full all righteousness." "Fill full" answers emptiness. When John had proclaimed "the way of righteousness," "tax collectors and harlots" believed him, but Jesus' critics were left empty. Mt 21:32

Thus Jesus made the dual crossing. When he passed back through the Jordan and came up out of the water, so the memory says, "the Spirit of God descended on him out of heaven like a dove and remained on him"—for life. With it a voice spoke from heaven, "This is my son, my beloved, with whom I am well pleased." The memory, preserved in all the Gospels, would not have become known had Jesus not told it himself. I suspect he told it freely and often. The word he heard from heaven was as personal and powerful for him as it became for me generations later. The liberation of heart it effected was more profound than Israel's deliverance from slavery under a mere Pharaoh. "Blessed are those who hunger and thirst for righteousness, for they shall be satisfied," a beatitude says. Mt 5:6 The sonship-word had satisfied Jesus' own hunger and thirst. His authentic identity and worth was of God from the beginning. It was not a matter of racial descent, or performance, or recognition and applause. No accuser or critic, accusation or criticism, could detract from or nullify his name, either.

"My beloved son," the voice named him from heaven, and "with whom I am well pleased!"

That simple word was "spirit and life" to Jesus, the rock-foundation of a house which no storm could shake. Jn 6:63; Mt 7:24-25 It opened the scriptures to him. It blossomed into a full understanding of Johwah's covenant with Israel—the wonder of chosenness, of God's people as pure receivers. It proclaimed a wisdom and knowledge of God from outside any human "self," which no one in the world could ever imagine. Every preserved memory of Jesus— his temptations, his preaching, his appeal to the scriptures, his parables, his conflicts with the authorities, his death and resurrection, and the young church's confession of him, is rooted in that initial revelatory "voice from heaven" covenant-word.

After his baptismal crossing, Jesus was led by the Spirit (Mark has "driven") into the wilderness to be tested by the devil. Mt 4:1-4; Mk 1:13; Lk 4:1-4 He wanted to go there, just as he had wanted to be baptized. Thus he followed in John's steps again, and Israel's of old. "Why should you need this?" John may have wondered. "What can you expect to learn that you do not already know?" Jesus did not argue, but just went. This too belonged to "filling full all righteousness."

He returned from the wilderness, eager to tell John how the revelatory word of the LORD had broken through into his hunger, "Man does not live by bread alone." But John was gone, his ministry abruptly cut off. People of Bethany told what they knew. John had been arrested by order of Herod, whose territory this was.

Josephus, mentioned earlier, cites Herod's "fear, lest the great influence John had over the people might put it in his power and inclination to raise rebellion." Rome had laid it on the high priest and council to maintain order in Judea, but John stayed across the Jordan in Perea. What could they do about him then? An open-eyed "knowledge of good and evil" was not free to do nothing. They would work through Herod—stir him to suspect John as the leader of a potential rebellion. Though John's testimony to "the kingdom of heaven" explicitly rejected a kingdom of violence, the wisdom of "knowing good and evil" saw no need to trouble Herod with this. No one knew where John had been taken or whether he was still alive. His disciples, helpless and with nothing else to do, had gone home. Home for Andrew and John was Bethsaida in Galilee. For Jesus it was Nazareth. Mt 4:12; Mk 1:14

CHAPTER EIGHT

The Son of David

"Hosanna to the son of David! Blessed be he who comes in the name of the Lord."　　*Matthew 21:9*

That Jesus should have been called "son of David" became a puzzle to me. Given his name from heaven, "my beloved son" and what it meant to him, he would hardly have been concerned about his human ancestry. John the Baptist could trace his descent from Aaron and thus Abraham, yet even he claimed no advantage by it. What mattered to both Jesus and John was the covenant-righteousness God had declared to Israel of old, "Israel is my son, my first-born; let my son go that he may serve me." Ex 4:22-23

Yet the Gospels testify persistently to Jesus as "son of David." People appealed for healing by this name: "Jesus, son of David, have mercy on me." Mt 9:27; 15:22; 20:30-31 An enthusiastic crowd sang it as they escorted him into Jerusalem, "Hosanna to the son of David!" Mt 21:9 "Blessed be the kingdom of our father David that is coming," is the Marcan variation. Mk 11:10 Luke has "Blessed be the King who comes in the name of the Lord," similarly John. Lk 19:38; Jn 12:13 Evidently "son of David" implied "king" or "anointed" ("christ" or "messiah"), as David had been anointed a millennium before. 1 Sam 16:13 "Christ, a king!" Jesus was accused before Pilate. Lk 23:2 The language of "king" and "kingdom" did not derive from the exodus history, as John's baptism and Jesus' sonship did, but from the history of David.

Might references to Jesus as descended from David be "new testament overlay," a picture-language applied to him later by the young church? I gave that a thought but quickly gave it up.[12] This had to be direct memory. People

---

[12] Oscar Cullmann observes, "Most scholars...argue that the Christians invented the tradition (that Jesus was the son of David) and was an apologetic answer to the Jews, who commonly believed

must have known Jesus so within his ministry. If he did not claim descent from David for himself, others must have imposed this on him. But why?

Genealogical Consciousness

Judeans were conscious of their genealogy. Their fathers had returned from exile in Babylon generations earlier. In Jeremiah's vision, those exiled were a basket of "good figs," and the remnant who remained in the land "very bad figs." Jer 24:1-10 Under the priest Ezra, the "good figs" recommitted themselves to the law of Moses. They must keep themselves "good" and not turn "bad," like that remnant. Many restored their racial integrity by putting away their foreign wives and mixed-race children. Ezra 10:2-4; Ex 34:12-16 Ability to document or recite their genealogy marked their "belonging to Israel." Ezra 2:1-63 Genealogical archives in Jerusalem recorded every qualified birth. A name entered on earth signified its inscription in God's own book. Is 4:3; Dan 12:1 A faithful son would identify himself not only by his immediate father but by reciting his ancestry all the way back to Abraham.

None of this mattered for Jesus and the young church, however. Their treasure was not genealogy, but the covenant-word from heaven. God could name and record as "my beloved son" anyone he pleased. "Rejoice that your names are written in heaven," Jesus assured Galilean disciples whose names were not recorded in Judean archives. Lk 10:20 "Names in the book of life" or "the assembly of the first-born enrolled in heaven" designated God's people of the young church in contrast to claims of human ancestry. Rev 13:8; 17:8; Heb 12:23

Judean consciousness of racial purity generated subtle rankings—a genealogical Israel over a merely circumcised Israel. Isaiah's word concerning "Galilee of the nations," quoted in Matthew, is pointedly significant. Is 9:1-2; Mt 4:15-16 Formerly "the land of Zebulon and Naphtali," Galilee had been conquered by Tiglathpileser of Assyria about 732 B.C., its people deported and scattered into lands similarly conquered. 2 Kgs 15:29 This practice is described vividly in the case of Samaria. 2 Kgs 17:6,24 The loss of its major population and their replacement by foreigners accounted for what Isaiah pictured as the "anguish" and "contempt" and "deep darkness" of "Galilee of the nations." Yet God's promised light would fall on that land by the covenant-character of a David reborn, with no concern for racial purity.

---

that the Messiah must be of Davidic descent." *Op. cit.*, p. 128. Cullmann concludes as I do, however, that this tradition can be accounted for only as direct memory.

Josephus is the source for the period of Judea's independence after the purification of the temple in 164 B.C. and subsequent wars. Priestly Maccabean kings expanded their territory by conquest. Idumea (Edom) to the south was taken about 129 B.C., cleansed and made habitable to Judeans by the forced circumcision of its male population, thus submitting them to Judean laws and worship.[13] King Herod, an Idumean, belonged to Israel by circumcision but not genealogy. The conquest and forcible circumcision of Iturea to the north is dated 104 B.C.[14] As for Galilee, John Reumann reports that it "had been conquered by the Maccabees and 're-Judaized' only in 80 B.C."[15] Why so late? One would think that lower Galilee, blessed with broad valleys and even a lake, would have been targeted for conquest first. Yet it had been part of Samaria. Samaritans worshiped the LORD and practiced circumcision, yet long ago, when they had asked to participate with the returned exiles in re-building the temple, Zerubbabel had refused them. "You have nothing to do with us in building a house to our God." Ezra 4:1-3 Hard separation resulted. Only when this area of Samaria was decreed to be not of Samaria after all, could it be conquered, cleansed, subjected to the law, thus made fit for immigrants from Judea.

Idumeans, Itureans, and Galileans participated in pilgrimages to Jerusalem for feasts, yet their genealogical deficiency demoted them in the eyes of Judeans. Ranking of this sort is evident in Ezra. Some "sons of the priests ... sought their registration among those enrolled in the genealogies, but they were not found there, and so they were excluded from the priesthood as unclean." Ezra 2:62 Indications are preserved of contempt for Jesus as even a Samaritan. "Are we not right in saying that you are a Samaritan and have a demon?" his critics could argue. Jn 8:48 "Search and you will see that no prophet is to rise from Galilee," someone proposed. Jn 7:52 Moses had said, "The LORD your God will raise up for you a prophet like me from among you, from your brethren—him you shall heed." Dt 18:15 Since Jesus did not qualify as a "brother," he could not be a prophet. "We (unlike you) were not born of fornication" is a slur implying mixed ancestry. Jn 8:41 Racial dysfunction

---

[13] Antiquities 13:9,1 "Hyrcanus subdued all the Idumeans; and permitted them to stay in that country, if they would circumcise their genitals, and make use of the laws of the Jews, and they were so desirous of living in the country of their forefathers that they submitted to the use of circumcision, and of the rest of the Jewish ways of living."

[14] Antiquities 13:11,3

[15] John Reumann, *Jesus in the Church's Gospels* (Philadelphia: Fortress, 1968), p. 13. Reumann gives no source for this dating, neither have I been able to confirm it elsewhere, yet it provides a significant clue for me, testable in the very use of it.

accounted for his undisciplined teaching.

This leads to my question. It seems clear from the crowds that escorted Jesus into Jerusalem that the common folk viewed Jesus enthusiastically as descended from David. Yet if he did not qualify within Israel by his racial origin, how could he be this?

Solving the David Puzzle

I inferred that the awareness of Jesus as "the son of David" was direct memory, even if it was rooted in no more than a good-humored family claim-to-fame. Though it had little significance for Jesus himself, someone who heard of it had reason to take it seriously. Genealogies in Matthew and Luke make it a matter of public record. Mt 1:2-16; Lk 3:23-38

Both genealogies link Jesus to David. Other than that, they do not correspond at all. One possibility did occur to me. Suppose that the date of Galilee's conquest and cleansing was indeed around 80 B.C. Suppose a Judean family with known Davidic roots chose to migrate to Nazareth about that time and settle there. In that case a son of that family, his name still recorded in the archives, could have been Jesus' great-grandfather. So notable a circumstance would likely have been remembered in the family tradition. The two genealogies of Jesus ought then to converge at least here! Sure enough, there it was— Matthat in Luke, Matthan in Matthew—essentially the same name, meaning "gift"! Lk 3:24; Mt 1:15 I took the variation to be merely of dialect, "Matthat" in Judea (source of Luke), "Matthan" in Galilee (source of Matthew).

Both genealogies link Jesus to David by Joseph, his known father. Who was Joseph's father then? The genealogies differ on this, as usual. "Jacob" in Matthew may have been entered from the father of "Joseph" in the Genesis history. "Heli" in Luke is the oddity. Jesus' mother or his brothers would have been able to supply it. Both genealogies have a "Zerubbabel," but these differ, too. Matthew's Zerubbabel traces to the well-known line of Davidic kings. Luke's shows no familiar link whatever.

I inferred that Matthew's genealogy was not intended to be literal, but designed to put an end to the whole notion of genealogy as a claim on God. Mt 1:2-17 Three sets of fourteen generations (six sevens) culminate in Jesus— this seventh seven implying a "rest" from genealogy and a better claim. This genealogy features notorious impurities in the lineage of David and Solomon, as though to invalidate the prevailing concern for purity of bloodlines. Tamar played the harlot to Judah. Rahab was of Canaanite Jericho. Ruth was by race a Moabitess. David's adultery was with "the wife of Uriah," a Hittite.

The sequence in Luke backs up from Jesus to David, the way genealogies were actually recited. It reaches David by a line unknown, by a "Nathan" hardly known. He is recorded in Chronicles as the third of four sons borne to David by "Bathshua, the daughter of Ammiel." Solomon is last of the four. Lk 3:31; 1 Chr 3:5; 2 Sam 5:14.[16] I inferred that the Lucan genealogy was authentic, actually researched from the archival records in Jerusalem. The researcher found Jesus' great-grandfather Matthat and worked back to David from him. The search would have had purpose within Jesus' ministry. I assume copies were distributed to select persons who would appreciate their significance. Luke found a copy among fragments preserved in his Gospel.

Who might have been so excited about establishing Jesus' link to David, and for what reason? That is the next question.

Zealotic Piety and the "Christ"

Modern speculation concerning Jesus' "messianic self-consciousness" proposes that he, though aware of being the christ, was keeping it a secret.[17] A more likely possibility is that someone of zealotic piety, suspecting that Jesus might be the christ, heard the family rumor of his descent from David and researched it in order to confirm or disprove his hope.

Zealotic piety pervaded the self-awareness of God's chosen and determinedly faithful people. It was sustained by the Feast of Dedication or Lights (Hanukkah). Celebrated festively at the new moon around the shortest day of the year, the darkest of times, it relived the purification of the temple and its rededication in 164 B.C., when God had given his people victory against impossible odds over the Syrian tyrant, Antiochus Epiphanes. The religion had come alive in those days. A company of those faithful to the sabbath law had endured ruthless slaughter rather than fight back when attacked, though if it happened again, it was decided that they would fight. 1 Macc 2:32-41 "Show zeal for the law, and give your lives for the covenant of our fathers," the priest Mattathias had urged his sons as he died. 1 Macc 2:50 "In the sight of Heaven there is no difference between saving by many or by few," Judas had exhorted

---

[16] The tradition of Bathsheba as Solomon's mother appears to have suppressed that of Bathshua and her four sons. David's Jerusalem-born sons are listed also in 2 Samuel 5:14. Nathan and Solomon are third and fourth, but the name of their mother, Bathshua, does not appear.

[17] Oscar Cullmann, *op. cit.*, p. 124, traces the issue of "the messianic secret" to W. Wrede, *Das Messiasgeheimnis in den Evangelien*, 1901. The classic text is Peter's confession, "You are the Christ," and Jesus' response, "He charged them to tell no one about him." Mk 8:30

his diminished and weary army, and they had won! 1 Macc 3:18 He and his brothers, sons of the righteous Mattathias, were heroes. Their names became popular—John, Simon, Judas, Eleazar, and Jonathan.

Parents recited such stories dramatically to their children. Other narratives of faithfulness and deliverance were cherished, too—Joshua's conquests, Samson against the Philistines, David against Goliath. Gideon defeated the Midianites with an army reduced from thirty-two thousand to just three hundred. Judg 7,8 "Nothing can hinder the LORD from saving by many or by few," Jonathan told his armor-bearer, whereupon the two had won a great victory. 1 Sam 14:6-15

Stories and prophecies of Daniel were also prominent. The LORD had delivered three who were faithful from the fiery furnace and Daniel from the den of lions. Dan 3,6 Momentary losses were not the end of the story. "The court shall sit in judgment," to consume and destroy arrogant kings who defied the God of Israel. "And the kingdom and the dominion and the greatness of the kingdoms under the whole heaven shall be given to the people of the saints of the Most High; their kingdom shall be an everlasting kingdom, and all dominions shall serve and obey them. Here is the end of the matter." Dan 7:24-28 "The vision is for the time of the end." Dan 8:17; 12:4,9 "But go your way till the end; and you shall rest, and shall stand in your allotted place at the end of the days," the book of Daniel concludes. Dan 12:13

It was a call to be faithful even to death. Many will "forsake the holy covenant" so as to win favor from alien tyrants, "but the people who know their God shall stand firm and take action." "Some of those who are wise shall fall, to refine and to cleanse them and to make them white, until the end of the time." Dan 11:30-35 Even death will not exclude these from the kingdom and glory promised them. "And there will be a time of trouble, such as has never been since there was a nation till that time; but at that time your people will be delivered, every one whose name shall be found written in the book. And many of those who sleep in the dust of the earth shall awake, some to everlasting life, and some to shame and everlasting contempt. And those who are wise shall shine like the brightness of the firmament; and those who turn many to righteousness like the stars for ever and ever." Dan 12:1-3

Zealotic piety in Jesus' day looked expectantly to this "end of the days," when "the greatness of the kingdoms under the whole heaven shall be given to the people of the saints of the Most High"—"an everlasting kingdom" in which "all dominions shall serve and obey them."

Yet ambiguities remained. The end-time kingdom could not be hoped for through the priesthood in Jerusalem, for they had profaned Israel's covenant by their comfortable and self-serving accommodation with Rome. Daniel had warned also that the initiative must be of God, not of human ambition. "Men of violence among your own people shall lift themselves up in order to fulfil the vision, but they shall fail." Dan 11:14 Jesus warned similarly, "From the days of John the Baptist until now the kingdom of heaven has suffered violence, and men of violence take it by force." Mt 11:12

In a soil of such expectation and desire the seed-idea took root, that God might intend Jesus, even though he was a Galilean, to be "the christ" who should lead his people toward this kingdom. In him the "time of the end" might actually be pending. Realization that "he taught as one who had authority and not like the scribes" implied a perception of emptiness in the tradition of synagogue and temple. Mt 7:28-29; Mk 1:22 Jesus came from outside the establishment, yet he was bringing the religion to life! "What is this? A new teaching!" people marveled, seeing his power even over unclean spirits. Mk 1:27 If his teaching could revive or cleanse synagogue and temple, what a blessing that could be! It might yield the ultimate realization of Israel's glory!

As the thought that he might be "the christ" dawned on some, the rumor that he had family roots back to David encouraged it the more. Prophecies of a new David, perceived as predictive, fueled the speculation further. A piety ambitious for Israel's destiny of glory began to subordinate what Jesus taught and did to speculations regarding his person. "Eyes opened" to "know good and evil" looked eagerly for further confirmatory evidences. Rumors of what people saw spread, anticipating also what it might mean. Jesus' disciples became infected, too. The sons of Zebedee (James and John), recalling how the LORD had once rained fire and brimstone upon Israel's enemies, proposed that they call down "fire from heaven" in Jesus' name on an inhospitable Samaritan town. Ps 11:6; Is 30:30-33; Lk 9:54 Mark's list of the apostles preserves a surname Jesus gave these brothers, "Boanerges," meaning "sons of thunder." Mk 3:17

Jesus' gospel of sonship and grace and gathering effected healings, but "eyes opened to know good and evil" began to see these as signs of divine power, pointing to greater wonders still to come. Imaginative leaders developed case studies by analogy from the scriptures. A pool of rumor grew. The more people heard, the more excited they were to see "mighty works" of his themselves—as though such works should define him. Lk 4:23; Mk 6:2-6 Eyes opened to watch what he might do blocked ears from hearing what he taught. Rumor-mongering developed into a purposeful tactic. Harness Jesus to a strategy, count on the hand of God to show.

Having grown up in this piety himself, Jesus was aware of what was going on. Stories of "signs and wonders" he did became an alien planting, fruitless and destructive. His parable of sowing depicts a soil on which his word fell and began to grow, only to have thorns spring up and choke it. Mt 13:7 "Unless you see signs and wonders, you will not believe," he grieved. Jn 4:48

The memory of a withdrawal to the area of Caesarea Philippi is revealing. Mk 8:27-30; Lk 9:18-22 "Who do the people say I am?" Jesus asked. His disciples had returned from a mission and should know. It was awkward. They did not want Jesus to know that they knew, or how they knew, or how much they knew. They assured themselves that he must know, longed for him to say so, but did not dare ask him. He was entitled, after all, to keep it secret as long as he wished. Secrecy was necessary in any case. Herod and Rome, if they heard such rumors, would sense subversion and respond accordingly—as when Herod had arrested John.

So they hedged. "Some say you are John the Baptist, others Elijah, others one of the prophets." Matthew's account adds Jeremiah. Jesus waited, but they were silent. Finally he forced it into the open. "But who are you saying I am?" They had been saying it, Jesus knew, though not to him. Simon Peter broke down. "You are the christ," he confessed. It was good to have it out. Now perhaps their master could open up with them.

Yet Jesus had not sent them to talk rumors or be swayed by what others said of him. Their mission was to teach his word as he had made them learn it, without addition or subtraction, according to the spirit and method of all the prophets. "He strictly charged the disciples to tell no one that he was the christ," Matthew's account recalls vividly. Mt 16:20 *They did not get this teaching from him!* Zealotic ambition was imposing it on him! Were it not that the young church confessed Jesus as indeed "the christ" (though redefined as "the son of God"), the answer as recorded might be exactly what John the Baptist had said earlier, "I am not the christ!" Jn 1:20

This exchange, in the context also of John's death, became a turning point in Jesus' ministry. The temple authorities need not send more delegations to investigate him; he himself would go to Jerusalem. Pharisees urged him to leave, citing Herod's threat to kill him as he had killed John. Jesus called Herod a "fox," a fearful coward. No, Herod would not do it again. Jerusalem must do it this time. "It cannot be that a prophet should perish away from Jerusalem." Lk 13:31-33

As for Jesus, he would "set fire on earth." Lk 12:49 He would proclaim his Father's word to the authorities face to face, clearly and uncompromisingly, undeterred by threat or fear—no alliances needed, no conspiracy, no secret swords, no misconstrued enemy, no revolution. How would it come out? The council of priests, scribes, and elders would not listen any more than zealotic piety did. They would trust their open-eyed wisdom of desire and fear. They had authority to judge themselves righteous and Jesus the blasphemer. All Jesus had was his Father's promise, "On the third day he will raise us up, that we may live before him." Hos 6:2; Mt 16:21

Who told all this afterwards? It must have been Simon Peter, named "rock" by Jesus initially, not as a badge of honor but as stubborn and unlistening. "They have made their faces harder than rock," Jeremiah said. Jer 5:3 "Is not my word like fire, says the LORD, and like a hammer that breaks the rock in pieces?" Jer 23:29 It was a rock-head Peter who protested, "God forbid, Lord! This shall never happen to you!" to which Jesus answered as in the mountain temptation, "Get behind me, Satan! You are an impediment to me. You are not on the side of God, but of men." Mt 16:22-23; 4:10

Other confessions from the post-resurrection side recall how the zealotic delusion had consumed the disciples and blocked their hearing. "They did not understand the saying, and were afraid to ask him." Mk 9:32 They argued jealously who should rank highest in his court some day. Mk 9:33-34; 10:37 In the upper room they pushed to sit next to him. Lk 22:24 They hid their miserable arsenal of two swords until Jesus forced it into the open. Lk 22:35-38 Rallied by Peter, they pledged to be faithful even to death. It took Jesus' dying to destroy their illusion. Only by and after his resurrection did they begin to know him for what he had been and taught all along, rather than by the open-eyed fantasy they tried to impose on him.

Simon the Zealot (Cananaean)

The populist conspiracy could not have developed or sustained itself without imaginative and aggressive leaders. Someone or other must have seen this possibility in Jesus, watched for confirmatory signs, found supportive evidences in the scriptures, whispered such awesome ideas, thus stirred excitement and hope in those who heard it. The pilgrim crowd that escorted Jesus from Bethany into Jerusalem, met by another crowd from the city, did not happen by chance. It took forethought and planning for people to lay their robes before Jesus in royal processional, cut and wave palm branches, and turn the "Hosanna, save us" of a pilgrim psalm into a chant to "the son of David" or "king," which children continued to sing in the temple. Ps 118:25-

26; Mt 21:9,15

The demonstration had a purpose. Jesus should know how widely and enthusiastically the people supported him despite their rulers, thus be persuaded to accept the messianic kingship they were thrusting upon him. There was risk, too. A procession so well organized would have the look of an insurrection, defying not only the priesthood but the Roman authority which the priesthood supported. But confidence in God prevailed. Hidden swords in that crowd were ready for action, courageous and determined, needing only a small signal from Jesus to turn violent, counting on angels to help. The promoters did not see their conspiracy as evil. They were the faithful! They would help Jesus fulfill his destiny. By promoting and supporting him so, they would also save him from a priesthood they knew was plotting to destroy him.

Who incited all this? Jesus' disciples were in on it, but they could not have originated it. One name does emerge. All four lists of the apostles have a Simon surnamed "the Cananaean" (Aramaic) or "Zealot" (Greek). Mt 10:4; Mk 3:18; Lk 6:15; Acts 1:13 "Zeal" was in itself a noble piety, implying faithfulness and dedication. What began as a piety turned into a party, however, with leaders and visions, weaponries and strategies, allies and enemies. That sense of "zealot" is common in Josephus. In the Gospels it occurs only here. As it turned out, the plot to make Jesus king succeeded only in getting him crucified by the Romans. When the wonder of his resurrection revealed him as the savior and "Christ" he truly was, this Simon, raised from a death of his own, surnamed himself "the Zealot." Thus he openly confessed and identified himself with the misguided plot of which he was now thoroughly ashamed. Nothing else is said of him, yet for the young church to list him so testifies that he became a notable apostolic witness and leader.

I infer that he was a Galilean, close to Jesus almost from the beginning. He must have been a gifted leader, able to inspire trust, knowledgeable in the scriptures, trained to read and write. He noticed "signs" Jesus did, sensed their potential implications, and rumored these in awe—looking toward a day when Jesus might reveal himself openly as the christ.

There is further evidence. A curious note in John identifies the disciple Judas as "(son) of Simon Iscariot." Jn 13:26 Simon Iscariot? Could this have been another self-designation for the Simon who also called himself "the Zealot"? Judas came to be called "Iscariot" in retrospect, meaning "deceiver" or "traitor." Yet Simon, his father, confessed himself to be the real "Iscariot." He had fathered the treachery! His corrupted piety had misled a courageous Judas into the plot that delivered Jesus up to be crucified. This Simon was to blame not for the death of Jesus only, but for the despair and death of his own son! Surely he was the real "Iscariot."

If this Simon was Judas' father, he was a generation older than the youthful disciples. Through Judas he gained access to all of them. They respected him for his age. His ideas and insights inspired trust. Seemingly on Jesus' side, he caught their ear secretively and became to them another teacher, the enemy-sower of thorns that sprang up to choke Jesus' own sowing. Mt 13:7,24-28 Drawing on familiar hero stories, Simon could project what a glorious role the disciples might play in the coming kingdom, if they were only faithful and courageous.

"Zealot" and "Iscariot" as surnames confess the same guilt. That Matthew and Mark list "Simon the Cananaean" (Aramaic) just before "Judas Iscariot," may likewise suggest a father-son linkage. John, whose memoir preserves this link, must have been in on the plot himself, close to both Judas and his father. He and James were the "Boanerges" brothers on the list of apostles.

There were many "Simons," of course. Simon and Judas were hero-names out of the Maccabaean wars, the most admired of Mattathias' five sons. 1 Macc 2:2-4 Jesus had brothers so named. Mt 13:55; Mk 6:3 Since these two scraps of memory derive from a single history, however, it makes sense to assume that the Simon they identify is one and the same.

The Genealogy

The era of zealotic enthusiasm for Jesus yields further questions. Who might have known the prophecies of David so well as to link the "signs" Jesus did with these? Who might have been struck by the rumor that Jesus, though a Galilean, was nevertheless a blood-descendant of David? Who would imagine that this link, if it could be substantiated, would not only confirm him as the christ but also qualify him as to race! Who, seizing the slim hint of Jesus' great-grandfather Matthan, might have been both capable and driven to search this out in the genealogical archives in Jerusalem? Who, having found what he sought, might have copied Jesus' lineage from his father Joseph, through Matthan to David, then circulated it among strategic leaders, so that Luke found a copy among his fragments? Who other than Simon, Judas' father?

Searching in the archives for a bloodline that ended four generations back with a "Matthan" was hard enough in itself. Discovering that it did indeed trace back to David was exciting indeed! The variant form "Matthat" in the archives might have disconcerted Simon for the moment, but he would readily perceive this as merely a matter of dialect. More troublesome would be the finding that Matthat's genealogy did not trace to David by the familiar line of Judah's kings, as expected, but by a "Nathan" hardly known. Yet such obscurity accorded remarkably with Isaiah's prophecy of the tree of Jesse cut down to a stump. Is 11:1 The "branch" would not grow from prior branches but from the root—a beginning totally new.

Jesus' genealogical link to David was firmly established in the young church. Other writings remember it, too. Paul confessed Jesus as "descended from David according to the flesh." Rom 1:3; 2 Tim 2:8 "The lion of the tribe of Judah, the root of David," the church sang of him. Rev 5:5; 22:16 Yet his genealogy "from David according to the flesh" ceased to be pertinent to the church's confession of him. He was indeed the anointed-messiah-christ, not of "the house of David," however, but as son and servant of God. Is 7:13-14; 42:1 He was indeed "the king of the Judeans," as the sign on the cross said, not as a zealotic "son of David" conqueror, however, but in the kingdom of his Father. Mt 25:34; 26:29; 27:29,37

Significantly, the genealogy in Luke extends beyond David to Abraham, beyond Abraham through Noah and the antedeluvian patriarchs to "the son ... of Seth, of Adam, of God." Lk 3:38 Why this? Because the life that distinguished Jesus was not of human genealogy but of the "voice from heaven." The covenant-word and Spirit of God established his name, sonship, honor, righteousness, freedom, calling, and eternal hope in relation to God his Father. That is the wonder of our identity also—and the hope of the world.

CHAPTER NINE

The Kingdom-*now*

"Repent, for the kingdom of heaven is at hand."
Matthew 3:2; 4:17; 10:7; Mark 1:14

The "kingdom" of which Jesus spoke, and John before him, countered the piety of a futurist glory. "The kingdom of heaven is at hand!"—here now, to be entered now. "Repent" summoned God's people to give up the fantasy of divine favoritism with its hope of their future exaltation over the nations. "Of heaven" in Matthew preserves a common euphemism for God.

"Kingdom" language derived from the era of David. Jesus' "gospel of the kingdom," founded on the covenant of the LORD by Moses, sees the two themes as one message. Mt 4:23 The young church derived the title "gospel" for what Jesus preached from Isaiah: "Get you up to a high mountain, O Zion, herald of good tidings; lift up your voice with strength, O Jerusalem, herald of good tidings, lift it up, fear not, say to the cities of Judah, 'Behold, your God!'" or again, "How beautiful upon the mountains are the feet of him who brings good tidings, who publishes peace, who brings good tidings of good, who publishes salvation, who says to Zion, 'Your God reigns,'" or "The LORD has anointed me to bring good tidings to the poor." Is 40:9; 52:7; 61:1

Gathering and Scattering

"He who does not gather with me scatters," Jesus said. Mt 12:30 Gathering was the very nature of the covenant-word from of old. "I will bless you ... so that you will be a blessing," the LORD told Abraham, even to "all the families of the earth." Gen 12:2-3 "If you obey my voice and keep my covenant ... you shall be to me a kingdom of priests and a holy nation," God promised his

121

people Israel. Their priestly calling was to mediate his covenant "among all peoples, for all the earth is mine." Ex 19:5-6 The principle, "You shall love your neighbor as yourself," extended to foreigners: "The stranger who sojourns with you shall be to you as the native among you, and you shall love him as yourself; for you were strangers in the land of Egypt." Lev 19:18,34 They were not to view the stranger as inferior, not dominate or enslave him as the Egyptians had them. "Behold, I have taught you statutes and ordinances, as the LORD my God commanded me," Moses said, "that you should do them in the land which you are entering...; for that will be your wisdom and your understanding in the sight of the peoples, who, when they hear all these statutes, will say, 'Surely this great nation is a wise and understanding people.'" Dt 4:5-6

Under David a holy confidence prevailed, that the nations around would gladly embrace Israel's covenant. Ruth, a Moabitess, told Naomi, "Your people will be my people and your God my God," and was not refused! Ruth 1:16-18 She married Boaz and become David's great-grandmother. Ruth 4:17 Obededom, a Gittite, was blessed to have the ark rest at his house. 2 Sam 6:11 Soldiers loyal to David included Ittai the Gittite and his six hundred, also Uriah the Hittite. 2 Sam 15:18-22; 23:39 Solomon's prayer of dedication pleads "that all the peoples of the earth may know your name and fear you, as do your people Israel." 1 Kgs 8:43

Prophecies of a new "David" do not look to his genealogy or a geographical kingdom, but to the character of the LORD manifest in him. "The earth shall be full of the knowledge of the LORD as the waters cover the sea. In that day the root of Jesse shall stand as an ensign to the peoples; him shall the nations seek, and his dwellings shall be glorious." Is 11:9-10 "I will raise up for David a righteous branch, and he shall reign as king and deal wisely, and shall execute justice and righteousness in the land.... And this is the name by which he shall be called, 'The LORD is our righteousness.'" Jer 23:5-6 "My servant David shall be king over them.... They shall follow my ordinances and be careful to observe my statutes.... I will make a covenant of peace with them... and I will be their God and they shall be my people. Then the nations will know that I the LORD sanctify Israel, when my sanctuary is in the midst of them forever." Ezek 37:24-28

But there was trouble. A contrary impulse of scattering was seeded very early. Evidences associated with Solomon signal an illusion of Israel's superiority in the eyes of God. "All the people who were left of the Amorites, the Hittites, the Perizzites, the Hivites, and the Jebusites, who were not of the people of Israel, these Solomon made a forced levy of slaves, and so they are to this day. But of the people of Israel Solomon made no slaves; they were the soldiers, they were his officials...." 1 Kgs 9:20-22 This perversity affected the history, then infected the writings. A retrojection appears in Joshua: the Gibeonites "continue to this day" as "hewers of wood and drawers of water for the congregation and for the altar of the LORD." Josh 9:27 Dramatic stories present the LORD as a warrior fighting on Israel's side against the nations, commanding them even to wipe out the nations. God's people, if faithful, could look to more and greater victories. On the other hand, if they disobeyed, God would punish them by delivering them up to their enemies.

Fear that the nations would pervert Israel supplanted David's confidence that Israel's covenant would assimilate them. Priestly control of sacred documents could write an enforced separation into the law ascribed to Moses, under the illusion of holiness. "When the LORD your God gives them (the seven nations) over to you and you defeat them, then you must utterly destroy them. You shall make no covenant with them and show no mercy to them. You shall not make marriages with them, giving your daughters to their sons or taking their daughters for your sons. For they would turn away your sons from following me to serve other gods. Then the anger of the LORD would be kindled against you, and he would destroy you quickly." Dt 7:1-5; Ex 34:12-16 Thereby Israel's holy writings spoke with a double tongue—the covenant of gathering against a piety of scattering.

Writings were subject inevitably to the authority of those who could write and read, in this case the priesthood. Their authority depended in turn on the authority of their documents. But if authority was ascribed to documents considered sacred, what authority remained for the covenant itself, which had created Israel as God's people in the first place? Prophets might hear the original covenant-word and delight in it. They might proclaim it as the "word of the LORD." Priests and kings could oppose them, however, by the authority of written texts, turned to their advantage by their own self-interested understanding.

The Kingdom of Gathering

For Jesus, the God named "Father" in the exodus history, or "King" in the David saga, was one. "Your heavenly Father knows that you need all these things. But seek first his kingdom and righteousness." Mt 6:32-33 "My Father's kingdom," he could call it. Mt 26:29 "The righteous will shine like the sun in the kingdom of their Father." Mt 13:43 "Father,... your kingdom come." Lk 11:2 How would his Father's kingdom come? Not by the strategies and powers of zealotic activism, not by a sudden divine end-time stroke, but by the seeding and slow growing of his covenant-gospel even now! "The kingdom of heaven is like a grain of mustard seed which a man took and sowed in his field... like leaven which a woman took and hid in three measures of meal, until the whole was leavened." Mt 13:31-33

The kingdom Jesus proclaimed was of peace, not war. It bound up wounds and did not inflict them. It measured worth by the honor of a sonship and inheritance open to all without partiality. The "sons" of this kingdom are "peacemakers." They do not consent to rankings or enmities. They break down walls of division. By a meekness without pride or envy, by a glad willingness to love and suffer injustices without defense or retaliation, by forgiving an abusive "enemy" rather than be divided from him, they put the weapons of zealotic warfare and of a self-serving priesthood to shame.

"My covenant of peace," the LORD called it. Is 54:10 "Come, behold the works of the LORD, what sort of desolations he has wrought in the earth! He makes wars to cease to the ends of the earth. He breaks the bow and shatters the spear. He burns the chariots with fire! Be still and know that I am God. I am exalted among the nations, I am exalted in the earth." Ps 46:8-10 "The mountain of the house of the LORD shall be established as the highest of the mountains, and all nations shall flow to it and say, 'Come, let us go up to the mountain of the LORD, that he may teach us his ways and that we may walk in his paths.' For out of Zion shall go forth the covenant, and the word of the LORD from Jerusalem. He shall judge between the nations and shall decide for many peoples; and they shall beat their swords into plowshares, and their spears into pruning hooks; nation shall not lift up sword against nation, neither shall they learn war any more. O house of Jacob, come, let us walk in the light of the LORD." Is 2:2-5

When the zealotic crowd hailed Jesus as king, he enacted Zechariah's prophecy of peace. "Lo, your king comes to you; triumphant and riding on an ass.... I will cut off the chariot from Ephraim and the war horse from Jerusalem; and the battle bow shall be cut off, and he shall command peace to the nations." Zech 9:9-10 Jesus lived by his Father's promises joyfully, even if all alone: "I keep the LORD always before me; because he is at my right hand, I shall not be moved. Therefore my heart is glad and my true worth rejoices, my body too rests secure.... You will show me the path of life. In your presence is fullness of joy, in your right hand are pleasures for evermore." Ps 16:8-11

The passwords of the kingdom Jesus preached were of the exodus—"receive," "enter," "inherit," "possess." "You shall do what is right and good in the eyes of the LORD, that it may go well with you, and that you may enter and take possession of the good land which the LORD swore to give to your fathers." Dt 6:18 "Blessed are the poor in spirit, for theirs is the kingdom of heaven," Jesus said. "Blessed are the meek, for they shall inherit the earth... Blessed are those who are persecuted for righteousness' sake, for theirs is the kingdom of heaven." Mt 5:3,5,10

Activist zealotry, by contrast, was not "poor in spirit," not "meek," not willing to be "persecuted." The disciples, when they argued which of them should be the greatest, were strong in spirit, aggressive, ready to persecute any who got in their way. Jesus set a child among them and warned, "Unless you turn and become like children, you will never enter the kingdom of heaven." Mt 18:3 Israel at Kadeshbarnea fell into panic at the report of the spies. "Not one of this evil generation shall see the good land which I swore to give to your fathers," the LORD decreed then, but "your little ones, who you said would become a prey, and your children, who to this day have no knowledge of good and evil (are not driven by lust and fear), they shall go in there, and to them I shall give it, and they shall possess it." Dt 1:35,39 Jesus modeled the kingdom "at hand" in his Jordan crossing. He heard the sonship-word, believed it, received his Father's Spirit, and like a little child entered.

He illustrated for his people the trap into which their tradition had fallen. God offered them a blessed feast now, yet "all alike began to make excuses." Lk 14:18 An eager youth asked, "Good Teacher, what must I do to inherit eternal life?"—parallel with "enter the kingdom of God." Mk 10:17-25 He had done everything the law required. He stood ready to do anything further that Jesus might ask. Yet when Jesus summoned him to "sell everything" he had (meaning give up his zealotic piety and start over with nothing), thus possess "treasures in heaven" now, he could not do it. "It is easier for a camel to go through the eye of a needle than for a rich man to enter the kingdom of God," Jesus said. The camel signified uncleanness, as of the nations. To view a camel through the eye of a needle is simple, to bring it through is impossible. Yet unclean nations will enter the kingdom of God more readily than a people who cannot "sell" or give up their illusion of superiority.

The gospel of the kingdom expects hearts who hear it to believe what they hear. Any who judge and reject this gospel, however, will be judged and rejected themselves. "Tell the righteous that it shall be well with them, for they shall eat the fruit of their deeds," Isaiah put it, but "Woe to the wicked! It shall be ill with him, for what his hands have done shall be done to him." Is 3:10-11 John the Baptist pictured an ax laid to the root of a tree planted in hope but stubbornly fruitless. He pictured a winnowing fan in God's hand, ready to blow away the proud pretense of empty chaff. Mt 3:10,12 The determining judgment was not for God to render in some distant future. It was the judgment his people were rendering against their God here and now.

The gospel breaks through nevertheless in holy joy and wonder. Its primal declaration, "You are my beloved son, with whom I am well pleased," reveals the Father's verdict of love on us from the very beginning, before we have thought or done anything. It confers an honor and hope and calling from outside our self, which no natural heart could ever imagine. Thereby it liberates us from the very system of "being judged."

Such freedom is beyond imagination! We do not live in self-conscious fear of being watched and criticized. We do not crave attention and compliments. We do not labor under anxiety to make a good impression. We are not subject to comparisons and competitions. We have no need to cover failure or hide from guilt. Of his own will and character, our Father in heaven forgives us when we fail. He cleans up our messes in patient hope without reproach. The kingdom of God knows only our authentic worth and honor—the grace and gift from a Father in heaven, whose patient love does not run out, whose foundational and impartial mercy does not know rankings. Since external diversities are not a measure of worth, they can be honored and enjoyed in holy freedom and mutual thanksgiving, rather than suppressed.

The God of mercy will not change, however. "I am who I am," Johwah defines himself. Ex 3:14 He will not yield to sinners who think they possess "heaven and earth" by right of their own creating, who tell God the Giver what he ought to be and do, who then, if he does not do what they think right, rule him out of existence. "The fool says in his heart, 'There is no God.'" Ps 14:1

"Judge not, that you be not judged," Jesus said. Mt 7:1 If anyone, confident of his rightness and proudly independent, prefers to live under the system of judging and being judged, of ranking and being ranked, of accusing and being accused, he shall have it. His way is slavery and death, however. The verdict he renders against the God of pure mercy is stamped "eternal." Not even the living God himself can force love and truth on him.

"He who scattered Israel will gather him, and will keep him as a shepherd keeps his flock," Jeremiah said. Jer 31:10 "Gathering" was for Jesus a conscious principle. He sought out the lost. Lk 15:4-7; 19:10 He received sinners and ate with them. Mt 9:10-11 A variety of images express this. Fishermen gather with their net. Mt 13:47 A hen "gathers her brood under her wings." Mt 23:37 Shepherds gather a people "harrassed and helpless." Laborers gather the harvest. Mt 9:36-38 The wolf scatters the sheep; the good shepherd gathers them from even beyond "this fold." Jn 10:11-16 Jesus died "not for the nation only, but to gather into one the children of God who are scattered abroad." Jn 11:51-52 His summons to entrust every anxiety or ambition to "your heavenly Father" is a classic invitation to the kingdom-now, with liberation for any human heart. "Seek first the kingdom of God and his righteousness" is his call. "All these things shall be yours as well" is his promise. Mt 6:25-35

When Jesus sent his disciples on their assigned tours, he set a practical limit: "Go nowhere among the Gentiles, and enter no town of the Samaritans, but go rather to the lost sheep of the house of Israel." Mt 10:5-6 Yet when outsiders came to him, he (and the young church in his image) could not turn them away. "Whoever comes to me I will not cast out, for I have come down from heaven, not to do my own will but the will of him who sent me." Jn 6:37-38

The secret of his Father's will was to "love your neighbor as yourself." Lev 19:18; Mt 22:39 Jesus knew and valued his own "self," the personhood he had from his Father. Thereby he loved and honored the "self" of every "neighbor" too, whose life touched his. He did not weigh people by outward diversities—like male or female, pure or impure, Jew or Gentile, rich or poor, likable or unlikable, healthy or sick, strong or weak, young or old, in authority or under authority, righteous or sinner, friend or enemy. Beneath any visible externality he saw, loved, and addressed the true and real "self" of the other as from God, a "self" no different than his own.

Images of manifest and abhorrent uncleannesses illustrate this. Not leprosy, not a woman's flow of blood, not even death, could contaminate the "self" given by God to him or to that neighbor. Mt 8:3; 9:22,25 In love and without fear Jesus closed the gap, touched and was touched, thus took the uncleanness of another upon himself. "He took our infirmities and bore our diseases," the young church testified later, quoting Isaiah. Mt 8:17; Is 53:4

The Covenant Prayer

Zealotry set its hope on a futurist kingdom. Creedal Christianity sets its hope in the future, too—"the resurrection of the dead and the life of the world to come." Praying Jesus' covenant prayer, however, focuses the kingdom-now as he believed and prayed it himself. Mt 6:9-13

To pray "Our Father in heaven, holy be your name" is to look to the Giver-Creator-God for identity and worth—rather than to our human descent or to any name we can achieve for ourselves. To keep his name holy is to embrace for ourselves the character and works of God our Father, whose "son" and people we are, as testified by Moses, prophets, and psalmists.

To pray "Your kingdom come, your will be done on earth, as it is in heaven" is to submit in glad servanthood to our Father-King. The angels bless the LORD and do his will in heaven. Ps 103:20 Our calling as children is to do his will on earth, in the bodies he gives us here and now. His kingdom is not a future reward. We live in it here and now.

To pray "Give us this day our daily bread, and forgive us what we owe, as we forgive those who owe us," is to be aware that we are pure receivers. We depend honestly and gladly on our Father's giving. Trusting him to pour out his gifts as he pleases, we pass the flow of his generosity on by our own. He does not ask payment for his giving and forgiving. We, who are formed in his image, seek no payment, either. Love remains love. Gift remains gift.

By praying "And lead us not into temptation, but deliver us from evil," we commit ourselves to follow our Father's lead in everything we are and do. His way includes testings. Seductions of gain or threats of loss will indeed come into view, which tempt us to turn our eyes from our Father and pursue instead the slithering lusts and escapisms of the snake. Trusting our Father to "deliver us from (what threatens) evil" frees us from fear and the impulse to save ourselves. We can walk his way true and upright even when it leads squarely into trouble, giving thanks regardless, confident that he will accomplish his purpose through us and make it good for us. That is what Jesus did and what his challenge means: "If anyone will come after me, let him deny himself and take up his cross and follow me. For whoever would save his life will lose it, and whoever loses his life for my sake will find it." Mt 16:24-25

"Signs and Wonders"

What of testimonies concerning Jesus' "mighty works" or "signs and wonders" then? Creedal Christianity accounts for these by assuming that the name "my beloved son" or "son of God" for Jesus means deity, and that the power to do "miracles" is evidence of his deity. My principle of coherence does not allow this explanation, however. The name "son of God" for Jesus is a language of covenant, not of deity. The gospel Jesus preached and lived is the LORD's covenant-word to his people. Any works of power told in the preserved memory must have been of his gospel, not of his omnipotent deity, because there was no such thing. This is my premise, my principle of coherence. If it does not work out in some instance, that testimony must be accounted for in some other way. "Why was this said the way it is said?" remains the question. Jesus' authentic gospel remains the climate for any answer.

The phrase "signs and wonders" derives from the exodus history and Daniel. Ex 7:3; Dt 4:34; Dan 6:27 Jesus cites it in warning against zealotic illusion. "Unless you see signs and wonders, you will not believe." Jn 4:48 "On that day many will say to me, 'Lord, Lord, did we not prophesy in your name, and cast out demons in your name, and do many mighty works in your name?' Then I will say to them, 'I never knew you; depart from me, you whose works are iniquity.'" Mt 7:21-23 "False Christs and false prophets will arise and show great signs and wonders, so as to lead astray, if possible, even the elect." Mt 24:24; Mk 13:22 Such sayings testify to a piety which loved to tell how God had miraculously delivered his people in the past. The common folk believed in a God of miracles. They counted on him to come through with spectacular works on the day of his kingdom, to raise and restore the faithful who had suffered death rather than forsake his law.

Jesus' "gospel of the kingdom" did effect healings, sometimes noticeably, in body and behavior. He could hardly have been accused for healing on the sabbath day if he did not in fact heal, or taunted at the cross, "He saved others," if he did not in fact save. Mt 12:9-14; 27:42 "He casts out demons by Beelzebul, the prince of demons," critics warned, to which Jesus responded, "If I cast out demons by Beelzebul, by whom do your sons (your own physicians) cast them out?" Mt 12:24,27 A summary observation, twice in Matthew, expresses his integrality: "He went about teaching in their synagogues and preaching the gospel of the kingdom and healing every disease and infirmity among the people." Mt 4:23; 9:35 Teaching, preaching, and healing were one.

Something happened, however, to distort evident healings into a promotion of "signs and wonders." Propaganda of this sort preceded Jesus when he visited Nazareth on his way to Jerusalem. The preserved memory suggests what had happened. "Doubtless you will quote to me this proverb, 'Physician, heal yourself,'" he began his sermon. "What we have heard you did in Capernaum, do here also in your own country!" Lk 4:23-30; Mt 13:54-58; Mk 6:1-6 His homefolk were not interested in hearing and believing his gospel. They wanted to see him do "signs and wonders," then marvel as others had, "Where did this man get this wisdom and these mighty works?" He disappointed them. The memory says they "took offense at him," viewed him as a fraud, even wanted to hurl him over a cliff.

Rumors like those which reached Nazareth were whispered throughout Galilee, even in Tiberias, Herod's capital. Lk 9:7 A memory from Jesus' trial, likely reported by Herod's steward, "Chuza," mentions that "Herod had heard about him and was hoping to see some sign done by him." Lk 23:8; 8:3

Miracle stories are a distraction also to creedal Christianity. Jesus, being God-incarnate, had power to do any miracle ascribed to him, it explains. The "mighty works" reported of him confirm his deity. This is his glory! As for the glad news of covenant-sonship, which Jesus heard from heaven at his baptism, by which he prayed, which he served even to death, and by which he is our savior Christ—it is shunted aside, not known, not recognized, not even heard. Yet it alone created this embattled history. It alone raised up the disciples and the young church out of Jesus' resurrection. It alone revealed the living and loving God in him. It alone brought into being every testimony to Jesus preserved in the Gospels.

The miracle stories must be accounted for. "Historical imagination" would not generalize but deal with each individually, asking why it was said the way it is said. More than one level of mind can sometimes be detected. Memory of an original event is a first level. Zealotic retelling could add a second. A third level might be a thought interpolated later by a copyist. Some miracle stories turn out to be post-resurrection metaphor. I treat these in Part Five.

Simon and his son Judas would have had part in the distraction I call zealotic. "Historical imagination" can reasonably infer how they came to be involved with Jesus. They were among the crowds that heard him while he was still gathering disciples. The vitality of his heart-message astonished them, too. As a memory has it, "He spoke as one who had authority and not like the scribes." Mt 7:29 Judas became a disciple. His father followed Jesus and heard him often. At some point Simon's focus shifted from Jesus' message to his person. "Eyes opened" to "know good and evil" perceived a glorious possibility in him. Might Jesus be "the messenger of the covenant" God had promised, who would "purify" the manifestly corrupted and compromising priesthood, "the sons of Levi," and so bring Israel into its own? Mal 3:1-4

Simon would observe a "wonder" Jesus did, then reinterpet it to Judas and the disciples in accord with the piety of miraculous "signs and wonders" in which all of them had been brought up. Without realizing it, the disciples became double-minded. By Jesus' mind, they memorized messages from him which they would then teach others. By Simon's mind, they talked secretively about "signs" and their possible implication. They did not tell Jesus about this, however, or ask him. "No one can serve two masters," he warned, but they were caught in between. Mt 6:24

In the post-resurrection era, it appears to me, some stories that had served to promote Jesus' "mighty works" (like rumors that reached Nazareth from Capernaum) were remembered and retold among other testimonies without distinction, written down, added to the "libraries" of the young church, and so preserved in our Gospels.

The memoir to which John affixed Jesus' warning, "Unless you see signs and wonders, you will not believe," is instructive. Jn 4:46-53 An official from Capernaum asked Jesus to come and heal his dying son. Jesus spoke a word of barren power, "Go your way, your son will live." The man "believed the word" Jesus told him and left. Servants met him and reported that his son was living. The man established that "the fever left him" at the very hour Jesus had spoken this word, whereupon "the man himself believed and all his house." What "word" did he believe? A word of power, signaling greater wonders to come. What kind of "believing" was this? A "signs and wonders" believing, reconfirmed by the servants who met him. What word did he and all his house not hear, not believe? Jesus' covenant-gospel.

Each miracle story needs to be searched in its own right, but a pattern emerges in some which is at least suggestive. A malady of body is described. Cure seems impossible. Witnesses are on hand. An appeal is made to Jesus or he notices it himself. He has compassion. He speaks an authoritative command directed toward bodily healing. "Be clean!" Mt 8:3 "Go, be it done for you!" Mt 8:13 "Stretch out your hand!" Mt 12:13 "Talitha cumi," or "Little girl, arise!" Mk 5:41 "Ephphatha" or "Be opened!" Mk 7:34 "Be silent and come out of him!" Lk 4:35 "Young man, I say to you, arise!" Lk 7:14 "Woman, you are freed from your infirmity!" Lk 13:12 "Receive your sight!" Lk 18:42 In John's memoir, "Go, your son lives." Jn 4:49 Full restoration follows instantly. Witnesses are awed. They tell it everywhere. If Jesus commands silence, they disregard him.

I may not have caught all this rightly. Some of these stories may yet make sense as post-resurrection metaphor. What matters is my principle of coherence, Jesus' own gospel. It created the history and its testimonies. Let it illuminate every interpretation.

The real wonder is that the sonship-word out of Moses and the prophets was heard again at all! Jesus heard it from heaven and believed it for himself. It persisted in him despite the distortions of zealotic piety, despite the overt opposition of synagogue and temple, despite the conspiracy to silence his gospel by putting him to death. That word was Jesus' power through death into resurrection and triumph at the right hand of God.

It is so still. "The words that I speak to you, they are spirit and they are life." Jn 6:63 The words his Father spoke to Jesus were his own spirit and life. They are the seed of ours. Our need is to hear and understand them, as Jesus himself understood them.

The Five Thousand

The feeding story needs special attention. All four Gospels have it. Matthew and Mark have also a variation, the feeding of the four thousand. I shall concentrate on John's account. Jn 6:1-15 It needs to be read at three levels—copyists, zealotry, and Jesus himself.

The uppermost layer is a misperception of copyists. In their mind, what distinguishes God from man is his almighty power. The miracles Jesus performed derived from his deity, among them this feeding story. The problem with this should by now be clear. To know God by his power and to believe Jesus by his miracles is paganism. It is not the covenant-gospel.

The middle layer is of zealotry. The kingdom it hoped for lay in the future. The God of Israel had set a day when he would exalt his people above all nations in an eternal kingdom, as his prophets promised. So confident did this piety become of Jesus as its heaven-sent "son of David," that leaders figured out even "the day and the hour." They rallied people to escort him like a king into Jerusalem, counting on God to show his mighty hand that very day. "Of that day and hour no one knows, not the angels, not even the son of man," Jesus warned. Mt 24:36 But their ears were closed to anything he said.

Secretive propaganda had been preparing for that climactic moment. John, who wrote this memoir in retrospect, had been part of it himself. What he tells is compact, in the style of oral literacy. Not a word is wasted. Every detail is meaningful.

"A multitude followed him," not for love of Jesus' covenant-gospel, but "because they saw the signs he did on those who were diseased." This kind of "following" was zealotic. Jesus would have none of it. He "withdrew to a hill with his disciples." "The Passover was near"—when this distortion would climax. "So the men sat down, in number about five thousand." All accounts of the feeding have "men," specifically males. In Matthew a copyist felt constrained to interpolate "besides women and children." Mt 14:21; 15:38 The number "five thousand men" did not derive from anyone's literal counting. Its source was Joshua's warrior ratio, "One man of you puts to flight a thousand, since it is the LORD your God who fights for you." Josh 23:10 Zealotic imagination, multiplying this by the boy's five loaves, projected a symbolic "five thousand men," well fed, at Jesus' disposal, each man capable of putting a thousand to flight.

Five thousand men! Gathered with Jesus! Fed miraculously by him from just five loaves! That awesome story was whispered everywhere. Compilers of all four Gospels found it in the fragment-libraries from which they worked—variations of "four thousand men" besides. Mt 15:32-38; Mk 8:1-9 "This is indeed the prophet who is to come into the world!" the people inferred from the amazing miracle. They did not hear his covenant-word. They only "saw the sign which he had done." A parallel fragment in John recalls, "Now when he was in Jerusalem at the Passover feast, many believed in his name when they saw his signs which he did." Jn 2:23

The plot to "take him by force and make him their king" depicts the crowd that gathered to escort Jesus into Jerusalem with palms and songs and ready violence. Jesus would have none of it. "He withdrew to a hill, himself alone." Ultimately, this is Gethsemane. He was truly alone, nobody hearing him, nobody understanding him.

Beneath the zealotic level, but still detectable, lies the original event. It is of the covenant-gospel. The hunger Jesus addresses is not the sort that can be satisfied by grocery stores or food pantries. "Why do you spend your money for that which is not bread, and your labor for that which does not satisfy? .... Hear, that your soul may live," Isaiah had said. Is 55:1-3

Jesus saw a crowd coming to him and asked Philip, "Where shall we buy loaves that these people may eat?" (The verse, "This he said to test him, for he himself knew what he would do," is a copyist's deity-enhancement.) In the art of the story, Philip responded in terms of food for the body. "Two hundred denarii would not buy enough bread for each of them to get even a little."

Andrew reported, "There is a lad here who has five barley loaves and two fish, but what are they among so many?" Jesus borrowed the boy's literal lunch to make his point.

"Drink" was not in his sermon, neither were the two fish (though a copyist felt he should get them in), but only those five loaves. "There was much grass in the place." To sit down and listen is not hard for those willing to do it. Jesus took those loaves in hand one at a time, gave thanks for each, then "fed" a covenant-message by it to the people who had gathered to hear him. That boy was the first to be fed as it were, and by him all the rest. The covenant-word is for children. Only as children can adults hear it, receive it, eat it.

John's story as such is a bare skeleton. It needs the covenant-word to fill it out. With a bit of imagination, what Jesus actually said by those five loaves can be at least approximated. Holding up the first loaf, he fed the people on the Father's covenant-naming, like "my beloved son, with whom I am well pleased." By another he spoke the Father's promises, like daily bread and deliverance from evil. By a third he pictured the kingdom-now as their noble calling to do the Father's will on earth, here and now. By another loaf he pictured their testings, how an attractive fantasy might seduce them from their Father's way, or a looming threat drive them to flee in fear. Holding up the fifth loaf, he fed their hearts on thanksgiving and praise as pure receivers of the Father's unfailing gifts. The disciples carried the distribution on. "And they all ate their fill."

The gathering of the leftovers supplements the story. The disciples and the young church, at Jesus' command, gathered abundant fragment-memories, beyond what anyone could eat and digest. Twelve baskets, symbolic number of the apostles, were filled full. By these, Jesus' feeding provided food unlimited for all nations! The variation in Matthew and Mark counts seven loaves and seven baskets of leftovers. Seven may indicate an alternative number for the apostles.

Is not this covenant-feeding the miracle above all miracles? Who will disparage it? Mothers bake for their children, markets display bread for sale. But this bread is of God alone. Our privilege is to "eat" what he so willingly feeds us, receive and believe it, give thanks, live by it, and pass it on. To "eat" the covenant-gospel is to know its revelatory wonder.

"Man does not live by bread alone, but man lives by every word that proceeds out of the mouth of the LORD." Dt 8:3 "Blessed are those who hunger and thirst for righteousness, for they shall be satisfied." Mt 5:6 "Do not labor for the food that perishes, but for the food that endures to eternal life." Jn 6:27

The Raising of Lazarus

This memoir of John is rooted in an event directly remembered, yet it exhibits the ultimate of both zealotic tampering and copyist interpolations. Jn 11:1-53

Jesus, threatened with stoning at the Feast of Dedication (December), withdrew across the Jordan, then carried on his ministry where John the Baptist had preached. Jn 10:22-42 Some weeks later, perhaps in March, Mary and

Martha of Bethany sent him word, "Lord, he whom you love is ill." Mark's reference to "the house of Simon the leper" suggests that their father was not at home but living among lepers. Mk 14:3 A memory of Martha's anxious serving while Mary sat and heard his word so intently, suggests that the sisters had hosted Jesus during his ministry in Jerusalem. Lk 10:38-42 That Jesus did not heal their father and bring him home indicates that "the good portion, which would not be taken away from (Mary)," was not zealotry's notion of "signs and wonders." That the sisters were unmarried but in charge of the house suggests that their mother was dead, that they were young, and that their brother was younger still.

As John tells it, Jesus waited "two days," then said, "Let us go into Judea again." The disciples worried, "Rabbi, the Judeans were but now seeking to stone you." Jesus responded by picturing his life on earth, and theirs too, as a limited twelve-hour day, given by his Father. He would not press to extend his day beyond what God gave, but walk by its light without stumbling, trusting the outcome to the Giver. The original memory continued with Thomas' gloomy expectation, "Let us also go, that we may die with him."

John preserves two versions of what happened upon Jesus' arrival. Both begin with the plaintive greeting, "Lord, if you had been here, my brother would not have died." The Martha version tells of the young church and its confession. The Mary version preserves what zealotic minds concocted as "signs and wonders" propaganda.

The Martha Story. Jesus does not weep, does not say a tearful "I know," or "I'm sorry." He accepts the death, does not protest or seek to undo it. When Martha adds, "Even now I know that whatever you ask God, God will give it to you," he does not intercede (as though his praying would be more influential than hers). What the text offers as Jesus' promise, "Your brother will rise again," is a copyist's interpolation based on Martha's self-consolation, rooted in Daniel. Dan 12:2 "I know that he will rise again in the resurrection at the last day," she says.

Jesus turns her from such futurist hope to the kingdom-now. "I am the resurrection and the life! He who believes in me, even if he dies, will live. And whoever lives and believes in me will not ever die. Do you believe this?" To believe in me is to disbelieve all distortions of zealotry and all accusations of temple and synagogue. What matters eternally for Martha, as for Jesus himself, is the resurrection and life she lives in her body here and now.

"Do you believe this?" Jesus asks Martha—this resurrection and this life. "Yes, Lord," she replies, then adds the young church's confession, "I believe that you are the Christ, the son of God, who is coming into the world." This "christ" is not of zealotic ambition, but "the son of God" who lived out his name in love and servanthood to the end. He "is coming into the world" now, to gather the world and raise it to life. He is not coming on some futurist "last day" (as zealotic piety understood Daniel), to exalt "the people of the saints of the Most High" by power, so that "all dominions shall serve and obey them." Dan 7:27

Jesus' idea of "resurrection and life" ruled him throughout. He would do the will of his Father to the finish of his "twelve-hour day." "Now is my soul troubled, and what shall I say? Father, save me from this hour? No, for this purpose I have come to this hour. Father, glorify your name." Jn 12:27 Covenant-promises as in Hosea sustained him: "After two days he will revive us, on the third day he will raise us up, that we may live before him." Hos 6:2 What should his disciples pray in Gethsemane? Not for a futurist kingdom and glory but "that you may not enter into temptation," thus live out the calling that is theirs now to its very end. Mt 26:41 What should Martha pray? Not to have her brother back, whose "twelve-hour day" on this earth is finished and returned to the Father who gave it. She has a "twelve-hour day" of her own to fill full! To invest every next hour in serving the God from whom she received it is her very life!

Every "I am" saying of Jesus in John's memoirs is of this order. "I am the light." Jn 8:12; 9:5 "I am the good shepherd." Jn 10:11 "I am the way and the truth and the life." Jn 14:6 "I am the vine." Jn 15:1 The kingdom of God "at hand," present tense, is an eternal now. Mk 1:15 Its great "either-or" is not what God will judge on some distant last day, but what those who hear his word decide and do in every today of their life. "He who believes in me now (as I believe in my Father), even though he die (as I die), yet shall he live (as I live). And whoever lives and believes in me shall never die." The life he lives in the body is of God's "forever," even now.

On the day and hour Jesus gave up the life of his body, he "finished" the servanthood for which his Father sent him. Jn 10:14-18; 19:30 His resurrection-victory revealed the whole of his twelve-hour bodily "day" to be eternal. "This is eternal life, that they may know you, the only true God, and Jesus Christ whom you have sent." Jn 17:3 God's promises liberate his people to serve him in patient hope here and now. This is not just Jesus' idea. It is what the scriptures have said all along. "Surely goodness and mercy shall follow me all the days of my life, and I shall dwell in the house of the LORD forever." Ps 23:6 "Let the beauty of the LORD our God be upon us; let him establish the work of our hands upon us." Ps 90:17

The Mary Story. Mary's repetition of the plaintive cry, "Lord, if you had been here our brother would not have died," now introduces the zealotic version. A name is supplied for the brother who died: "Lazarus." Four days after the death and burial, the Judeans who came to weep are with the sisters still. Jesus weeps in compassion. "Where have you laid him?" he asks. "Lord, come and see," they answer. Mary leads him to the tomb, a large crowd following. "Remove the stone," Jesus commands. Martha's response dramatizes the impossible, "Lord, by this time there will be an odor, for he has been dead four days already." Jesus is not deterred. The word he speaks loudly is a command of sheer power, "Lazarus, come out!" Lazarus does so.

Zealotic leaders needed this story. They expected the coming Passover to be the end-time and dedicated themselves toward making it so. The timing was critical. Caiaphas and council were conspiring to arrest Jesus and kill him. They must not succeed. A counter-strategy was needed to save Jesus, but also to exalt his authority decisively over the corrupt priesthood. "The day and the hour" would be that of his coming to Jerusalem for the Passover. Mt 24:36 Rally a huge crowd to escort him into the temple, and within it a hidden army ready to fight for him against any temple police or even Romans who stood in the way. Surely God will exalt his beloved son over priests and elders who connive with alien oppressors to sustain their own authority, so as to secure and enrich themselves.

What should happen, once Jesus and his escort reached the temple? An accusation in Caiaphas' court, preserved in Matthew and Mark, suggests what the conspirators had in mind. "This fellow said, 'I am able to destroy the temple of God and to build it in three days.'" Mt 26:61; Mk 14:58 The mockery at the cross repeated it: "You who would destroy the temple and build it in three days, save yourself!" Mt 27:40; Mk 15:29 That is what the promoters of Jesus thought he could and would do—not the temple as architecture, but the corrupt, dead and decayed priesthood that ruled it! The temple had attacked the prophet John first and gotten rid of him. Now it was attacking Jesus and plotting to kill him, too. Let Jesus declare himself and take over! They were ready with secret swords to help him.

"Build it in three days" expressed a literal hope. Between Monday, the tenth of the month when lambs for the Passover were purchased and set aside, and the fourteenth when they were sacrificed, lay just three days, Tuesday to Thursday. Ex 12:2,6 In that time-frame, the rebuilding of the temple would be fully done! "The Lord whom you seek will suddenly come to his temple,"

Malachi had promised, and "he will purify the sons of Levi." Mal 3:1-2 "And you will tread down the wicked, for they will be ashes under the soles of your feet, on the day when I act, says the LORD of hosts." Mal 4:3 Surely the LORD would act!

John's memoir reports that the strategy was effective. "The Judeans who had come with Mary and had seen what he did believed in him." Jn 11:45 "The crowd that had been with him when he called Lazarus out of the tomb and raised him from the dead bore witness. The reason why the crowd went to meet him was because they had heard he had done this sign." Jn 12:17-18

But John reports also an emergency meeting of the council, told him afterwards perhaps by Nicodemus. "This man performs many signs," it was said. "If we let him go on thus, every one will believe in him, and the Romans will come and destroy our holy place and our nation." Jn 11:47-48 The high priest's counsel prevailed, "that one man should die for the people and the whole nation not perish." Jesus should be arrested on sight. Jn 11:54

Reflecting on this afterwards, John recast the zealotic fantasy into a sign which Jesus himself spoke and actually fulfilled: "Destroy this temple and in three days I will raise it up." Jn 2:18-19 By his willing death, he did indeed "destroy" the temple religion. By his resurrection, he did indeed raise it up in three days—to its authentic life. They needed only to receive it.

Copyist Interpolations. Interpolations into John's text by copyists yield a third story. Enhancements clutter what was concise. "Lazarus" is named repeatedly. Jn 11:1,2,5,11,14,17 Mary is identified knowingly as the one who anointed Jesus. Jn 11:2; 12:3 That "Jesus loved Martha and her sister and Lazarus," is said again. Jn 11:3,5 That Lazarus has been in the tomb four days is likewise said again. Jn 11:39,17 That "Mary stayed in the house" does not need saying. Jn 11:20 "Now Jesus had not yet come into the village, but was still in the place where Martha met him" does not need saying, either. Jn 11:30 "So the Judeans said, 'See how he loved him'" derives from an earlier verse. Jn 11:36,5 The assumption that materials on the scroll were in chronological sequence, together with copyists' view of Jesus as deity, has witnesses cry out, "Could not he who opened the eyes of the blind have kept this man from dying?" Jn 9; 11:37 The visualization, "the dead man came out, his hands and feet bound with bandages, and his face wrapped with a cloth," derived from mummified burials familiar to a copyist. It required the further command, "Loose him and let him go." Jn 11:44

Most serious is the "deity-trap." Jesus exhibits his glory as the son of God by knowing everything in advance and by his almighty power. A copyist has him predict, "This illness is not unto death; it is for the glory of God, so that the son of God may be glorified by it," and again, "For your sake I am glad that I was not there, so that you may believe"—meaning, believe Jesus' deity. Jn 11:4,15 A dialogue on death as "sleep" draws on a saying in Daniel, "Many who sleep in the dust of the earth shall awake." Jesus is made to say, "Lazarus our friend has fallen asleep, but I go to awaken him." Jn 11:11-15; Dan 12:2 At the tomb he reminds the witnesses, "Did I not tell you, if you believe, you would see the glory of God?" Jn 11:40

Martha had expressed her confidence, "Even now I know that whatever you ask of God, he will give you." Jn 11:22 A copyist, so prompted, has Jesus pray at the tomb. "Father, I thank you that you have heard me. I knew that you hear me always, but I have said this on account of the people standing by, that they may believe that you have sent me." Jn 11:41-42

Here are three distinct "believings." The Martha story tells the covenant-believing of the young church. The Mary story tells the "signs and wonders-believing" of zealotic piety, harnessing Jesus to its dream of a futurist kingdom. Zionist-believing is its heir. Greek copyists subsequently interpolated a "deity-believing," to be confirmed by seeing Jesus, "the son of God," perform this miracle. Christianity's "creedal-believing" is the latter sort, supplemented by doctrines like two natures of Christ and the Trinity. "Bible-believing" is yet another. It equates the Bible with "the word of God," reads it flat as it were, believes everything it says, does not ask or need to ask what a text like this one means, or why it was said the way it is said.

Portrait

The portrait of Jesus that emerges shows nothing of his bodily appearance. It is not of zealotry's "christ"; neither does it show a deity "son of God" as in Christianity's Creed.

It shows rather "the son" who prays the covenant Prayer and teaches us to pray it with him. Mt 6:9-13 The portrait displays his "heart," the selfhood he had from his Father and returned to his Father, the "eternal life" he lived bodily among bodily people like himself. The "blesseds" amplify it. "Blessed are the poor in spirit, for theirs is the kingdom of heaven" describes Jesus himself first before anybody else, likewise "Blessed are the meek, for they shall inherit the earth" and all the rest. Mt 5:1-12 There is nothing of the raging warrior in this portrait, only the sonship to which the LORD had called Israel from the beginning, as when he told Pharaoh by Moses, "Let my son go that he may serve me." Ex 4:22-23

The disciples, purged of zealotic fantasy by his death, saw Jesus in his resurrection for what he had been in reality all along. They marveled how covenant-images from the prophets depicted him truly. "Behold, my servant whom I have chosen, my beloved with whom my soul is well pleased. I will put my spirit upon him, and he shall proclaim justice to the Gentiles. He will not wrangle or cry aloud, nor will any one hear his voice in the streets; he will not break a bruised reed or quench a smoldering wick, till he brings justice to victory. And in his name will the Gentiles hope." Mt 12:18-21; Is 42:1-4

The biblical record presents Jesus as imaging in his body on earth the character of his Father in heaven. His concern was not to qualify for some future kingdom, but to serve the kingdom of his Father's eternal now. The war he waged was not against human enemies or injustices, but against any snake-like temptation that might divert him from such servanthood. His purpose in love was to restore his people to the freedom and fullness of covenant-sonship which was their heritage and glory as well as his own—thus deliver them from the anti-kingdom that had imprisoned them for so long and from an emptiness they did not even know. His weaponry was the revelatory covenant-word alone—the name, the promise, and the calling they had from heaven. He believed that word himself and lived by it to the very finish. And he won!

PART FOUR

Deciphering the Conflict

Wheat and Weeds

The distinction Judeans drew between themselves and Galileans is symptomatic. I signal it by rendering the Greek *ioudaioi* "Judeans" rather than "Jews." Conflicts between Jews and Christians came later and are of a different order. That Jesus, a Galilean, met increasing opposition from Judean authorities of synagogue and temple is hardly deniable. That he pursued his steadfast way regardless is hardly deniable either. His way was straight. He did not slither right to pursue some "good" or left to escape some "evil." His way was also level. In the image of his Father, he acknowledged no mountains or valleys, no degrees of human worth.

Authorities who opposed him were neighbors still, not enemies. He yearned to free them from seductive falsities they did not even know. "Love your enemies," he taught his disciples, "and pray for those who persecute you, so that you may be sons of your Father who is in heaven." Mt 5:44-45 His prayer from the cross testifies to the sonship-gospel he lived by and preached all along: "Father, forgive them, for they do not know what they are doing." Lk 23:34

A parable has servants ask their master in dismay, "Lord, did you not sow good seed in your field? How then has it weeds?" Mt 13:24-30 "An enemy has done this," he replied, that is, seeded weed-words unnoticed "while people slept." Who is this "enemy"? Not the weed-persons themselves but lies which have perverted them and robbed them of their true heritage. "Do you want us to go and gather them?" the servants asked. "No," their master answered, "lest in gathering the weeds you root up the wheat with them." The alternative is startling. "Let both grow together until the harvest!" God does not worry how pure his field looks or does not look. His reapers will tend to that at harvest time. The servants, trusting this promise, do not judge weeds or fear them but devote themselves confidently to the wheat-seed of the kingdom-*now*.

People who look like weeds need healing, not exclusion. They are corrupted by deceits they do not know. They may be of wheat still. They may yet become wheat. Recover for them their true honor. Set before them "life and good," as Moses put it, in contrast to "death and evil"—so that they have a chance at least to "choose life." Dt 30:15,19 Keep sowing the life-giving covenant-truth as from God himself. It will work then by its own power.

That this parable was preserved is one evidence among others that the young church in Jesus' image kept sowing his gospel truth at all costs just as he had done, even among persecutors. It refused to cut them off or to be cut off.

The contrast is stark. It is *weeds*, seeded by the enemy, that invoke the name of God on a standard of purity they devise, then enforce conformity by institutional authority, cut-off, and division. Weeds purify their field by pulling up what is authentic wheat. This was the "eyes-opened" tactic of temple and synagogue against Jesus and the young church. The field called "Christianity" has been infected similarly. Secretly "while people slept," the enemy sowed weeds into it too. If Jesus' seed-gospel had prevailed, Christianity would not have been divided within itself, or from Judaism, or from Islam either.

On the other hand, if Jesus' seed-gospel is sown and takes root again, its spirit of truth will infiltrate a field of weeds with life and healing. It will not create division or cut anyone off.

The task in the next chapters is to examine the weed-seed in the light of Jesus' own sowing so as to know what it was and how its deception worked.

C H A P T E R   T E N

The Chosen People

"For many are called, but few are chosen."

Matthew 22:14

This saying of Jesus is drastic, unheard of. That "many are called" testifies to God's love and generosity toward all, even me. A calling so noble anticipates a joyful "Yes!" from those who hear it. That "few are chosen" testifies that a "Yes" is not automatic. God compels no one to hear and belong to him. Racial descent from Abraham does not guarantee that those so privileged will understand and believe and live their own covenant-name. A glitteringly deceptive counterfeit is available. Since many opt for it rather than for the true, the "chosen" turn out to be few.

The Marriage Feast

"Many are called, but few are chosen" is the end-verdict of a striking parable. Mt 22:1-14 "The kingdom of heaven is like a king who gave a marriage feast for his son," Jesus begins. "Son" and "chosen" and "worthy" in the parable are covenant-names spoken on Israel by God himself. The marriage feast depicts the joyous fulfilment for which his people have long been waiting. It is here. The kingdom is not future but *now.* "Come! Everything is ready *now!*"

The parable visualizes a history. It pluralizes the king's "son" (Israel as a people) into the "invited" who hear the call individually, then into the "guests" who actually come. Many who heard Jesus' "gospel of the kingdom" "made light of it." It did not meet their expectations. A vision of Daniel said, "The kingdom and the dominion and the greatness of the kingdoms under the whole heaven shall be given to the saints of the Most High." Dan 7:27 Where was this "greatness" in Jesus' preaching? Where did he credit the faithfulness of "the saints of the Most High," who ought rightfully to receive it? The kingdom he preached was not what God had promised! Hence "they would not come."

Other servants, the young church, pressed the invitation. Everything is ready. The kingdom is *now!* "But they went off, one to his farm, another to his business." The work and property they controlled was *real*. They would wait for a kingdom of God that was *real*. The servants persisted, the story goes on, only to be arrested, treated shamefully, even killed. An interpolation follows, entered when the destruction of Jerusalem had become known: "The king was angry, and he sent his troops and destroyed those murderers and burned up their city."

The issue of the parable, however, is not whether the kingdom-*now* which Jesus preached was real or worthwhile. The issue was *chosenness*. "The king said to his servants, 'The wedding is ready, but those invited were not worthy.'" Claims of worthiness by genealogy and law do not hold when the joy and hope of the kingdom-*now* is rejected. In the drama of the exodus, no Israelite slave was forced to leave Egypt and go home to the land of the fathers. Some may have been comfortably willing to stay. To stay, however, would be to refuse their covenant-honor and calling. The judgment "not worthy" would apply to them.

The parable extends chosenness now to nations considered "unworthy." Forget those who think that to be on the invitation list makes them superior, the king tells the young church, his servants. Go to the highways. Invite randomly anyone you find, "bad and good," undesirable or desirable. Count anyone who hears the invitation and comes as the king's "son" or "chosen" or "worthy," a full participant in the "marriage." "So the wedding hall was filled with guests."

A subparable pictures the feast in progress. All guests wear a common wedding garment, in praise of the "God merciful and gracious" to whom they belong. Their worthiness is nothing else than this. This secret commonality levels and liberates all outward diversities and visible rankings. The king visits with the guests. He notices one who has crashed the feast wearing a worthiness of his own, as though wanting to stand out from the rest. A Judean shows off his pure-blooded ancestry. A Pharisee shows off his obedience to the law. The king offers him a last chance to face reality. "Friend, how did you get in here without a wedding garment?" Will he repent? Will he throw himself on God's mercy, thus be in on the wedding by grace alone? He cannot answer, just as the authorities of synagogue and temple could not answer. Yet he will not bow, either. "Bind him hand and foot," the king commands. "Whatever you bind on earth will be bound in heaven," Jesus put it elsewhere. Mt 18:18 "Outer darkness" excludes him from God's covenant-light altogether. "Weeping and gnashing of teeth" depicts his self-pity and grinding rage against the God who is "not partial," the God who will not applaud the delusion of self-achieved worth which would set him above others.

The conclusion of the parable is soundly realistic: "Many are called, but few chosen."

Parables were not framed to judge and divide, but to focus the issue and keep the invitation open. This parable was framed in hope of persuading those who needed to hear it. Judgment has not yet fallen. It is not too late. Come to the wedding still! His true kingdom, long lost, is here for you *now*, not later. It waits only for you to enter. The wedding feast of sonship in the joy of oneness is *real*, a belonging and servanthood of love and purpose and glory no circumstance can negate or enemy steal away. This is what your God and king has intended for you. So come!

God's people had long sung such an invitation in a psalm, "O come, let us worship and bow down, let us kneel before the LORD our Maker! For he is our God, and we are the people of his pasture and the sheep of his hand." However, the temptation to reject it is real, too. Hence the psalm sang on, "O that today you would hearken to his voice! Harden not your hearts... as when your fathers tested me and put me to the proof, though they had seen my work... Therefore I swore in my anger that they would not enter my rest." Ps 95:6-11

The song carried on into the wedding hall filled with guests. "You are a *chosen race*, a *royal priesthood*, a *holy nation*, *God's own people*, that you may declare the wonderful deeds of him who *called you* out of darkness into his marvelous light. Once you were no people, but now you are *God's people*; once you had not received mercy, but now you have received mercy." 1 Pet 2:9-10 Peter drew this last from Hosea: "In the place where it was said to them, 'You are not my people,' it shall be said to them, '*sons of the living God.*'" Hos 1:10

The Impending Conflict

In Jesus' mind, "chosen" belonged to the covenant which his Father had declared to him from heaven, "This is my son, my beloved, with whom I am well pleased." In the Judean mind, chosenness was measured by racial descent and purity under the law. That standard, as indicated earlier, disqualified Jesus as a prophet and scorned him as a Samaritan. Jn 7:52; 8:48 The drama played out to the end. "Let him come down from the cross, if he is the Christ of God, his *chosen,*" critics mocked Jesus as he hung dying. Lk 23:35

The issue had lurked all along. The LORD who decreed Israel to be "my first-born son" did not exclude the "mixed multitude" that came with them out of Egypt. Ex 4:22; 12:38 Abraham himself was not God's "chosen" for his race or circumcision. The LORD called him by his own gracious will, with no reason or condition whatsoever, to "leave your country and kindred and father's house" and go to a land he would show him—promising to make him a great nation and a source of blessing to all nations. Gen 12:1-3 Abraham believed that call and left everything to follow it. That was his chosenness! In the imagery of the parable, he "came" to the wedding feast. The LORD repeated that promise to Isaac and then Jacob. They came too.

Generations later, Isaiah comforted his people by that same covenant-word. "But you, Israel, *my servant,* Jacob, whom I have *chosen,* the *offspring of Abraham, my friend....* You are *my servant,* I have *chosen* you and not cast you off; fear not, for I am with you, be not dismayed, for I am your God...." Is 41:8-10 Chosenness did not depend on purity of racial descent, but on God's covenant alone. "For *you are our Father, though Abraham does not know us, and Israel does not acknowledge us, you, Johwah, are our Father,* our Redeemer from of old is *your name!*" Is 63:16 To be chosen implied the noble call to work with God in oneness. "Behold, *my servant,* whom I uphold, *my chosen,* in whom my soul delights; I have put my spirit upon him, he will bring forth justice to the nations." Is 42:1 "I have given you as a covenant to the people, a light to the nations, to open the eyes that are blind, to bring out the prisoners from the dungeon." Is 42:6-7

A memoir of John preserves a dialogue between Jesus and the Judean authorities on the theme of Abraham. "You judge according to the flesh," Jesus said, meaning fleshly genealogy. "You are from below, I am from above; you are of this world, I am not of this world." Jn 8:15,23 You get your identity from physiological birth, I get mine from my Father in heaven. "I know that you are descendants of Abraham; yet you seek to kill me, because my word finds no place in you." Jn 8:37 "Your father Abraham rejoiced that he would see my day, and he saw it and was glad." Jn 8:56 Abraham does not rejoice in you for the purity of your bloodlines, but for the blessing God has spoken to me as well as to him, and to the world through me. You mock me as "not yet fifty years old," but the covenant-word will not be contained by time. "Truly, truly, I say to you, before Abraham was, I am." Jn 8:58 The "self" given me derives from a word of God older even than Abraham. That word was the ground of Abraham's believing and hope and joy, of his walking with God and serving him. It is so no less for me, and for you. The Judeans rejected this as arrogant blasphemy, however, and were ready to stone him for it. Jn 8:59

Jesus' concern was to recover for his people their real treasure. The distortion that snared them had been passed down from their fathers over many generations. It happened all too easily. To be declared God's "chosen people" felt "good." God must have perceived some "good" in them which he did not perceive in other nations! Such logic is of "the tree of the knowledge of good and evil." It sees "good" in a God who is "partial" to them. Those so favored feel close to God. Their special access offers opportunity to wheedle, bribe and manipulate him. "You shall not make my Father's house a house of trade," John's account of the temple cleansing has Jesus say. That depicts what their worship has in effect become—a bargaining with God for the best deal. Jn 2:16

"Who then is the faithful and wise servant, whom his master has set over his household, to give them their food at the proper time?" Jesus asked. "Blessed is that servant whom his master when he comes will find so doing. Truly I say to you, he will set him over all his possessions." Mt 24:45-47 This is the wedding-garment, the kingdom-*now*. The glory of chosenness is the honor and gift of serving God in freedom, needing no supervision, concerned not to achieve "good" or to avoid "evil" but only to fulfill so privileged a life and calling—rejoicing to belong, stretching every talent toward doing what is given to be done, waiting to see what God may have in store next, trusting tomorrow and its outcomes to him.

While Jesus was teaching in a crowded house, word came to him, "Your mother and your brothers are outside, asking for you." "Who is my mother, and who are my brothers?" he replied. Gesturing toward those around, he answered, "Here are my mother and my brothers! Whoever does the will of my Father in heaven is my mother, and sister, and brother." Mk 3:31-35; Mt 12:46-50 This was no rebuff to his human family. He only illustrated the kingdom-*now*—a kingdom not of human parentage, but of the covenant-sonship or chosenness spoken from heaven by the Father. The calling to "do the will of my Father" on earth yields a "brother and sister and mother" oneness which gathers all nations.

A Roman centurion stationed outside Capernaum declared himself "not worthy." Jesus' word of healing made him worthy, nevertheless. A saying preserved in that context upsets the whole tradition of worthiness. "I tell you, many will come from east and west and sit at table with Abraham, Isaac, and Jacob in the kingdom of heaven, while the sons of the kingdom will be thrown out into the outer darkness. There will be weeping and gnashing of teeth." Mt 8:5-13

Nicodemus

The sequence of John's Gospel has Jesus' night conversation with Nicodemus early, after the temple cleansing. Jn 2:13-25; 3:1-12 Both events actually occurred during the week of Jesus' death, however. Nicodemus, a Pharisee and member of the council, appears to have agonized over the council's determination to arrest Jesus and put him to death. He and a small minority, notably Joseph of Arimathea, felt repressed and helpless. If he could talk to Jesus, something might still be done. John, who recorded this memory, must have been in on it. I infer that Nicodemus caught him in the temple, drew him aside, told him he needed to talk to his master, and arranged to meet him after dark. John brought him to Gethsemane, where Jesus and his company were camping out for the Passover.

Nicodemus confessed his distress. "We know that you are a teacher come from God, for no one can do the signs you do unless God is with him." What made this conversation worth preserving was not Nicodemus' concern to save Jesus, however, but Jesus' concern to save the Judeans and the council. "Truly I say to you, unless one is born from above (as by the covenant-word from heaven), he cannot see the kingdom of God."

Nicodemus stated his problem in terms of natural birth. "How can a man be born when he is old? Can he enter a second time into his mother's womb and be born?" For Judeans to start over was not possible. How can they give up the birthright they have boasted for centuries and preserved at so great cost? The nation was too old, the tradition too old, Nicodemus too old!

Jesus would not compromise. "Truly, truly, I say to you, unless one is born of water and the Spirit, he cannot enter the kingdom of God." Moses had warned his people similarly. "You were unmindful of the Rock that bore you, and you forgot the God who gave you birth"—the God who brought you out of Egypt through the sea to be his "sons and daughters." Dt 32:18-19 Be mindful of your beginning! Your fleshly descent will not confer the life of God, Jesus said. Hear the covenant-word of your God again, so that his breath can start your life over. "That which is born of flesh is flesh, and that which is born of the spirit is spirit."

"Don't marvel at this or be so shocked!" Jesus comforted Nicodemus. "The spirit is like breathing. Your breath breathes involuntarily on its own. If you listen, you can hear yourself inhale and exhale, but even then you cannot tell where your breath comes from or where it goes. So it is with God's breathing in you. You cannot will that breathing, either, but only receive it. So don't try to control what God does. Hear what he says. Let him do with you as he wishes!"

Nicodemus heard this, understood and believed it. So did Joseph of Arimathea and others. John told the wonder later: "To all who received him, who believed in his name, he gave authority to become children of God; who were born, not of blood nor of the will of the flesh nor of the will of man, but of God." Jn 1:12-13

A related saying is equally drastic. "If your hand is blocking you from the kingdom, cut it off; it is better for you to enter life maimed than with two hands to be thrown into Hinnom...."[1] And if your foot is blocking you, cut it off; it is better for you to enter life lame than with two feet to be thrown into Hinnom. And if your eye is blocking you, pluck it out; it is better for you to enter the kingdom of God with one eye than with two eyes to be thrown into Hinnom, where their worm does not die and the fire is not quenched." Mk 9:43-48; Mt 5:29-30; 18:8-9; Is 66:24

Imagine what Nicodemus might say to that! "It's too much, Jesus! You are asking us to cut off our heritage as God's chosen people—and our law, for which our heroic fathers, the sons of Mattathias, fought the Syrian persecutor Antiochus and won! Was that all a mistake? Are you saying Ezra was a mistake? I tell you plainly, we Judeans, the council, will never consent to this!"
But Jesus could not yield. "Yet this very worthiness of yours is blocking you, corrupting you, robbing you of the life and kingdom to which your Father in heaven is calling you. Give it up! Cut yourself free of it! Glorify your Father in truth and yourself as his son. Enter the kingdom that is yours *now*!"

The Maccabaean revolt, for all its zeal and momentary glory, did not bring in the kingdom of God. Indeed, it yielded only new corruptions, generation upon generation. It must stop! The iniquity of the fathers has been visited upon the children long enough. The body can still be saved, but any member that impairs it must go. The eye that boasts it sees but does not, pluck it out. The hand that boasts it serves but does not, cut it off. The kingdom God's people long for cannot tolerate deceits. It cannot tolerate mass

---

[1] The Greek *geenna* transliterates the Hebrew *ge-(ben)-hinnom*, "land of the son of Hinnom." This valley bore the curse of idolatry and thus exclusion from the God of Israel. Jer 7:30-32 It bordered Jerusalem on the west and south. The Kidron valley, along the east side of Jerusalem and the temple mountain, signaled hope and blessing.

politics or armies. What the council decides has no authority. Let each decide for himself. Be born with God's life yourself. Pluck out your own right eye, cut off your own right hand. What you give up is only a debilitating rot.[2] "Everyone will be salted with fire," another graphic imagery insisted. Your open wound will burn fiercely for the moment, but it is for healing. "Salt is good!" What good is salt if it does not burn? Mk 9:49-50

Nicodemus knew that Jesus spoke the truth. But he knew the council, too. It could never vote to pluck out its right eye or cut off its right hand or submit to the burning salt. "What the tyrant Antiochus could not achieve by force, this Jesus would accomplish by subversion from within!" it would argue. "His way will mean the end of us as a people!" It would do what it had already determined—silence the message by killing the messenger.

Jesus offered Nicodemus no counter-strategy. He would fill full the honor of his sonship, trust promises like, "that you may live and that it may go well with you," and do the will of his Father steadfastly to the end. Dt 5:33

---

[2] Paul's transition from persecutor to Apostle illustrates what it meant to be "born again"—to "pluck out and cast away one's right eye" or "cut off one's right hand." "Though I myself have reason for confidence in the flesh also... circumcised on the eighth day, of the people of Israel, of the tribe of Benjamin, a Hebrew born of Hebrews, as to the law a Pharisee, as to zeal a persecutor of the church, as to righteousness under the law blameless. But whatever gain I had, I counted as loss. Indeed, I count everything as loss because of the surpassing worth of knowing Christ Jesus my Lord." Phil 3:4-8 A verse follows which expresses well what has been my own longing: "That I may know him and the power of his resurrection, and may share his sufferings, becoming like him in his death, that if possible I may attain the resurrection from the dead."

CHAPTER ELEVEN

◼ The Law

"If you believed Moses, you would believe me, for he wrote of me."   John 5:46

The first perversity of weed-sowing was the fantasy that names like "chosen" and "my first-born son" for God's people marked them superior in his sight over other nations. To Jesus, such names conferred a life of honor and hope, purpose and freedom in oneness with God—by which Israel would be seeded as a blessing to other nations.

A second weed, the piety I call zealotry, branched from the first. It twisted God's promises of care and blessing into predictions of a futurist kingdom and glory. God would reveal Israel's favored status visibly and eternally some day, so that other nations would see it and be humbled before it. Those who died faithful would be raised in their bodies to participate, nevertheless. To Jesus, God's kingdom comes as his people do his will on earth freely in the bodily life he gives them *here and now.* His *promises* liberate them from covetousness and fear, so that they can serve him only. "Therefore... do not be anxious about your life." Mt 6:25 "Your heavenly Father knows that you need all these things." Your calling is to "seek first his kingdom and his righteousness." Do it, *"and all these things shall be yours as well!"* Mt 6:31-33

A third perversity was the need to be faithful, so as to qualify for this futurist kingdom and glory. Israel must keep itself apart. Laws of genealogical purity, sabbath rest, and cleannesses made the distinction visible. God's judgment at the last day would exalt the faithful, but consign the unfaithful to wrath. Dan 12:2 To Jesus, such law did not yield the free servanthood God desired, but a self-conscious "put-on" and "show." He called it *hypocrisy*, hiding one's true person under a mask. Mt 6:2,5,16 Calculated performance displaced the commandment to "love the LORD your God with all your heart," and "your neighbor as yourself." Mt 22:37-39

Such perversions are natural to a psyche of self-determinism. They have snared Christianity, too. The *name* that counts is *Christian*, for *Christianity* is "the only true and saving religion." The *promises* point to a *futurist salvation, eternal life* and *bodily resurrection—going to heaven* (a better place) when you die and not to hell. The *calling* that counts is to *believe rightly and sincerely,* and to show this by doing right, so as to pass judgment on that last day.

The Torah

Instances of conflict with respect to "the law" were remembered after Jesus' resurrection, written down, and so preserved. In the background lay the writings we call "Old Testament." "Moses *wrote* of me," Jesus said. Jn 5:46 "The law and the prophets" were the writings.

Writings preserved a literacy once oral. That was and remains their blessing. But they were also a problem. Oral literacy structured sayings and stories concisely for memorizing, then transmitted these person to person, mouth to ear. Much background understanding was also conveyed in that process. Authority lay in the message itself. Written literacy, by contrast, was a speciality of scholars. They read and studied documents in private. Meanings depended on what they brought to words and sentences out of their own background. A tradition of interpretation developed. The common folk trusted the authority of those who could read.

When the writings were not yet fixed, new material could readily be entered as copies were made. The need to be concise also vanished. The account of Moses' call and signs at the bush, for example, including the sonship-word which Jesus heard at his baptism, originated as oral literacy. Ex 3:1-4:9; 4:21-23 Written literacy preserved this, but embellished it with an extended drama of signs and wonders. So elaborate and graphic was this drama, that the simple original fell into obscurity. Additions could corrupt meanings. Once they were written into the sacred scrolls, they gained sacred authority from these.

The corruption is evident in changed meaning. "Torah" in oral literacy was a synonym of "covenant"—God speaking his grace from heaven to hearts. "Blessed is the man ... whose delight is in the *torah* of the LORD, and in his *torah* he meditates day and night," the people sang in celebration. Ps 1:1-2 "The *torah* of the LORD is perfect, reviving the soul," another psalm sang, then amplified the wonder by parallel terms: "making wise the simple ... rejoicing the heart ... enlightening the eyes ... more to be desired than gold ... sweeter also than honey." Ps 19:7

The term "covenant" had a lively heart-sense. When this meaning was lost, "covenant" was made a title for documents. Moses "took *the book of the covenant*, and read it in the hearing of the people." Ex 24:7 "And he wrote upon the tables *the words of the covenant*, the ten words." Ex 34:28 At some point "the book of the covenant," perhaps enlarged, came to be called "the book of the law (*torah*)." "*This book of the law* shall not depart out of your mouth," the LORD told Joshua, "but you shall meditate on it day and night." Josh 1:8 "In the presence of the people of Israel, he wrote upon the stones a copy of *the law of Moses,* which he had written." Josh 8:32 Next, a set of five scrolls associated with Moses was called "the law of Moses," or "Torah."

Written scrolls, an admirable achievement of human art, took on an authority of their own. Authority shifted then to scholars who could write and read. From writings attributed to Moses, a line of scholars abstracted specific "laws" which the people would need to learn and do. Further details could even be written into copies of documents ascribed to Moses.

Trouble developed when the Galilean Jesus heard the voice of his Father speak to him, not by scribal authority or documents, but directly as from heaven, "You are my son, my beloved, with whom I am well pleased." This word grew in him like a lively seed. He came to perceive it as the very essence of Israel's "covenant" and "law" out of Egypt, thus of "Moses and the prophets." He treasured the documents, but understood them always by the covenant-declaration that had made Israel God's people in the first place.

Scribes and Pharisees

Scribes, whose profession was writing and reading, were highly valued in business, government and record-keeping. Associated with the Pharisees, they were specialists in the holy writings. They read and taught these in worship, studied them in private, consulted with one another regarding interpretations, and taught youths to read as well as well as recite. When copies were needed, they made them. Some became rulers of synagogues. The title "Rabbi" settled on them eventually, but Jesus and John as teachers were called this, too. Jn 1:38,49; 3:2,26

Interpretation maintained the tradition of Ezra, scribe and priest of the returned exiles. Ezra "had set his heart to study the law of the LORD and to do it, and to teach his statutes and ordinances in Israel." Ezra 7:10 He taught his people to cherish and preserve their integrity by faithful obedience, for it was disobedience that had brought exile upon their fathers. Ezra 9:7 The Maccabaean wars had been fought on this principle. Mattathias the priest, "burning with zeal for the law," had resisted the forced imposition of idolatrous pig-sacrifice by murdering not only a Judean who consented to it, but also a king's officer who stood by. 1 Macc 2:26 "Show zeal for the law and give your lives for the covenant of your fathers!" was his dying word. 1 Macc 2:50

Among the heroes of that noble era were "a company of Hasideans, mighty warriors of Israel, every one who offered himself willingly for the law." 1 Macc 2:42 The books of Maccabees were written in Greek, but *hasid,* another covenant-name for God's people, was transliterated from the Hebrew. English translations render it "saint" or "holy one" or "godly." Ps 16:10; 116:15 In spirit and in company, Hasideans were antecedents of the Pharisees.

Pharisees, laymen of any occupation, were a distinct party. By devoting themselves to doing rightly whatever the law required, they became a visible model of faithfulness. They not only recited the great *shema* verse daily, "Hear, O Israel," but took literally the prescription to "bind these words as a sign upon your hand and as frontlets between your eyes." They strapped on arm or forehead leather boxes, or "phylacteries," containing written texts which commanded this. Dt 6:4-9; Mt 23:5 Distinctive tassels on the four corners of their cloak were another signal of their commitment to know the LORD and do his commandments. Num 15:37-39 Tithing was a visible discipline too, giving to the LORD the first tenth of all his blessings, even of garden condiments— likewise prayers, fastings, and giving of alms. Mt 6:2,5,16; 23:5,23 They did all this not in pride, but to mark and preserve Israel's unique identity and destiny as God's chosen.

Jesus, by contrast, had heard his covenant-identity fresh from heaven by the voice that named him "my beloved son," as it had named Israel out of Egypt long before. He did not regard this as a mark of favoritism or as promising a superior destiny, but as a privileged call to know Johwah his Father, be formed in his image, and serve him. He taught this honor without discrimination to any who would hear. The common folk responded appreciatively. "A new teaching!" they exclaimed, for they had never heard this before. Mk 1:27 "They were astonished at his teaching, for he taught as one who had authority and not as their scribes." Mt 7:28-29 Words and forms that had seemed empty came alive. Jesus' covenant-gospel drove out alien spirits that had controlled them and filled their place with the spirit of God. It lifted burdens and effected healings even of body, but from the heart out. All this was refreshing, awesome and wonderful.

Tax Collectors and Sinners

But it was also trouble. By forgiving past sins and freeing people to start over new, Jesus negated scribal discipline. When friends of a paralytic brought him for healing, Jesus' first word was, "Take heart, child, your sins are forgiven." Mt 9:2 His authority lay in the character of his Father—"a God merciful and gracious, ... forgiving iniquity and transgression and sin." Ex 34:6-7 The God of covenant-mercy longed for his errant children to know him as their Father, not as accuser and judge, so that they could return to him without fear and start over freely and at peace. The tradition of the synagogue did not know this gospel, however. God alone would render the final judgment as to who of his people qualified for the coming kingdom and who did not. Surely God could forgive sins to anyone he wished. But that any man on earth could take it on himself to speak for God in this way seemed arrogant to the point of blasphemy. Nevertheless, says the witness of the young church, something powerful happened to this paralyzed sinner by Jesus' gospel! The bed did not carry him any more, he carried it! He walked home on his own!

In the case of "tax collectors and harlots," the need for disciplined exclusion seemed obvious. Any man who profited by collecting taxes from his own people on behalf of Herod, and thereby Rome, was subjecting the holy race to the rule of idolatrous Gentiles rather than to God alone. Any woman of Israel who sold her sexual favors to Romans or mercenaries encamped in the land was doing likewise. Rome would not allow her to be stoned, but the synagogue must at least cut her off.

Yet Jesus accepted invitations into the homes of excluded sinners and ate with them. A notorious instance was a feast which Levi, chief tax collector in the district of Capernaum, prepared for his colleagues, so that they too could meet Jesus. Lk 5:27-31 In the view of his critics, Jesus had no business being there, no matter how good the food and the wine. Mt 11:19 "I hate the company of evildoers, and I will not sit with the wicked," the people were taught to sing in worship from childhood. Ps 26:4 But Jesus said, "Those who are well do not need a physician, but those who are sick. I have not come to call the righteous, but sinners to repentance." In the case of Zacchaeus, tax collector of Jericho, he said, "Today salvation has come to this house, for he also is a son of Abraham. For the son of man came to seek and to save the lost." Lk 19:9-10

When Jesus as guest was reclining at table in the house of Simon, a Pharisee, a woman burst in uninvited. Lk 7:36-50 She obviously knew him, for she wept as she anointed his feet, "washing them with her tears," Jesus put it. Simon and others perceived the discipline of the synagogue to be breaking down. "How could he not know that she was a sinner?" Yet Jesus not only allowed her to touch him, he also signaled by a parable of two debtors that her sin had been great indeed, and how very much she had been forgiven. Simon, Jesus' host, must have been personally moved. This memory, including thoughts that went through his own mind, could hardly have been known and preserved had he not told it afterwards himself.

Jesus could not be excused as merely lax or ignorant. He taught and acted so deliberately and repeatedly. The common folk were impressed, but the authorities had principles to uphold. Should the whole sacred system change for the sake of this Galilean? What would become of Israel's distinctive chosenness, if tax collectors and harlots were received back into synagogue worship as though their idolatrous compromise did not matter? By sitting with sinners in their homes and eating with them, Jesus contaminated himself, too. Could the synagogue continue to receive him without forfeiting its own holiness? Must he not finally be cut off too—and the young church after him? If he were allowed to continue, what would become of the holy people? God's judgment would fall on them again. It would be their end!

The Sabbath

Jesus viewed the sabbath as a wisdom and gift from God. Six days of labor sanctified the seventh of rest, which in turn sanctified the six of labor. Ex 20:5-11 Both labor and rest belonged to the service of God, not by force but in freedom. Scribal interpretation, concerned to do the law right for the sake of Israel's special status and hope, hedged the sabbath rest with specific prohibitions, however. Clashes were inevitable.

Some testimonies recall healings which Jesus performed publicly on a sabbath day, even within synagogue worship. With respect to the element of miracle, I shall say more in the next part. Let me repeat here, however, that Jesus' power to heal lay in his gospel. It was indeed a power. The revelation that my worth is given me in full from the beginning, that I have no need to make myself worthy or demonstrate or defend my importance to anybody, comes as a blessed relief! It is the most fundamental of all healings! It truly *is* a miracle—like opening the eyes of the blind or the ears of the deaf. It can take hold and transform a heart in a moment! Jesus knew this power. He saw how it worked in people who heard him. He acknowledged it when he said, "Those who are well do not need a physician but those who are sick." Mt 9:12

Whatever the language may mean in specific cases, critics did not argue the reality of Jesus' healings. Their concern was for what appeared to be his deliberate violation of sabbath law. Physicians among them healed too, but they did not violate the sabbath rest. The law allowed for emergencies, but no healing Jesus did on the sabbath could be construed an emergency.

He was teaching in a synagogue on a sabbath. A woman was there who had suffered "a spirit of infirmity for eighteen years, bent over and unable fully to straighten herself." Lk 13:10-17 Jesus said to her, "Woman, you are freed from your infirmity." (That he also "laid his hands upon her" strikes me as a copyist enhancement.) "Immediately she was made straight and praised God." Troubled by Jesus' apparent violation of the sabbath rest, yet not wanting to reprove his guest-preacher directly, the ruler of the synagogue warned his people, "There are six days in which work ought to be done. Come on those days and be healed, but not on the sabbath day." Jesus could not let the woman go home guilty and robbed of her joy. "Does not each of you on the sabbath untie his ox or his ass from his manger, and lead it away to water it?" he observed. "And should not this woman, a daughter of Abraham, whom Satan has bound for eighteen years, be loosed from her bond on the sabbath day?" What better day to give her rest? The people rejoiced. That "the adversaries were put to shame" expresses the tension, however.

Another account depicts a man with a withered hand. Matthew and Mark locate the incident in a synagogue, Luke in the home of a ruling Pharisee. Mt 12:9-14; Mk 3:1-6; Lk 14:1-7 Jesus saw the man's condition and asked, "Is it lawful to heal on the sabbath?" A variation in Mark reads, "Is it lawful on the sabbath to do good or to do harm, to save life or to kill?" When no one answered his question, Jesus asked another: "Who among you, if he has one sheep and it falls into a pit on the sabbath, will not lay hold of it and lift it out? Of how much more value is a man than a sheep? So it is lawful to do good on the sabbath."[3] Then he turned to the man and said, "Stretch out your hand." He did so and was healed. The Markan fragment adds a reaction: "The Pharisees went out and immediately held counsel with the Herodians against him, how to destroy him." Herodians served the Herod who had arrested John and subsequently put him to death.

Jesus' disciples were criticized for harvesting on a sabbath. Mk 2:23-29; Mt 12:1-8; Lk 6:1-5 Perhaps two of them, on a journey for him, were hosted over the sabbath by a family whose grain field was ripe for harvest. The law invited

---

[3] Curiously, the so-called "Zadokite Document," generally associated with the Qumran community, offers a stricter view at this point. "No one is to foal a beast on the Sabbath day. Even if it drop its young into a cistern or a pit, he is not to lift it out on the Sabbath." Theodore Gaster, *The Dead Sea Scriptures in English Translation*. Garden City, New York: Doubleday Anchor Books, 1956, p. 78.

a neighbor or wayfarer to sample the grain, thus partake of the generosity God was pouring out on the owner. Dt 23:25 Knowing this privilege, the disciples went to the field, plucked a head of grain, rubbed the kernels loose between their hands, blew away the chaff, and ate it. Someone of Pharisaic mind saw this and rebuked them for harvesting on the sabbath. It troubled them. On their return they asked Jesus about it.

He cited an episode well known. David and his company, in flight from Saul, came to Ahimelech, priest at the tabernacle (Mark has Abiathar). 1 Sam 21:1-4 He had nothing to feed them except the covenant bread, loaves brought by women and put on display each sabbath, a gift from the gifts of God, to be eaten by the priests. Lev 24:5-9 Caught between priestly privilege and human need, Ahimelech "inquired of the LORD," then gave the bread to David and his men. The Pharisees of Jesus' day would not fault him for this. "The sabbath was made for man, not man for the sabbath," Jesus inferred. He might have said similarly, "The covenant bread was made for man, not man for the covenant bread." Sabbath rest is a wise gift of God for his people to receive and enjoy. It is not intended as a tyranny of law to control them. If God himself offered the taste of ripened grain, should the disciples not receive and enjoy it even on the sabbath? "So the son of man is lord even of the sabbath." "Son of man," a humble variant of "son of God," means Israel as God's children or people. Their Father in heaven grants them freedom to decide such details on their own. Let scribes and lawyers grant them such freedom, too.

Cleannesses

A third area of dispute concerned laws of cleanness. Soiled hands could contaminate even the most carefully selected and prepared foods. Ritual hand washings signaled respect for such law. A preserved memory tells how the Pharisees, accompanied by investigators from Jerusalem, complained to Jesus that "some of his disciples ate with hands defiled, that is unwashed." Mk 7:1-23; Mt 15:1-20 This too may have been observed on one of their journeys.

Jesus yearned for his critics to recover the "heart-person" within the bodily act, the "self" that gave meaning to any external performing. He quoted a complaint of the LORD by Isaiah, "This people honors me with their lips, but their heart is far from me. In vain do they worship me, teaching as doctrines the precepts of men." Is 29:13 A piety of "do right" performance does not help people know and serve God from the inside heart. On the contrary, it stifles their knowing him. "There is nothing outside a man which by going into him can defile him, but the things which come out of a man are what defile him," Jesus said. "For from within, out of the heart of man, come evil thoughts, fornication, theft, murder, adultery, coveting, wickedness, deceit, licentiousness, envy, slander, pride, foolishness. All these evil things come from within, and they defile a man." Mt 15:18-20 The distinction was a very heart-truth of Israel's God. But it was of God's kingdom-*now*—not of a futurist hope for which his people must qualify by doing the law right.

Jesus had his disciples memorize this response precisely, then sent them out to teach it throughout Galilee. When they returned, they reported the reaction: "Do you know that the Pharisees were offended when they heard this saying?" Mt 15:12-14 Yes, of course! But the issue was vital. Would his disciples be "sons of God" with Jesus in freedom, or would Pharisaic law reduce them to self-conscious performers? Would they walk in the way of the LORD and his promises, or would an illusion of superiority snare them? "Every plant which my heavenly Father has not planted will be rooted up. Let them alone; they are blind guides. If a blind man leads a blind man, both will fall into a pit." Here was Moses' ultimate choice—"life and good" or "death and evil." Dt 30:15 It allowed no space in between.

Another incident dramatizes the issue further. Lk 11:37-41 That Pharisees would invite Jesus for dinner on occasion testifies that some respected him and were trying to understand. In this instance, he startled his host by declining a bowl of water and towel, brought around by a servant for one more ritual hand-washing.[4] Jesus' explanation, tightly condensed, comes off as harsh and accusatory. In the event, however, he would have yearned to win his host and others at that dinner. "You Pharisees cleanse the outside of the cup and of the dish, but inside you are full of extortion and wickedness. You fools! Did not he who made the outside make the inside also? But give alms for those things which are within, and behold, everything is clean for you." External cleansings cannot make a heart clean. A clean heart cleanses everything else.

Moses and the Law

"We are disciples of Moses. We know that God has spoken to Moses," the Judeans said. Jn 9:28-29 To be zealous in doing what Moses prescribed, ready

---

[4] Alfred Edersheim suggests a setting for this from the Talmud(Ber. 43a). "As the guests enter they sit down on chairs, and water is brought to them, with which they wash one hand. After this the cup is taken, when each speaks the blessing over the wine partaken of before dinner. Presently they all lie down at table. Water is again brought them, with which they wash both hands, preparatory to the meal..." *The Life and Times of Jesus the Messiah* (Grand Rapids: Eerdmans, 1936), II, p. 207.

even to die for it, was their very life. Faithfulness required sharpening the law so as to know what is right, then to do it right. Samples of such reasoning are preserved in the Gospels. More may be found in the *Mishnah,* the accumulated "instruction" of past teachers, long memorized, written down about 200 A.D.[5]

But Jesus claimed Moses, too. The voice-from-heaven name at his baptism, "my beloved son," was of Moses: "Thus says the LORD, Israel is my firstborn son; let my son go that he may serve me." Ex 4:22-23 Israel's passage through the sea, which sealed this word to them and set them free to this day, was of Moses. By words preserved in the scriptures, God made his name "Johwah" known to Moses. By Moses, he commanded his people to swear by this name alone and not use it in vain or emptied of meaning. Ex 3:15; 20:7; Dt 6:13 To Moses on the mountain, the LORD even defined his name: "Johwah, Johwah, a God merciful and gracious, slow to anger and abounding in steadfast love, keeping steadfast love for thousands, forgiving iniquity and transgression and sin." By Moses, he added the warning, "but who will by no means clear the guilty, visiting the iniquity of the fathers upon the children to the third and fourth generation." Ex 34:5-7 The name "Father" for Johwah was rooted in a song of Moses: "Do you thus requite Johwah?... Is he not your *father*, who created you, who made you and established you?" Dt 32:6

The Moses Jesus knew affirmed the LORD's name as uncompromisingly holy. "For Johwah your God is God of gods and Lord of lords, the great, the mighty, and the terrible God, who is not partial and takes no bribe." Dt 10:17 This Moses faced Israel and every subsequent generation with the choice between the tree of life and the tree of the knowledge of good and evil: "Behold, I have set before you this day life and good, death and evil... therefore choose life, that you and your descendants may live." Dt 30:15,19 Jesus cited Moses in reply to each of his temptations: "It is written, man does not live by bread alone, but man lives by every word that proceeds out of the mouth of Johwah." "It is written, You shall worship Johwah your God, and him only shall you serve." "It is written, You shall not tempt Johwah your God." Dt 8:3; 6:13,16 Moses proclaimed walking with God to be a noble wisdom and joy and freedom and power: "You shall be careful to do therefore as Johwah your God has commanded you; you shall not turn aside to the right hand or to the left. You shall walk in all the way which Johwah your God has commanded you, that you may live, and that it may go well with you, and that you may live

---

[5] In English, Herbert Danby, *The Mishnah*, translated from the Hebrew with introduction and brief explanatory notes. (London: Oxford University Press, 1933).

long in the land which you shall possess." Dt 5:32-33

Jesus did not view the law as commandments laid end to end, each claiming in its own right the full authority of God.[6] To him the law had a heart-pulsing center. "Hear, O Israel, Johwah your God is one Johwah, and you shall love Johwah your God with all your heart, and with all your soul, and with all your might." Dt 6:4 From this flowed the implication, "You shall love your neighbor as yourself. I am Johwah." Lev 19:18 "On these two commandments depend all the law and the prophets," Jesus said. Mt 22:37-40 His practical commentary on "as yourself" is also preserved. "So whatever you wish that men should do to you, do so to them; for this is the law and the prophets." Mt 7:12; Lk 6:31

Significantly, the law of Moses did not limit love of neighbor to Israel. "The stranger who sojourns with you shall be to you as the native among you, and you shall love him as yourself; for you were strangers in the land of Egypt. I am Johwah." Lev 19:34 You shall not treat a stranger (not of your race) as the Egyptians treated you!

Jesus appealed also to the prophets. Two contexts in Matthew cite him as urging from Hosea, "Go and learn *what this means*, 'I desire steadfast love, and not sacrifice, the knowledge of God rather than burnt offerings.'" Mt 9:13; 12:7; Hos 6:6 What the God of Israel desires is not complexities of law and performance, but that his own steadfast love flow onward through his people as their very character. It was so with Jesus. Knowing himself as "beloved" of his Father, he saw every neighbor as equally "beloved." On that premise he could tell his anxious critics, "Do not think that I have come to abolish the law and the prophets. I have not come to abolish them but to fill them full." Mt 5:17

Jesus could not surrender the liberating covenant-word of Moses to the authority of those who claimed Moses for their law, yet did not really know him. "They *have* Moses and the prophets, *let them hear them*," he pleaded. "If they do not *hear* Moses and the prophets, neither will they be convinced if someone should rise from the dead." Lk 16:29-31 "Do not think that I shall accuse you to the Father; *it is Moses who accuses you*, on whom you set your

---

[6] From Danby's introduction, *op. cit.*, p. xvii: "These topics are all included within the single divine revelation; all are part of the inspired Word of God; the scrupulous fulfilment of the laws about Fringes and Phylacteries is as much a fulfilling of God's purpose as abstention from idolatry and murder. Granted the acceptance of the Written Law as God's will for Israel, Israel's teachers had not the right to determine the relative importance of this or that injunction. Therefore the Oral Law preserves with equal piety customs and decisions arising out of the 'lightest' as out of the 'weightiest' precepts of the Law revealed to Israel at Sinai." A footnote here refers to Aboth 2:1: "And be heedful of a light precept as of a weighty one, for thou knowest not the recompense of reward of each precept." (See p. 447)

hope. If you believed Moses, you would believe me, for he wrote of me. But if you do not believe his writings, how will you believe my words?" Jn 5:45-47

The "be right and do right" reasoning into which the scribes and Pharisees had fallen derived from the snake and the tree of death. With eyes wide open to their own advantage, they invoked Moses to dominate, judge, accuse, command, and discipline others. But it was slavery, not for their people only, but for themselves. A memoir of John preserves the diagnosis: "Truly, truly, I say to you, everyone who commits sin is a slave to sin. The slave does not dwell in the house of the LORD forever, the son continues forever. So if the son makes you free, you will be free indeed." Jn 8:34-36 The psyche of "sin," taking the form of superiority and comparison-making and self-justification, cannot comprehend the grace of gladly dependent receiving and thanksgiving. "Sin" harnesses law to personal rights and advantage. "Sin" does this with great success, no less in religion than in government, politics, business, war, sports, education, or any other arena.

There is no escape, no freedom, except by the revelatory sonship-gospel which Jesus himself heard from heaven, believed, preached and lived. His mission of intervention was not prideful and self-determined. It was of the LORD's own covenant-grace, proclaimed by Moses and the prophets, also by John the Baptist—intended not to give his people Israel some advantage over others, but to make them his instrument for gathering and healing the nations.

CHAPTER TWELVE

▪ Authority

"By what authority are you doing these things, and who gave you this authority?"   Matthew 21:23

Authority in common understanding is the right and responsibility of a certain few to decide for the many in some specific area and to enforce their decision. The controlling priesthood had written its authority ages ago into sacred documents ascribed to Moses. These documents told how the LORD had commanded Moses to assign the ministry of sacred things to the tribe of Levi and the priesthood to Aaron and his sons. Ex 28-29; 40:12-16; Num 1:47-54; 6:22-27 Aaron was anointed to his office, as were the priests after him. The authority of the council of elders, scribes, Pharisees and rulers of synagogues, derived from the priesthood. Authority structures were needed to lead the worship, preserve the doctrine, mediate disputes, execute discipline and keep the peace.

Contrasting Authorities

Authority in this sense is structured in layers of "hierarchy," like government or the military or business operations. "I am a man under authority, with soldiers under me," the centurion of Capernaum told Jesus. Mt 8:9 He knew where he fitted in, neither top nor bottom but somewhere in the middle. The "chief priests and elders" ranked near the top of their authority structure, only the high priest above them.

Jesus embodied another order of authority, however. "Let justice roll down like waters, and righteousness like an everflowing stream," Amos said. Amos 5:24 The head of this stream was his Father. Jesus was given his place in it by his Father's word and call. He looked upstream in the praise and glad dependence of a beloved son. Upstream were likewise all givers and gifts between— parents, John, Moses, prophets and psalms. He hoarded nothing of what flowed to him, but invested his gifts and passed on what he received in wisdom, love, and servanthood. "It is fitting for us to fill full all righteousness," he told John. Mt 3:15 That expressed his very life, without comparison-making or competition, without pride or envy, without covetousness or fear. The stream would keep flowing. Where it would take him was his Father's business.

That was Jesus' freedom, his prayer, also his *authority*. He needed no other. On the last day of the Feast of Tabernacles, he spoke stream-language in the temple, "If anyone thirsts, let him come to me and drink. He who believes in me, as the scriptures say, out of his heart shall flow rivers of living water." Jn 7:37-38 More flows out than went in! Here is the authority of *life!*

This vision of "righteousness," having a place in a stream that originates in God, pervades the biblical wisdom. Children "honor their father and mother" as upstream "givers" through whom they receive their very life. A "place" upstream or down from someone else has nothing to do with rankings or worth, but with the gift and call and opportunity of servanthood. Children will one day be upstream givers to their children. Visible diversities are unlimited. Yet all are downstream from the Father, source of their world, life, purpose and hope.

Each has "authority" to fill full his own unique time and place with all gifts, energy, and love. This is a noble trust and freedom from God. Jesus understood and lived it. "My Father is greater than all," John's memoir has him saying, or "greater than I." Jn 10:29; 14:28 To be in everything a receiver from his Father was his all-sufficient honor, joy, security, and purpose. No "authority" of external hierarchy could add to or diminish the name "my beloved son" his Father had given him, or deny the freedom of his servanthood, or suppress his talents and opportunities, or revoke his calling to love his Father with all his heart and every neighbor as himself, or negate the promise that it would go well with him. To pass this "glory" on was his yearning desire.

Such wisdom is of the gospel from heaven. It is known only by *revelation*, as when Jesus heard it at his baptism. The joy of a humanity gifted by God for dominion and creativity over this earth is to remain in the stream of the Giver. To usurp instead an authority not given, to become "like God, knowing good and evil," to abuse power by what "opened eyes" can see and judge, is to choose instead the seductive wisdom of "Satan and his kingdom," as Jesus called it. Mt 12:26

When the disciples fell prey to zealotic ambition and comparison-making, Jesus warned them, "A disciple is not above his teacher, nor a servant above his master; it is enough for a disciple to be like his teacher and a servant like his master." Mt 10:24-25 Their calling and glory was to be downstream "receivers" from him. By usurping authority to teach him, they reverted to hierarchy, competition and lust to dominate. The end could only be disaster and death.

Authority Dialogues

After John's arrest, Jesus "returned in the power of the Spirit to Galilee." A memory in Luke adds that "he came to Nazareth, where he had been brought up, and he went into the synagogue, as his custom was, on the sabbath day." Lk 4:14-22 Invited to teach, Jesus arose, received the scroll of Isaiah from the attendant, read the lesson of the day, then sat down to teach the people from it. The theme he announced was, "Today this scripture is filled full in your hearing." Hearers wondered at "the gracious words which proceeded from his mouth."

This illustrates his authority. It did not lie in his person or certification, but in the covenant-truth he shared from familiar readings. That truth recovered for his hearers the flow of grace which originated in the God who was their Father. It gave them a place of honor in his kingdom. It summoned them to know God and serve him as their free and noble calling. It took hold of hearts without need for external proof or enforcement.

The covenant-gospel Jesus taught was Israel's authentic glory. It had made them God's people in the first place. When it was obscured ages ago, a counter-authority rushed in to fill the vacuum—the authority of office, of institutional hierarchy. The priesthood took charge. Scribes were assigned their place in the system. Law and ritual were defined and approved by recognized authorities. The system kept the people dependent, under judgment, self-conscious and rank-conscious, prideful or fearful, competitive and defensive, needing to know what was right so as to do right and be right and so please God.

Hierarchical authority does not welcome criticism. Troubled by the enthusiasm of many for Jesus' teaching, some scribes and Pharisees asked him for a "sign from heaven," that is, from God. Mt 12:38; 16:1 He had not studied in their schools, after all, or been certified for any regular teaching office. Jn 7:15 Synagogue authorities did indeed invite him to preach on occasion, but that hardly constituted a license—particularly when his teaching upset their tradition. Moses had done signs to confirm his authority. Ex 4:1-9 Without some sign, Jesus could hardly expect them to trust and believe him. Yet it was not that simple. If he gave them a sign, by what authority would they judge it? Slanders they circulated were already negating the sign-value of his healings. "It is only by Beelzebul, the prince of demons, that he casts out demons," they said. Mt 12:24

"An evil and adulterous generation seeks a sign," Jesus answered. Mt 12:38-41; 16:4 The problem was their "evil and adulterous" hearts—adulterous meaning idolatrous. The word of the living God and his kingdom asked only to be heard and believed. This "generation," however, by relying on the visibly hierarchical, resisted Jesus' covenant-word and fought to save itself from it. If his inquisitors would only hear and see seriously what he was really saying, they would not need signs. Their own hearts would testify that he spoke from God.

"No sign shall be given to it except the sign of the prophet Jonah," Jesus went on. "The men of Nineveh...*repented at the preaching of Jonah!*" Ninevites were long-standing outsiders and enemies of Israel, yet they heard and believed what Jonah preached as *revelation* from God without any sign! By hearing Israel's covenant-truth, they let go the hierarchical domination and supremacy that had consumed them for so long. They chose the covenant-righteousness and peace of Israel's God instead! By his word alone the LORD conquered Nineveh!

Such was "the sign of Jonah." "Something greater than Jonah is here," Jesus added, meaning his gospel. If the king of a proud and ruthless Nineveh could repent at the preaching of Jonah and urge his people to hear him, why cannot the authorities of synagogue and temple repent and urge their people to hear Jesus' teaching? Their "evil generation" is doing it to them. By their delusion of superiority, they expect God to raise Israel up by putting the nations down. This is idolatry! It must stop! The iniquity of the fathers has been visited upon their children and children's children long enough! Ex 20:5; 34:7 This generation must not pass it on to yet another!

Jesus' metaphor of new wine and old wineskins dramatized the issue further. Mt 9:16-17 The hierarchy-authority of temple and synagogue was empty of the covenant-wine. Its forms were dried-out and brittle. The new wine of Jesus' covenant-word had authority. They were right to fear that their system would burst under its ferment, destroying the tradition they defended and spilling the wine as well. New wineskins were needed, a starting-over of containers and content alike. A parallel metaphor pictured Israel's tradition as a garment under constant repair for generations, but beyond further patching. A whole new garment was needed.

When Jesus arrived in Jerusalem and was teaching in the temple, the chief priests and Pharisees of the council sent a squad of temple police to arrest him. Faulted for returning without him, these officers replied, "No man ever spoke like this man!" Jesus' teaching had drawn them into the stream of grace and truth by its own authority without any sign. The Pharisees appealed to the authority of hierarchy. "Are you led astray, you also? Have any of the rulers or of the Pharisees believed in him? But this crowd, who do not know the law, are accursed." Jn 7:32,45-48

"I do nothing on my own authority but speak thus as my Father has taught me," Jesus said. "He who sent me is with me; he has not left me alone, for I always do what is pleasing to him." Jn 8:28-29 This was his place in the flow. The Father was "well pleased" with him, even if his critics were not. He would not yield to threats or bluff, but fulfill his calling straight through to the end. "I have authority to lay down my life, and I have authority to receive it again. This commandment I have received from my Father." Jn 10:18

The tragedy that loomed was not for himself. It was for those who ought to be in on this flow of grace with him, but whose "evil generation" would not allow it. "Woe to you, scribes and Pharisees, because you shut the kingdom of heaven against your own people; for you neither enter yourselves, nor allow those who would to enter." Mt 23:13

Malachi recalled a "Levi," once authentic: "My covenant with him was a covenant of life and peace.... He feared me, he stood in awe of my name. True instruction was in his mouth, and no wrong was found on his lips." Mal 2:4-6 The present leaders, however, perverted their authority toward preserving advantage and resisting disadvantage. They handed down verdicts, plotted strategies, and enforced commands—just like Herod or Pilate or Caesar. They exalted God "Most High" hierarchically above all heavens, thus conforming him to the authority structure that kept them in power. They directed the worship of the temple and of synagogues everywhere. By the authority of Rome, they maintained civil order in Judea. They invoked such authority against Jesus now to silence the word of the living God and suppress his kingdom. "Do not weep for me, but weep for yourselves and for your children," he said, as he was led out to die. Lk 23:28

John's Baptism

"By what authority are you doing these things, and who gave you this authority?" they asked. Mt 21:23; Mk 11:28; Lk 20:2 All three synoptic Gospels locate this challenge of "the chief priests and scribes and elders" near the crisis-end of Jesus' ministry. They meant it as judgment, not as an invitation to dialogue. As for Jesus, to explain his authority by logic or even the stream was no use, for their purpose was only to refute and silence him. Yet his question faced them with an authority they did not know. "The baptism of John, was it from heaven or from men?" Mt 21:25-27

The common folk knew John's authority simply by having heard him. Crossing to him through the Jordan, thus out of the land and into the wilderness, was for them as ennobling and liberating an act as passing out of Egypt through the sea had been for their fathers. "My son, my first-born," they heard the LORD name them through John, and "Let my son go, that he may serve me!" That word satisfied the hunger of their hearts for worth. It filled the emptiness they sensed in their tradition. It gave meaning to their call as God's chosen people. It started them over new.

No one perceived John's "baptism" (as it came to be called) to have been his invention. God spoke to them by it from heaven, drawing them into the flow of grace as receivers not only of this gift, but of all his gifts. John had needed no further sign or proof of his authority. Indeed, the people could not grasp why the authorities of the temple were so unwilling to listen to him—unless they saw their own authority threatened. A rumor persisted that the council itself had seduced Herod to arrest and kill John, lest he one day rally hosts of zealotic-minded enthusiasts to revolt—a threat not so much against Herod as against the reigning priesthood.

The issue of John's authority had died with him, but Jesus' teaching resurrected it. The common folk of Judea heard his word in the temple as gladly as they had heard John's in the wilderness. Hence Jesus could ask concerning John's authority, "was it from heaven or from men?" "From heaven" would mean by revelation from God. Authority "from men" was what many saw in a conniving and self-perpetuating priestly hierarchy. The memory testifies that the priests and elders could not answer. To acknowledge John's baptism as "from heaven" would invite a next question, "Then why did you not believe him?" But if they answered that John's baptism was "from men," that would inflame the latent anti-priestly sentiment all the more.

The Wonder of Oneness

"I do not pray for these alone," Jesus said, "but also for those who are to believe in me through their word, that they may all be one; even as you, Father, are in me and I in you, that they also may be in us, so that the world may believe that you have sent me. The glory which you have given me I have given to them, that they may be one even as we are one, I in them and you in me, that they may become perfectly one..." Jn 17:20-23 His prayer depicts the flow of righteousness, the authority of giving and receiving, receiving and giving, by which oneness and peace happen.

Each child of God receives his place in the stream from the Giver-Creator. Each fills it full with all gifts and opportunities. Each passes the flow onward in relation to the place and gifts of every other in the freedom of love and servanthood, trusting the outcome to God. The patient forgivingness of God draws home those who are seduced away. The authority of his children to suffer hurt and to forgive rather than defend themselves makes them "blessed peacemakers" in a world of judgment and division. Mt 5:9 "My covenant of peace," the LORD called it. Is 54:10; Ezek 34:25 Jesus understood this, lived by and taught it. So did the young church in his image.

The authority of hierarchy, driven to defend its self-worth, could not comprehend this. The crucial issue behind Jesus' conflict with "the Judeans" was precisely his covenant-name, "son of God," and his oneness with his Father. Accused for healing a man on the sabbath, he said, "My Father is working even now, and I am working." Jn 5:17-20 His hierarchy-minded critics "sought to kill him, because he not only broke the sabbath, but also called God his Father, thus making himself equal with God." Yet Jesus was not "making himself" anything. He was only filling full what his Father had named him to be and called him to do. "The son can do nothing of his own accord, but only what he sees the Father doing; for what he does, the son does likewise." To the mind of hierarchy, however, this was intolerable blasphemy.

Another dialogue has the Judeans claim, "Abraham is our father," and infer, "we have one Father, even God." Jn 8:39-59 Jesus proposed oneness as a test: "If God were your Father you would love me, for I proceeded and came forth from God ... not of my own accord, but he sent me." Why can they not hear Jesus' word? Because they are captive to the devil's delusion of worth. "You are Samaritan and have a demon," they charged, thus ranking him inferior. "I honor my Father and you dishonor me," Jesus answered. From their posture of humility before the God they called "Most High," they heard this as sheer arrogance. "Who do you think you are?" they accused him in effect. Jesus replied, "If I glorify myself, my glory is nothing. It is my Father who glorifies me, of whom you say that he is your God. But you have not known him. If I said I do not know him, I would be a liar like you; but I do know him, and I keep his word"—meaning his covenant-honor and hope and calling, like the word, "Let my son go that he may serve me."

Winter came—the Feast of Dedication. John's memoir tells how Jesus was teaching in the temple, in the portico of Solomon along the eastern wall. The Lord GOD had accused the priesthood by Ezekiel, "Ho, shepherds of Israel who have been feeding yourselves, should not shepherds feed the sheep?" Ezek 34:2 Jesus declared his own shepherding to be one with his Father's. "My sheep hear my voice, and I know them, and they follow me, and I give them eternal life, and they shall never perish, neither shall anyone snatch them out of my hand," he said, then added, "My Father, who gave them (these sheep) to me, is greater than I and no one is able to snatch them out of my Father's hand. I and my Father are one." Jn 10:22-39

Once again the Judean authorities, hearing only blasphemy, looked for stones to stone him. "We stone you not for any good work, but because you, a man, make yourself God," they said. Jesus cited a familiar psalm, in which God's voice from heaven affirmed with even greater daring, "I say, *you are gods*, sons of the Most High, all of you!" Ps 82:6 If God names his people "gods" as well as "sons of the Most High," how can it be it blasphemy for Jesus to receive, believe, and cherish the name "son of God" which God conferred on him—yet on them, too? To hear what God says and to live by it in oneness with him cannot be blasphemy! But if they cannot receive Jesus' *words*, will they not at least acknowledge his *works*? He is serving his Father! People are finding life, joy, and healing in his ministry "... that you may know and understand that the Father is in me and I am in the Father," Jesus concluded. They could not receive this, but they could not answer it, either. The defensive impulse of hierarchical authority was to arrest him.

PART FIVE

Penetrating Metaphor

History in Pictures

A literacy of reading and writing can hardly imagine a literacy purely oral—formed in the mind, communicated precisely voice-to-ear, understood by hearers, preserved by disciplined memorizing, published by parents to children. In such literacy, metaphor was a natural art. It framed truth in picture images or story. The Eden metaphor, for example, marvelously portrays a universal humanness that is inherently noble but desperately self-corrupted. Gen 2-3

A memory of Jesus notes that he "did not speak without a parable." Mk 4:34 I take parable here to be metaphor in a broad sense. The disciples afterward continued that art. By stories of mountain and lake, healing and mission, they pictured Jesus as they had come to know him. Luke cites among his sources, "ministers of the word." Presumably these were of the young church, but other than the apostles. Lk 1:2 They would have known and spoken metaphor, too.

People of oral literacy perceived the humanness depicted in the Eden story as their own. They did not see "Adam" as the progenitor of the human race, or wonder whether he had a navel or lacked a rib. They realized that Isaiah's imagery of valleys raised and mountains brought low meant people, not highway construction. They sensed at once that to "pluck out a right eye" or to "cut off a right hand" so as to enter the kingdom was not about self-mutilation, but about giving up whatever was perverse in the tradition, no matter how much a part of "self" it had become.

The common folk of oral literacy knew "life" on the heart-level to be real and enduring above the "life" of mere body. They were aware of a warfare within themselves between being ruled by the holy spirit of God and being possessed by an unclean spirit or demon. They knew the metaphoric blindness, deafness, lameness, leprosy, paralysis, poverty, and even death, which Jesus healed by his gospel. They saw how, in parable upon parable, he exposed weed-seedings which had corrupted their tradition, and how the truth and freedom he offered was authentically of Moses and the prophets. When the apostles proclaimed Jesus by stories like walking on the sea and coming to them at night, such metaphor made graphic an inside-history which eyes could not see—his walk through abuse, darkness, and death into resurrection and life for their sakes.

People found it exciting and stretching to hear such carefully crafted messages and talk about their implications while memorizing them. The issue was of heart and very real. But it was also a testing. Zealotic voices, drawing their fantasy-faith out of familiar piety, misdirected what Jesus said and did toward their hope of a futurist kingdom. Authorities of synagogue and temple published slanders against him orally too, and afterwards, against those who believed him.

Sayings of Jesus and stories about him were written down in abundance and so preserved. Written words were not able to convey the person-to-person life of oral literacy and tradition, however. Scholars trained to read and write studied in private. The culture they brought to bear on their work did not know metaphor or even suspect it. Indeed, reverence for the authority of sacred documents precluded any search for meaning beneath the flatly literal impression of a text.

"Blessed are your eyes, for they see, and your ears, for they hear," Jesus said. Mt 13:16 "Eyes and ears" of the heart can be so blessed even today, but they need to be opened boldly and without fear. Metaphor waits to divulge the history and conflict that produced it. Once penetrated, every detail of stories so purposefully crafted reveals why it was said the way it was said.

The backside gain of penetrating metaphor is the capacity to notice in the Gospels a wealth of direct memory that *cannot* be metaphor, and to pursue this with like intensity.

CHAPTER THIRTEEN

Word Pictures

*"The words that I have spoken to you, they are spirit
(breath) and they are life."*   *John 6:63*

The life of the body comes by parents and genealogy. It is sustained by breathing (Hebrew *ruach* or *nishmah*, Greek *pneuma*, Latin *spiritus* or *animus*, English *breath* or *ghost*) and by eating foods that derive from the aliveness of plants and animals. It is marked by a beating heart. When breathing and heartbeat cease, it is over.

The "breath" and "life" of which Jesus spoke had to do with human personhood beyond mere body. This was metaphor as old as Eden. The LORD God "breathed into his nostrils the breath of life, and the adam-man became a living person." Gen 2:7 To sustain this "living person," God planted "the tree of life" in the garden for his people to "eat," but also "the tree of the knowledge of good and evil." When the adam-man chose the latter, he "died" to the "life" of God in him. Here are the two "psyches" (as I called them), which Moses set before his people—one of "life and good," the other of "death and evil." Jesus in his temptations chose "life and good."

The language of "holy spirit" in contrast to "unclean spirit," or demon-possession, parallels those two psyches. Jesus could not set the choice between these before his people, however, as Moses did, for they *did not even know* the covenant-sonship, which was their very life and glory! The psyche of "death and evil" (the "unclean spirit") ruled them even under the forms of their religion. His "gospel of the kingdom" *invaded* the kingdom of unclean spirits or demons which held them captive, so as to heal them and set them free.

Metaphor stories picture the controlling psyche of "death and evil" under forms like seizures, paralysis, sickness, mad or violent behaviors. To take these literally is to miss the point, that the psyche of self-determinism is itself the issue! The measure of normalcy, healing, sanity, or right mind, is the psyche of "life and good." Deliverance from the other cannot come by laws or a display of decent behavior. It comes only by the gospel and spirit of sonship.

Spirit

Jesus received the covenant-life of word and spirit from his Father at his baptism. Isaiah called it "the spirit of wisdom and understanding, the spirit of counsel and might, the spirit of knowledge and the fear of the LORD." Is 11:2 In his temptations, the devil, by the weaponry of an eyes-opened "knowledge of good and evil," fought to negate his sonship and holy spirit. Jesus' ministry was a counterattack *to set his people free* from the unclean spirits that bound them. "The words that I speak to you, they are spirit and they are life," he said. Jn 6:63 Those *words* are *spirit and life* still. To hear and believe him is to be alive and free, breathing the spirit of God.

The War of Spirits. Mk 1:21-27; Lk 4:33-36 A striking fragment makes the warfare graphic. Mark and Luke both found it already grouped with other fragments, and entered it near the beginning of their scrolls. It depicts in summary-metaphor the battle of Jesus' entire ministry. The synagogue is the battleground. "A man with an unclean spirit" depicts an Israel possessed by distortions of chosenness, law and authority. The unclean spirit knows it is under attack. The cry of the man represents its resistance against Jesus and the young church after him.

"What have you to do with us, Jesus of Nazareth?" Go away! Leave us alone. That he is "of Nazareth" disqualifies him. What does he know? Where has he studied? "Have you come to destroy us?" Jesus is attacking the secure and authoritative religion, subverting it from within. Yet the "unclean spirit" knows well who and what it is up against: "I know who you are, *the holy one of God*." That name, a variant of "son of God," is the embattled issue through-out. Unclean spirits can handle a Jesus merely "of Nazareth," but the Jesus *whose holy spirit is from God* is too much. Another parallel fragment has the scribes and Pharisees turn the attack against Jesus, as though he is the one so possessed! "He casts out demons by Beelzebul, the prince of demons." Jesus replies, "If it is by the spirit of God that I cast out demons, then the kingdom of God has come upon you." Mt 9:34; 12:24,28 It is a warfare of spirits indeed, and they are in it.

In this case Jesus commands, "Be silent and come out of him!" That command capsules his gospel of covenant-honor and freedom. It refutes and silences every lying voice that is raised against him. "He would not permit the demons to speak, because they knew him," a parallel verse says. Mk 1:34 The enemy is not the man himself, but the spirit that has usurped control and turned him against the word and spirit of God. The man's convulsion and loud cry pictures a battle within himself, though seeming to make Jesus the enemy. The outcome is clear. The holy spirit of Jesus prevails over the unclean. The man healed depicts the young church still worshiping in that same synagogue—but cleansed and alive and free.

"What is this word and authority?" witnesses asked. "A new teaching" they called it, "not like the scribes." What Jesus taught seemed new, yet it was the covenant-word God had spoken to his people Israel from the beginning. The young church, which confessed him and breathed his spirit, was not an enemy or threat to the people of Israel and their authorities. The enemy was unclean spirits that had taken possession of them, from which they too could be free.

The House of Seven Haunts. Mt 12:43-45; Lk 11:24-26 "The house of Israel" is familiar language in the Prophets (75 times in Ezekiel). Jesus likened his people to a house from which an unclean spirit had been evicted, as when God had taken Israel to himself out of Egypt. That spirit needed a home. It sought rest in waterless (uninhabitable) places, but finding none, decided to "return to my house from which I came." On coming, he found it to be agreeably "empty, swept, and put in order"—externally well-administered but void of covenant-substance.

Emptiness was the problem. The house had been emptied of the name Johwah, for example, and thereby of "a God merciful and gracious, slow to anger and abounding in steadfast love...." Ex 34:6-7 A law required the faithful to wear the *Shema* verse externally in phylacteries and to recite it daily, "Hear, O Israel, the LORD our God, the LORD is one, and you shall love the LORD your God with all your heart." Dt 6:4-5 Yet how could they love with all their heart a "Johwah" whose name was silenced and whose character they did not even know? The people had their own name from the LORD, as in Moses' word to Pharaoh, "Thus says Johwah, 'Israel is *my son, my firstborn*; let *my son* go that he may serve me!'" Ex 4:22-23 But if they exalted the name "Johwah" and their own name as his "son" so high that they dared not even speak it, how meaningless their calling would be to know their Father, walk with him, and serve him only!

The unclean spirit rushed to fill the vacuum. He brought with him "seven other spirits more evil than himself," so that "the last state of that man is worse than the first." This parable was diagnosis, not insult. Let "the house of Israel" realize what had happened to it. Jesus may have had people memorize this as he began a sermon, then filled in what it meant. His disciples would then have taught it throughout the land.

Spirits, though unseen, are knowable by their effects. "You shall know them by their fruits," Jesus said. Mt 7:16 To penetrate this metaphor, consider effects that would prompt so drastic a diagnosis. Only an unclean spirit would incite Israel to suppress the name, "son of God," which the LORD had spoken on all his people and which Jesus cherished. Only an unclean spirit would pervert the wonder of Israel's chosenness into an illusion of superiority. Only an unclean spirit would deform God's call to freedom, "that he may serve me," into self-conscious performances designed to keep Israel special. Only an unclean spirit would accuse Jesus of violating laws that kept Israel apart, thus suppressing the great commandment to "love Johwah your God with all your heart" and "your neighbor as yourself." Only an unclean spirit would absolve the authorities of any need to hear the covenant-word Jesus proclaimed, on the ground that a Galilean was not their brother and so did not "qualify" as a prophet. Only an unclean spirit would conspire to silence God's message by killing his messenger, even his "beloved son." Only an unclean spirit would see to it meanwhile that the temple remained magnificent, gold trim gleaming, priestly vestments beautifully crafted, sacrifices and feasts efficiently administered, holy city Jerusalem glorified.

On the other hand, by the spirit of his sonship-name, Jesus defied the unclean spirits. All alone, he went to their headquarters, exposed hypocrisies, offered freedom and healing. He persisted in setting "life and good" and "death and evil" before his people, as Moses had done. Dt 30:15 Longing for them to "choose life," he fought to expose and drive out their unclean spirits. For all their abuse, he would not turn against them as enemy, even to his own death.

The Distraught Father. Mk 9:14-29; Mt 17:14-21; Lk 9:37-43 Mark has this in greatest detail. Jesus' disciples (the young church) and the scribes of the synagogue are engaged in a dispute. A crowd of common folk do not know what to make of it. The distraught father (think Abraham) appeals to the disciples, then to Jesus, on behalf of his son, the present Israel, whose actions are driven by an alien, self-destructive spirit. Contorted prescriptions of scribal religion are pictured metaphorically as epileptic seizure. "Dumb" suggests the silencing of God's authentic word. The spirit "dashes him down" so that he cannot walk nobly and upright before the God he is called to serve. "He foams and grinds his teeth" in rage against Jesus and the young church. "He becomes rigid," unable to change. Clearly, the "enemy" is not the boy himself but the unclean spirit that is doing this to him. The father loves his son, has brought him to the disciples (the young church), but the torment goes on. Now he (and they) turn to Jesus himself.

"O generation without faith." This *generation* has refused the *faith* of Abraham, of Jesus himself, and of his disciples. "How long am I to be with you? How long am I to bear with you?" pictures God's frustration and yet patience with a recalcitrant people. "Bring him to me," Jesus says. He does not evade the problem or give up on it. Neither can his young church.

Confronted by Jesus and the holy spirit, the unclean spirit drives the boy into yet another convulsion—depicting fits of defensive irrationality into which synagogue and temple have been driven for fear of Jesus. "How long has he had this?" Jesus asks in Mark's version. "From childhood," the father replies. He tells how this spirit "casts him into the fire and into the water to destroy him." Every action and reaction serves not to honor God, but to ruin the son himself. "But if you can do anything, have pity on us and help us," he pleads. "You dumb and deaf spirit, come out of him," Jesus commands. "Deaf" is another symptom. Deaf ears block hearts from hearing the word of honor or hope which alone can lift them up and set them free.

The authority of Jesus' command is his loving and obedient sonship, even to death, on behalf of a people who could not hear. The disciples had been convulsed themselves at Jesus' death and left like a corpse, yet he by his resurrection had raised them up, free of the unclean spirit, alive with the spirit of his Father.

Mark's account has the father struggling, "I believe, help my unbelief." Dare Abraham hope that his son, embodied in the rulers of synagogue and temple, can yet be freed from the unclean spirit they do not even know? The disciples, caught in that struggle, ask, "Why could we not cast it out?" "This kind cannot be driven out by anything but prayer," Jesus replies, a call for unwavering confidence in God, despite their dismay. Matthew's account adds, "Truly I say to you, if you have faith like a grain of mustard seed, you will say to this mountain, 'Move hence to yonder place,' and it will move; and nothing will be impossible to you." Not the size of their faith will move the mountain, but courage even in weakness to keep walking straight on through. Let the mountain do the moving.

The Centurion of Capernaum. Mt 8:5-13; Lk 7:1-10 What of the Roman forces which occupied the land? A corrupt but pervasive piety turned against

Rome a hatred it considered holy. "Do I not hate those who hate you, O LORD?... I hate them with perfect hatred; I count them my enemies," a Psalm sang. Ps 139:21-22 Yet Jesus' word had somehow affected a Roman officer. Touched by its power, he pleaded with Jesus (the young church) on behalf of a servant who "lies paralyzed at home, terribly distressed." The symptoms are of an alien spirit that possesses the centurion's people. (Luke's account is corrupted by an intercession of "elders of the Judeans" with Jesus on behalf of this centurion: "He is worthy, for he loves our nation and has built us a synagogue." Such reasoning may free Jesus to respond in this particular instance, but at the price of validating the Judean spirit of superiority over and separatism from foreigners.)

"I will come and heal him," Jesus says, without hesitation. The centurion honors Israel's special "cleanness," however. "I am not worthy to have you come under my roof, but speak the word only, and my servant will be healed." He explains his own place in the authority structure of Rome, and how he can give orders and have them obeyed. He can manage that kind of kingdom. But the authority to heal his servant is beyond him. It requires the authority of Jesus' word.

The young church understood this difference. The zealotic notion of Israel's superiority had died in Jesus' death. Rome and its forces of occupation were not the enemy. The kingdom Jesus proclaimed did not exalt one nation over another. If a Roman comes in hope of covenant-healing, let God's people rejoice! That the covenant-word of God, Israel's unique heritage, should spill over to the nations and heal them also from the heart out is the true kingdom and glory.

The warfare of spirits continued within Israel, however. "Truly I say to you, not even in Israel have I found such faith," Jesus said. The compiler of Matthew attached a fragment here, which Luke has in another context. Lk 13:28-30 "I tell you, many will come from east and west and sit at table with Abraham, Isaac, and Jacob in the kingdom of heaven, while the sons of the kingdom will be thrown into outer darkness; there men will weep and gnash their teeth."

The Demoniac(s) of Gadara/Gerasa. Mk 5:1-20; Lk 8:26-39; Mt 8:28-34 Variations suggest that this fragment-story, initially Galilean (so preserved in Matthew), was expanded before it reached Judea, where Mark and Luke came upon it.

This metaphor was told as a kind of mission report to the young church in Galilee from across the lake. Gadara (Matthew) and Gerasa (Mark and

Luke) were cities of the Decapolis, a Gentile territory mostly east of Jordan. Its native population was Aramaic, but Greeks had colonized it long ago. That two different cities are named suggests that the mission was reaching the whole territory. The young church identifies itself with Jesus. The Judean variation (Mark and Luke) has the man cry out, "What have you to do with me, Jesus, son of God Most High?" The version in Matthew has "two," which I take to envision male and female. "What have you to do with us, son of God?" the two cry out against him. Either represents in metaphor the whole population. The covenant-name, "son of God," is the issue of this warfare.

"Out of the tombs" signifies obsession with death. Anxiety for worth, a driving need to be noticed, to prove oneself or cover oneself, is a function of this demonic obsession. The man is fighting his fear of unworth. His self-assertive struggle is desperate. "No one could bind him any more, even with a chain; for he had often been bound with fetters and chains, but the chains he wrenched apart and the fetters he broke in pieces, and no one had the strength to subdue him. Night and day among the tombs and on the mountains (Luke has also the desert), he was always crying out, and bruising himself with stones." Society enforces restraints against the violent to preserve its peace, but destructive forces break through, anyway. A frantic need for attention, to win, be liked, be right, be rich, have everything one's own way, is symptomatic of self-destructive demonry—likewise raging frustration, lies, bluster, and evading shame.

Through the young church another spirit, that of Jesus, was now confronting people of these towns. His name, "son of God," is shorthand for his message. Sonship and worth, life and hope, purpose and calling in the use of one's gifts, are given from heaven at the very beginning. Such honor requires no proof or payment. It needs only to be received and put to use. Jesus, serving his Father and people even to death, yet raised to life again, embodies this message not to Israel only, but to the nations. His kingdom knows no mountain-people or valley-people, but only brothers and sisters walking upright and side-by-side as one people. For all their diversities, they share a wondrous commonality—to be named children of one Father in heaven, from whom they all come and to whom all will return. Their joy and glory is to know and serve him freely.

The mission across the lake is portrayed in bold cartoon-like strokes. "When he saw Jesus from afar (a first glimpse), he ran and worshiped him." But the implication became frightening.

"What have you to do with me, Jesus, son of God Most High? I adjure you by God, do not torment me." "Don't get involved," the unclean spirit tells the man. Stay in control. You wouldn't want his sonship. It only mocks you! Look how it destroyed him! Why should he care about you, anyway? "'What is your name?' Jesus asked. 'Legion,' he replied," like a division of the Roman occupation army. Yet his legion of demons could not withstand the simple name and gospel of Jesus, the son of God.

That was the heart of this mission report. But there was also a problem. Could these Gentiles be received into the people of God so easily, by Jesus' mere word and name? Gentiles raised swine and ate the meat of swine—the most graphic of all uncleannesses! The metaphor addresses this concern as well. Their legion of demons, driven out of one home, needed another. They did not want to be sent out of their country, like to Galilee or Judea, where they might encounter Jesus again. So they begged him, "If you cast us out, send us away into the herd of swine." It was an appropriate match—unclean spirits for unclean pigs. "Go!" Jesus said.

Whoever formed this metaphor envisioned pigs as feeding on hillsides like sheep or goats and tended by herdsmen. Viewed from Galilee, hills on the eastern shore of the lake appear to descend steeply into the water. The fragment in Mark numbers the pigs at two thousand—ten cubed to signal totality, multiplied by humanity as male and female (like the two of Matthew). The metaphor pictures them, possessed by demons, as running precipitously down the slope into the water and drowning themselves. To worry about the economic loss of literally-drowned pigs is to miss the metaphor. The point is Jesus' sonship-gospel cleanses and gathers Gentiles without partiality. When his new and clean spirit possesses them, their external lives are cleansed also.

A final testimony suggests that the mission was continuing. The herdsmen ran to the city and told what had happened. People came and saw the man "clothed and in his right mind"—clothed by God with righteousness and honor, his mind free, honest, upright and in the service of God. Fearing what deliverance from unclean spirits might do to them, they asked Jesus to leave them alone. He returned to Galilee, the account says, but the mission went on. The man, himself healed, became God's voice of mercy and life to his whole region.

The gospel of covenant-sonship has power by the spirit of God to liberate and heal still. Let it drive out the unclean spirits of our culture from people so possessed—then send these spirits down their own precipitous slope to be drowned like the pigs of Gadara in wholesome suicide!

Life

"The words that I speak to you, they are *spirit* and they are *life*." As "spirit" (breath) is metaphor throughout the scriptures, so is "life." "You shall walk in all the ways the LORD your God commanded you, that you may *live*," Moses said, adding "that it may go well with you, and that you may *live long* in the land which you shall possess." Dt 5:33 "I am the LORD your God. You shall keep my statutes and my ordinances, by doing which a man shall *live*." Lev 18:5 "Life" in this spirit-sense does not disparage the aliveness of the body but honors and rules it.

John's memoir begins with Jesus' feeding the five thousand. Jn 6:1-15 A metaphor follows, which reveals the inside history of the disciples in the dark night of Jesus' death. They were at sea, rowing futilely against a strong wind, getting nowhere. They saw Jesus walking on that sea, as though he were its master, and coming to them. Fear gave way to joy. When they received him into the boat, they were immediately at their destination. Jn 6:16-21 (A copyist, not perceiving the metaphor, imagined how the crowd Jesus fed got home the next day. "Boats came near from Tiberias," so "they got into the boats and went to Capernaum, seeking Jesus." Jn 6:22-25)

John's extended discourse on life and the bread that sustains life derives from the post-resurrection witness of the young church in Capernaum. Jn 6:26-59 In the background is the "manna" of Israel's wanderings. "The LORD your God ... humbled you, and let you hunger, and fed you with manna,... that he might make you know that man does not *live* by bread alone, but that man *lives* by every word that proceeds out of the mouth of the LORD." Dt 8:2-3; Mt 4:4 "Labor not for the food that perishes but for the food which endures to *eternal life*, which the son of man will give you," Jesus said similarly. "My Father gives you the true bread from heaven." "Your fathers ate the manna in the wilderness *and they died*. This is the bread which comes down from heaven, that a man may eat of it and *not die*."

The gem-theme of John's memoir goes beyond metaphor to God's word and life in Jesus *himself*. Many people had known him humanly. "Is not this Jesus, the son of Joseph, whose father and mother we know?" they remembered rightly. True enough, yet the identity that directed Jesus' life in the body was not of his human parents. He heard the voice of his Father declare to him personally what the LORD had said of Israel in Egypt: "This is my beloved son, with whom I am well pleased. Let my son go that he may serve me." That word was *bread* to him. He *ate* it. The life it gave him was of God, thus *eternal* in distinction from the passing life of his body. "The living Father sent me, and I live because of the Father," he said. It should be the life of his people, too! "They shall *all* be taught by God," Jesus quoted Isaiah. Jn 6:45; Is 54:13 "Everyone who hears and learns from the Father comes to me," he added.

His name "son of God," with "the Father" as its corollary, was the very essence of Israel's covenant. That he took it with utter seriousness was neither usurpation nor arrogance. His Father had named him so. It implied also his calling to serve his Father. "I have come down from heaven not to do my own will, but the will of him who sent me." Others asked, "What must we do, to be doing the works of God?" "This is the work of God, that you believe in him whom he has sent," he answered. To receive his "bread of life" message is to receive *him*, the messenger who also embodied it. This is the point of the "I am" sayings in John's memoir. "I am the bread of life. He who comes to me will not hunger, and he who believes in me will never thirst."

"The bread *which I give is my body*, for the life of the world." (The Hebrew/Aramaic *basar* may be translated either *flesh* or *body*. I prefer *body*.) Jesus gave as "bread" for their life the covenant-sonship he himself ate and lived by in his body. "How shall this man give us his body to eat?" some asked? How? By *choosing* to live and do his Father's will even to the crucifixion and death of his body! Do you want this bread from heaven for yourself? Then come to terms with him! "Unless you eat the body of *the son of man* and drink his blood, you have no life in you.... For my body is food indeed, and my blood is drink indeed." (That Jesus was willing to call himself "the son of man" in deference to the prevailing piety did not obscure the issue).

The choice is drastic. You who are heirs yourselves of that covenant-name, "my beloved son," what will you do? Will you take the side of those who rejected his sonship and condemned him to death for claiming it? Will you shrug him aside as though what happened does not matter? Will you care only about the desires and fears of bodies doomed to die? Will you keep performimg the emptiness of self-serving law as before? Will you cling to the illusion of a God who regards you as superior to all nations, who should one day glorify you by crushing others? Will you not see how Jesus *saved you* from that? By putting his own life in between, he stopped an insurrection which the Romans would have crushed without mercy!

Or will you receive and believe in the son whom the Father sent, and who *gave himself* for you? Will you eat the body and drink the blood of his dying for your very life? Will you confess his name and so become what he is? For his body is food indeed and his blood is drink indeed!

"This is a hard saying; who can listen to it?" many worried. "Do you stumble at this?" Jesus answered. "What if you were to see the son of man ascending where he was before?" Jesus, the son of God crucified, has ascended to the bosom of the Father who sent him. He is sealed in the eternal life and glory he filled full as servant to the very finish! That is your glory too! Fill it full in your own holy serving. "It is the spirit that gives life, the body of itself counts for nothing. The words that I speak to you, they are spirit and they are life."

A memory is preserved that "many of his disciples cringed and withdrew from him." "Will you also go away?" Jesus asked the twelve. Simon Peter's reply is the confession of the young church. "Lord, to whom shall we go? You have the words of eternal life. And we have believed and know that you are the holy one of God."

Copyist Interpolations. Corruptions in the extant text of John 6 need to be detected and set aside. Some are merely repetitious enhancements: "And he said, 'This is why I said that no one can come to me unless it is granted him by the Father.'" Jn 6:65 from 44 "This he said in the synagogue, as he taught at Capernaum." Jn 6:59 from 17

In John's memoir, "eternal life" is the life of God in his people *now*. A copyist saw it as a future restoration and eternal extension of bodily life, however. Borrowing Martha's pious hope, "I know that he will rise in the resurrection at the last day," he had Jesus promise at four places, "And I will raise him up at the last day." Jn 11:24; 6:39, 40, 44, 54

Some interpolations presume Jesus' deity and invite a deity-believing. "I told you that you have seen me and yet do not believe." Jn 6:36, from 30 and 40 "Not that anyone has seen the Father, except him who is from God, he has seen the Father" makes Jesus an exception to the "No one has ever seen God" of John's prologue. Jn 6:44; 1:18 A deity-Jesus knows everything, thus a copyist adds, "knowing in himself that his disciples murmured at it." Jn 6:61

Jesus' "foreknowledge" of Judas as traitor encumbers John's memoir twice, to say nothing of distorting Judas himself. Jn 6:64-65,70-71

Resurrection: The Sadducees

"Life" or "death" in the *visible* sense are biological terms. With respect to plants and animals they have no other meaning. With respect to human self-awareness, they have also an *invisible* or metaphoric sense. "Life" is to be righteous and have worth by the voice-from-heaven word of God. "Death" is to depend for righteousness and worth on our own self-creation and self-asser-tion. The metaphoric sense is no less real than the biological.

So also with the term "resurrection." Taken visibly, it is biological. Thus Martha said of her brother, "I know that he will rise again in the resurrection at the last day," looking to the futurist resuscitation of his corpse. Jesus di-verted her to the *invisible* "resurrection" that happens in the body *now,* as focused on himself. "I *am* the resurrection and the life. Whoever believes in me, though he were dead, yet shall he live. And whoever lives and believes in me will never die. Do you believe *this*?" "Yes, Lord, I believe that you are the Christ, the son of God," she replied. Jn 11:24-27 The pious hope of corpses resuscitated for another bodily life in the future only diverts God's people from the *eternal life* of belonging to and serving God in the bodies they have *now.*

A dialogue of Jesus with some Sadducees (of the priesthood) makes the same point. All three synoptic Gospels have it, Luke's version more ample than the others. Lk 20:27-39; Mt 22:23-33; Mk 12:18-27 The Sadducees were prac-tical and realistic. By a crude joke based on Mosaic law, they mocked the piety of a futurist "last day" bodily resurrection. A wife whose husband died child-less must be given to his brother, to raise up an heir for him. Dt 25:5 Suppose a woman were given successively to seven brothers, each of whom died child-less. Finally, she died also. "In the resurrection, therefore, whose wife will she be? For all seven had her as wife."

"You are misled," Jesus answered, "for you do not know the scriptures or the power of God." Mt 22:29 Human genealogy is sexual. They "marry and are given in marriage," thus have children. God counted Israel "worthy" to attain "life" on a different order than body, however. By his covenant-word and spirit he named them "my first-born son." In so doing, he raised them up in a "resurrection-life" unknown to other nations. They are rightly called "the sons of God," even "sons of the resurrection"—not futurist, but *now.*

Jesus cited the angels. "Bless the LORD, O you his angels, you mighty ones who do his word, hearkening to the voice of his word ... his ministers that do his will," the people sang. Ps 103:20-21 Angels live and serve God, yet their life is not of sexuality and marriage. "The living God" they serve is not of body, either. But if "the living God" names us to be "the sons of the living God," he has resurrected us in our mortal bodies to a life like his own. Hos 1:10 By his life in us, our "heart and body sing for joy to the living God" and "thirst for the living God." Ps 84:2; 42:2 Jesus knew this of himself: "The living Father sent me, and I live by the Father." Jn 6:57 When those named "the sons of the living God" die as to their visible bodies, they do not lose the "eternal life" of God in them, no more than angels can lose their life and die! "They cannot die any more, but are equal to angels and are sons of God, being sons of the resurrection."

The patriarchal fathers passed a life of sexuality and marriage on through many generations to this day. The Sadducees honored this when they recited their genealogies. Yet if this were all their fathers had to offer, what worth or hope would Israel enjoy beyond other nations? The patriarchs were dead, likewise every descendant of theirs! Only by another level of life were they "accounted worthy to belong to that age and the resurrection from the dead."

Jesus cited the text in which God identified himself to Moses out of the bush, "I am *the God of* your father, *the God of* Abraham, *the God of* Isaac, and *the God of* Jacob." Ex 3:6,15; 4:5 "*The God of, the God of!*" By God's initiative, God's choice, God's voice, the patriarchs belonged to the eternal Giver-Creator-God and he to them! Who but *God* was the true life and worth of the fathers out of Egypt? "I will be *your God*, and you shall be *my people*," the LORD said, and "Israel is *my first-born son*." By that *invisible* covenant-word they were the sons—not of the patriarchs only, or "of this age" only—but "of the living God"!

Your bodies are a grand gift, but they cannot be your glory! Your true glory is the eternal life of your God in you, calling you by his name, breathing his breath in you! He is "not the God of the dead, but of *the living*; for *all live to him*." "Live to him" the "life" he desires and makes possible for you as his sons! By his life in you, *your bodily life on this earth is eternal even now*, defying the death of your body. Only by "the God of" the patriarchs does your descent from them count for anything at all.

The piety of Jesus' day had lost metaphorical meanings. Its hope was visible-literalist. The kingdom and glory, and the resurrection of the faithful who had died before it came, were of the body, like other nations, only "superior." Since none of this was being experienced here and now, it had to be future. Jesus diverted both resurrection and kingdom from visible to invisible, from future to present, from what God should do for his people to what his people should do in serving their God. Resurrection to the life of God is *now*, just as the kingdom is *now*. The invitation of the sonship-gospel is *now*.

He prayed it: "Our Father, your kingdom come, your will be done, *as in heaven, so on earth*." Mt 6:10 He sang it: "Surely goodness and mercy shall follow me all the days of my *life*, and I shall dwell in the house of the LORD forever." Ps 23:6 He taught it: "The slave does not continue in the house forever, the son continues forever." Jn 8:35 He continued "forever" in his Father's house precisely by *not saving* the life of his body. God's promises enabled his serving: "After two days he will revive us, on the third day he will raise us up, that we may *live* before him." Hos 6:2 "Truly, truly, I say to you, unless a grain of wheat falls into the earth and dies, it remains alone; but if it dies, it bears much fruit. Whoever loves his life loses it, but whoever hates his life in this world will keep it for *eternal life*." Jn 12:24-25

"When Jesus knew that his hour had come to depart out of this world to the Father, having loved his own who were in the world, he loved them *to the finish*.... Knowing that the Father had given all things into his hands, and that *he had come from God and was going to God*," he rose from supper and washed his disciples' feet. Jn 13:1,3 This was *resurrection and eternal life* for him, here and *now!* He looked for no futurist reward, kingdom, resurrection, or life. "My food is to do the will of my Father and to finish his work," he said, and did it. Jn 4:34 When he said "It is finished" and died, he had eaten what he called "my food" to the full. Jn 19:30

Light and Blindness

"Light" and "blindness" are likewise metaphor. "I have given you as a covenant to the people, a light to the nations, to open the eyes that are blind, to bring out from the prison...those who sit in darkness," Isaiah said. Is 42:6-7 "The eye is the lamp of the body," Jesus pictured it. "So, if your eye is sound, your whole body is full of light; but if your eye is not sound, your whole body will be full of darkness. If then the light in you is darkness, how great is the darkness!" Mt 6:22-23 Of the "blind" who will not acknowledge their blindness, he said, "Let them alone, they are blind guides. If a blind man leads a blind man, both will fall into a pit." Mt 15:14

A Man Born Blind. Jn 9:1-41 This metaphor preserved, under the form of story, a history of conflict in the young church. The blind man whom Jesus and the young church encountered in Jerusalem depicts a people who could neither "see" nor fill full their honor and calling as sons of God. "Rabbi, who sinned, this man or his parents, that he was born blind?" Whose fault was it? Jesus' disciples (the young church) puzzled over this while he was still with them. The man had been born into that condition. It did not seem fair to blame him. Yet to blame his parents, thus previous generations, did not make sense, either. Should a son suffer for the iniquity of his father? How many generations back should one go to assign fault?

Jesus directed his disciples to a more fruitful outlook. What mattered was not to fix blame but to heal. "It was not that this man sinned, or his parents, but that the works of God might be made manifest in him. We (Jesus and the young church) must do the works of him who sent me while it is day, before the night comes when no man can work. As long as I am in the world, I am the light of the world." To know and live by the light is to be doing the work God gives each to do, while it is still day.

The metaphor-story has Jesus spit on the ground, mix this tiny moisture of life from within himself with the dirt into a paste, anoint the man's eyes with it, and send him to the pool of Siloam to wash his eyes. ("Which means Sent" is a distraction, entered by an officious copyist.) The link in metaphor is to "the waters of Shiloah that flow gently," meaning the covenant-promises which, in Isaiah's context, "this people have refused." Is 8:6 Those gently flowing waters are a parallel metaphor to "light." For the blind man to wash his eyes there, as Jesus directed him, is to return to those promises, believe them, and thus see the light. His "seeing" is a miracle, "the work" of God in him. By it he is no longer a depressed beggar, but a free and honored "son of God!" Thus Jesus, "the light of the world," and the young church with him, are doing "the works of him who sent me while it is day."

The witness which the man bore, likewise the resistance he endured, pictures the young church. His "neighbors" function in metaphor as the community which sees the change in him, but remain caught in the familiar tradition. They asked him about it, heard his witness, and were filled with wonder. The flow of gentle grace originating in God reached out toward them, too— opening their eyes to glimpse what they had not seen or known, either. "Where is he?" they asked, concerning the Jesus who had done this wonder. The man did not know. In the post-resurrection era, the *where* of Jesus was not geographical. He came to people, not they to him.

The neighbors brought the man to the Pharisees of the synagogue to get their opinion. These leaders and teachers evaded the wonder of the man's "seeing" by invoking the sabbath law against Jesus, as they had often done before. "This man is not from God, for he does not keep the sabbath." The neighbors were not convinced. "How can a man who is a sinner do such signs?" they wondered. The "sight" which the man experienced could not be lightly shrugged off. So they asked him, "What do you say of Jesus, since he opened your eyes?" The man knew his former blindness. He knew how he had been awesomely enlightened. So he answered, "He is a prophet." Jesus did not speak and act by his own word, but by God's.

The metaphor story shifts to "the Judeans," the priesthood and council. They knew what was at stake. Jesus had not stayed dead. The pernicious infection they had thought to eliminate was continuing in his disciples and the young church. They summoned the man's parents. Parents are responsible to transmit the tradition properly to their children. They are accountable for their children's aberrations, in this case for the "sight" their son had received.

"Is this your son?" these authorities asked. His parents acknowledged it. "Do you say that he was born blind?" they asked. To answer yes might suggest a blindness in the tradition itself, in which the Judeans as well as these parents had been brought up. The parents confirmed it regarding their son, however. He was indeed blind and from birth. The ultimate question followed, "How then does he now see?" Even these critics acknowledge that something good had happened to the man. He could see! The metaphor suggests that the authorities could not readily deny the "sight" and understanding of the young church, or dismiss it as evil.

The parents were caught in between, however. To acknowledge that their son did really see, and that Jesus had done it, would seem to make Jesus right and the authorities wrong. They might be accused of joining their son in confessing Jesus to be "a prophet," to be the "light" for their darkness, too. The warning had been issued. Anyone who confessed Jesus as the young church was confessing him would be "cast out of the synagogue." So they retreated. "How he now sees we do not know, neither do we know who opened his eyes. He is of age, ask him."

The authorities summoned the man and proposed a compromise. Leave Jesus out of it! "Give God the praise; we know that this man is a sinner." See and know God apart from Jesus! Say it was God and we will acknowledge the miracle too, even join you in praising him for it! Keep whatever sight you received as a miracle from God himself! The compromise was tempting. It would resolve the tension. The Judeans would even join him! Of course, they would be acknowledged as right in condemning Jesus. They would keep control.

The blind man now seeing would not argue their theology. "Whether he is a sinner, I do not know." He only repeated the miracle of revelation: "Though I was blind, now I see." The defensive accusers could not let it go at that. "What did he do to you? How did he open your eyes?" they asked. "I have told you already, and you did not listen," he replied. Why did they need to get into this again? Were they probing for further grounds on which to accuse Jesus? Or, might it be possible that one or another among them actually wanted to hear more, so as to get in on the wonder of sight himself? Assuming the latter, the man's answer would be not taunt but invitation: "Do you too want to become his disciples?" The metaphor story makes clear, in any case, that the young church would not consent to dividing Jesus from his Father.

The authorities tried next to divide Jesus from Moses. "They reviled the man, saying, 'We are Moses' disciples. As for this man, we do not know where he comes from.'" This Jesus, who is he? What are his credentials? The man once blind appealed to another authority, however. The miracle of revelation into which he was drawn did not originate in Jesus but in God his Father. "Why, this is a marvel!" he replied. "You do not know where he comes from, and yet he opened my eyes!... Never since the world began has it been heard that anyone opened the eyes of a man born blind! If this Jesus were not from God, he could do nothing!"

The stifling tradition, defending its darkness as though it were light, had no answer. Its final tactic was derision backed by institutional power—superior over inferior. "'You were born in utter sin, and would you teach us?' And they cast him out." Excommunication was the lot of any who steadfastly confessed that Jesus, shining like light into the darkness of his people, was from God. Jn 9:22; 12:42

What shall the young church do? The narrative tells how Jesus heard of it, found the man, and comforted him. "Do you believe in the son of man?" he asked. His self-designation here as "the son of man" (modest pseudonym for "the son of God") suggests that this metaphor-drama was told quite early. It was not long before the young church gave up that device and confessed Jesus boldly by the name on which his very gospel turned, "the son of God."

The man raised a counter-question in which the very identity of God's people was at stake. "Who is he, that I may believe in him?" "Son of God" is a covenant-name for Israel from Moses. It was the crux of Jesus' life and battle. Who is properly called "son of God" now? The council, which condemned Jesus as a blasphemer for confessing this of himself? The synagogue, which excommunicated the man born blind for confessing Jesus as the one who opened his eyes? Shall the temple authorities be called "the son of God," who claim Moses on their terms and turn him against Jesus? "Who is he, that I may believe in him?"

"You have *seen* him! It is he who is speaking to you!" Jesus answered. The man of the metaphor saw Jesus as the young church saw and confessed him. Jesus bore the name "son of God" by right of his Father's declaration from heaven. He lived that name and filled it full in love even to death. His Father certified him by raising him from the dead, and by "works" like this one—healing Israel's blindness from birth through him. To confess Jesus as the son of God is to reject every alternative. Flesh-and-blood descent from Abraham does not qualify Judeans for that name, neither does Jesus' blood-descent from David qualify him so, neither does the zealotic usurpation of the kingdom by violence qualify zealots so, neither does the Moses whom the authorities turn against Jesus qualify them so.

"Lord, I believe," the man confessed, "and he worshiped him." As glad receiver he looked upstream to Jesus the giver and beyond him to the Father. The wonder of oneness embraced him. He belonged, had a place. "Who sinned, this man or his parents, that he was born blind?" was the question. Jesus answered, "It was not that this man sinned or his parents, but that the works of God might be made manifest in him." The man saw. "The works of God" were manifest indeed.

"As long as I am in the world, I am the light of the world," Jesus added. The light shines still, even for those who have rejected it. Its "either-or" is decisive. "For judgment I came into this world, that those who do not see may see, and that those who see may become blind," Jesus said. Isaiah knew that battle, too. "Lord, who has believed our report?" "He has blinded their eyes and hardened their heart, lest they should see with their eyes and perceive with their heart and turn for me to heal them." Is 53:1; 6:10; Jn 12:38-40 God speaks his word of grace insistently but forces it on nobody.

What of the Pharisees who ridiculed the man and excommunicated him? "Are we blind also?" the narrative has them ask. "If you were blind, you would have no sin," Jesus answers, "but now that you say, 'We see,' your guilt remains." The blindness they manifest now is no longer "from birth" but chosen! That is their guilt. "Woe to those who put darkness for light and light for darkness," Isaiah said. Is 5:20

Even so they need not stay blind. The light of the world shines even on those who abhor it. "I have come as a light into the world, that whoever believes in me may not remain in darkness," says another fragment, "for I did not come to judge the world, but to save the world." Jn 12:46-47 Will they love their darkness still? Will they keep saying, "We see"?

CHAPTER FOURTEEN

Parables

> *"This is why I speak to them in parables, because seeing they do not see, and hearing they do not hear.... But blessed are your eyes, for they see, and your ears, for they hear."* Matthew 13:13-16

Jesus' parables were a vital weaponry toward setting before his people what Moses called "life and good" on the one hand, and "death and evil" on the other. Dt 30:15 "Life and good" was his gospel of covenant-sonship. "Death and evil" was a corruption that needed to be understood. Hearers would see what was at stake and thus "choose." When Jesus had framed a parable in his mind, he had his disciples memorize it and teach it throughout the land. Given his covenant-truth as the consistent "life and good," it becomes possible to grasp in each parable the contrasting "death and evil." Since the parables are metaphor, each opens a window into the depth-dimension conflict that gave rise to it.

It was a weaponry peculiar to the kingdom of God. Since the enemy was not people, conspiracy and alliances, money and sword, negotiation and compromise were alien to it. "He shall smite the earth with the rod of *his mouth*, and with the breath of *his lips* he shall slay the wicked," Isaiah said. Is 11:4 "A sharp two-edged sword out of his mouth," became a graphic metaphor later, once the power of his word was understood. Heb 4:12; Rev 1:16 His power lay not in denunciations or rhetoric, but in the penetrating truth of what he said.

But it called for steadfast faith and courage—also in the young church afterwards. By faith as small as a grain of mustard seed, his fearful disciples could stand up against the fake fig tree (sycamine), command it, "Be rooted up and planted in the sea" where you belong, and it would be done. Lk 17:6 When a mountain of opposition theatened to fall on and crush him, Jesus walked straight on through and commanded it to do the moving. Mt 21:21

The Sower. Mt 13:3-9 This parable pictures what the gospel-seed was up against and yet its hope. Some seed fell on the hard and well-trodden pathway of tradition, defended by scribes, Pharisees and priesthood. Before it could even begin to grow, the birds ate it. Other seed fell on shallow ground and began to grow. People heard and were enthusiastic at first, but when the heat of day came, when they noticed what the way of the Lord might cost them, they withered. Some seed fell on soil that was in itself good, but weeds sprang up with it and choked it. The dream of Jesus as a zealotic "christ" so enamoured the people of Galilee and even his disciples, that his word and seeding were not heard. Yet there was also the soil that yielded its full potential—a hundred-fold, sixtyfold, thirtyfold. "He who has ears to hear, let him hear!" Jesus yearned. His business was not to sort out soils in advance but to scatter his seed indiscriminately, trusting the LORD's promise by Isaiah, "So shall my word be that goes forth from my mouth; it shall not return to me empty, but accomplish what I purpose." Is 55:11

Sons as Servants

The sons of God image their Father's creativity toward the earth and his love toward people. When the LORD called Israel out of Egypt, "Let my son go *that he may serve me*," this was their liberation, not a new slavery. Yet enslavement returned under the guise of piety. Jesus saw it clearly. The self-serving and manipulative bondage under law, into which his people had been seduced, was a slavery to "sin" from which only "the son" and their own sonship could liberate them. Jn 8:34-36 Parable upon parable illustrates the trap.

Lost Sheep. Lk 15:1-7 "Now the tax collectors and sinners were all drawing near to hear him. And the Pharisees and the scribes murmured, saying, 'This man receives sinners and eats with them.'" In their view Jesus was not upholding their discipline, but undermining it. "Sinners" were people whom the synagogue had properly cut off for their deliberate and open defiance of God's law. This parable sets before them "life and good" in contrast to "death and evil." The God of Israel does not view "sinners" of his flock as outsiders to be cut off, but as sheep still his own, who have gone astray and are in trouble. To seek them out is to manifest the LORD's shepherding. Jer 23:4; Ezek 34:11-16 By a love and longing like God's own, Jesus will leave the ninety-nine righteous so as to find one who is lost. There is joy in heaven over one sinner who returns home to the honor and freedom of sonship, more than over ninety-nine righteous who need no repentance, but stand apart as judges and accusers. The leaders are called to be shepherds themselves. How can they presume themselves "righteous" if they resist the very shepherding they should be doing? To choose "life and good" will be to rejoice in Jesus' kingdom of gathering and get in on it themselves.

Wayward Sons. Lk 15:11-32 Each of the two sons in this parable illustrates the conflict. The younger son is the "sinner." He did not value the honor and freedom of his Father's house. Concerned not for thanksgiving but rights, not belonging but independence, he asked one day for everything he regarded as his possessions and headed for the far country. It was a "death and evil" fantasy. To be on his own in the world outside would be far more free and blessed for him than the irritating servanthood of home. The father gave him what he asked and let him go. To hold him forcibly would deny him the ultimate freedom inherent in his sonship.

What had seemed so much was soon spent, however. The alienated son ended up hungry and alone, nobody caring about him, eating with pigs. One day, he came to his senses. "How many of my father's hired servants have bread enough and to spare, but I perish here with hunger!" Though he had forfeited his right to sonship, his father might at least give him a job. Then came the great wonder. He was still the son, still beloved! His father was watching for him! He rejoiced to see him coming home, not by force but of his own will! Without a thought of law and rights or the hurt this thankless renegade had done him, the father ran to meet his son, embraced and kissed him, cleansed him, put the family ring and robe and shoes on him, prepared a great banquet, invited friends and neighbors to help celebrate his return. "This my son was dead and is alive again, he was lost and is found!" The resurrection-*now* imagery is powerful here! That was the mind of the father and the joy of his heart, everything else forgotten.

As it turned out, the older son did not know thanksgiving or the wonder of belonging any more than the younger. He came in from the field, heard the celebration, discovered it was for his brother, but would have no part in it. What mattered was his presumed rights. His father saw the alienation of his elder son, but did not give up on him. He even came out to invite him in. But the elder was angry and refused to go. "Not fair!" he cried. He had stayed home and worked, faithful and obedient, yet never once had his father appreciated his labors by putting on a party like this for him and his friends! "But when *this son of yours* (not brother of mine!) came, who has devoured your living with harlots, you killed for him the fatted calf!" he raged. "Son, you are always with me, and everything I have is yours!" his father pleaded. What more can I give you than myself and all I have? Get in on the joy! "It was fitting to make merry and be glad, for this *your brother* was dead and is alive again, he was lost and is found."

Thus Jesus set before his critics "life and good" over against the "death and evil" in which they were so deeply snared. Parables offer the choice but do not report the outcome. Did the renegade finally know the wonder of his Father, the honor of belonging, and the freedom of serving? Did the righteous scribe or Pharisee come to realize this same wonder, let go his indignation, and share the joy of having his brother home? The answer lies in each hearer.

The Laborers. Mt 20:1-16; Is 5:1-2 To serve God in his vineyard, the place he prepared for his people Israel, is not only a high privilege but their very life. Jesus' parable pictures the testing his people faced. "Death and evil" is justice based on superior status and comparative rights. "Life and good" is a God without partiality, who by pure mercy and gift gathers into oneness.

The metaphor draws on the history. Those who came into the vineyard at early morning, trusting the householder's promise of a "denarius," a full day's wage, were the Judeans. Descendants of Abraham, then called out of Egypt, they were the "good figs" of the exile and the return. They had avoided marriages with foreigners, obeyed the law, even suffered much for it. Truly, they had "borne the burden of the day and the scorching heat."

At the third hour, the householder saw others standing idle in the market place. They did not know what to do or what their lives were for. "You go into the vineyard, too," he said, promising to pay them "whatever is right." Glad and honored to be wanted, they went to work. At the sixth hour and the ninth, he found still others and gathered them into his vineyard, too, this time without a word about wages. At the eleventh hour, when the day was almost over, he found still another group. "Why do you stand here idle all day?" he asked them. "Because no one has hired us," they replied. His mercy honored them as well with a place and purposeful work.

A history is remembered here. In 140 B.C. Aristobulus, the Hasmonean ruler of Judea, made war against the Itureans north of the Sea of Galilee, conquered the great part of their territory, including the water-sources of the Sea and of the Jordan, converted the inhabitants by compelling the males to be circumcised. Thus he purified the land and made it safe for colonization by Judeans. Circumcision of males was the long-prescribed mode of adding foreigners to God's people. Ex 12:43-49 In 126 B.C. John Hyrcanus conquered Idumea, to the south of Judea, ancient territory of the Edomites including Hebron, and converted that population similarly. The Herods were Idumean by race. Around 80 B.C. lower Galilee, including the fertile valley of Jezreel (till then a part of Samaria), was similarly conquered and added to Judea.

What should be the status of these latecomer foreigners? Jesus' parable does not view them as conquered, but as invited by God himself to go into his vineyard and work there, thus fully of his people. "Why do you stand here all the day idle?" For one reason only, "Because no one has hired us." When the covenant-invitation honored them with a holy place and calling, however, they accepted willingly and eagerly. Jesus and the young church are among those latecomers. The voice from heaven that named Israel out of Egypt "my son, my first-born" and called them to "serve me" named *them* "my beloved son" too, and called them to his service no less than the first. Every blessing of the Judeans is theirs in full without discrimination.

"The end of the day" reveals this. "Give them their wages, starting with the last," the householder commands his steward. He does so. The eleventh-hour workers receive a full denarius. So do the others. How can it be otherwise? To belong is to belong. To have the promises is to have the promises. To be in on God's holy work is to be in on God's holy work. "Life and good" for the Judeans is to acknowledge this freely and with joy. God intends a full denarius for Galileans, too. He does not divide his kingdom into twelfths for some or multiply it twelve times for others.

"Death and evil" have befallen those who claim to be the original Israel, pure of blood, in on the covenant from the beginning. Thinking themselves superior, they expect the LORD to be partial to them. The kingdom for which they have worked all day should at the least grant them special recognition, extra credit. But they receive only their promised denarius. The parable expresses their indignation. "These last have worked only one hour, and you have made them equal to us who have borne the burden of the day and the scorching heat." Unwittingly, their hearts have turned the Father of pure grace into a God who plays favorites, a "merchant-God" with whom they can plead "rights" and negotiate a better deal. They are not happy and free son-servants of their Father, but bitter and complaining.

The householder does not apologize or change his character to suit them. "Friend, I am doing you no wrong. Did you not agree with me for a denarius? Take what is yours and go. I choose to give to this last even as I give to you. Do I not have the right to do what I wish with my possession, my vineyard? Is your eye evil, because I am good?" "So the last shall be first and the first last," Jesus concludes. Are the complainers willing to have it so? Let them choose "life and good." God will not bow to their "death and evil." Each hearer will personalize the ending.

The Devious Steward. Lk 16:1-9 A rich man (God) entrusts the management of his affairs to a steward—priests of the temple and scribal leaders of synagogues. Accusations are brought that the steward is not fulfilling his office, but misusing it. God, by his prophets, calls the steward to account. Perceiving his status and authority to be threatened, the devious heart of the steward summons his mind to devise a strategy. His concern is not to serve God but to maintain his superior status, hence honest responses are not viable. He cannot return on menial but honest labor like "digging," neither can he become as small as a "beggar" and throw himself on God's mercy. His strategy is to get people to like him, respect him, depend on him. Those who approve him will support him and take him in. In that case what God thinks or does will not matter.

His device is to discount their obligation. To "love the LORD your God" totally, "with *all* your heart and with *all* your soul and with *all* your might," and "your neighbor *as yourself*," is not really expected. Fifty percent will do in one case, eighty percent in another. The bill will be paid by observing external laws like the sabbath, cleannesses, worship, tithing and discipline.

It is a revealing imagery. The people are not being taught "life and good," that is, to know and love God as their Father and to belong confidently to him as he belongs to them. They are not being taught to regard God's house their own and live in it as his beloved children, thus to enjoy working with their Father honorably and freely in everything they do. They are being taught instead to think of God as a landlord and themselves as tenants. God is a businessman who bills them for his services. They have a right to live in his house, as long as they pay the rent.

The parable climaxes in what can only be sarcasm. "The master of the house commended the unrighteous steward for slithering so cleverly to achieve his purpose. For the sons of this world-order are far more clever in dealing with God and one another than the trustingly obedient sons of light (the young church)." Knowing what a miracle of the spirit it would take for the authorities of God's people to listen, give up their control and become sons of light, Jesus urges them on in their hopeless illusion. "But I say to you, Go ahead, trust your deviousness. Make friends for yourselves by perverting the gifts and calling God has entrusted to you. Then, when your time runs out, count on friends you have won by such briberies to receive you into the eternal homes you still claim as your right!" Will those bought-friends be there? Will they care? They are not in charge of God's "eternal homes." God alone is in charge.

The judgment is not future but *now*. Those "friends" will not decide it, neither will God. Each hearer will decide it for himself. "Therefore choose *life*," Moses said and Jesus with him, "that you and your descendants may *live*, loving the LORD your God, obeying his voice, and cleaving to him." Dt 30:19-20

The Diverse Talents. Mt 25:14-30; Lk 19:11-27 A man entrusts his property to his servants, then goes away. This is the Giver-Creator-God or "Father," from whom his people have their life, calling, and whatever comes into their hand. That he "goes away," leaves them on their own without prodding, supervision or specific directions, expresses his trust in their freedom.

The problem that arises is not caused by the inequities of common human experience. The version in Luke has the nobleman give ten "pounds" (Greek *mna*), one to each of ten servants. With respect to the grace and trust of God they are equal. Inequity appears at the outcome. One servant's pound has gained ten more, another's five more. In Matthew the inequity occurs at the beginning. "To one he gave five talents (Greek *talanta*), to another two, to another one, each according to his ability." The servants are not unequal in worth. The master is not ranking them or playing favorites. What appears unequal accords with visible reality, the special place and opportunity of each. The grace of God is not bound to human notions of justice and rights.

What matters is not equality but the attitude of each servant toward himself, master, and world. The "good and faithful" respond by investing their imagination and energies, abilities and resources, in opportunities of creativity and love they see before them. To belong to and build on the world they have from God is their very life. Hearts of honor and thanksgiving and trust impel their work. They do not try to create worlds of their own around themselves.

It proves exciting. Two servants, though their gifts differ, discover on their own how they have profited and their master with them. They delight to show how their talents have doubled by their labors! The master celebrates the wonder. "Well done, good and faithful servant! You have been faithful in a little; I will set you over much! Enter the joy of your Lord!"

A third servant illustrates the choice of "death and evil" over "life and good." He is no less capable than the others of multiplying his talent by eager work and of experiencing the joy. But a perversity impels him to bury God's gift and calling in the ground unused, then turn his mind and resources toward creating a life and world of his own. Suspicious and resentful, he accuses God as "a hard master" who exploits him unjustly to profit himself. The outcome is bitterness and division. "Cast the worthless servant into outer darkness (where there is no light of truth); there men will weep (in self-pity) and gnash their teeth (in rage against the injustice)."

Why might the one-talent servant have been chosen as the model for resentment and anger against God? Perhaps the temptation to feel worthless and to undervalue one's "self" is most powerful among ordinary folk. Those who succumb do not invest themselves as servants of God in the place and calling he has given them. They do not experience the surprise of achievement beyond expectation. They do not enter the joy of their Lord. Instead they denigrate their work, grumble against human masters who seem to profit from their sweat, feel they are being exploited. In truth they are turning in resentment against the tyranny of the God who put them there.

Who will fill the gap they leave in God's kingdom and theirs? "Take the talent from him and give it to him who has ten. For to everyone who has (the covenant-sonship) will more be given, but from him who does not have it, even what he has will be taken from him."

The Samaritan. Lk 10:25-37 The priestly authorities of Judea labeled Jesus a "Samaritan." Jn 8:48 The Galilee from which he came was originally of Samaria. They knew also that he did not separate himself from Samaritans, that he had even come to Judea through Samaria. Lk 9:52 Jesus stood firm. His Father had named him "my beloved son" without regard to his supposedly inferior descent. Rather than object to their slur, he made a point of it.

A lawyer asked, "Teacher, what shall I do to inherit *eternal* life?" The obverse of "eternal" would be a bodily life of racial purity. At Jesus' prompting, he cited the summary he had learned from Jesus and the scriptures: "You shall love the Lord your God with all your heart," and "You shall love your neighbor as yourself." "Do this, and you will *live*," Jesus replied.

"But who is my neighbor?" the lawyer asked. That question is the issue of this parable. Its setting, "Jerusalem to Jericho," as well as the inclusion of priest and Levite, suggests that it derived from Jesus' ministry in Judea. The priest who came by on that road, and then the Levite, diagnosed the man lying there as a "sinner," unclean, rightly excluded for violating or neglecting their law. Sinners had chosen their lot. So they passed him by. Compromising their discipline would make them partners in his sin and uncleanness.

The "Samaritan," however, looked beyond his evident guilt and shame to the "enemy" who had done this to him. Robbers had stripped him and beaten him, then departed leaving him half-dead. For all his sin, he still had a God-given "self" like Jesus' own "self," a heart like Jesus' own heart. Robbers had taken away his "robe of righteousness," his honored name and heritage in God's people. Is 61:10 Indeed, they had stripped the whole nation of the covenant-name Johwah—"a God merciful and gracious, slow to anger and of great mercy, keeping steadfast love for thousands, forgiving iniquity and transgression and sin." It was a frightful wounding. To silence God's holy name is to be robbed of its meaning, to be left wounded and half-dead. How can one so wounded do what God asks—"love Johwah your God with all your heart and with all your soul and with all your strength and with all your mind"? How can a people who do not know the enemy know their own "self," to say nothing of the "self" of a neighbor? The Judean religion of rightness under law was itself "half-dead," on the way to dying totally.

The "Samaritan" understood all this and had compassion. He stopped, diagnosed the injuries, bound up his wounds, poured on the oil and wine of his gospel, lifted him up on his own beast, brought him to the inn, took care of him. The next day, from his own wealth as God's beloved son, he contracted with the innkeeper for further care toward the man's full restoration, promising to pay whatever was necessary on his return. The imagery depicts Jesus' compassion for his wounded people, his longing to deliver them from their real enemy—entrusting further care to the young church after him. By him the covenant of "eternal life" triumphed over a self-conscious legal system.

"Who is my neighbor?" the lawyer had asked. Jesus inverted his question: "Who acted as neighbor to the man who fell among robbers?" "The one who showed mercy on him," he replied. "Go and do likewise," Jesus said. "Life and good" or "death and evil"—that was the choice. Which would priest and Levite choose? What of the lawyer? If he did indeed "go and do likewise," the cost could be great. Eternal "life and good" as the Samaritan Jesus understood and lived it would require him to give up as "death and evil" what scribe and Pharisee, priest and Levite, understood and enforced. The consequences could be severe.

The Rich Man and Lazarus. Lk 16:19-31 By this parable the young church of Judea (the poor man Lazarus) appealed to the authorities of temple and synagogue (the rich man at whose gate the young church sat) to know God's mercy while there is still time.

Both are descended from Abraham. There ought be no chasm between them. But there is. The priesthood, vested in purple and fine linen, feasts sumptuously every day on the tithes of the people and the prime cuts of their sacrifices. Its wealth includes also the library of "Moses and the prophets." As for Lazarus, he lives on crumbs from his brother's table, but experiences also judgment and rejection. What comfort and support he gets comes from "dogs" (as the crumb-seeking Canaanite woman willingly called herself)—thus from Gentiles and the mixed-race hangers-on of the time, who welcomed the gospel that gathered them also. "The dogs came and licked his sores." Mt 15:26-27 Nevertheless, Lazarus stays where he is. He can no more give up on his rich but deluded brother than Jesus could. He sits where his brother must see and hear him every time he goes out or comes in.

The brothers have something else in common: death. Death fixes eternally what has been true and real all along. "Lazarus was carried by angels to Abraham's *bosom*." *Bosom* signals heart. Moses' hand in his *bosom* lay over his heart. Ex 4:6 John's testimony to Jesus as "the only son *in the bosom of the Father*" celebrates his return to the heart of the Father who sent him. Jn 1:18 The rich man relies by contrast on his genealogical descent from Abraham's *sexual potency*. To this Abraham there is no return. As Jesus told the Sadducees, if "*the God of* Abraham, *the God of* Isaac, *the God of* Jacob" is not known, biological life counts for nothing. Lk 20:37-38

When the rich man dies and is buried, he does not return to Abraham but goes down to Hades (Hebrew *she-ol),* as low as heaven is high. "You are brought down to Sheol, to the depths of the Pit," Isaiah has it, a language the priesthood should know. Is 14:15 "I am tormented in this flame," he cries out. Hot shame and guilt utterly crush his former pride. The "chasm" fixed between him and Lazarus now had not existed before. He could have acknowledged the young church at any time, heard its truth of mercy and gift rather than law and performance, sat beside its brother, asked questions, even brought him into his house! Rivers of mercy were available then; but now, not a finger's drop to cool his tongue. Abraham with Lazarus in his bosom is far off. "Son, remember that you in your lifetime had your good things and Lazarus evil things. But now he is comforted and you are tormented."

The parable is meant for the five brothers whose lifetime is not yet over. They total six, signifying labor without rest. Lazarus, the young church, is their "seventh" of "rest," if they will only hear. "They have Moses and the prophets, let them *hear* them," Abraham says. They *have* the sacred writings complete and in sufficient copies, the finest and most durable of scrolls. "*Let them hear them!*" What of Moses and the prophets should they hear? Let them hear the name Johwah, "a God merciful and gracious," but not a God of partiality and rights. Ex 34:6-7; Dt 10:17 Let them hear the LORD say still, "Israel is my first-born son; let my son go that he may serve me." Ex 4:22 Let them hear Moses say, "Man shall not live by bread alone," or "See, I have set before you life and good, death and evil ... blessing and curse. Therefore choose life, that you and your descendants may live, loving the LORD your God and cleaving to him." Dt 8:3; 30:15-20 Let them hear people not of Abraham pray in hope to Abraham's God: "For you are our Father, though Abraham does not know us and Israel does not acknowledge us, you, O LORD, are our Father, our Redeemer from of old is your name." Is 63:16 That is what Jesus preached and lived, and the young church (Lazarus) after him.

But the rich man, even in Hades, cannot surrender control. "No, father Abraham, but if someone goes to them from the dead, they will repent!" he argues. Priestly authorities have set conditions for the young church. "You say he rose from the dead? Prove it! Let your gloriously risen Jesus display himself to us, too! Then we will believe!" They had mocked Jesus so at the cross: "Let him come down, then we will believe in him!" Mt 27:42 Empty of the life of God, they insist on a life and resurrection purely physiological. Their argument is not with Lazarus or even Jesus, however, but with Abraham, Moses and the prophets, even God. "If they do not hear Moses and the prophets, neither will they be convinced if someone should rise from the dead."

Which of the apostles compressed so much understanding into so striking a form cannot be known. His word forces nothing. It still speaks, however, and with power.

"Watch!"

"Watch, therefore, for you do not know (neither is it your business to know) on what day your Lord is coming.... Who then is that faithful and wise servant, whom his master has set over his household, to give them their food at the proper time? Blessed is that servant whom his master when he comes will find so doing. Truly, I say to you, he will set him over all his possessions." Mt 24:42-47

In the language of parable, "When he comes" fixes what is real. At that point, repentance or change will no longer be possible. "Watch!" does not mean, "Speculate about the day and hour when a future kingdom breaks in!" It does not mean, "Be ready to fight and die when the signal is given for the end-time warfare" (as zealotry thought). Neither does it mean, "Watch out, lest you be caught not working or doing something wrong." It means, "Pay attention to what you are doing *now!*" "Watch and pray that you may not enter into temptation," warns against being distracted from doing your Father's business *now*. Mt 26:41 The time and place God grants each of his son-servants is "his kingdom at hand" here and now. It is not his kingdom only but theirs too, the only kingdom they have. How it will come out is not their worry, but the Father's. Promises like "It shall go well with you!" are enough. Dt 5:33

The Divided Bride. Mt 25:1-13 "Ten" in this parable represents the whole of God's people. They wait for the groom and the joy of their wedding day, yet are also weary of waiting. Though alike in dress and lamps (outward forms of worship), they are significantly different. The five wise (the young church) have flasks of oil, a fullness of meaning, content to keep their lamps aflame, however long the night. By that light they will know the bridegroom when he comes and he them. The five foolish (of law and tradition) have the outward forms right but pay no attention to the oil, what the word and promise and call of God to them really means. Their lamps are empty. Lacking oil, they cannot give light. In this critical time, when the kingdom they have wanted is truly here, they have no flame to see what is really happening.

This division was real. In the era of the young church, the "ten" were still together in the worship of synagogue and temple. Yet only "five" had light to know the bridegroom, Jesus, when he came unexpectedly in the dark of night, by which he would also know them. The "five" recognized him and welcomed him in the full joy of the kingdom and their life together as one.

But the five foolish, empty of the light and power of their own religion, have missed out. They may want the bridegroom still, may even pound on the door saying, "Lord, Lord, open to us," but their tradition and outward claims are not sufficient to identify them as God's own. "I do not know you," their Lord, the groom says. They don't know him either, for the kingdom Jesus proclaimed is not what they expected and wanted. What is their hope? Oil for their lamps! Where can they get it? Where the five wise got theirs, "from those who sell"—the original source, Moses and the prophets—and Jesus who has revealed what the oil truly is, which alone can fill their emptiness.

"Watch, therefore, *for you know neither the day nor the hour.*" That accent recalls the carefully engineered escort of Jesus into Jerusalem, which in the mind of zealotic expectation ought to have been "the day and the hour" for Jesus to declare himself and God to act. But they did not know, neither was it their business to know. This is an ongoing theme. What matters in the kingdom of heaven is what you are doing *now*, the kind of servant you are *now*.

Outward forms are precious by their inner content. Seek and renew the oil always, keep the lamps burning, do the work of the day, leave the tomorrow to God. "Blessed are those servants whom the master finds awake when he comes...; he will come and serve them." Lk 12:35-40

Judgment. Mt 25:31-46 The intent of this parable is not to encourage speculations about a futurist judgment on the other side of death, but to dramatize "life and good" in distinction from "death and evil" even now, while a choice is still possible.

The authorities of synagogue and temple would not acknowledge Jesus as "the son of man" (meaning "the son of God")—not even when the Father had raised him from the dead and exalted him to his right hand as "Christ" and "King." Ps 110:1 Far from feeding hearts hungry and thirsty for righteousness, far from welcoming strangers or caring about the naked or sick or imprisoned, the rulers were excluding and persecuting the very brothers whom Jesus had loved and gathered and honored as "blessed of my Father." Yet those so blessed could not give up on the rulers who did this to them. They might look outwardly to be rich and powerful, in control and on top, but in reality these very rulers were "the least" among Jesus' brothers—hungry and thirsty of heart, strangers, naked, sick and in prison.

This parable extends the great "either-or" to all nations, sorted out like "sheep" and "goats," no in-between possible. To those on his right hand the king says, "Come, O blessed of my Father, inherit the kingdom prepared for you from the foundation of the world." The "blessed" receive, enjoy, and live by this inheritance even now. Without self-conscious concern for verdicts or rewards or rankings or costs or troubles, without evading risk and burden, they trust their God to make things good according to his promises and to deliver them from evil. The "judgment" expresses and seals as authentic a life that to them is simply natural. "Truly I say to you, as you did it to one of the least of these my brothers, you did it to me!" The love they received from Jesus and his Father and passed onward to "one of the least" is not measured by isolated incidents. It is the character of the whole stream.

Specific images illustrate the distress of a natural humanity alienated from God, and the young church as his instrument of gathering and restoration. "I was hungry and you gave me food, thirsty and you gave me drink," has to do with proclaiming God's covenant-sonship and honor to hearts hungry and thirsty for righteousness. "Naked, and you clothed me," delivers people from a shame like that of Eden and the dishonest futility of fig-leaf pretenses, covering them instead with "the garments of salvation" and "the robe of

righteousness." Is 61:10 "I was a stranger and you took me in" refers in metaphor to breaking down barriers of exclusion and gathering sinners and the
nations into God's people. "I was sick and *you visited me*, in prison and *you
came to me*" diagnoses the young church as not repelled by offensive and self-
destructive behaviors, but taking the initiative of love to heal and liberate
those so afflicted. "*He has sent me*," Isaiah said, "to bind up the brokenhearted,
to proclaim liberty to the captives and the opening of the prison to those who
are bound." Is 61:1

Such is the covenant-character of a people who, for themselves and others, "seek *first* the kingdom of God and his righteousness," trusting the promise of their "king" that "all these things will be yours as well." External bodily
needs implied in such an array of metaphor will be satisfied, too, and in full.
"When did we see you?" they ask in wonder, and the king answers, "Truly I
say to you, as you did it to one of the least of these my brothers, you did it to
me." They "see" by a heart-vision of which natural eyesight is not capable.
Beneath any person of any diversity, from greatest to least, they see a God-
given "self" like their own "self," whom they, following Jesus their king, are
not ashamed or fearful to call "my brother." Such is the kingdom inherited by
"the blessed," prepared for them by the Father from the foundation of the
world.

The possibility of choosing "death and evil" remains, however, and the
"son-of-man" king will not negate it. Lies and pretense are transparent to him.
"Depart from me, you cursed, into the eternal fire prepared for the devil and
his angels," he says to those on his left hand. When temple and synagogue
reject his kingdom, they become like any nation. For all their show of right,
they are choosing a destiny of hotly blushing "shame and contempt."
Dan 12:2. Thinking to be "like God," they devise their own kingdom, feed
their own hunger, pursue their own way. They display thanksgiving and trust
outwardly, but at heart they are concerned only to attain what looks "good" to
their opened-eyes and to protect themselves from what looks "evil." "Love" is
a strategy—to be put on when it offers advantage or when to "not love" might
invite criticism.

The real problem is emptiness. When the word of God is not heard or is
falsified, hungers of heart are not fed. Indeed, they are not even known. Self-
conscious impression-making may seem to compensate, but the king is not
deceived. "As you did it not to one of the least of these my brothers, you did it
not to me," he declares.

Telling this parable is itself an initiative of the young church to "visit" the very sick and imprisoned "brothers" who have cut them off. Let those who trust their delusion of control give it up. There is still time to join the "blessed of my Father" who "inherit the kingdom prepared for them from the foundation of the world." In that kingdom everything they are and have is pure "gift." The righteous live their eternal *now* in noble oneness with the Father and his son and one another—thanking, loving, trusting, and serving him in simple freedom, and no one else.

Tenants and the Heir. Mt 21:33-46; Mk 12:1-12; Lk 20:9-19 All three synoptic Gospels preserve what may be the last parable Jesus taught in the temple. The judgment of the priesthood and council against him was impending, yet the final verdict would be God's, not theirs. Jesus pictures the vineyard, Israel, in which God has invested much love and care. Is 5:1-7 The tenants, called to nurture and care for his vineyard-people, are the priestly authorities. They have departed from his flow of grace, however, and substituted a hierarchy of law under their control, as though the vineyard were their own.

The tragedy keeps repeating itself. When God sent his servants, the prophets, to receive his harvest, his priests or kings summoned their institutionalized authority to silence them as intruders—beating one, killing another, stoning a third. When God sent still other servants, they treated these the same way. Now God has sent his "beloved son." "Surely they will respect my son," he thinks. Surely they will see in the son what the Father is like, what their own true honor is from him, what God is really asking of them! But these tenants see Jesus as the last barrier to their own kingdom and glory. "Let us kill him, and the inheritance will be ours."

The God of grace will not forcibly stop them, neither will his son. But they will not win. Their verdict against Jesus will not stand. God will rescue his people. Priesthood and temple will come to a miserable end. The vineyard will be given to others. New tenants (like the young church) know God and serve him freely, delight in giving him his fruits. A psalm which pilgrims sang will be filled full: "The stone which the builders rejected has become the head of the corner. This is the LORD's doing, and it is marvelous in our eyes." Ps 118:22-23

A memory indicates that the authorities of the council, Pharisees and chief priests, understood very well that Jesus was speaking about them. They did not "repent," however, or let go their falsified authority, or return to the stream of righteousness. Unable to hear the message or refute it, their last defense and weaponry was to silence the messenger.

No parable is mere morality tale. Every parable opens a depth-perspective window into the heart-conflict that gave rise to it. Every parable summons a choice. Isaiah pointed out the irony, and Jesus knew it well, that the more clearly a thing is said, the more determined hearts will be to not understand it. "To you has been given the secret of the kingdom of God, but for those outside everything is in parables, so that they may indeed see but not perceive, and may indeed hear but not understand; lest they should turn again and be forgiven." Is 6:9-10; Mk 4:11-12; Jn 12:40

CHAPTER FIFTEEN

Jesus Stories

"And those in the boat worshiped him, saying, 'Truly you are the son of God.'"   Matthew 14:33

The "Jesus stories" are of the young church. The disciples, resurrected with him out of the zealotic illusion now dead, perceived what natural sight can never see—the kingdom of God as it actually was and how it had come. Jesus had done miracles in a depth they could never have dreamed. They heralded this in metaphor-stories, many of which are preserved in our Gospels. Whether of mountain or lake or healing or mission, each opens a further window into the young church regarding its Lord. The necessary question is always "What does this mean?" and "Why is it said the way it is said?" The covenant-gospel is the gate to understanding. That revelation, invisible to the natural eye, is the true glory of Israel, of Jesus, and of all the scriptures.

Mountain Stories

The Mountain of All Nations. Mt 4:8; 28:16-20 A mountain in metaphor is a height from which to see great distances, as when the LORD took Moses up to Mount Nebo (or Pisgah) in Moab and showed him the land which Israel was about to enter and possess. Dt 34:1 Jesus' temptation on "a very high mountain" stretched his vision far beyond what any literal mountain-view could offer. The devil showed him "all the kingdoms of the world and the glory of them," so as to offer him these by zealotic conquest. "All nations" were in view from a mountain in Galilee after the resurrection, ripe for conquest this time by the weaponry of Jesus' kingdom. "Go and make disciples of all nations," he commissioned his disciples, "baptizing them in the name of the Father and of the son and of the holy spirit."

That three-fold name capsules "righteousness like an everflowing stream," as Amos called it—gifts given and received, received and given onward, to be received by others downstream. Amos 5:24 The stream originates in "the name of the Father," who named Israel "my first-born son" and himself "Johwah, a God merciful and gracious." Ex 4:22; 34:6 Jesus, the Father's receiving and then giving "son," filled his name and the Father's full even into and through death. The stream flowed on by his resurrection and Spirit, drawing into itself the once errant disciples and so forming the young church. "Go, therefore," Jesus commanded them, thus sending the stream onward to gather "all nations."

God's holy name will not limit the flowing stream to a people of blood-descent from Abraham or to the authority of their priesthood. "All authority is given to me in heaven and on earth," Jesus said. His authority inhered in the stream of righteousness to which he belonged. "Teach them to observe whatever I have commanded you." Unlike laws designed to mark Judeans visibly as a "chosen race" above others, Jesus' command consisted in the simple wisdom on which "all the law and the prophets" depend—to "love the LORD your God with all your heart, and with all your soul, and with all your might," and "your neighbor as yourself." Mt 22:37-40

Furthermore, the place of God's special presence and name is no longer the visible holy city Jerusalem and its temple mountain. Dt 12:5 "Lo, I am with you always, to the close of the age." "Where two or three are gathered in my name, there am I in the midst of them." Mt 18:20 The Lord Jesus is "in the midst of them" wherever among the nations his gathered people hear his word, receive his gifts, know and depend freely on him, and live his righteousness as their own.

The Transfiguration. Mt 17:1-9; Mk 9:2-10; Lk 9:28-36 The mountain-metaphor in this instance depicts a revelation from heaven, as when Moses, and later Elijah, talked to God on Sinai (or Horeb). Ex 19:20; 24:9-18; 1 Kgs 19:8-18 The history that produced it is Jesus' resurrection.

Its pristine form is preserved in 2 Peter, not in the Gospels. 2 Pet 1:16-18 I cited this in my first chapter. Peter's structure of the word from heaven in Greek, literally translated "My son, my beloved, this is," matches the Hebrew of Moses' word to Pharaoh, "My son, my first-born, Israel (is)." Ex 4:22 Clearly, the name "my son" for Jesus at his baptism, transfiguration, and throughout, is covenant-language. Christianity's early and controlling assumption that "son of God" for Jesus means deity was tragic. It took Jesus' own gospel out of circulation and substituted a counterfeit.

Peter spoke the young church's continuing and urgent witness to those who still defended the Judean tradition. "We did not follow cleverly devised myths when we made known to you the power and coming of our Lord Jesus Christ, but we were eyewitnesses of his majesty. For when he received honor and glory from God the Father and the voice was borne to him by the Majestic Glory, 'My son, my beloved, this is, with whom I am well pleased,' we heard this voice borne from heaven, for we were with him on the holy mountain." Peter and the others had not invented this revelation. They had only heard it, received it, believed it.

The "power and coming" was of Jesus in his resurrection, as was the confessional name "our Lord Jesus Christ." From Caiaphas and the council he had received shame and mockery and a death verdict for blasphemy, but from "the majestic glory" of "God the Father, he received honor and glory." Jesus was with them on the holy mountain, but did not need to affirm his sonship again. The Father, whom he served to the end and whose verdict alone counted, did it for him.

The argument was over. The end-verdict affirmed the sonship which the Father had declared to Jesus at the beginning. Between beginning and ending lay everything Jesus had believed and taught and done as the beloved son-servant of his Father in heaven. By this covenant-name, he had chosen "life and good" even when faced with the "evil" of crucifixion. The authorities who thought to save themselves by condemning him had chosen "death and evil." Yet it was not too late. If they doubt the oral witness of Peter and the young church, they have "as a more sure witness the prophetic word" of their own covenant-sonship preserved in *their* scriptures. They do well to pay attention to it as to a lamp shining in a dark place. The day may still dawn and the morning star arise in their hearts. 2 Pet 1:19

The versions preserved in Matthew, Mark, and Luke testify similarly. Time-frames indicate the resurrection. Matthew and Mark have "after six days." The six of labor are over and the seventh of rest has come. Luke has "eight days after." Jesus' resurrection day was this "eighth," the day after the seventh or sabbath. Details are added of Jesus' shining glory, the cloud, the disciples' fear, the call "Listen to him," and the aftermath. These versions were written down out of testimonies once oral. Compilers of the Gospels translated them accurately, but located them on their scrolls in Jesus' pre-death ministry.

Moses and Elijah are a meaningful addition to the original. Moses stands for those who kept invoking Moses against Jesus. Elijah represents the disciples and constituents of John the Baptist. Mt 11:14; Jn 1:21; Mal 4:5 Tensions arose in the early post-resurrection era, for the idea did not make ready sense that Jesus' death was more than just another tragic injustice, as when John was beheaded. With trouble on both sides, Peter's proposal was tempting. "Lord, it is good that we are here. If you wish, I will make three tents, for you one, for Moses one, and for Elijah one." Let the Moses-people have their tent, the Elijah-people theirs, we ours!

(Copyists, not grasping what Peter meant, attributed their ignorance to him. Thus, Luke has the entry "not knowing what he said," and Mark "he did not know what to say." That Moses and Elijah talked with Jesus about his coming death is likewise a copyist's speculation.)

The voice-verdict from heaven was decisive. The God of Moses, of Elijah, and of Jesus, cannot be divided. The command, "Listen to him!" affirmed Jesus as a prophet of God by the very text which the Moses-people had cited to disqualify him. A Galilean was not their brother, they argued, but God declared of his prophet, "him you shall heed." Dt 18:15-19; Jn 7:52 Let John's disciples "listen to him," too! The straight and level way of the LORD is one, not three. The God of Israel has one beloved and chosen people, not three. Peace by schism is no peace at all.

Peter's original witness ended appropriately with the declaration from heaven. The addition in Matthew of the disciples' falling on their faces in fear and "Jesus' bidding them rise," is a copyist's enhancement. Coming down from the mountain is a transition entered by compilers who, not recognizing the metaphor, took the mountain as literal geography.

A puzzle remains. Where did the idea come from that the disciples not tell the vision until after Jesus' resurrection? Perhaps some in the church came to realize that it actually *did* testify to his resurrection! Copyists signaled this then as best they could.

Storm Stories

Certain lake stories are metaphor, too—a great catch of fish, a storm quieted by a word, Jesus walking on the sea. When the disciples said to him, "Truly, you are the son of God," they were confessing his covenant-sonship. Mt 14:33 Readers in the Greek world assumed that this confession of him meant deity, however. They took metaphor to be literal-visible reality. How could Jesus do such wonders? He was God! Why did he do them? To demonstrate himself so. When Jesus' covenant-sonship became unknown, his covenant-gospel was lost with it.

Jesus' gospel as the principle of coherency opens much that can only be metaphor. Zealotic piety remembered how the Syrian tyrant, Antiochus Epiphanes, had wanted to force God's people to give up the "law" that set them apart, but had been defeated in the Maccabean wars. A subsequent taunt pictures him as "thinking in his arrogance that he could sail on the land and *walk on the sea*, because his mind was elated." Another taunt has him "thinking that he could *command the waves of the sea*." 2 Macc 5:21; 9:8 Sea-stories of Jesus drew on these imageries. What was taunt against Antiochus became real in him. In meek obedience, as the son and servant of God his Father, he actually did it!

The language of a psalm was also familiar. "Some went down to the sea in ships, doing business on the great waters; they saw the deeds of the LORD, his wondrous works in the deep. For he commanded and raised the stormy wind, which lifted up the waves of the sea. They mounted up to heaven, they went down to the depths; their courage melted away in their evil plight; they reeled and staggered like drunken men, and were at their wits' end. Then they cried to the LORD in their distress; *he made the storm be still, and the waves of the sea were hushed*. Then they were glad because they had quiet, and he brought them to their desired haven." Ps 107:23-30 The thought of waking God up from sleep was also known: "Rouse yourself, why are you asleep, O LORD?... Rise up, come to our help!" Ps 44:23,26 Actual experiences of storms on the Sea of Galilee might contribute also. The metaphor dramatizes the *inside* of the external event—the fear and guilt and helpless futility of the disciples at Jesus' dying—the miracle Jesus worked *for them* in his passion and the unexpected deliverance of his resurrection coming.

Walking on the Sea. Mt 14:22-27; Mk 6:45-52; Jn 6:16-21 Jesus' ministry is pictured as over. Having dismissed the crowds, he was praying alone. He sent his disciples off to make this crossing on their own. When arrested he said, "Let these men go." Jn 18:8 The metaphor portrays night. They are in darkness. Contrary winds frustrate their hard and determined rowing. No God or kingdom of God is in sight. Nothing is going as they planned. Their ambitious self-confidence is at a dead end. Looking back, the disciples willingly confessed it.

In the fourth watch of the night, leading into dawn, they saw Jesus walking alongside them on that sea as though to pass them by—he doing it his way and they theirs. Whose way would it be? Jesus had not even a boat, yet he walked that storm and its waters as though he were its master. The darkness and wind and waves had no power over him. The metaphor pictures his walk

215

through his passion and death, in full mastery. They, however, pursuing their confident desires apart from him, found themselves helpless in the middle of nowhere and night.

On seeing him, their first reaction was fear. They had no expectation of seeing him again. "A ghost!" they cried out. A Jesus of disembodied "breath" signaled guilt and death. But he spoke comfort and reassurance, "Take heart, it is I, don't be afraid," then got into the boat with them. With that he was in charge and they were willing to have it so. The storm was over. John's account has them immediately at their destination, as in the psalm: "He brought them to their desired haven." Jn 6:21; Ps 107:30 The goal at which they arrived was not theirs but his, the kingdom of God! All was well but full of wonder.

Matthew's account adds a Peter-confession, a post-resurrection incident. Mt 14:28-31 Peter knew the metaphor of Jesus' walking on the sea, how he had not yielded to threat and fear, but walked through it straight and true with God and won! Peter wanted to do this, too. Some episode had truly tested him. "Lord, if it is you, bid me come to you on the water," he had prayed, despite his fears. He would walk into his hard situation whatever it was, as Jesus invited him, bearing steadfast witness and trusting the outcome to God. "Come!" Jesus said. Peter did so! He left the boat and began to walk that fearful sea, until a threatening wave panicked him and he began to sink. "Lord, save me!" he cried out. Jesus' hand was there for him immediately, his voice speaking encouragement and high expectation: "O man of little faith, why did you doubt?" The diagnosis is significant. Under pressure of visible threats, Peter had lost sight of God's word and promises.

The disciples on the "new testament" side knew Jesus' place and their own in the stream of grace and righteousness from his Father. To worship him was to receive and use his gifts. Their awed confession, "Truly, you are the son of God," as Matthew has it, identified them with his covenant-sonship, wanting nothing more than to fill it full in their own servanthood.

Stilling the Storm. Mt 8:23-27; Mk 4:35-41; Lk 8:22-25 This is a young church story, as the mention of other boats in Mark's account suggests. Jesus gets into a boat and the disciples follow, wanting to be with him and like him in every way. That he is sleeping pictures him as with them, yet leaving them on their own. A great storm comes up. They are being swamped by the waves. It is a situation of severe testing, a crisis of persecution, perhaps. They awaken him, crying out, "Lord, save us, we are perishing!" or "Teacher, do you not care that we are perishing?" "Why are you afraid, O men of little faith?" he asks them. "Then he arose and rebuked the wind and said to the sea, 'Peace! Be still!' And there was a great calm!"

The story is framed compactly so as to be memorizable. "Faith," in its original setting, was the spontaneous and transforming response of hearts to the covenant-word which had made Israel God's people in the first place. That word had declared the disciples' honored sonship from heaven. It promised them that their living God and Father was in charge of outcomes, that he would turn to "life and good" even what threatened "death and evil." It called them to serve him in the kingdom-*now* by simply doing his will nobly and without fear, day by day. Jesus believed and proclaimed and embodied that word even to death. "Little faith" meant that they had lost it.

In the midst of storm and fear, the disciples saw Jesus alive and awake with them, speaking the word of rebuke against threats that had seemed so overwhelming. "And there was a great calm." The calm they recovered was of Jesus himself, as he had walked nobly through the storm that raged so fiercely against him, and won. "What sort of man is this, that even the winds and the sea obey him?" they marveled at him. Yet by faith of their own, they became "that sort of man" themselves.

"Increase our faith." Lk 17:5-6 This fragment derived from a situation like that of the storm. Jesus pictured the threat against "the apostles" as a sycamine tree (Greek *sykaminos*), fruitless counterfeit of the fig (Greek *sykea* or *syka*). The counterfeit must be exposed and cast out. You are those called and privileged to do it. Don't look inside yourselves or worry about the size of your faith. "If you had faith like a grain of mustard seed, you could say to this sycamine tree, 'Be rooted up and planted in the sea,' and it would obey you." Let the resistant sycamine tremble for fear of you! Even against your fears, keep speaking the word your persecutors don't want to hear. The simple covenant-truth you proclaim, even in weakness and fear, is more powerful than all the lies, deceits and power they turn against you.

Fishing Stories

The memory of Jesus' calling the first of his disciples is direct and vivid. Mt 4:18-22; Mk 1:16-20 He came from Nazareth to populous Capernaum and centered his activity there. He went on to Bethsaida, home of Andrew and John, Galilean disciples of John the Baptist whom he had met earlier. Jn 1:37-40 There he found Andrew and his brother Simon washing their nets in the sea after a day's fishing. "Follow me, and I will make you fishers of men," he said, inviting both to become his disciples. Farther up the shore he found John. He and his brother James were sitting in their boat with Zebedee, their father, and some hired servants, mending their nets. He called them and they followed him, too. The parents understood what Jesus was asking for and released their sons to him. It appears that Jesus had a boat available to him at Capernaum and that he made retreats across the lake. At least once, he sat in Simon's boat and taught the crowd from off shore. Two metaphor-narratives of fishing draw on this background.

Fishing in John. Jn 21:1-14 Jesus' disciples had left Judea and gone home to Galilee. This episode names Simon Peter first, then Thomas, Nathanael of Cana, the sons of Zebedee, and two others. "I'm going fishing," Simon Peter said, and the others went with him. "That night they caught nothing." The "night" pictures the darkness and futility of zealotic ambition which had for so long blocked them from hearing or truly knowing their Lord.

As dawn broke out of their long and hopeless night, they saw him on the shore but did not yet know it was he. "Children, have you caught any fish?" he called. "No," they confessed. Fishing on the "left" side and in the night pictures the era of self-determined labor for a kingdom of superiority, stirring people to help bring it in at any cost, looking for Jesus to declare himself. His death had put an end to that kind of ambition. In the resurrection dawn, the disciples listened to Jesus as they had not before. Casting their net on the right side of their boat was their authentic mission as "fishers of men." The result was so many people glad to be caught by their gospel that they could hardly haul the net in. John said to Peter, "It is the Lord," that is, the Lord's doing. When they got out on land, they saw a charcoal fire and fish on it. "Come and have breakfast," Jesus invited them, the first meal with him of a new day. Their hesitance to ask "Who are you?" suggests the slow dawning of their resurrection awareness, yet "they knew it was the Lord." He took the bread and gave it to them, and also the fish, feeding them still on his word of life, as he had fed them before.

(Uncomprehending interpolations by copyists literalize the metaphor and clutter it with special attention to Simon Peter. Verses 7-8 tell what he wore, his aggressive leap into the sea and swimming to shore. Verses 10-11 tell Jesus' unnecessary command, "Bring some of the fish you have caught" [he had fish already on the fire], Simon Peter's hauling the net to shore a second time, the description of the fish as "large," and the count of 153. Whether this last represents the varieties of fish known in that day, or whether it plays knowingly on the sum of numbers 1-17, it only clouds the metaphor further. Verse 14, counting this episode as "the third time" Jesus appeared to his disciples, is yet another knowing intrusion.)

Jesus' thrice-repeated "Simon, son of John, do you love me?" follows. Jn 21:15-19 Free of the old illusion and conformed now to Jesus as he actually was, Peter answered each time in simple confession, "Yes, Lord; you know that I love you." (A copyist, assuming that he would be grieved to be asked this a third time, took the opportunity to have Peter remind Jesus of his deity-omniscience, "Lord, you know everything.") Each time Jesus responded with a call under the imagery of a shepherd, "Feed my sheep." He then contrasted what Simon had been with what he was now. "When you were young (confident and self-determined), you dressed yourself and walked where you pleased," needing no help, listening to nobody. "But when you are old, you will stretch out your hands like a little child for someone else to dress you (trustingly dependent), and carry you where you on your own would not wish to go." Such is the wisdom of a kingdom reserved to little children. Mt 18:3-4 (A copyist, knowing of Peter's death and assuming Jesus' omniscience as deity, explained that he said this "to show by what death he was to glorify God.")

Fishing in Luke. Lk 5:1-11 This account is again metaphor. Framed on a memory of Jesus' teaching out of Simon's boat, it weaves a great catch of fish into the original call of Jesus' fishermen-disciples to be "fishers of men." The form of Jesus' command was, "Put out into the deep and let down your nets." As in John's account, Simon confessed a night of futility: "Master, we toiled all night and took nothing." Now it was day, however, and he was ready to do it Jesus' way: "but at your word I will let down the nets." With Jesus in the boat, Simon's catch was so great that his partners, James and John in another boat, were summoned to help. The name "Simon Peter" enters the story at this point. Falling down at Jesus' knees, he confessed his unworthiness. "Depart from me, for I am a sinful man, O Lord." Jesus would not let him go, however. "Do not be afraid; henceforth you will be catching men."

The Peter of this confession and call is the prime actor in both fishing stories. It must have been a significant turning-point and memory, not for him only but for the young church which he represents. Luke would have found his version in the fragment-library of some Judean church. The account in John would have been preserved in Bethsaida among the memoirs assembled in the Gospel named for him.

Healing Stories

Metaphoric stories of mountain and lake tell "signs and wonders" which Jesus did in truth, unlike those which zealotic propaganda had imposed so as to rally people to him. Metaphors of healing effected by the power of his gospel are likewise "signs and wonders" in truth.

"Rise, Pick Up Your Bed and Walk!" Mk 2:9; Jn 5:8, 11-12 This healing word occurs in two contexts—a paralytic in Capernaum and a disabled man at the pool of Bethesda in Jerusalem. The point in each is that the religion of synagogue and temple, for all its promise, is disabled and disabling. Far from lifting its people up to walk tall and free with their God, it has stripped them of honor and paralyzed them "in bed," as it were. Jesus and the young church are not a threat but a God-blessed recovery of what synagogue and temple are capable of being and ought to be.

The metaphoric imagery of the paralytic at Capernaum is physiological, but the historic reality it pictures is of the heart. Mk 2:1-12; Mt 9:1-8; Lk 5:17-26 Its setting is the young church. Jesus "crossed over and came to his own city" is resurrection-memory. Great crowds press upon him. Friends bring this man on his bed, confident that Jesus can heal him, but the enthusiastic crowds block their way. Determined to get through, they open the roof and lower the man in front of Jesus. Metaphor does not need to be concerned with mechanical details—how this bed was constructed, how they managed to carry the man on it up to the roof, how they opened not only the tiles but the supporting beams to get him and his bed through, what tools they used, how the roof was strong enough to hold them, how they found ropes to lower him, how long all this took, what repairs they did afterwards. The point is that the young church, in faith and hope and love, is seeking out the lost who need healing, bringing them one by one to Jesus even against difficulty. The mission of healing is happening, of hope and freedom, of spirit and life.

Jesus speaks love and gathering. The Aramaic of his address to the man is clouded in translation. Matthew and Mark have "child," Luke has "man." The covenant-gospel is compacted into "Your sins are forgiven." Capernaum was home to a massive zealotic enthusiasm for Jesus. Its miracle-propaganda had not only obscured what he taught, but gotten him crucified in the end as an insurrectionist king. The paralytic represents the hopeless dismay of those consumed by a guilt and shame, like that which had befallen the disciples themselves at Jesus' death. Let the gospel of forgiveness and peace which had raised them by Jesus' resurrection raise Capernaum from its hopeless guilt, too.

The objection of the ruling scribes and Pharisees is standard. "Blasphemy! Who can forgive sins, but God alone?" Jesus (the young church) appeals to the healing effect of this very forgiveness. "Which is easier? To say 'Your sins are forgiven'? Or to say, 'Don't lie paralyzed on a bed that carries you! Rise!

Pick that bed up, carry it, and walk'? But that you may know that the son of man (son of God) does have authority on earth to forgive sins—Jesus tells the man, 'Rise! Pick up your bed and go home!'" The man rises, stands noble and free like the disciples, picks up his bed and goes home, full of honor and hope and divine calling, eager for any servanthood to which God summons him. "When the crowds saw it they were amazed and glorified God, *who had given such authority to men!*"—authority starting with Jesus alone, to heal not just physiological bodies here and there, but the whole religion from the heart out!

Bethesda. Jn 5:1-18 A parallel metaphor derives from the young church in Judea. Archaeologists suggest that "Bethesda" was a grid of streets north of the temple area, laid out under Herod the Great.[1] The Aramaic Bethesda (*beth chesedah*, "house of mercy") appears in the Copper Scroll of Qumran. A dual form there, "Bethesdatain," indicates "two Bethesdas." Herod had developed an elaborate water system for Jerusalem, aquaducts from the north flowing into rain-collecting cisterns. The huge double-pool archaeologists have uncovered, whose remains are pointed out to tourists, was part of that system. It could not have been the pool of John's account, however. Anyone who stepped into those cisterns would drown.

John's account suggests another double-pool, an elaborate *miqweh* at a northern entrance to the temple grounds. Worshipers would step down into it and cleanse themselves by immersion, before entering the temple. Its association with "the sheep gate" suggests that its twin was designed to cleanse sacrificial animals on their way into temple. Excavations show small *miqweh*s at the opposite (south) end of the temple complex. This one must have been an architectural triumph, however. "Five porches" suggests a miniature of the temple's colonnade-porches. To cleanse oneself in this pool would seem to have been very special.

The metaphor portrays this liturgical magnificence as promising much but delivering little. Its waters would occasionally be stirred and so effect healing.[2] John the Baptist, for one, had found truth and life in the scriptures treasured by both temple and synagogue. So had Jesus. The masses of people, however, "a multitude of invalids, blind, lame, withered," passed dutifully but

---

[1] John Wilkinson, *Jerusalem as Jesus Knew It: Archaeology as Evidence* (London: Thames and Hudson, 1978), pp. 53-68,95-104. Wilkinson shows how the variant "Bethzatha" originated by a mistaken transliteration of the Aramaic into Greek.

[2] Verse 4 in the King James Version picks up an explanation which was interpolated late enough that some preserved manuscripts do not have it: "For an angel went down at a certain season into the pool, and troubled the water; whosoever then first after the troubling of the water stepped in was made whole of whatever disease he had."

numbly through the prescribed routines, yet waited in vain for the waters to come alive and bring them the deliverance of heart that seemed never to happen.

One day the healing did come—not by temple doctrine and worship, however, but by Jesus and the young church. The metaphor preserves the testimony of a man thirty-eight years old at the time. "Do you want to be healed?" Jesus asked him. "Yes, but...," he replied. He would see the water stirring and healing happening to others on occasion, but had somehow never been quick enough to get in on it himself. Jesus' word accomplished what the officialdom of the temple could not. "Rise, pick up your bed, and walk!" is its summary, as in the Capernaum story. The effect was immediate. The man rose, picked up the bed that had signaled him ill for so long, walked tall, honored and free in the knowledge and service of his God. Let others in that multitude of the plodding-depressed do likewise!

An epilogue depicts the continuing conflict. "It is not lawful for you to be carrying your bed," the authorities accuse him. His violation of the sabbath illustrates what was to them the young church's indifference to the law. (The digression of verses 13-14, Jesus' finding the man in the temple and saying, "Sin no more, lest a worse thing come upon you," is not of the covenant-gospel. The man's "sin" has not been at issue. I take it to be a copyist interpolation out of Greek moralistic piety.) The man refers the critics to Jesus who has healed him. He refers them to his Father, for he did not do the healing on his own. "My Father is working still, and I am working." With that, their accusation intensifies. "He not only broke the sabbath, but also called God his Father, making himself equal with God." This should justify not only their condemnation of Jesus but also their continuing accusation against and persecution of the young church.

The Funeral at Nain. Lk 7:11-17 This metaphor tells how Jesus and his resurrection-gospel came to Nain. The widow stands for women and thus, ordinary folk. She, and a large crowd with her, has believed and served the religion in which she was brought up, trusting and depending on what leaders have taught. But grief has come upon her. Her father has died, and all by whom the sacred tradition came down to her. Her husband has died, who carried it on. Now her son has died, her "only son," her last hope. It is over. The sonship itself, Israel's glory and hers, is dead! There can be no other. The weeping widow, the crowd that weeps with her, can see only the cemetery.

Yet "at the gate," Jesus and his own crowd, the young church, meets this funeral and has compassion. He touches the bier, contaminates himself purposefully and without shame by this death, stops the funeral. He says to the woman, the common folk, "It's not hopeless. Do not weep." Then he speaks with authority his covenant-word to raise the dead, "Young man, I say to you, be raised up!" With that "the dead sat up and began to speak." The covenant-sonship came to life and spoke again. "And he gave him to his mother," to the folk who knew how to weep over such disaster, but who could also recognize and welcome the wonder of life! "Blessed are those who mourn, for they shall be comforted," Jesus said, and it was so. Mt 5:4

"Fear seized them all, and they glorified God saying, 'A great prophet has been raised up among us,' and 'God has visited his people.' And this word about him went out in all Judea and in all the country around!" This appears to be direct memory. It actually happened so. The witness of the young church and its life had power to raise up not only Nain and Galilee but Judea even, and the lands around—like Samaria and Phoenicia and the Decapolis.

The Daughter of Jairus. Mt 9:18-26; Mk 5:21-43; Lk 8:40-56 That Jesus "had crossed again in a boat to the other side" (so in Mark) indicates the post-resurrection era. Matthew's version would have been found in the fragment-library of Capernaum, the longer versions of Mark and Luke in Judea. Jairus' story could be his own telling. Though a ruler of the synagogue, he faced a desperate situation he could not handle, saw hope in Jesus, fell at his feet, and pleaded for the daughter he loved but could not save. She is an only daughter, at age twelve still a child. In metaphor, she depicts the state of his congregation, dying or dead. Prophets had spoken daughter-language similarly: "Rejoice greatly, O *daughter* of Zion! Shout aloud, O *daughter* of Jerusalem!" Zech 9:9 So had Jesus on his way to Golgotha: "*Daughters* of Jerusalem," he said, "Weep not for me but for yourselves and for *your children*." Lk 23:28 A delegation came to report the worst. His daughter was already dead.

The metaphor presents Jesus as the hope of an Israel otherwise hopeless. Crowds with their wailing and flute-playing accent the hopelessness. All three versions preserve Jesus' response, "She is not dead but sleeping," followed by ridicule. Jesus takes "Peter" (that he is not "Simon" here indicates that this testimony is post-resurrection), James, and John into the room with him. I take these three to have been early witnesses to Capernaum of Jesus' resurrection. Matthew's account has him take the girl by the hand, "and the girl was raised." Mark and Luke have her rise in response to a command. Metaphor can say this briefly, but what the daughter (namely Jairus' people) hears is the full covenant-gospel of sonship and life. The command to "give her something to eat" (so Mark and Luke), calls for sustaining her by that same word.

The Flow of Blood. Lk 8:43-49 This parallel metaphor was inserted at some point into that of Jairus. The doctrine and worship of the synagogue has left this woman (imaging the people) perpetually and irretrievably unclean. She has tried all physicians and prescriptions, but in vain. She hears about Jesus but is hesitant, knowing how the synagogue disapproves of him. Perhaps if she touches him secretly just a little (like the fringe of his garment) in that large crowd (the young church), she can receive his healing without being noticed, without offending her tradition. She does so, fearful and trembling, and is cleansed immediately—not by bare power but by the sonship-gospel her people had lost, which Jesus lived and taught, by which he died and was raised again. The young church, embodied in Jesus, draws her into the open so that she can confess Jesus fully. "Your faith has saved you," he says, namely "faith" in the word of honor and hope and calling that has liberated her heart. His gospel adds the joyous blessing, "Go in peace."

Mission Stories

Mission stories imaged as driving out "unclean spirits" were told earlier—Jesus' gospel in Gadara and Gergesa, to Romans (the centurion's servant), as well as to Jesus' own people (the distraught father). But the mission appears also in other forms.

Philip and "Some Greeks." Jn 12:20-26 A Philip memory from the era of the young church tells of some Greeks who came to him saying, "Sir, we wish to see Jesus." Its location on the scroll of John is misleading. A copyist made sense of it by explaining that they came to Jerusalem "to worship at the feast." When this is set aside, the incident can be seen as having occurred in Galilee. Greeks of the Decapolis approached Philip of Bethsaida. Philip and Andrew made the glory of Jesus known to them by the metaphor of a seed, sown into the earth as he died and was buried, yet by his servanthood to death bringing forth much fruit. "Eternal life," the honor of belonging to and serving Jesus and his Father, overflows to these Greeks as well.

The Canaanite Daughter. Mt 15:21-28; Mk 7:24-30 The message of the young church was spilling over likewise to the region of Tyre and Sidon, northwest of Galilee. A Canaanite woman cries out to Jesus, "Have mercy on me, Lord, son of David. My daughter is grievously demon-possessed." In metaphor the daughter is her people. Mark's version identifies her as Syrophoenician. What shall the young church (Jesus) do? If his healing gospel gathers even Canaanites, how will it justify this to the authorities of synagogue and temple? Ever since Ezra, the returned exiles of Judea had observed Moses' stricture regarding seven nations, among them Canaanites, whose land Israel had conquered. "You shall make no covenant with them and show no mercy to them. You shall not make marriages with them.... For you are a people holy to the LORD your God... a people for his own possession out of all the peoples on the face of the earth." Dt 7:2-4

The metaphor depicts the strain of a decision that took time to emerge. As Mark's version has it, Jesus wanted to hide himself but could not. Matthew's account has him silent at first. When the woman persists, his disciples suggest that he "send her away," but he cannot. A limitation comes to mind, which Jesus had imposed when he sent them out to their assigned towns: "Go nowhere among the Gentiles, and enter no town of the Samaritans, but go rather to the lost sheep of the house of Israel." Mt 10:5-6 "The lost sheep of Israel" were the young church's immediate concern, especially since they now encompassed the "ninety-nine" of Jesus' parable, who (so they assured themselves) "never went astray." Mt 18:13

But the woman would not hear this. She knelt before Jesus, pleading, "Lord, help me." The young church demurred yet again: "It is not right to take the children's bread and throw it to the dogs." "Yes, Lord," the woman conceded, "yet even the dogs eat the crumbs that fall from their master's table." She would not be insulted, would not compete to sit with the children at their table. All she asked was to eat the spill-over crumbs. Surely the master's "children" would not miss crumbs already fallen!

Her hunger for Israel's covenant-word and her confidence of the healing it can effect is "faith"—"great faith" even, Jesus says. Let the children at table learn from a Canaanite "dog" then, to cherish the bread which is their heritage in abundance! The table does not exist for itself but for the bread! Let Israel's crumbs fall where they will, for they have power to drive out demons from anyone anywhere. They can gather even Canaanites into the eternal honor of God's elect, to know and serve him only. To eat a crumb of Israel's bread is to hear and believe the voice that speaks from heaven, "You are my beloved son, with whom I am well pleased!" This spirit-word of the living God has power to drive out demons of lust and fear, aggression and defensiveness, pride and despair, from anyone on earth—thus to set both heart and body eternally free!

The Samaritan Leper. Lk 17:11-19 This episode too, condensed for memorizing, would have been preached, then written in the form preserved to us. The command, "Go and show yourselves to the priests," suggests that it was Judean, for it honors the priestly authority. Lev 14:2

"On the way to Jerusalem he was passing between Samaria and Galilee.

As he entered a certain village..." is a transition supplied by Luke. The original story would have begun, "Ten lepers met him, who stood far off." The law required such separation. Lev 13:45-46 Jesus could visit Mary and Martha of Bethany "in the house of Simon the leper," but their father was quarantined outside the village. Mk 14:3; Jn 12:1-3

Leprosy in metaphor pictures a corruption that is consuming God's people, compromising their identity, and cutting them off from the community. "Ten" signifies completeness. That the ten call out to "Jesus, Master" suggests that they know, trust, and set their hope in him. As healed, they are of the young church. The sermon-story has in mind a time, however, when they were among the leprous of God's people, isolated and under judgment. They knew their disease and looked to Jesus for healing in a way that their fellow Judeans and the priesthood did not.

The prayer, "Have mercy on us," draws on the psalmody of temple and synagogue, in which the young church still participated. Ps 51:1 The ten do as their worship has taught them, confess their dependence on "a God merciful and gracious, slow to anger, forgiving iniquity and transgression and sin." Ex 34:6; Ps 103:8 That they look to Jesus as "Master" and agent of their healing implies that they know what his "mercy," imaging his Father's, has done for them.

His command, "Go, show yourselves to the priests," summons the priesthood to do the service which the law of leprosy asks of them. Let the regular priesthood examine the young church and certify that it is healed! Let it then turn to "Jesus, Master" for its own healing.

"As they went, they were cleansed!" The ten hear what Jesus says, trust him, and do it. To turn and go is to "repent." They let go their leprosy, their superiorist spirit and the isolation it causes. Being out from under law and judgment, they are now under "mercy." This is the heart of Jesus' preaching, a gospel not original with him but echoing Moses and the prophets.

All ten are lepers, all ten cry for mercy, all ten hear Jesus' word, all ten turn to go, all ten receive mercy, all ten are cleansed! That is the wonder of Jesus and the Father as the young church knows and proclaims him. One horrible disease, one mercy, one healing, granted freely and without judgment to all. This gospel ought to bind all together as one—young church to its fellow Judeans and to the priesthood alike! That is the thrust of this metaphor-sermon. Jesus is not a threat to a people still so contemptuous and suspicious of him, but the instrument of their cleansing! He breaks down barriers of the sort that keep the lepers so "far off"!

But the story reveals a problem which afflicted the young church from within. "Where are the nine?" One of those ten was different. "When he saw that he was healed, he turned back, praising God with a loud voice; and he fell on his face at Jesus' feet giving him thanks. And he was a Samaritan!" Samaritans were hearing Jesus' gospel! Long isolated from racially-pure Judeans, treated as lepers, they too were crying "Jesus, Master." Thrilled to be gathered and to belong, they were full of thanksgiving to the God who through Jesus loves and gathers even Samaritans! The simple unabashed "receiving" of "this stranger" acknowledges a "mercy" that knows no barrier.

Thanksgiving in response to mercy closes the circle of oneness between Giver and receiver—but also between leper and leper. Mercy negates rights. Mercy levels visible rankings. Mercy disallows comparison-making. What can be more equal than pure gift? Mercy is the same for Judean, Galilean, Samaritan, Canaanite, Greek, or Gadarene. The Father's mercy to Jesus, a Galilean, was pure gift. His mercy to Judeans, who looked down on and judged Jesus from their illusory height, was likewise pure gift. Here is hope for oneness between the young church and fellow Judeans. Here is hope for oneness between Judeans and Samaritans, even all nations!

But the young church itself, to whom this sermon is preached, has not as yet caught this wonder in full. A lifetime piety of separatist contempt for Samaritans is not easily broken. Thus the Jesus of this metaphor-sermon asks, "Were there not ten cleansed? But where are the nine? Was no one found to return and give glory to God, except this foreigner?" If mercy and cleansing are equal, how can faith and thanksgiving be unequal? Let the nine cease looking at "this foreigner" with suspicion. Let them look instead to the God he is praising and praise him with the same joy! Then the leprous division between God's people and the nations will be no more!

If the priesthood will not certify the Samaritans as healed, Jesus and the young church must do so and will. "Rise up and go," is resurrection-language. "Your faith has saved you."

By simply believing the word of mercy spoken to him, the Samaritan is one with the God who spoke it, with Jesus and the young church, and with all who return to give thanks.

The Woman at the Well. Jn 4:5-42 A fragment of direct memory in Acts remembers Philip as the voice of the gospel to Samaria. Acts 8:5-13 Since he had been with Jesus on his journey through Samaria to Jerusalem, Philip would likely have sought out the woman of Jacob's well and the people of her town first, eager to tell them about Jesus' death and resurrection and how he was the messiah indeed. A mission to Samaria from Galilee would not be burdened by the anti-

Samaritan inhibitions of Judeans. I infer that this memoir was from Philip and that it was preserved among John's memoirs at Bethsaida, which was Philip's home, too. Though it contains metaphor ("living water," "five husbands," and "fields ripe to harvest"), it is not itself metaphor but direct memory. I enter it here for what it tells of the young church's spill-over to Samaria.

(Copyist interpolations need to be detected and set aside. I explained earlier why a copyist felt the need to invert Jesus' journey, making it from Judea to Galilee rather than from Galilee to Judea. Another interpolation has the woman say what the man healed of blindness said in another context, "Lord, I perceive that you are a prophet." Jn 4:19; 9:17 A copyist, missing the metaphor of the woman's "five husbands" and the "living water," but captivated by Jesus' deity, had her testify merely to his supernatural knowledge: "He told me all that I ever did." Jn 4:29,39 Borrowing Andrew's word to his brother Simon, "We have found the messiah," a copyist interpolated the woman's anticipation of "the messiah." Jn 1:41; 4:25-26,29)

Such clutter aside, a significant story emerges. The long schism between Judeans and Samaritans is acknowledged. Jn 4:9b Two evidences indicate, however, that it is being healed. Geographical locations, "on this mountain" (Gerizim) or "in Jerusalem," are becoming irrelevant. "The hour is coming *and now is*, when the true worshipers will worship the Father in spirit and in truth." Jn 4:20-24 Jesus' vision of "fields already white to harvest" views the young church as "reaping" what he sowed, "so that sower and reaper may rejoice together." Jn 4:35-38

Much that is told appears to be direct memory of an original event. Jesus was journeying with his disciples and the women from Nazareth to Jerusalem for the Feast of Tabernacles. They reached Jacob's well at noon. He sent his disciple to the town of Sychar to buy food, for no town had developed around this well. Though of sacred memory, it was too deep (a hundred feet) for ordinary use. Jacob had bought this property from the sons of Hamor, father of Shechem. Gen 33:19 The sellers may have watched with amusement as Jacob's servants dug and dug, deeper and deeper, day after day, refusing to admit defeat, until at last they hit water. To draw water from a well that deep, also for cattle, became an unsustainable effort, however. Jacob moved on, but the property remained a possession central to what became the inheritance of the Joseph tribe Ephraim. When Israel came out of Egypt, they buried Joseph's bones here. Josh 24:32

That the woman came to this well alone and at noon suggests that she was an outcast even from her own people. Jn 4:7-15 She perceived that Jesus was "a

Jew." Her comment, "You have nothing to draw with," suggests that the well had no apparatus, that she had to bring a hundred feet of rope as well as her jar or bucket, then drop and raise it by sheer strength. When she had finished, taken a drink herself, and was ready to go, Jesus broke the silence. "Give me a drink," he said. That he was not embarrassed to ask, then receive and drink from her cup, broke the barrier and honored her. The metaphor of "living water" depicts Israel's covenant of sonship. That Jesus offered it implies that it did not exclude her heart, "thirsting for God, for the living God," as the Psalm says, or "for righteousness," as he would say. Ps 42:2; Mt 5:6 Those who heard Philip's memorable report afterwards, here condensed, would fill out this water-word without need for further definition, since they "drank" it themselves and "lived" by it. As naming and hope and calling from God, it had indeed become in them "a spring of water, welling up to eternal life." "Give me this water," the woman said, "that I may not thirst." ("Nor come here to draw" could be yet another literalist enhancement by a copyist).

Then Jesus addressed her evident aloneness. "Go, call your husband," he said. "I have no husband," she replied. His diagnosis of "five husbands" and a sixth who is "not your husband," was metaphor. Six, without a seven, depicts a labor that never attains "rest," an endless burden without hope. She would understand. What this meant specifically, whether she was outcast from her village by harlotry perhaps, or what "rest" Jesus may have offered, is again not told. His word touched her, however, and lifted her to honor.

When his disciples returned, they wondered that he was talking to her, but said nothing. She left her jar for them and went off, not home but to the town, urging her people to come and hear Jesus themselves. The lonely outcast became the gatherer. Meanwhile, Jesus marveled at how she "received" him. His own people in Nazareth had not received him so. "A prophet has no honor in his own country," he observed by contrast. Jn 4:44 Jerusalem, where he was going, would not receive him, either. But this woman drank deeply of his "living water." When his disciples urged him to eat, he answered memorably, "I have a food to eat that you do not know." They wondered whether he might have already eaten, but he explained the metaphor, "My food is to do the will of him who sent me and to finish his work."

Many Samaritans of Sychar came to see and hear Jesus, as she urged them. They invited him and his disciples into the town. He stayed with them two days—thus delaying his arrival in Jerusalem for the feast even more. "We know that this is indeed the Savior *of the world!*" is post-resurrection confession, but appropriate for so compacted a history. To Philip and the young church, it became a blessed memory. Samaria, an eager soil for Jesus' sowing, signaled a breakthrough into "the world" beyond Judea and Judeans. "Behold, the lamb of God who takes away the sin of *the world!*" Jn 1:29 "God so loved *the world.*" Jn 3:16 The living water of Jesus' covenant-gospel was gathering the world. "All nations and kingdoms and languages" were joining Israel freely in serving the kingdom of the one eternal God, as the prophets had said. Dan 7:14 The vision on the mountain in Galilee was becoming reality, "Go and make disciples of all nations." Mt 28:19

But there was a dark side, too. The defensive resistance of Judean authorities against that very gospel is evident in parable. "The wedding is ready, but those invited were not worthy. Go therefore to the thoroughfares and invite to the marriage feast as many as you find." Mt 22:8-9 "I tell you, none of those who were invited shall taste of my banquet." Lk 14:24 "There you will weep and gnash your teeth, when you see Abraham and Isaac and Jacob and all the prophets in the kingdom of God and you yourselves thrust out." Lk 13:28

Much history of the young church, in Galilee as well as Judea, is revealed by sayings and stories like these. The resistance climaxed when persecution at one blow wiped out its libraries of fragment-memory. With the testimony to Jesus thus suppressed, zealotic violence was free to revive until it brought about the destruction of Jerusalem. Mt 11:12; Dan 11:14 Late interpolations into the Gospels testify that the disaster did indeed happen. Mt 22:7; Lk 19:12,14,27

PART SIX

Choosing Life

The Finish

The passion narrative is pieced together from the memory of witnesses who were actually there. Details are preserved in four accounts, derived from separate collections of fragments, assembled without awareness of each other. Since all four Gospels testify to the same event, historical questioning can take note of passing evidences in any of them, fit these into the whole, and bridge gaps between them. The history that emerges is as sound as any can be.

Threads of conflict traced earlier converge. Zealotic leaders envisioned the hour of the kingdom and pushed Jesus to be its "christ." Judeans defended their racial advantage against him, scribes and Pharisees their law, the priests their authority. The council, responsible for maintaining order, countered the threat of insurrection by drawing Rome into the drama.

Yet the force of the event was Jesus himself. His covenant-name, "my beloved son," had grown like a mustard-seed into the full tree. Mt 13:31-32 His "gospel" taught his people the honor of their own sonship, the promises that assured the Father's care in every tomorrow, and the calling to belong to and serve him freely in the kingdom-*now.* Jesus set before them also the essence of Israel's covenant-wisdom—the distinction between "life and good" or "death and evil." Dt 30:15 "Therefore choose life!" Moses had said. In parable after parable Jesus pleaded the same. To eat "the tree of life" as in Eden was to hear and believe the covenant-word, trust "good" and deliverance from "evil" to the love and wisdom of the LORD God, and "live" as children-servants by doing his will. To eat the tree of death was to "die" by pursuing whatever the self-assertive wisdom of "opened eyes" might judge to be "good" and to evade any threatened "evil."

Jesus, knowing the alternatives, "chose life." That was the inside secret of the passion event. Alone, threatened by powers on every side, betrayed and

233

forsaken by his own disciples, he would not be silenced or compromise to save himself. He was the son-servant of his Father in heaven. His covenant-sonship was at stake. So was the "life" of his people. He brought the battle climactically to headquarters, the temple itself. As events developed, he faced the ultimate test—to "choose life" when doing so meant giving himself up to death even by crucifixion.

In remembering and telling this, the disciples did not conceal their own failures. They made clear that Jesus was not a victim, that this awful thing did not just happen to him. He *chose* it. What he did was an incredible miracle, like walking on the dark sea in control of its ragings, then coming to rescue them from their own lost night. He did it all alone! That there could be one like him was unimaginable. Yet when it was over, that is what they wanted to be themselves.

He had trusted his Father to make "good" what looked to be utterly "evil." A sermon of Peter in Acts cites a Psalm: "I keep the LORD always before me; because he is at my right hand I shall not be moved. Therefore my heart is glad and my glory rejoices; my body also dwells secure. For you do not give me up to Sheol, or let your godly one see the Pit. You show me the path of life. In your presence is fullness of joy, at your right hand are pleasures forevermore." Ps 16:8-11; Acts 2:25-28 Most prominent in the memory was a saying from Hosea. "Come, let us return to the LORD, for he has torn, that he may heal us; he has stricken, and he will bind us up. After two days he will revive us; on the third day he will raise us up, that we may live before him. Let us know, let us press on to know the LORD. His going forth is like the dawn." Hos 6:1-3

Jesus' "choosing life" was the pivot of the history. Yet only by looking back after it was over could the glory of what he had done, and the hand of God on him, be seen.

CHAPTER SIXTEEN

Jerusalem

"Now before the feast of the Passover, when Jesus knew that his hour had come to depart out of this world to the Father, having loved his own who were in the world, he loved them to the finish."

John 13:1

The Chronology in John

The Gospel of John provides a precise and sustained chronology. Having decided to go to Jerusalem and speak his word to the authorities directly, Jesus left Capernaum and went home to Nazareth for a last visit. Jn 7:2-13 The Feast of Tabernacles was near, about October. His brothers invited him to join their party for the pilgrimage, but he held back. They went off on the customary route to the Jordan and southward on its far side, avoiding unclean Samaria. Jesus did not cut himself off from Samaria and Samaritans, however. His region of Galilee had been taken from Samaria by Judeans for the sake of its rich valley only a little over a century ago. He was himself of Samaritan descent. Jn 8:48 To pass through Samaria was his purposeful choice.

His party included not only his disciples but a group of loyal women—among them Mary Magdalene, Salome ("the mother of the sons of Zebedee"), and Susanna. His own mother joined them for the journey. It appears that she was introduced in Judea as mother of one or another of his brothers, not of himself—a device for her protection. Luke has her as "the mother of James" (whom Paul called "the Lord's brother"). Lk 24:10; Gal 1:19 Matthew has "the mother of James and Joseph," or "the other Mary." Mt 27:56; 28:1 Mark has

"Mary, the mother of James the younger (brother of Jesus) and of Joseph," or "Mary, the mother of Joseph," or "Mary, the mother of James." Mk 15:40,47; 16:1 John knows Jesus as "the son of Joseph," but leaves Mary unnamed as simply "his mother." Jn 1:45; 2:1; 6:42; 19:25-27 "His mother's sister" in this last reference may have gotten into the record as still another name for her.

Jesus' encounter with the woman at Jacob's well and the people of Sychar delayed him two days. Jn 4:5-44 When a Samaritan village refused him lodging, he went on to another—possibly the "Ephraim" to which he made a retreat later. Lk 9:51-56; Jn 11:54

As John's memoir tells it, he arrived in Jerusalem about the middle of the feast and began to teach in the temple. Jn 7:14 The council moved to arrest him, for they had decided that, once he came into their jurisdiction, they would take care of him. Jn 7:32 On the last day of the feast his theme was, "If any one thirsts, let him come to me and drink." Jn 7:37 John's memoir reports that the temple police failed to pursue the arrest, explaining that "No man ever spoke like this man." Jn 7:45-52 Despite Nicodemus' protest, the chief priests and Pharisees of the council inferred that Jesus, being a Galilean, did not qualify as their "brother," hence could not be a prophet. Dt 18:15 Another dialogue exalts their claim of racial purity over Jesus' name from his "Father." A dispute here regarding "Abraham" ends in an attempt to stone him. Jn 8:31-39

Whoever found the Bethsaida fragments and compiled them into the Gospel of John digressed from his memoir at this point to enter the metaphor of the blind man, followed by the post-resurrection testimonies of Jesus as the door of the sheepfold and the good shepherd. Jn 9; 10:1-18 John's own memoir continued with the Feast of Dedication at the December new moon, near the shortest day of the year. Jn 10:22-39 That Jesus, of Galilean-Samaritan extraction, should openly call God his Father and himself God's son, a language which violated all modesty, was blasphemy. Threatened again with stoning, Jesus left Jerusalem and the temple for Bethany beyond the Jordan, the place of John the Baptist's ministry, Herod's territory. Here he remained as long as three months. Many people came out to him there. Jn 10:40-42 Two Gospels locate a divorce dialogue here. Mt 19:1-12; Mk 10:1-12 I assume that Jesus sent his disciples with carefully crafted messages to towns of Judea, as he had to Galilee. Many preserved parables may have reached the common folk this way.

News from Mary and Martha of their younger brother's illness brought Jesus back to Judea in spite of the danger. Jn 11:1-17 "Let us also go, that we may die with him," Thomas said memorably. Episodes which other Gospels associate with Jericho would fit this return—healing a blind man and Jesus' overnight stay with Zacchaeus. Lk 18:35; 19:5-6 The zealotic propaganda of the raising of Lazarus, widely told, stirred much enthusiasm for Jesus as the messiah. The council, perceiving a threat of insurrection and responsible for keeping order, met in emergency session. Jn 11:45-53 Crowds of Galileans would be coming for the Passover. Fanatics, secretly armed and viewing the priestly authority as hopelessly contaminated by collaboration with Rome, might rally to Jesus at any signal and fight to overthrow them, confident of angelic intervention. If such a rabble were to win a skirmish or two, Rome would return in strength and ruthlessly "wipe out both our holy place and our nation." (Forty years later, that actually happened).

These proceedings would have become known to John through Nicodemus. Caiaphas' advice seemed unarguable, "It is expedient for you that one man should die for the people, and the whole nation not perish." That Jesus was not stirring up the insurrection himself was irrelevant. He must be held accountable. The threat could be dissipated by putting to death just this one man. That would spare the nation a fearful war and save many lives. The council would turn Jesus over to the governor to be crucified as an insurrectionist. John, looking back on all this after the resurrection, noted in his memoir that the high priest spoke here as God's own prophet. One man, Jesus, did indeed die for the people so that the whole nation might not perish—not for that nation alone either, but for the children of God scattered among all nations. Jn 11:51-52

Jesus knew how the plot and rumormongering of his misguided supporters must end. His passion-prediction in a later form anticipated that the chief priests and scribes would deliver him to the Gentiles to be mocked and scourged and crucified. Mt 20:19; Mk 10:33-34 He did not go to Jerusalem after visiting Mary and Martha in Bethany, but withdrew northward to Ephraim, a town of Samaria which he may have visited before, staying there perhaps two weeks. No one knew where he was. Pilgrims arriving early for the Passover wondered whether he would come. An order went out that anyone who saw him should notify the authorities so that they might arrest him. Jn 11:53-57

The Last Week

John's dating is precise. Six days before the Passover, Jesus returned to the home of Mary and Martha in Bethany, on the southeastern slope of the Mount of Olives, two miles from Jerusalem. Jn 12:1 That would have been Sunday, following the sabbath rest. Mary anointed him with a valuable oil—"for my burial," Jesus said, lest anyone take this as a sign that he was the "messiah" or "christ." His disciples regretted the waste. The ointment might have been sold and the money given to "the poor," they said piously, meaning any cause they preferred, such as more weapons. (A copyist imagined Judas as having instigated the complaint, picturing him as a thief who would steal from the money box, of which he was in charge. Jn 12:4,6)

The next morning, Monday, was the grand processional, plotted and promoted by zealotic leaders including Simon, father of Judas, who confessed himself afterwards as "the Zealot." Three significant expectations contributed to the enthusiasm. One concerned the day of the LORD as prophesied in Zechariah: "Then the LORD will go forth and fight against those nations as when he fights on a day of battle. On that day his feet shall stand on the Mount of Olives which lies before Jerusalem on the east; and the Mount of Olives shall be split in two.... Then the LORD your God will come and all the holy ones with him.... And the LORD will become king over all the earth.... The LORD will smite all the peoples that wage war against Jerusalem.... And on that day a great panic from the LORD shall fall upon them... and the wealth of all the nations around shall be collected, gold, silver, and garments in great abundance...." Zech 14:3-4 This was the day of the kingdom! The Mount of Olives, over which Jesus would pass, was the place! "You do not know the day or the hour," Jesus would say, but they thought they did. Mt 24:36

The second expectation concerned a priesthood perceived to be corrupt and compromising. It had opposed Jesus, but on this day it would be purified and join in supporting him. "Behold, I send my messenger to prepare the way before me, and the Lord whom you seek will suddenly come to his temple; the *messenger of the covenant* in whom you delight, behold, he is coming, says the LORD of hosts.... And he will purify the sons of Levi and refine them like gold and silver, till they present right offerings to the LORD." Mal 3:1-3

An accusation, raised against Jesus in the preliminary hearing before the high priest, makes sense as a hope which zealotic minds had ascribed to him. "This fellow said, 'I am able to destroy the temple of God and to build it again in three days.'" Mt 26:61 (I take "made with hands" and "made without hands" in the Marcan parallel to have been interpolated later by a copyist. Mk 14:58) The saying recurs in the mockery at the cross. "You who would destroy the temple and build it again in three days, save yourself!" Mt 27:40; Mk 15:30 The Johannine variation, "(You) destroy this temple and in three days I will raise it up," associates the saying with his cleansing the temple, but recasts it as filled full in Jesus' death and resurrection. Jn 2:19

High priest and council knew the rumored saying to be a plot against their authority. The zealotic crowd expected it to happen, however. Jesus, "the messenger of the covenant," was preparing the way for the LORD of hosts to come and do whatever purifying was necessary. It would be painful, yes. "Who can endure the day of his coming, and who can stand when he appears? For he is like a refiner's fire." It had precedent. David of old had brought the ark of God to Jerusalem with festive song and revitalized the Levites and priesthood. 1 Chr 15:26; 16:43 Hezekiah and Josiah, of the line of David, had cleansed the religion of ungodly abuses and restored its integrity in their day. 2 Chr 29-31; 34-35 Jesus, the son of David, should do the same. This strategy would also subvert the conspiracy of the priesthood to arrest Jesus and kill him.

"Destroy this temple" (*naos*, the internal sanctuary) and "build it" or "build another" was code language for transforming a dead and corrupt priesthood into one alive, true and visionary. Only so could the promised kingdom of God arrive for his people. "Through three days" set a time-frame—Tuesday, Wednesday, and Thursday of this very week. By Preparation-Day, Friday, the miraculous purifying in anticipation of the kingdom would be finished. The Passover would then inaugurate it, as when Israel of old came out of Egypt.

The third expectation was a call to courage and hope, inspired by the wonder-story of Jesus' raising Lazarus. If enemies stood in the way, if war broke out, let those who were armed fight for the cause of the kingdom, boldly without fear! The LORD of hosts and his angels would fight with them. The promise of resurrection, evidenced in the raising of Lazarus, stood firm. Any who died faithful in battle would not miss out on the coming kingdom and glory!

Crowds of enthusiasts came from Jerusalem to help escort Jesus over the Mount of Olives. Everything they did had been planned in advance. They sang psalms and waved palms in holy anticipation. Many spread their garments before him like a royal carpet, retrieving them when he had passed. From a pilgrim psalm they chanted him "blessed," and "coming in the name of the Lord," then named him boldly "the son of David" and even "king." Ps 118:26 This was the place and the day! "On that day his feet shall stand on the Mount of Olives, and the Mount of Olives shall be split in two," the prophecy said, but no such thing happened. "Then the LORD your God will come, and all the holy ones with him," it said, but he did not come. As for Jesus, he rebuked the zealotic vision by riding a borrowed donkey, signaling Zechariah's prophecy of a king meek and creating peace, not war. Zech 9:9-10

The crowd was his protection, but only for the moment. It led him down into the Kidron Valley, across the brook, then up the temple mountain. Jesus would have dismounted at some point and returned the donkey to its owner. An exterior Herodian staircase along the eastern wall ascended to a porch at the level of the temple area. A broken remnant remains of the spring of the arch which once supported that porch.

Cleansing the Temple

The procession arrived, but had no idea what to do next. Nothing had happened as expected. The fragment in Matthew tells of children singing on and on, "Hosanna to the son of David." When "the chief priests and scribes" objected, Jesus quoted a psalm regarding praise "by the mouth of babes and infants." Mt 21;15-16; Ps 8:2 A variation in Luke may be post-resurrection. Some Pharisees in the crowd said, "Teacher, rebuke your disciples." He replied, "If these were silent, the very stones would cry out." Lk 19:39-40

That Monday was "the tenth day of the month," on which the people must select their lamb for the Passover, then keep it until the fourteenth day— which happened this year to be Friday, the Preparation-Day for the sabbath. Ex 12:1-8 On the fourteenth day, "between the two evenings," that is, from noon when the sun began its descent until its final setting, the lambs would be sacrificed and prepared for eating. The Passover meal would begin after sunset on the fifteenth or full moon day of the lunar month, which fell this year on the sabbath.

Thus, the Monday when Jesus arrived was big business in the temple. Pilgrims were purchasing lambs for the Passover, also animals for other sacrifices. The lambs, male, born the previous spring, cattle too, and cages of doves had been certified as without blemish by inspectors of the priests or Levites. The animals were led or driven through one of the twin pools north of the temple compound. Thus cleansed, they entered the temple grounds through the sheep gate. Moneychangers made it convenient for those from distant lands to pay the shepherds and other sellers in local currency. The process was organized efficiently by long experience.

Jesus took time to fashion a whip of cords, an art learned perhaps from his carpenter father. Did that crowd of zealotic enthusiasts, still watching for him to do something, expect him to cleanse the temple by violence? He would demonstrate what violence could accomplish. Business was at its height when he interrupted it by an act carefully premeditated. Quickly, before anybody could stop him, he rose and lashed out with whip and shouts to drive the startled cattle out of the temple, upsetting the cages of doves and the tables of the moneychangers along the way. Jn 2:13-22 "What do you think you are doing?" would be the angry cry. Other than stir up anger, what had his violence accomplished? Nothing! The cattle returned. Scattered coins were gathered and tables reset in short order.

Thus Jesus mocked the perverse hope of a zealotic kingdom and its kind of warfare. Whips are for animals, not people. Weapons and strategies of violence can never change human hearts or bring in the kingdom of God. Only the covenant-word can cleanse God's house and people. That word would be his weaponry, even if the authorities responded by turning their violence against him. Jesus cast his whip aside, then withdrew to teach any who would listen.

"I have persistently sent all my servants, the prophets, to them, day after day; yet they did not listen to them, or incline their ear, but stiffened their neck," the Lord had complained to Jeremiah. Jer 7:25-26 Yet cleansing would be possible only by that persistent word. Lonely Jeremiah had deplored the temple's uncleanness and predicted its destruction. Jer 7:1-14 "My house shall be called a house of prayer, but *you make it a den of robbers*," Jesus quoted him—your haven of safety when you have finished your self-centered scheming. Mt 21:13; Is 56:7 "You shall not make my Father's house a house of trade!" is John's variation. Jn 2:16 Temple worship had taken on the character of negotiation—God a merchandiser out to sell his services, his people shopping for the best deal. "Pay me this and I do this for you." Prophets had protested such dickering for ages. "With what shall I come before the Lord, and bow myself before God on high? Shall I come before him with burnt offerings, with calves a year old? Will the Lord be pleased with thousands of rams, with ten thousands of rivers of oil? Shall I give my first-born for my transgression, the fruit of my body for the sin of my soul?" Mic 6:6-7 "Sacrifice and offering are not what you desire.... Burnt offering and sin offering are not what you have required." Ps 40:6

The alternative to violence or deceitful manipulation is consistent and graphic. "He has showed you, O man, what is good," Micah continued, "and what does the Lord require of you but to do justice, and to love kindness, and to walk humbly with your God?" The Psalm went on, "I delight to do your will, O God; your law is within my heart." When a woman in another setting cried out to Jesus in admiration, "Blessed is the womb that bore you, and the breasts that you sucked," he replied, "Rather, blessed are those who hear the word of God and keep it." Lk 11:27-28

Did Jesus on this tenth day of the month buy a lamb for his own Passover with his disciples, to set aside till the fourteenth day? The Gospels give no such indication. If the disciples thought to ask him, "Where is the lamb for our Passover?" he might have responded as Abraham did to Isaac long ago, "God will provide himself the lamb, my son." Gen 22:8-9

The Plottings

Only at great effort and risk had the zealotic leaders stirred up that huge crowd to escort Jesus and hail him as king, yet he frustrated their dream again and again. He had ridden a lowly donkey. When Jerusalem came into view, rather than lift his voice in celebrative hymnody, he had wept for the disaster and devastation about to come upon it. Ps 122; Lk 19:41-44 His mode of temple cleansing mocked the cleansing they had hoped for. When his disciples hailed the beauty of the temple that evening, hoping he might say something about its greater glory to come, Jesus predicted its destruction once again, not one stone left upon another. Mt 24:1-2 The common folk, so enthusiastic that morning, were disaffected and at a loss. Far from encouraging their support, Jesus was isolating himself in even greater danger.

Yet for some, at least, the fantasy would not die. Might God only be testing them? Might he be deliberately reducing the number of his faithful as in the day of Gideon, so that the few who remained would rely on God alone and not on themselves? Judg 7:2-7 That could make the victory, when it came, all the more glorious! "In the sight of heaven there is no difference between saving by many or by few," Judas Maccabaeus had said, quoting Jonathan of old. 1 Macc 3:18; 1 Sam 14:6

Jesus and his disciples returned to Bethany that night. Mt 21:17 On Tuesday he taught in the temple again, then camped out at Gethsemane on the lower slope of the Mount of Olives across the Kidron from the temple. Lk 21:37; Jn 18:1-2 Here John brought Nicodemus to him. Jn 3:2 He taught on Wednesday again, but John then reports one more withdrawal. "He departed and hid himself from them." Jn 12:36 Jesus assured his disciples once again of his coming death. "You know that after two days the Passover is coming, and the son of man will be delivered up to be crucified." Mt 26:1-2 They still did not believe it could happen.

Caiaphas and the council knew the zealotic mind. Since the kingdom had not broken in as yet, the enthusiasts would focus now on the Passover itself, looking for a repeat of Israel's miraculous departure from Egypt long ago. To avoid the threatened turmoil, Jesus must be arrested secretly away from the crowds and disposed of before the feast day came. Mt 26:3-5

Judas formed a counter-conspiracy of his own and shared it with Peter and the others. The vision of the LORD's mighty intervention on the Mount of Olives, which his father Simon had derived from Zechariah, might yet be fulfilled. That the once huge crowd had been reduced to just themselves was God's own doing! He would save by just them! That they were not trained in war did not matter. They needed only to be faithful! It was a grand idea, revelatory! The council, for all their plotting against Jesus, would not be able to withstand the coming of "the LORD your God." Did they want to arrest him? Very well, Judas would direct their forces to the Mount of Olives. He and the disciples would stand firm there with their master. In that dark hour, the LORD with hosts of angels would deliver his son from the priestly conspiracy against him, purify his holy temple, give Jesus the kingdom, and exalt Israel to its proper glory.

Judas perceived himself as acting in faith, even manipulating the enemy to help the cause. He visited the house of Caiaphas secretly and conspired to deliver Jesus up before the Passover, as the high priest wished, away from the crowds loyal to him. Mt 26:14-16 He pretended to do it for money, but in reality to make the Mount of Olives the site of the climactic battle. The others would do their part. Their determined courage and the intervention of angels would do more than save Jesus. It would bring in the kingdom! Mt 26:53

Wednesday should have been the night, but Jesus thwarted it by his withdrawal. He understood "the knowledge of good and evil" calculation which unclean spirits were working on all sides. He knew what the council was plotting, what his disciples had in mind, what Judas was up to. A comment of John, which the compiler entered early on the scroll, is appropriate for this moment: "Now when he was in Jerusalem at the Passover feast, many (the zealotic enthusiasts) believed in his name (that he would be their christ and king), when they saw his signs which he did; but Jesus did not trust himself to them, because he knew all men and needed no one to tell him what they had in mind, for he knew what was in man." Jn 2:23-25

The Supper

Jesus had planned this last meal with his disciples. The combined memory suggests that he knew the house with the upper room, had been a guest there, and had arranged to use it on the night before his host's own Passover. They had agreed that Peter and John, sent ahead to prepare the meal (the women perhaps with them), should find the house by noticing a male servant draw-ing water around noon at the pool of Siloam and following him home. Mk 14:13-16; Lk 22:7-13 The host would have the room ready. Homes overlook-ing the old city of David and the Kidron Valley from the west would have been of noble, even priestly, families.

"Having loved his own who were in the world, he loved them to the finish," John's memoir reflects of Jesus, and "knowing that the Father had given all things into his hands, and that he had come from God and was going to God." Jn 13:1-3 "With desire have I desired to eat this Passover with you before I suffer," Luke's account has Jesus saying as they sat down to the meal. Lk 22:15

He and his company would have arrived after dark, the beginning of Friday. "A dispute also rose among them, which of them was to be regarded as the greatest," suggests that some pushed to sit next to Jesus even then. Lk 22:24 John managed to seize the place "on his breast," that is, on his right as they reclined at the table. Jn 13:23-27 Judas secured the place at Jesus' left. Appar-ently Simon, having been squeezed out, humbly took the lowest place. (Greek copyists, obsessed with Judas as the betrayer and assuming the other disciples to be innocent, corrupted this chapter with many interpolations concerning him. Jn 13:2,10-11,18-19,27,28-29)

Jesus' first act contradicted once again his disciples' stubborn fantasy of a kingdom of conquest and superiority. He, the beloved son, took the role of a servant to wash their feet, one after the other, including Judas'. Jn 13:4-17 Only as receivers from him and then servants in their own right, could they be part of him in the kingdom-*now*. If they could not grasp this at the moment, they would later, John's memoir notes. A parallel memory in Luke has him say, "I am among you as one who serves." Lk 22:25-27

Next Jesus let them know he was aware of their secretive plotting. Jn 13:21-30; Mt 26:20-24; Mk 14:17-21 "Truly I say to you, one of you will deliver me up," he said. Their plan to rescue and exalt him would only hand him over to the authorities, thus leave them empty and overwhelmed by guilt. "Lord, is it I?" they began to ask uneasily, wondering how much he really knew. John tells how Simon Peter signaled him to ask Jesus directly, "Lord, who is it?" and how Jesus dipped a morsel in the sauce and gave it to Judas. Judas rushed off into the night, not believing that the plot could fail. That John calls him here "the son of Simon Iscariot" suggests that Judas' father had originated this daring illusion and afterwards took the disgraceful name "Iscariot" as his own.

Body and Blood

The prime memory of that meal is the word which made it the young church's Passover. Mt 26:26-28; Mk 14:22-24; Lk 22:17-22; 1 Cor 11:23-25 Implications perceived later were retrojected into the memory of the meal itself. At the very next Passover, Jesus would already have been seen as the true "lamb." Language like "new covenant" marked a conscious turn from the failed "old." "Forgiveness of sins" heralded the wondrous effect of his willing death. Ex 24:8; Jer 31:31-34 "Do this in remembrance of me" overlaid the memorial mandate of Israel out of Egypt. Ex 12:14 "For many" perceived the gospel validated in Jesus' death as embracing even Gentiles.

Then there is "the blood." Preserved manuscripts of Luke suggest that this was not in the original event, but only the bread, of which Jesus said, "This is my body." Lk 22:19a "Given for you, ... in remembrance of me, ... the new covenant in my blood"—all this was written into Luke's text later. Lk 22:19-(20)

Luke's account has Jesus begin the meal by blessing the cup. "And he took a cup, and when he had given thanks he said, 'Take this, and divide it among yourselves; for I tell you that from now on I shall not drink of the fruit of the vine until the kingdom of God comes.'" He would not celebrate their fantasy-kingdom with them, but only the true kingdom. The account continues: "And he took bread, and when he had given thanks he broke it and gave it to them, saying, 'This is my body.'" Lk 22:17-19a In Luke, that is all!

The imagery of *eating* human *flesh* or *body* (the Hebrew/Aramaic *basar* can be translated either way) is familiar metaphor in psalms and prophets. "Have they no knowledge, all the evildoers, *who eat up my people as they eat bread*, and call not upon the LORD?" Ps 14:4; 53:4 "When evildoers came upon me *to eat my body*, my adversaries and my foes, they stumbled and fell." Ps 27:2 "Each devours his neighbor's *body*," Isaiah said. Is 9:20 Micah depicts "the heads of Jacob ... who hate the good and love the evil, who tear the skin from off my people and their flesh from off their bones; who *eat the body of my people*." Mic 3:2-3

That is what Jesus' disciples were doing to him, even to his body. By their conspiracy they were devouring him, even his body and life! They wanted him for their own kingdom, not for the kingdom he taught. They did not care how they were abusing him. It was the final prediction of his death and of their part in it. When this took form in the sacrament, eating his "body" was a confession of guilt and horror at what they had done to him, yet of wonder at his and the Father's "giving," which had become their very life.

245

Though drinking Jesus' blood was not of that original event, it did become part of the young church's meal of remembrance. *Shedding* or *pouring out* the blood is an imagery of death. The law required that the blood of an animal be reverently drained, before its meat could be eaten as food. Gen 9:3-4 A priestly commandment applied this to animal sacrifices. "The life of the body is in the blood, and I have given it upon the altar to make atonement for your lives," it said. Lev 17:11 Jesus' crucifixion had not been a legally-correct blood-sacrifice of temple worship, however. It had come about by a conspiracy of guilt involving his own people, his disciples, and the Gentiles. Yet it was ultimately God's doing, his "giving" his beloved son "for you" and for "the forgiveness of sins." Jesus had prayed so himself, "Father, your will be done."

The young church understood this by and after Jesus' resurrection. The "covenant of blood" in animal sacrifices, as administered by the priests, was over. Legal niceties, like not eating blood, had not saved them from condemning Jesus and sending him to be crucified. Their covenant was over. "The blood of the covenant" in Jesus' death, "poured out for many" and "given for you," superseded it. This was God's doing, utterly new. The horror of "eating" the body of Jesus' death, matched by the horror of "drinking" his blood, must not be evaded. "Unless you eat the body of the son of man and drink his blood, you have no life in you," John's memoir put it later. Jn 6:53 It was like facing through the flaming sword of Eden, not for death but for life. Gen 3:24 Jesus' death did not end in horror! The wonder of "forgiveness" and "life" was in it from the living God and Father. His love for his son, his people, and the world had not failed! Thus the meal of guilt and shame emerged in a life of joy and honor, peace and freedom.

During the meal Jesus exposed their arsenal, two swords. Simon was hiding one beneath his robe. The other was likely Judas'. Not daring to be armed on his mission to Caiaphas, he entrusted it perhaps to John. "Two swords" were quite "enough," Jesus said, to get him "numbered with the transgressors" as one who "perverted the nation," and so condemned to death. Lk 22:35-38; 23:2; Is 53:12 He made them recite another word from Zechariah, on whose prophecy they so relied: "I will strike the shepherd, and the sheep will be scattered." Mt 26:31; Zech 13:7 Peter objected. The rest might run off, but he would be faithful even to death. The others agreed. They would not fail Jesus either. The boast was folly. "This very night, before the first cock crow of morning, you will deny me three times," Jesus told him. All four Gospels have this in some form. It became known because a transformed "Peter" confessed it freely.

Gethsemane and Arrest

After supper Jesus and his disciples sang a psalm together, then set out for Gethsemane to spend the night there again. It would be the darkest of nights. The memory is again from Peter, though James and John, mentioned also as witnesses, told it too. They recalled Jesus' distress and how he withdrew to pray alone. "My soul is very sorrowful, even to death," he said. That they record him as praying, "All things are possible to you," may reflect their own hope in a God of power who will endorse their fantasy and miraculously destroy any unrighteous who stand in their way. Mk 14:36 To Peter in particular Jesus said, "Could you not watch with me one hour? Watch and pray, that you may not enter into temptation. Your spirit is determined, but your body is weak." Mt 26:40-41; Mk 14:37-38

In the second chapter I linked Jesus' Gethsemane temptation to that of the pinnacle of the temple, in full view against the night sky. Mt 4:5-7 Nowhere is the choice Moses set between "life and good" and "death and evil" more dramatic than here. "If you are the son of God, cast yourself down," the devil said, for that is what your Father is asking you to do. No matter what he says, no angels will rescue you. Give yourself to those who come to arrest you and you know what will happen. You will end up crucified. Is that what you want? Is that what the God you call Father wants of his "beloved son," after all you have done for him? It's madness, Jesus! Save yourself while you still can! What good can come of it anyhow? This people cannot hear and never will, not even your own disciples! Give it up!

But Jesus chose *life*. "Knowing that the Father had given all things into his hands, having loved his own, he loved them to the finish." Jn 13:1,3 "My Father, if it is possible, let this cup pass from me; nevertheless not as I will but as you will." Mt 26:39 That is how the kingdom came.

Judas drew Caiaphas into his plan at this last moment, thinking still to trick him into a battle Jesus would win. The high priest did not believe in angels or fear their intervention. Knowing the zealotic mind, however, he could not discount a larger conspiracy. What secret army might Judas have in mind to ambush his temple police? Caiaphas summoned a strong force quietly, so as not to stir up the city. Their leader was Malchus, a Nabatean name, perhaps a second-generation slave out of a conquest by Herod the Great. That John preserves his name is significant. Jn 18:10 He is the likely source of much inside information.

John's memoir indicates that the temple police were reinforced by "a band of soldiers and their captain," a Roman force likely stationed in the Tower of Antonia under a "tribune." Jn 18:3,12 In that case the governor himself must have been asked to support the impending arrest of an insurrectionist leader, thus help dissipate the zealotic threat. Caiaphas would not have bothered to tell Pilate that the leader they planned to arrest was, in fact, Jesus of Nazareth.

Judas received his thirty pieces of silver, another link to Zechariah. Zech 11:12-13 Caiaphas, suspecting his motives, would not let him return. Malchus would need him to identify Jesus, he explained. For Judas this must have been disconcerting. He wanted to be at Jesus' side in the crucial hour. His offer to identify him by a kiss was a tactic to put him there still.

The disciples had gone to sleep, but Jesus awakened them. "The hour is at hand and the son of man is delivered up into the hands of sinners," he told them—the exact opposite of their expectation. Mt 26:45 When the arresting force arrived, John's account depicts Jesus in calm control. Jn 18:4-8 "Whom do you seek?" he asked. "Jesus of Nazareth," an officer replied. "I am he," he said. They were taken aback, unprepared to deal with one who would not fight. (The note that "they fell to the ground" is a copyist's notion, designed to glamorize Jesus' power).

Nothing happened as the disciples expected. "Lord, shall we strike with a sword?" one of them offered. Lk 22:49 John identifies Peter as the one who actually drew a sword and slashed out with it, ready to kill but managing only to cut the right ear of Malchus. His term for "ear" (Mark's too) is a diminutive, suggesting a little piece of ear. Jn 18:10-11; Mk 14:47 Peter would have been promptly disarmed. Another disciple, John perhaps, was drawing a sword too, but Jesus stopped him. "Put your sword away," he said, "for all who take the sword will perish by the sword." Mt 26:52 (A Greek copyist of Luke, assuming Jesus' divine power and compassion, interpolated that "he touched his ear and healed him." Lk 22:51) A saying in Matthew, that Jesus could have prayed to his Father for "twelve legions of angels" but did not, suggests that the disciples had expected a legion of angels to fight with each of them. Mt 26:53-55

"Have you come out as against a robber, with swords and clubs to capture me?" Jesus asked. "Robber" indicates an insurrectionist with a subversive army, the sort Caiaphas expected. Jesus was not that at all. Everything he had said and done was in the open, no conspiracy whatsoever. Jn 18:20 "I taught daily in the temple," he reminded them. If they thought him an insurrectionist, they could have arrested him at any time. "But all this has taken place, that the scriptures of the prophets might be fulfilled," he said. Mt 26:56 The scriptures, as Jesus and the young church fulfilled them, were not about predictions come true but about the covenant-God, the great "either-or," and choosing life.

"If you seek me, let these men go," John's memoir records him as saying, thus putting himself in between. Jn 18:8 That the officers released even Peter, that they arrested only Jesus, indicates that they sensed in him an authority other than mere power.

The disciples fled without interference. As for the ambush Caiaphas had anticipated, there was none—only a youth who, caught momentarily, left his linen garment in the hands of one of the temple police and ran home naked. Mk 14:51-52 I take him to be the "Mark" of this Gospel. His home would likely be that in which Jesus and his disciples had eaten supper. Apparently, it became later a gathering place for the young church in Jerusalem, remembered as "the house of Mary, the mother of John, whose other name was *Mark*." Acts 12:12

CHAPTER SEVENTEEN

The Trial

"We have a law, and by that law he ought to die, because he made himself a son of God." John 19:7

It was late, the city asleep, when Jesus, hands bound like a criminal, was led quietly into the city to the palace of the high priest. John mentions Annas, formerly the high priest, father-in-law to Caiaphas. He had quarters still in that house and appears to have played a considerable background role in the proceedings. Jn 18:13,24

Simon Peter

John preserves another detail: "Simon Peter followed Jesus, and so did another disciple." Jn 18:15-27 But why? Were they still thinking desperately to save Jesus—that the vision of Monday's procession, reduced to his determined disciples, reduced further to just the two of them, could not be mistaken?— that somehow they might yet win a glorious victory, like Jonathan and his armor-bearer against the Philistines of old? 1 Macc 4:30; 1 Sam 14:6 This is another Peter story. That other disciple, "known to the high priest," known also to the maid at the door and the guards inside, can only have been Judas. Now Peter was with Judas again, an army of two, frightened, no strategy left, yet hoping somehow to save Jesus still, counting on divine help. "God forbid, Lord! This shall never happen to you," he had protested already in Galilee. Mt 16:22 He believed it still. No, this could not be happening to Jesus! It must not!

But why does the preserved text say "another disciple," rather than name Judas explicitly? Peter, who told this on himself later, would not have concealed this. John would not have obscured it, either. I suspect that a Greek copyist, idealizing Peter and abhorring Judas, could not accept Peter's complicity with Judas and so concealed it.

Judas told Simon Peter to wait in the courtyard while he went inside to see what he could see. Peter felt uncomfortable. He had no business being there. Yet here he was, standing at the fire with some of the temple police who had arrested Jesus. When Judas got him in, the maid at the door had asked the obvious, "Are you also one of this man's disciples?" to which he had lied by instinctive fear, "No, I am not." The guards did not know him, either, so it was natural for them to ask the same question. Peter had set his course. "No, I am not," he said, but did not identify himself otherwise. They knew he was lying. His accent gave him away as a Galilean. One of them claimed to recognize him from the garden at Jesus' arrest, not to threaten him but curious to know, then perhaps ask about his master. But Peter was guilty and caught. He denied it this time with an oath, "I do not know the man!"—which was, in a sense, true. Then he heard a cock crow and ran out, no one pursuing him, and wept bitterly. He told this afterwards, when Jesus' resurrection had set him free. He had not saved Jesus. Jesus had saved him.

The Condemnation

Varied memories of Jesus' trial suggest that a hearing was held in Caiaphas' palace already that night, representatives of the council present, to set the strategy for an official session in the early morning. Charges were needed. It seemed simple at first. "I am able to destroy this temple and in three days I will build another," someone claimed to have heard him boast, thus inciting his followers against the priesthood God himself had established. He had exhibited glaring disrespect also by disrupting the business of the temple that Monday. Yet witnesses could not agree on what Jesus had actually said, or even that it was he who said it. Mk 14:55-59 When Jeremiah predicted the destruction of the temple generations before, no one considered that to be blasphemy. Jer 7:14 Caiaphas proposed the charge on which they had been ready to stone him, his claim to be "the son of God"—"calling God his Father, making himself equal with God," "even making himself God." Jn 5:18; 10:33 Blasphemy, they had called it. Jn 10:36 They, the pure race of Abraham, would never use such language! For a Galilean "born of fornication" to claim this was intolerable. Jn 8:41 If he could be made to say it openly before the whole council, he would condemn himself.

John's account introduces the morning session. The high priest began by questioning Jesus about his disciples and his teaching. In summarizing his message, he would surely refer to God as his Father and himself as God's son! Jesus gave them no help. If they cared about his message, they could have heard it all along. "I have always taught in synagogues and in the temple, where all Judeans come together; I have said nothing secretly. Why do you ask me? Ask those who have heard me what I said to them." One of the officers standing by struck Jesus and said, "Is that how you answer the high priest?" Jesus answered simply, "If I have said something wrong, bear witness to the wrong. But if what I said is right, why do you strike me?" Jn 18:19-23 Whoever reported this exchange, most likely Nicodemus, must have been impressed by it.

Other questions were asked, but Jesus remained silent. The high priest then put him under oath: "I adjure you by the living God, tell us if you are the christ, the son of God." Mt 26:63; Mk 14:61 ("Christ" came to be defined as "the son of God" only after the resurrection, hence I take this to have entered the text later from the young church's confession). It was to his name "the son of God" that Jesus replied, "You have said so." They might condemn him for it now, but God's verdict would overrule theirs. "Hereafter you will see the son of man sitting at the right hand of God, and coming with the clouds of heaven." Dan 7:13: Ps 110:1

Luke's account seems the clearest at this point. Lk 22:69-71 Realizing that "the son of man" and "the son of God" were equivalent, Caiaphas pressed Jesus to say the bolder name outright. "Are you the son of God then?" he asked. "You say it, I am," Jesus replied—as they knew he must, for this was the issue of his whole life. "What further testimony do we need? We have heard it ourselves from his own lips!" Caiaphas cried out in horror. Matthew and Mark have him tearing his robe. "He has uttered blasphemy. Why do we still need witnesses? You have now heard his blasphemy. What is your judgment?" The verdict, "He deserves death," was declared to be unanimous. They inflicted on him the required beating, spitting, and mockery. Mt 26:63-68 They did not take him out to stone him though, but bound him as planned and led him away to be tried, sentenced, and executed by the Roman governor.

Judas

Meanwhile the tragedy of Judas was unfolding to its end. Mt 27:3-10 "When Judas saw that Jesus was condemned," the account begins. Waiting in the entrance room of Caiaphas' house he could see messengers go out and members of the council come in for the night meeting. No sign of divine rescue was evident, only the grim silence of leaders doing an unpleasant but necessary duty. When they came out after a while, Judas got one of them to tell what happened. The council would meet in early morning, condemn Jesus for blasphemy, then deliver him to Pilate to be crucified as an insurrectionist king. It was all set.

Only then did Judas' expectation of angels and a miraculous divine intervention die. Now the magnitude of his own part in Jesus' disaster began to dawn on him. His plot had failed. Far from saving Jesus, he had delivered him up to the enemy he despised. Next morning Judas waited at the council chamber to catch Caiaphas or any of the priests and elders with whom he had dealt. He abhorred his bag of silver pieces. He was desperate to undo the damage, retrieve his horrible mistake, buy Jesus back. "It was I who sinned, not Jesus. I delivered innocent blood to you!" Those he tried to stop had no use for him, however. If any paused, it was only to rebuff him: "What is that to us? See to it yourself." One of them must have remembered this later and told it.

The next scene was the sanctuary, a magnificent edifice within the temple complex, walled in marble and trimmed in gold. Its porch, a hundred cubits square, gave access to the holy place where the priests burned incense and offered prayers. Behind was the holy of holies, which the high priest could enter through the veil, yet even he only once a year. A court reserved to the priests surrounded the sanctuary. Eastward from it was the great altar whose fire never went out. This was the morning of pre-Passover devotion, the sacrificing of lambs to begin at noon.

Suddenly a nondescript Galilean leaped the low wall, invaded the court, mounted the porch, and before anyone could think to stop him, hurled his silver pieces clattering into the holy place itself. It was blasphemy! He ought to be dragged out immediately and stoned! That, in fact, is what Judas wanted. He, the guilty, would die with Jesus, the innocent. But it did not happen. The officiating priest, possibly Caiaphas himself, recognized him, appreciated how distraught he was, and ordered those who held Judas to let him go.

The final scene was the pinnacle. Climbing the interior steps to the top of the temple wall at that dramatic southeast corner, Judas cast himself over and down. He hit the slope, then tumbled wildly until his torn body came to rest on the floor of the Kidron Valley. There he was found, "all his bowels gushed out," a sight so abhorrent that all Jerusalem heard of it. Acts 1:18-19 They buried him in what came to be called Akeldama, "Field of Blood," in the valley of Hinnom south of the city. The council bought that field with Judas' blood money as a burial site for strangers. Mt 27:6-8 Someone must have known and told this, too.

There was still Simon, Judas' father, who after Jesus' resurrection labeled himself not only "the Zealot" but the real "Iscariot," or deceiver. How did he find out? Was he perhaps in on that awful burial? Who probed Judas' story and made its agonizing details known? One thing is clear. Judas' grievous end, together with Jesus' death, marked the death of zealotry for Simon, and by Jesus' resurrection, transformed him into a voice of the new beginning.

Pilate

Abundant memory from independent witnesses is preserved of the trial before Pilate. The event was humanly real, single, and coherent. A preliminary assumption is vital. "The chief priests and elders" or "the Judeans," who brought Jesus to Pilate, were not the entire council but a delegation. The delegation in turn did not speak in a chorus but by an appointed leader, trusted to present their case and respond to any new situation. The man who spoke for them was knowledgeable, committed, alert, quick-witted, even brilliant. Since he is the voice of the delegation throughout this trial and beyond, it is useful to supply a name for him. Let me call him "Perez."

Pontius Pilate governed Judea and Samaria from his seaport capital, Caesarea. He came to Jerusalem for every major feast of the Judeans, however, bringing an adequate force to augment the legion stationed year-round in the Tower of Antonia, which overlooked the temple area from the north. For his headquarters in Jerusalem, Pilate had taken over the palace of Herod the Great at the western wall of the city. A gate here opened toward Joppa on the Mediterranean. Another road led northeast, linking the palace with Antonia. Along it was the hillock called Golgotha, its racks mounted firmly in the ground, ready always for a next crucifixion.

The zealotic impulse posed a constant threat of insurrection—against the priesthood for its satisfied complicity with Rome, but ultimately against Rome itself. When a leader emerged to whom enthusiasts could rally, the unrest could become dangerous. In this instance it was Jesus of Nazareth. On Monday a great crowd had escorted him into the temple with songs and palm branches, hailing him even as king, expecting him to somehow displace the priesthood. Caiaphas and the council had kept things under control, but Roman forces were on the alert, too. The suspicion that some in that crowd were secretly armed was confirmed by a hot-blooded skirmish. A Galilean named

Barabbas had gotten into a fight and killed somebody. Mk 15:7; Lk 23:19 He and two companions, promptly subdued, were awaiting execution.

Pilate's own spy network indicated that this Jesus was a threat only to the authority of the priesthood and council. Far from plotting or stirring up revolution, he had consistently disavowed the fanatics. When put to the test on the issue of Roman taxes, he had commanded the people to pay them, saying that their problem was not with Caesar but with their own God. Mt 22:15-22 An undercurrent of an expectation ready to become violent remained, however, stirred by bizarre stories of signs and wonders and looking for greater wonders still to come. Pilate had reason to appreciate the initiative of Caiaphas toward arresting one such potential troublemaker during the night, his own forces standing by, before the situation got out-of-hand. Remove the leader and the crowds would go home after the Passover, without incident.

"Perez" and his delegation stood back while the temple police turned Jesus over to a Roman centurion and his squad. Pilate's response in John suggests dismay. The man whom Caiaphas had arrested and was sending him for trial was not a zealotic conspirator at all, but the Jesus he knew to be innocent and had even come to respect. Jn 18:28-38 "What accusation do you bring against this man?" he asked. The answer, voiced by "Perez," suggests that Pilate had already received the charges. "If he were not an evildoer, we would not have handed him over to you." Luke has the detail. "We found this man perverting our nation, and forbidding us to give tribute to Caesar, and saying that he himself is Christ a king." Lk 23:1-5 Not a word of this was true. The strategy, however, was to hold Jesus accountable for what zealotic enthusiasts promoted in his name.

"Take him and judge him by your own law," Pilate responded, wanting no part in it. "Perez" replied that they had already judged him, but needed the governor to issue the death sentence. "It is not lawful for us to put any man to death." That was true in principle, yet when a situation demanded it, they did their stonings anyway.

Pilate turned to enter the judgment hall, called the praetorium, and summoned Jesus before him. To conduct an inquiry for which he already knew the answer was awkward. All four Gospels preserve his opening question, "Are you the king of the Judeans?" Matthew and Mark indicate that Jesus acknowledged it but would not answer further questions, to the point that the governor marveled. John's memoir preserves a bit of conversation, however.

Jesus asked Pilate, "Is this your own idea, or are others accusing me of it to you?" Jn 18:33-38 "Am I a Judean?" the governor replied. "Don't expect me to understand how Judeans think! Your own nation and the chief priests have handed you over to me. So what have you done?"

Jesus explained, "If my kingdom were the sort these zealots want, I would have had an army of them with me last night. They would have fought bitterly to keep me from being arrested and handed over to the council and to you. But that is not my kind of kingdom."

"Are you a king then?" Pilate pressed on. "Yes, I am a king," Jesus said, "but I was born to it. I don't need to fight for it. My calling in this world is to tell the truth of God's kingdom, so that my people may be born to it, too. Those who care about the truth listen to what I say."

"What is truth?" Pilate asked, cutting him off. That Jesus was no threat to Caesar might be the truth of it, but what good was that? Only power mattered now, Pilate's power against Caiaphas and the council, their power to pressure him. He knew why they were doing this. It was envy, fear of being wrong, fear of losing control. Mt 27:18 They would not stand for it, so they had found reason to condemn Jesus. Now they wanted Pilate to do the dirty work of executing him, while they stood back to keep clean for their Passover. Jn 18:28

The governor went out to the accusers and told his verdict: "I find no crime in him." All the Gospels report this. The delegation from the council could not accept it, however. Luke's account has "Perez" urge the case intently: "He stirs up the people, teaching throughout all Judea, from Galilee even to this place." "Galilee!" Pilate seized his opportunity. Jesus was a Galilean, of Herod's jurisdiction! Herod was in the city for the Passover. Let him handle it! Lk 23:5-12

Herod's house in Jerusalem was on the same western slope overlooking the old "city of David" and the Kidron Valley beyond it. That the trial should be diverted so would have irritated "Perez" and his delegation. This business was taking too long. They had the Passover to prepare for and the devotions that attended it. The city was well awake by now, and word of Jesus' arrest was bound to get out. There was nothing to do, however, except accompany the Roman guard that brought Jesus to Herod and state their case all over again.

The likely source for what went on at this trial was Chuza, named in Luke as Herod's steward. Lk 8:3 Chuza would have known John the Baptist during his imprisonment in Tiberias. His wife, Joanna, had joined the women of Jesus' company in Galilee and had rejoined them now. Perhaps it was through her that the news of Jesus' arrest and impending death spread quickly to the other women and throughout Jerusalem, even to pilgrims encamped around.

Herod had never met Jesus but was glad to see him—hoping he might even see a "sign" from him of the sort that so enamoured people of zealotic piety. "Perez" told how urgent it was that Jesus be put to death. Jesus said nothing to defend himself. Herod decreed him innocent and sent him back to the governor. He had no desire to kill another prophet. Let Pilate do this one. Knowing the inevitable outcome, Herod had his soldiers costume Jesus in an old royal robe, then turned him back to the centurion and his squad. He could commiserate with Pilate. To have authority is not necessarily to be free. The episode bridged a certain enmity between them.

Barabbas

Now came the Barabbas incident, preserved most clearly in Mark. Mk 15:6-15 "The crowd came up and began to ask Pilate to do as he customarily did for them"—release at Passover any one prisoner whom they desired. The memory indicates that these petitioners were of the zealots who had been looking to Jesus so eagerly as their "christ-king," and that Pilate realized this. They had in mind to rescue Barabbas, imprisoned and under sentence of death with others who had committed murder in an act of insurrection—an enthusiasm likely associated with the zealotic escort of Jesus into the temple. This crowd viewed Barabbas as a hero, one of their own and dear to them. A zealotic leader, possibly Simon, Judas' father, summoned them to this mission. They came to Pilate knowing nothing of Jesus' arrest that night.

While they were presenting their case, the council's delegation returned silently, wanting to attract no attention, bringing Jesus back from Herod. Two groups stood before Pilate now, neither of whom knew what the other was about. "Perez" and his delegation pressed through the zealotic crowd to finish their business with the governor. Simon and his party were here first. If these others had in mind to ask for another prisoner, they would hold their ground. It must have been shocking to see that the man in the purple robe was a prisoner, and that it was Jesus.

Pilate perceived his opportunity and played it well. He reviewed the case with "Perez" and his company, so that the zealotic crowd would know what was going on. "You brought me this man as one who was perverting the people," the record in Luke has him saying. "After examining him before you, I did not find him guilty of any of your charges against him. Neither did Herod, for he sent him back to us. I will therefore chastise him and release him." Lk 23:13-17 The council's delegation, of course, could settle for nothing less than Jesus' death.

Pilate turned then to the zealots. Knowing that they were of the crowd that had hailed Jesus as their king only a few days ago, he offered him to them an alternative: "Do you want me to release for you the king of the Judeans?" Confident what their decision must be, he withdrew into the praetorium.

He turned Jesus over to the guard then, so as to amplify the mockery of Herod's robe and to make sure these fanatics understood the folly of imagining he could ever be their king. In the interim, a maid brought a message from his wife. She had heard of the prisoner and the council's determination to crucify him. It terrified her. "Have nothing to do with that righteous man," her message said, "for I have suffered much over him today in a dream." Mt 27:19 "Tell her it's troublesome to me, too," he sent word back to her, "but I think now I have it under control."

By now the council's delegation realized who this other crowd was and why they had come. It was a crisis. What if they asked to have Jesus released instead of Barabbas? "Now the chief priests and elders persuaded the people to ask for Barabbas and destroy Jesus," a memory says. Mt 27:20 How "Perez" and his company accomplished this may be deduced in part from yet another memory—the "mockery" at the cross. Mt 27:40-44; Mk 15:29-32 "Perez" mounted a step and beckoned for attention. Knowing the zealotic mind, their persistent hope and expectation of a miracle even at the last desperate moment, he challenged their noble undying faith.

They must surely regret with great pain, he said, that in choosing Barabbas they would have to abandon his two courageous companions. Still, it might not have to be so! If Jesus is indeed the christ, as they have firmly believed, he will surely save not just himself but them, too! Has he not always saved others? Let their faith not fail! The living God, who loves his son, will not bring him low to abandon him, but only to let his glory shine the more! Watch and see what God will do! Even if it goes so far as actual crucifixion, Jesus the christ can still come down from the cross—and bring those other two down with him!

As for "Perez" himself and the council—true, they have had a problem believing Jesus or setting their hope in him. Nevertheless, if this great miracle were actually to happen, if Jesus were to come down from the cross, that would be the sign of all signs! Be assured, he and the council would not be so blind as to miss it or so hardened as not to believe! They too would embrace Jesus, invite him to take over, follow his lead into the glorious fulfillment of the kingdom of God! As for this faithful and expectant crowd, their opportunity of the moment is to save Barabbas. Let them see that intention through!

Then watch and see how Jesus will save himself, and the others also, even if it comes to crucifixion! God is greater than all! Believe it!

To Simon and his zealotic companions, the case "Perez" made was persuasive. This could be God's way to purify the temple, to rally the whole nation!

Pilate returned to hear the decision. Jesus followed, attended by the centurion and his squad. He wore again the robe of royalty in which Herod had clothed him, but it was plain that he had suffered cruel scourging. The soldiers had also plaited a crown out of thorns and pressed it on his head. His hands were bound, but they had put a reed in his right hand for a scepter. They bowed before him in pretense. "Hail, king of the Judeans!" they said, mocking not only Jesus but those who had hailed him just this way. Pilate let the charade play on for a bit, then put an end to it. "Here he is, look at him!" he said. All of them, priestly party and zealotic enthusiasts together, must know that the Romans were in charge. Jesus would never be their king. He signaled the soldiers, and they led him back into the praetorium.

Now let them establish what is truth. Do they want Barabbas, insurrectionist and murderer? Or Jesus, whose innocence they must know, whom they had honored with such expectant devotion? "Which of the two do you want me to release for you?"

They answered in chorus, "Barabbas!"

Pilate could not imagine it. Had he heard right? How could they do this? "What shall I do with Jesus then, who is called Christ?" he asked helplessly.

"Let him be crucified," the cry came back.

"Why? What evil has he done?"

But they shouted the more, "Let him be crucified!" Mt 27:21-23

Pilate could not bring himself to do it. Jn 19:6-15 "Take him yourselves and crucify him, for I find no crime in him," he protested.

"Perez" reassured him, "He is not as innocent as you think, governor. We have a law, and by our law he ought to die, because he has made himself the son of God." This left Pilate the more afraid. "Son of God" suggested descent from deity, a god disguised as a man.

He turned back into the praetorium and faced Jesus again. "Who are you?" he asked. "Where are you from?" Jesus did not answer. Pilate could not comprehend his silence. He was looking for any clue to save him, but Jesus seemed not to care. "You will not speak to me?" he said. "Don't you know that I have authority to release you, and authority to crucify you?"

Jesus tried to comfort him. "Don't blame yourself, or even the Judeans.

You would have no authority over me at all, unless it were given you from above. It is my God who has delivered me to you. If you need to blame somebody, blame him."

Pilate was the more determined to release him, but the delegation of chief priests and elders was adamant. Jesus was responsible for this zealotic furor and must be held accountable. "Perez" put it to Pilate again, "If you release this man, you are not Caesar's friend! Everyone who makes himself a king sets himself against Caesar."

In the background lay Caiaphas' realism, "It is expedient for you that one man should die for the people and that the whole nation not perish." Release Jesus now and the insurrection, about to be quenched, will burst forth in his name all the more fearfully! This crowd, ever eager for signs and wonders, will perceive his release as a divine miracle, then expect more such miracles. The council was fulfilling the responsibility assigned it by Rome to avert such a disaster. Pilate must do his part. To send one man to death, even one he might consider innocent, would be a cheap price to pay if that single death were to spare both Rome and the Judeans a fearful and bloody warfare. Even Caesar would see it as good governing!

The Sentence

Pilate brought Jesus out once more, then took his place on the seat of judgment built up out of the stone porch. John's memoir notes that this was called the Pavement. The translator preserves the Hebrew, Gabbatha. The day was the Preparation (Friday), looking to the sabbath-Passover. The time reference in John, "about the sixth hour" (counting from sunrise), namely noon, would link Jesus' dying with the sacrificing of lambs, to start as the sun began its descent from zenith. Jn 19:14 Mark has what was likely the actual time, nine in the morning. Mk 15:25

From his seat of judgment, the governor appealed to the zealotic party one last time. "Here is your king," he said, gesturing to Jesus, the very king they had hailed only four days ago. They remained unmoved. "Away with him, away with him, crucify him!" they chanted. The governor could still not comprehend it. "Shall I crucify your king?" "Perez" and his delegation answered firmly, "We have no king but Caesar."

Pilate had done all he could. Mt 27:24-26 Bowing to the pressure, he asked for water. A bowl was brought. He washed his hands openly as a sign to them, saying, "I am innocent of this man's blood. It is your doing. See to it yourselves."

They accepted the responsibility, for they had done what they must. "His blood be on us and on our children," they said, confident that this was not the sort of iniquity God would visit on a next generation. Ex 20:5

Pilate had Barabbas brought up and released him to Simon and his crowd. Then he handed Jesus over to the centurion and his squad to be crucified. For the zealotic party, the reunion with Barabbas was joyful. They had reason to stay on, however. If Jesus was truly their christ and king, as they were determined to believe, not even crucifixion would thwart him. He would show his glory by coming down even from the cross. They must be there to see it, the first to receive him! "Perez" and his associates needed to stay as well, until the crucifixion had safely accomplished its end.

Who would have remembered all this afterwards and told it? Much would have come as confession from those zealots, Simon perhaps among them.

Other questions arise for which no answer is preserved. It must have occurred to Simon quickly to wonder about his son Judas and the other disciples. Last night they were to have gathered for supper with Jesus. What had happened? Where were they now? Such an anxiety might have diverted him from the still-anticipated miracle. He must find Judas and the others, give them hope, possibly even bring them to Golgotha! One question leads to another. When and how did Simon come to know his son's tragic end? What did that discovery do to him? Might he even have been in on the burial? Was it he, perhaps, who pursued Judas' story and told it in such detail, so that it is preserved in the record? No such information is preserved. Nevertheless, there must have been a story, painful indeed.

CHAPTER EIGHTEEN

■ Golgotha

"So they took Jesus, and he went out, bearing his own cross, to the place called the place of the skull, which is called in Hebrew Golgotha. There they crucified him, and with him two others, one on either side, and Jesus between them."

John 19:17-18

The Procession

The crucifixion squad organized the procession. They took the purple robe off Jesus and put his own garment on him. Matthew and Mark have the scourging here, the crown of thorns and reed and mockery, which John has earlier. Mt 27:27-31; Mk 15:16-20 They brought the two who were to be crucified with Jesus, each to carry the crossbar on which he would be nailed. Jn 19:17

Meanwhile Pilate prepared a sign to identify Jesus and state the charge for which he was being executed. "Jesus of Nazareth, the king of the Judeans," it said in three languages, Hebrew, Latin, and Greek. Jn 19:19-22 A Galilean, king over the Judeans! Pilate liked it. Perhaps he had in mind some residual notion of Jesus' kingdom of "truth" over mere power. In any case he wanted it fixed over Jesus' head. It conveyed his own protest against the incongruity of it all.

If he hoped it might annoy Jesus' accusers, he got his wish. "Perez," voice of "the chief priests of the Judeans," saw the sign as the procession formed and protested. The zealotic illusion must not be encouraged. Responsible Judeans had not acknowledged Jesus as king and never would. Let him die anonymously like the others. But if there must be a sign, let it be accurate. "Your sign, governor, it's not true!" he cried out. "He is not the king of the Judeans, and you know it! He only tried to be. Let it read, 'He said, I am the king of the Judeans!'"

Pilate, glad to reclaim his authority, retorted, "What you say is not true, and you know it! He did not claim, 'I am the king of the Judeans.' You only accused him of it. No, my sign stands. What I have written, I have written." The young church came to perceive Pilate's sign as a divine irony, God himself testifying to the truth in what seemed total disaster, putting it in writing even for all the world to read. "He who sits in the heavens laughs!" Ps 2:4

Who would have overheard this exchange? More than that, who witnessed everything that had gone on within Pilate's praetorium, was affected by it, and told it afterwards, so that it is on record to this day? The centurion, head of the crucifixion squad, is mentioned at the end. He had stood dutifully alongside Jesus throughout these proceedings, thus had heard and seen everything. Glimpses of his silent role may be detected behind other elements of direct memory.

The centurion would have conscripted Simon of Cyrene to carry the crossbar for Jesus. Mt 27:32; Mk 15:21; Lk 23:26 He was "coming in from the country" just as the procession headed out toward the site of the execution. Cyrene lay eight hundred miles west across the Mediterranean, on the north coast of Africa in today's Libya. If Simon was only now arriving for the Passover, he must have been grievously delayed. The Roman right to conscript anyone for "a mile" of burden-bearing delayed him further, to say nothing of assaulting his dignity. Mt 5:41 Why should he be made to bear the crossbar of some criminal he did not know to the site of the execution? Yet it turned out to be the privilege of Simon's lifetime. He came to know Jesus by it. He was the very first, in fact, to literally "take up Jesus' cross and follow him," a language that became metaphor later. Mt 10:38; 16:24 All three synoptic Gospels preserve Simon's name. Mark's account identifies also two sons of his, Rufus and Alexander, known in the young church.

But if the centurion conscripted Simon for this task, what might have been the need? It was not Jesus' physical collapse, as tradition has supposed. The need was the centurion's, to lighten Jesus' burden ever so slightly in protest of a dreadful injustice, which he was nevertheless compelled to execute to its end—a silent but eloquent kindness.

News of the unfolding trial must have spread rapidly and systematically through the city, even to pilgrims camped outside. Joanna, wife of Chuza, had gotten word to the Galilean women, including his mother. Zealots, hoping to see the climactic miracle still, rushed to gather others of like mind. Someone met John and told him, the only one of Jesus' disciples to be at the cross. Thus, when Jesus passed through the gate, a considerable crowd was there to join the procession to Golgotha, including "women who bewailed and lamented him." Lk 23:27-31

I take this testimony to derive from direct memory, also the report that Jesus stopped, turned to speak to them, and what he said. Still, by what authority could a condemned prisoner interrupt the procession to Golgotha this way? Why didn't the execution squad brutally shove him on? The centurion alone could have permitted it and signaled a halt.

Someone who was there remembered what Jesus said and retold it in compact form, so that it was written down and preserved among the fragments which Luke afterwards incorporated in his Gospel. "Daughters of Jerusalem," Jesus said, "weep not for me, but weep for yourselves and for your children of a next generation." He had stopped similarly a few days before on the Mount of Olives. There he had wept for a Jerusalem that "did not know the time of your visitation." Lk 19:41-44 The LORD had been "visiting the iniquities of the fathers upon the children" for generations. Ex 20:5; 34:7 Now, in this generation, he was offering them "the things that make for peace," yet they coveted instead a glory that could only end in their destruction. That was real cause for weeping! So also here. "Blessed" that there be no next generation! "Blessed" that "wombs not bear and breasts not give suck!" "Then they will begin to say to the mountains, Cover us, and to the hills, Fall upon us." Hos 10:8 Jesus is a green tree of life, but they will not know it. "If they do these things to the green wood, what will happen to the dry?"

The procession resumed and came to Golgotha. Mark and Matthew tell the memory, "They offered him wine mingled with myrrh (in Matthew, gall), but he did not take it." Mk 15:23; Mt 27:34 This wine, whatever its quality or ingredients, was not intended for those being crucified, but for the squad. By offering some to Jesus, the centurion was again showing respect for him. There is no indication that he offered it also to the others. Why did Jesus not accept it? He had said at supper, "I shall not drink again of the fruit of the vine, until that day when I drink it new in the kingdom of God."

The Crucifixion

And so they crucified him, and the other two on either side. Archaeology explains the procedure and the death process. The biblical record knows the event by the minds and hearts of those who took part in it, however. It is not interested in the engineering.

Their task done, the soldiers sat down to divide their normal booty, garments which those crucified would no longer need. Ps 22:18 All the Gospels take note of this. John, who was there, tells it in detail. "In four parts, to each soldier a part," he observes, but adds that they cast lots for Jesus' tunic, since it was "woven seamless from top to bottom." Jn 19:23-24 Some woman, I think of Mary or Martha, must have made it and given it to him. By wearing it, he honored the giver.

Luke has Jesus praying, "Father, forgive them, for they know not what they do." Lk 23:34 The Father's love flows onward through his son toward sinners. But who are "they" and what was their ignorance? The crucifixion squad knew what they were doing, at least the technique of it. Pilate too, for all his regret, knew what he was doing. So did "Perez" and the colleagues for whom he spoke. Even the zealotic enthusiasts knew what they were doing, or thought they did—Jesus' disciples included. Yet "what they were doing" conspired to get the son of God, the embodiment of Israel's covenant, crucified! "If they do these things to the green wood, what will happen to the dry?" Lk 23:31 Here is the great "either-or" again—"life and good" or "death and evil." Jesus alone knew what he was doing. Who else could even imagine such a prayer?

What appears to be mockery follows. Mt 27:39-43; Mk 15:29-32; Lk 23:35-38 It began with the plaintive cry of a zealot. He had come expecting to see the grand reversal. The sign on the cross encouraged him further. Yet after long and anxious waiting, his faith was failing. Breaking the silence, he pleaded aloud for Jesus to do even at this ultimate hour what he and others still hoped. "Come down from the cross!" With that, other voices gave expression to every element of zealotic hope. "The chief priests, with the scribes and elders" ("Perez" and his delegation) had infiltrated the zealots, identified with them. They appeared to support them. "Yes, Jesus, king of Israel! Give us the sign we ask for! Come down from the cross, and we will believe in you, too!"

The plea deteriorated into mockery, not just of Jesus but of the zealots and their fanatical faith. "Is he the king of Israel? Let him come down from the cross." "He saved others, let him save himself, if he is the christ, his chosen one." "You who would destroy the temple of God and build it again in three days, save yourself!" Matthew's text draws on a psalm: "All who see me mock at me, they wag their heads, saying, 'He has committed his cause to the LORD; let him deliver him, let him rescue him, for he delights in him.'" Ps 22:8 Then, like the devil in Jesus' temptations, they cite the critical issue: "for he said, 'I am God's son!'"

That the "robbers" (insurrectionists) crucified with Jesus would join in this plea might be expected. Some zealot, as the procession was forming, would have whispered to them how Jesus at this dark hour would yet reveal his glory by coming down from the cross, and so bring them with him. Luke has the detail. Lk 23:39-43 "Are you not the christ? Save yourself and us," one of them pleaded. His companion was beginning to know Jesus, however. "Do you not fear God, since you are under the same judgment? And we indeed justly, for we are getting what we deserve. But this man has done nothing wrong." Seeing the kingdom now as Jesus had taught it, longing to share the hope of the one who had not lost hope but said, "Do not weep for me," he prayed, "Lord, remember me when you come into your kingdom." Jesus' answer defied death for them both. "Truly, I say to you, today you will be with me in paradise."

The zealotic illusion finally died. There would be no miracle. Jesus was not asking for one, had never asked for one. He would not come down from the cross. Numb with despair, the enthusiasts began to drift away. "Perez" and his party had no reason to stay, either.

The faithful Galilean women had been standing far off. They came nearer now. Mary Magdalene and Jesus' mother are listed, her identity variously concealed. Matthew's "the mother of the sons of Zebedee" appears to be Mark's "Salome." Mt 27:56; Mk 15:40 Luke mentions Joanna in the resurrection context. Lk 24:10 John has "Mary, the wife of Clopas." Jn 19:25 If his "Clopas" is the "Cleopas" of Emmaus in Luke, she would be Judean. Lk 24:18 Simon of Cyrene may have stayed on, perceiving more in this strange Passover than he would ever have dreamed. John may have hidden himself until then among the zealots, but no longer.

"Woman, see your son," Jesus said, directing his mother to him and him to her, "See, your mother." Jn 19:26-27 That John called himself "the disciple whom Jesus loved" does not imply favoritism. Jesus had not given up on him for all his sin, but loved him to the end even at so great a cost. "Whom Jesus loved" plays also on his name "Jochanan" ("Johwah is gracious"). Jesus' love for him is Johwah's. That John from that hour took Jesus' mother (he does not name her) to his own home indicates that he and his mother, Salome, brought her home with them to Bethsaida in Galilee after the resurrection, and that she lived out her life there rather than in Nazareth.

The Psalm

Matthew and Mark preserve only one saying from the cross, "My God, my God, why have you forsaken me?" Mt 27:46; Mk 15:34 The time is the ninth hour, three in the afternoon. Jesus' agony was almost over. In Matthew this saying is transliterated from Hebrew, then translated. Mark transliterated it in Aramaic. Both Gospels preserve a triviality in that context. "Bystanders," likely the soldiers, thought Jesus was calling on "Elijah" for help. "Eli" or "My God" of Matthew's Hebrew matches "Elijah." Mark's Aramaic "Eloi" does not.

That a soldier responded quickly by dipping a sponge in vinegar, putting it on a reed, and holding it to Jesus' mouth, may indicate again the centurion's care for him. Mk 15:36; Mt 27:48 John's memoir reports that Jesus said, "I thirst," and thereby received the drink. Jn 19:28 That he drank now what he refused earlier accords with his final word in John, "It is finished." This does not indicate escape, but a task accomplished in full. He had walked the way of righteousness to the end, straight and level, serving his Father and his people, drinking the cup his Father gave him to drink, returning to the God who sent him. "I will not drink this fruit of the vine until the kingdom of God comes," he said at the meal. Lk 22:18 Now he drank it! This was the kingdom!

Aramaic was the language of common speech, but scripture readings in worship were still Hebrew, also singing of psalms and prayers. Psalms were memorized with their tones and readily sung by those brought up in them. Jesus, nearing his last breath, began to sing a psalm familiar to them all, "My God, my God, why have you forsaken me?" Ps 22 His little flock picked it up and sang it through for him. What they sang called attention to details they might not have noticed but told later—mockery, dry thirst, divided garments. Mt 27:35,43; Mk 15:24,29a; Jn 19:23-24,28

The psalm ebbs and flows between despair and hope. Metaphor upon metaphor expresses torment, yet the memory and promise of God's grace keeps returning. The cry of forsakenness is answered by recalling how the fathers cried out in similar distress and were delivered. Mockery of God's promises is answered by remembering how life from the mother's womb was sustained and kept safe on her breast, an imagery of infant-like dependence on God even now. Bones out of joint, heart melting like wax, parched tongue cleaving in thirst to the jaws, ribs standing out so as to be counted, garments divided and lots cast—the accumulating torment is answered by a cry to the LORD. He will not be far off. He alone can deliver "my soul" from a host of enemies. Enemies are pictured graphically—sword, dog, lion, horns of wild oxen.

Suddenly the strife is over, and after that only praise. "I will tell of your name to my brethren, in the midst of the congregation I will praise you." "He has not despised or abhorred the affliction of the afflicted, and he has not hid his face from him, but has heard, when he cried to him." "May your hearts live forever!" Israel's covenant has no boundaries. "All the ends of the earth shall remember and turn to the LORD; and all the families of the nations shall worship before him." The iniquity of the fathers will no longer be visited upon children and children's children. "Posterity shall serve him; men shall tell of the LORD to the coming generation, and proclaim his deliverance to a people yet unborn, that he has done this."

The little company at the cross sang this as never before. It was grievous, yes, but the story was not over. Matthew and Mark mention a loud cry. Luke has Jesus praying from another psalm, "Father, into your hands I commend my spirit." Ps 31:5 With that, he breathed his last.

The Signs

"Signs" of the sort the zealots expected failed to happen. When this story was told in the young church, however, it was full of signs. Graphic metaphor indicates a turning point, the very day of the LORD—like seeing God from the back after he has passed by. Ex 33:23 From noon to Jesus' death, the sun was darkened and gave no light. Mt 27:45 "'And on that day,' says the Lord GOD, 'I will make the sun go down at noon and darken the earth in broad daylight... I will make it like the mourning for an only son, and the end of it like a bitter day.'" Amos 8:9-10 "The curtain of the sanctuary was torn in two from top to bottom." Mt 27:51 God had moved out, as in Ezekiel's vision. Ezek 10:4,18-19; 11:23 Priesthood and people would have to look for him elsewhere. "The earth shook and the rocks were split," as in Elijah's vision and Haggai's. Mt 27:51; 1 Kgs 19:11; Hag 2:6 "The tombs also were opened, and many bodies of the saints who had fallen asleep were raised, and coming out of the tombs after his resurrection, they went into the holy city and appeared to many." The dead religion was shaken to life, evident in people raised up with the disciples and confessing Jesus' name. Mt 27:52-53

The centurion witnessed all this from the moment Jesus was delivered to Pilate. He knew how the issue turned on the accusation, "He made himself God's son." Jn 19:7 His spontaneous verdict became indelible memory, "Truly, this was God's son!" Mt 27:54; Mk 15:39

John witnessed signs of his own. Jn 19:31-37 Pilate honored the need of the

Judeans to cleanse their land by having those crucified buried before sunset, especially in view of the coming sabbath. Dt 21:23 He ordered his execution squad to hasten the deaths by breaking their legs. Suspended purely from their arms, they would quickly suffocate. John watched the soldiers break the legs of the two crucified with Jesus but pass him by, since he was already dead. One soldier thrust his spear upward into his heart, nevertheless. Blood and water poured out. John testified to blood literally shed. He recalled the Passover law, that the lamb be eaten in one house, no bone broken. Ex 12:46 No bone of Jesus was broken! He recalled a prophecy of Zechariah on the piercing: "And I will pour out on the house of David and the inhabitants of Jerusalem a spirit of compassion and supplication, so that, when they *look on him whom they have pierced*, they shall mourn for him, as one mourns for an only child, and weep bitterly over him, as one weeps over a first-born.... On that day there shall be a fountain opened for the house of David and the inhabitants of Jerusalem to cleanse them from sin and uncleanness." Zech 12:10; 13:1

The Burial

Two minority members of the council came to Golgotha toward the end. All four Gospels name Joseph of Arimathea, a town north of Jerusalem. Mt 27:57-61; Mk 15:42-47; Lk 23:50-56; Jn 19:38-42 John adds Nicodemus. Luke's account recalls that Joseph "had not consented to the council's purpose and deed." The moment Jesus died, Joseph rushed to Pilate and asked for his body, intending to bury him in a tomb rather than have the soldiers dig a pit for him with the others in the cursed valley of Hinnom. Mark's fragment reports that Pilate summoned the centurion to confirm that Jesus was already dead, then granted his body to Joseph.

Returning to Golgotha with servants and a supply of ointments, spices, and burial cloths of linen, all this planned in advance, they lowered the body and brought it to a nearby garden area outside the city wall, a burial site authorized by the council. Joseph had hewn out a tomb for himself and his family in a hillside of rock. It was as yet unused. Here they cleansed Jesus' body, prepared it for burial, and laid it reverently to rest. When they came out, they rolled the heavy stone-disk back in its track to cover the opening. Matthew and Mark report that the Galilean women witnessed this, in particular Mary Magdalene and "the other Mary" or "the mother of Joses" (Jesus' mother). Mt 27:61; Mk 15:47 John would have been with them still.

The fragment on the guards (temple police) in Matthew can only be direct memory. Mt 27:62-66; 28:4,11-15 It explained what in the young church was a nagging mystery—the accusation of the council that Jesus' own disciples had violated Joseph's tomb and stolen his body. One of the bribed guards must have confessed some time later what had actually happened. What he told was written down, then found among the fragments that yielded this Gospel.

The story had two scenes. The first, a conversation of "the chief priests and Pharisees" with Pilate, concluded with his command to "make the tomb as secure as you can." The second told the report of the guards the next morning and the bribery. The compiler of Matthew inserted a resurrection-fragment between these scenes, however. He then linked the return of the guards with the return of the women: "While they were going." A Greek copyist perceived a gap in the account before him. What did the guards do at the tomb? From Pilate's instruction he entered, "They went and made the sepulchre secure, sealing the stone and setting a watch." Mt 27:66 That opened another gap. What did the guards do when the resurrection angel appeared? A copyist's imagination supplied, "For fear of him the guards trembled and became like dead men." Mt 28:4

Traditional interpretation views the guards as reporting *Jesus' resurrection* the next morning and being bribed to conceal it. In its original untampered unity, however, the fragment tells something very different. The first scene has "the chief priests and the Pharisees" express their concern to Pilate regarding his authorizing Jesus' burial in a tomb. In the second they bribe the guards to account for the violated tomb and missing body by blaming it on Jesus' disciples.

The council as such would hardly have met and become involved in either scene, however. At Jesus' trial "the chief priests and elders" are a delegation charged with seeing the council's resolution through. In this fragment, they are not even a delegation but just one man, the one who led that delegation and argued the council's case so effectively, whom I for convenience have named "Perez." The mention of "Pharisees" here may remember him as such.

"Perez" could have slept well that Passover night, his mission successfully accomplished. Next morning, however, he heard what Joseph and Nicodemus had done and was enraged. Pilate had no business granting such a request. The council had authorized this holy burial site for Joseph and his family, not for a blasphemer! The crucifixion squad should have treated Jesus like the others—dropped him into an unmarked pit in the cursed valley of Hinnom! Jer 7:31-32

The emergency was sufficient to justify breaking the sabbath rest. "Perez" confronted Pilate on his own that Passover-sabbath morning, but representing the council still. Why had he granted Jesus' body to Joseph? "How should I know?" Pilate might answer. "Isn't he a member of your council? He asked for the body and I granted it to him." I suspect Pilate was glad for Jesus to receive this honor, glad to annoy the domineering "Perez" by it.

"Perez" could not leave it at that. The psyche of "death and evil" is not concerned for truth and honesty, but about *being right* and *in control*. The zealotic threat was truly over, but "Perez," needing to put the governor in the wrong, invoked it again. "That deceiver" had predicted his death while he was still alive, but always with the assurance that, "after three days I will be raised again!" What might Jesus' "disciples," his fanatical followers, do when they heard that he had been buried in a tomb? Plot again to help God out! Come by night, steal his body, then whisper throughout their crazed network that he had been raised up, just as he had said—a greater miracle than if he had come down from the cross, greater even than raising Lazarus! This last deception would threaten violence and sword worse than the first! "Perez," needing to dominate still, ordered the governor, "Command that the tomb be held safe until the third day!"

Pilate would not be manipulated again. That Jesus' disciples would even imagine what "Perez" envisioned, much less pull it off, was past believing. The council had had its way. Jesus was dead. What more could "Perez" want? "If you're so worried about it, use your own guard!" he taunted him. "Go ahead, make the tomb as secure as you can!"

If the original fragment-memory had stated explicitly what the guard was ordered to do during that night—rebury Jesus in Hinnom, where he ought to have been buried in the first place—the translator-compiler of Matthew could hardly have divided it and inserted his resurrection piece between. The information the fragment supplied was not about Jesus' reburial, however (that was already known), but how the *lie* came about, which the guard had told and the council was still telling—that Jesus' own disciples had violated Joseph's tomb and stolen his body.

"Use your own guard!" Pilate had said. Very well! The angry "Perez" would do it! He waited till dark, when the sabbath was over, then summoned a squad and gave them their orders. The next morning, they reported "all that had taken place to the chief priests," the fragment says—that is, to "Perez," who embodied their authority. What exactly had "taken place"? They had removed Jesus' body, as ordered, and reburied it!

It appears that a sudden fear struck "Perez." Had the squad closed the tomb again, or had they left it open? They had left it open! What would Joseph do when he found out that his tomb had been violated? He would complain to the governor! What would Pilate think? He would hold "Perez" responsible! What then? He would arrest and crucify him—for violating his burial order, yes, but in revenge also for pressuring him to order the crucifixion of the Jesus he had pronounced innocent! "Perez" should not have brought his complaint to Pilate at all! Why had he not simply done on his own what needed to be done? But it was too late. What to do? The obvious cover-up would be to blame the open tomb and the missing body on Jesus' madly-zealotic "disciples," against whom he had warned Pilate already. "Perez" needed the lie to cover "Perez"!

He must have confessed his dilemma to the guards in full. His prior argument with Pilate would make their lie believable. To have them lie to their own hurt, that they were sleeping when they ought to have been watching, required a considerable bribe, but they negotiated it—"Perez" paying it from the temple treasury. He would go to Pilate immediately and report in anguish how his guard had failed him, how they had slept that night while Jesus' disciples were ravaging Joseph's tomb. Pilate might rail against the guards but would entrust their discipline finally to "Perez." "If the governor should hear this, we will persuade him and keep you out of trouble."

"Perez" would explain the situation immediately also to the council—how he had undertaken to cleanse the burial site of such abuse, but also why he had needed to bribe the guards. If ever the matter came up, the council would confirm what "Perez" and the bribed guards were saying. That is how the lie of the empty tomb came about, which was being told still "among the Judeans to this day." Mt 28:15

As for the disciples and the women, finding out *why* the tomb was violated and empty did not affect their conviction of Jesus' resurrection in the least. The young church knew about Jesus' reburial in Hinnom all along. It was not embarrased to preserve this memory.

A tantalizing residuum of oral memory, "he descended into hell" (so the Apostles Creed), can only have derived from the young church. *Gehenna* ("hell") is Greek for "land of Hinnom." The creed confesses Jesus' degradation in five stages—"suffered under Pontius Pilate, was crucified, dead, buried, descended into Hinnom." This last testifies to his reburial in the valley of total uncleanness, thus to be obliterated from memory. St. Paul knew this, too. He paraphrased "Hinnom" for Gentile readers as Jesus "*descended into the lower parts of the earth,*" as low as anyone can get, lower even than crucifixion and death and burial in Joseph's tomb. Eph 4:9

Ironically, by reburying Jesus, the council itself created the shocking first sign of his resurrection, the open and empty tomb, timed even for the literal "third day."

PART SEVEN

Raising the Dead

The Resurrection

No imagination could have plotted the varied motives and random circumstances that converged in this event. Why should zealotic enthusiasts have tried to exalt Jesus as "the christ" of a futurist kingdom? But they did. How did Caiaphas and the council manage to persuade Pilate to crucify him, thus silence his sonship-gospel? But they did. How did Jesus dare "choose life," even at the cost of being crucified? But he did. Why did he prompt the little company at the cross to sing a psalm of hope, even as he was dying? But he did. How did it happen that he, though executed for blasphemy and insurrection, was not dropped into a pit of Hinnom like the others, but buried in a tomb? But he was. Why should an intervening Passover-sabbath have made Hosea's "third day" a literal time-frame? But it did. Why should temple police have been sent to rebury him secretly that very night? But they were. Why did the women, who witnessed his burial, return at early dawn to anoint him? But they did. Why should the shock of finding the tomb open and empty have recalled to their minds, as by angels, the promise of Hosea, which Jesus had taught and lived by? But it did. How could this revelatory-memory have turned them from their grief and sent them to tell the disciples about his resurrection and life? But it did. How could their word have raised the disciples from death to life—so that they *saw* Jesus *alive* and were formed in his image? But it did! How could the newborn church have remembered and recited so many testimonies to Jesus, as preserved in the Gospels to this day? But it did!

The miracle of Jesus' resurrection was *not* a resuscitated corpse. The faith and witness of the young church did *not* proceed from the "eyes-opened" logic of a barren "Wow!" The miracle was that the *sonship-gospel* Jesus *embodied*, which the council tried to kill by killing *him, did not stay dead!* It *arose* in the women as by the voice of angels, and in the disciples by their witness. The

Jesus who *appeared* to them was *embodied* in that *gospel*. They *saw* him by that *gospel!* Such was the resurrection to which King Herod testified memorably when Jesus had become known in Galilee. "John, whom I beheaded, has been raised from the dead," he said. Mk 6:14-16 The miracle was the revival of John's gospel, not his corpse.

"I *am* the resurrection and the life," Jesus told Martha, but more! "Whoever believes in me, *though he were dead, yet shall he live!* And whoever lives and believes in me *shall never die.*" Jn 11:25 "He who hears my word and believes him who sent me, *has eternal life*; he does not come into judgment, but *is passed from death to life*," Jesus said. Jn 5:24 The Sadducees needed to know "*the God of* Abraham," not just bodily descent from Abraham. Then, as "sons of the resurrection," they would serve their God in the bodies they had *now!* Lk 20:34-38

The promises Jesus believed were not about a life-after-death *body*. He "knew that he had come from God and was going to God," John testified of him, and "No one has ascended into heaven but he who came down from heaven, the son of man." Jn 13:3; 3:13 "My food is to do the will of him who sent me and to finish his work," Jesus declared. Jn 4:34 When he died, saying, "It is finished," he was "in the bosom of the Father" from whom he had come. Jn 19:30; 1:18 This was his fullness of life, his very *gospel!* As for the "glory" and "much fruit" that might grow from his sowing, Jesus did not need to *see* such outcomes. He entrusted them to his Father. Jn 12:23-26

Copyists, however, could conceive of his "resurrection" only as the resuscitation of his corpse. The only "God" they knew was of power. "Believing" came by "seeing" miracles! Hence, they interpolated bodily "proofs" of Jesus' resurrection into copies they were making. Then, to explain why he was no longer being *seen* in his resurrected body on earth, they invented a visible bodily departure. The disciples *saw* him "carried up into heaven." Lk 24:51; Acts 1:9

Such is the deceit of the tree of death, of "eyes opened" to "know good and evil." Gen 3:5

CHAPTER NINETEEN

■ The Third Day

*"After two days he will revive us; on the third day
he will raise us up, that we may live before him.
Let us press on to know the LORD. His going forth
is as sure as the dawn."*   Hosea 6:2-3

Mary Magdalene in John

John's memoir can only be direct memory. Jn 20:1-18 "On the first day of
the week Mary Magdalene comes to the tomb early, while it is still dark, and
sees the stone removed from the tomb. She runs therefore and comes to Simon
Peter and to the other disciple, whom Jesus loved, and says to them, 'They
have taken the Lord from the tomb, and we do not know where they have put
him.'" "We" implies other women with Mary, but she alone is named.

Peter and John ran to see for themselves. John outran Peter, peered into
the tomb, but did not go in. When Peter came, he entered and John followed.
They saw the linen burial cloths lying in a heap, but the napkin that had
covered Jesus' face rolled up neatly by itself. Apparently, men of different tem-
perament had been involved in removing the body. John recalls that he "saw
and believed," natural sight confirming what Mary had reported.

A distinction points to what came later: "As yet they did not know the
scriptures, that he *must rise* from the dead." Their knowledge of and testimony to Jesus' resurrection did not come by natural sight, John is saying, but
by the scriptures, like the covenant-promise Jesus believed for himself and
taught his disciples from Hosea. He chose life! In that case, for him to stay
dead was not possible. Not just Hosea's word would have failed, the LORD's

whole covenant by Moses and prophets and psalms would have failed with it. Anyone who knows God by that covenant, as Jesus did, will know that it cannot fail. "He *must rise* from the dead."

Mary Magdalene's story follows, as John wrote it into his memoir. It is her way of telling what happened to her. Concise as in oral literacy, not a word wasted, it appears to be the earliest preserved testimony. Mary returned to the tomb and stood outside weeping. Stooping to look in, she saw two angels in white sitting where Jesus had lain, one at the head and the other at the feet. The point is not the angels as such, but a question she of herself would not have thought to ask: "Woman, why are you weeping?" Mary had been weeping for a whole sabbath about the cruel injustice and haunting tragedy that had befallen the Jesus she so loved, believed and trusted. Now she poured out the new grief as she had told it to the disciples: "They," whoever that may be, "have taken away my Lord out of the tomb, and I do not know where they have put him."

Turning around she "saw Jesus standing," but did not know him. "Woman, why are you weeping?" he repeated the angels' question, then added another, "Whom do you seek?" Obsessed with the missing body and thinking him to be the caretaker, she acknowledged an uneasiness over this burial site. Joseph had buried Jesus here on his own, disregarding the council's authority. "Sir, if you have carried him away, tell me where you have laid him, and I will take him away." Whom was she seeking? A dead Jesus still! A corpse!

Now came the revelation. Jesus called her by name, "Mary!" By that voice of familiar love Mary was suddenly in his world, seeing him and all that had happened in a way she could not have dreamed. She turned to him fully, never to worry about his corpse again. "Rabboni," she called him. She had him back, the "teacher" from whom she was ready to learn as never before.

"Touch me not," he said. A touchable body was not the point. (The addition, "for I have not yet ascended to my Father" is of a copyist who thought of Jesus' "ascension" as future, thus keeping him touchable for now, after all.) What Jesus actually said, as Mary reported it, was about his calling filled full. "But go to my brothers and say to them, 'I am ascending to my Father and your Father and my God and your God.'" Jn 3:13; 6:62 He had not been a helpless victim. Far from the disastrous loss his bodily death appeared to be, he had finished his sonship and serving, thus was returning to the Father who had sent him. Jn 13:3; 16:5,28 The disciples are his brothers, sons of the same Father and God. Let it be so for them in their calling, too!

"I have seen the Lord," Mary said, as she told them what Jesus had told her. Among them was the John of this memoir. Such sight and hearing is not physiological, no more than Mary's seeing and hearing the two angels was physiological. It took the language of metaphor to express to others how the revelation broke through to her own heart.

The Women in Luke

Luke's account is independent. Lk 24:1-12 It names Mary Magdalene but also Joanna and Jesus' mother. The time was "the first day of the week at early dawn." They came to the tomb with spices and ointments to anoint Jesus further. Seeing the stone rolled away, they entered the tomb but did not find the body. They were perplexed. Two men stood by them in dazzling apparel, but they were only instrumental. The dawning came by what they said.

"Why do you seek the living among the dead?" Jesus was "living" even in his dying, but by a life other than natural eyes could see. "Remember what he told you while he was still in Galilee." They remembered it well, for he had made them and the disciples learn it. "The son of man," he called himself—implying the sonship-name his Father had spoken to him when he passed through the Jordan. His true life came from his Father, not from his human genealogy. "The son of man *must* be delivered into the hands of sinful men, and be crucified, and on the third day rise," he had said. Here is that "*must*" again! Let this "third day" signal what Jesus taught from Hosea: "After two days he will revive us; on the third day he will raise us up, that we may *live* before him." Jesus had "lived before him," even to death. How then could he *not* be raised, as his Father promised? Seek a dead body in a cemetery, but seek the living Jesus by remembering what he said to you, and in remembering, *listen* to him!

The dawning broke upon the women by the word of God. They returned from the tomb and told it to the disciples. The men, however, seeing and thinking with natural eyes only, dismissed their witness as an idle tale. Hosea's "third day" was of another dawning than the sun's.

Emmaus

Memories across all four Gospels speak of the same event and people. "Clopas" in John, whose wife "Mary" is named among the women at the cross, is likely the "Cleopas" of Luke. Jn 19:25; Lk 24:13-25 The variation is simply of accent, Galilean or Judean.

Cleopas and his wife told afterwards how they were walking home to Emmaus after that Passover-sabbath, grieving over all that had happened. "Jesus himself drew near and went with them," they reported, "but their eyes were kept from recognizing him." They reviewed for him "what had happened in Jerusalem these days," thus providing background for anyone who might hear this carefully worded testimony. It was about "Jesus of Nazareth, a prophet mighty in deed and word before God and all the people." Their hope that he would be "the one to redeem Israel" had come to nothing. The chief priests and rulers had delivered him up to the Romans to be condemned to death and crucified. They told of strange happenings on the morning of this third day. Some women went to the tomb early, did not find his body, but reported seeing a vision of angels who said he was alive. "Some from our company went to the tomb and found the body missing, just as the women had said, but him they did not see."

As they told it, the risen Jesus did *not* answer, "O fools, can't you see who I am?" Clearly, they did not come to know him by natural sight. He directed them instead to the covenant-word. "O fools and slow of heart to believe all that the prophets have spoken! Was it not *necessary* that the christ should suffer these things and enter into *his* glory?" *Necessary?* Here again is that *"must!"* They had looked for a christ who would redeem Israel for the sake of their own glory. The true christ *must* serve his Father faithfully to the end regardless of cost, trust his promises, and so win! "Then, beginning with Moses and all the prophets he interpreted to them in all the scriptures the things concerning himself."

The texts were familiar from what Jesus had long taught, from readings in worship and from psalms. Now, however, Cleopas and Mary heard by them the covenant-honor and hope and calling which Jesus had believed and filled full in love and obedience even to death. A psalm sang, for example: "I keep the LORD always before me; because he is at my right hand, I shall not be moved. Therefore my heart is glad and my soul rejoices, my body also shall rest in hope. For you do not give me up to Sheol or let your godly one see the pit. You show me the path of life; in your presence there is fullness of joy; at your right hand are pleasures for evermore." Ps 16:8-11; Acts 2:25-28 By such faith and hope the "christ" had "entered into *his glory*" through suffering.

Cleopas and Mary told how they invited their companion to stay the night. That "their eyes were opened and they knew him" by his blessing and breaking the bread at table suggests that Jesus had been their guest previously. At that point "he vanished out of their sight." They did not marvel at this, however, but at what he had taught them. "Did not our hearts burn within us while he *talked* to us on the road, while he *opened to us the scriptures?*"

No longer were they "fools and slow of heart to believe all that the prophets have spoken." In Jerusalem with the others, they told "what had happened on the road and how he was known to them in the breaking of the bread." This was *revelation,* not sense-perception. They did not talk about how he looked bodily, or about touching him bodily, or about what he ate bodily, or about his appearing and disappearing bodily.

The resurrection accounts in John and Luke are prime, the oldest and fullest. They cohere with the covenant-gospel Jesus believed and lived and died for, as exhibited in the notable "on the third day" text from Hosea. They cohere with the account in Matthew concerning Jesus' reburial in Hinnom during the night after the sabbath. They cohere with the understanding of "resurrection and life" in Jesus' response to Martha, and his "sons of the resurrection" response to the Sadducees. They cohere with his teaching of the kingdom-*now* rather than futurist, of life and servanthood in freedom *now*. They cohere with Abraham's hard rejection of the rich man's plea that a visible return from the dead might persuade his five brothers: "If they will not believe Moses and the prophets, neither will they be persuaded though one rose from the dead."

For "Christianity" to accept that Jesus' resurrection and appearances are not physiological but of the gospel he embodied, will be as difficult a "repentance" as it was for the authority and piety of synagogue and temple in that day to accept the resurrection-gospel of the young church. The problem is humanly mutual. Let Christians and Jews face it together.

Matthew and Mark

The resurrection memory in Matthew would have been found among fragments gathered in Capernaum, Mark's in Jerusalem or Judea. Mt 28:1-10; Mk 16:1-8 At early morning after the sabbath, Mary Magdalene went to the tomb with Jesus' mother. Mark names also Salome. "They bought spices to anoint him," says Mark, as in Luke. An anxiety on the way can only be direct memory: "Who will roll away the stone for us from the door of the tomb?" Matthew's account perceives the tomb to have been opened by the hand of God: "An angel of the Lord" rolls away the stone and sits on it. In Mark the women enter the tomb and see "a young man sitting on the right side, dressed in a white robe."

Despite these variations, the narrative in both is compacted as though readers already know the resurrection-witness and do not need to hear its details again. The angel does not ask whom the women seek, but tells them. They do not find the body missing, the angel tells them. They do not learn Jesus has been raised by remembering his words as in Luke, or by hearing his voice as in John. The angel tells them. What makes these accounts special is their accent on Galilee. The women are to tell the disciples, not so much that Jesus has been raised from the dead (which Mark does not even mention), but that he is going before them to Galilee and that they will see him there. "As he told you" in Mark refers to this, not to the resurrection.

A copyist of Matthew interpolated a bodily appearance of Jesus to the women as they were returning from the tomb. "They came up and took hold of his feet and worshiped him." He had Jesus then repeat what the angel had said, "Do not be afraid. Go and tell my brothers to go to Galilee, there they will see me." "Brothers," rather than "disciples," derives from John. Jn 20:17

Why this stress on Galilee? Perhaps it entered when attention was shifting from Galilee to Jerusalem. The record in Mark stresses Peter: "Go, tell his disciples and *Peter*." Indirectly, it calls attention to James, Jesus' brother. At the cross his mother is "Mary the mother of James and Joseph," but in the resurrection she is "the mother of *James*." Mk 16:1; Lk 24:10 Memories in Acts testify to Peter and this James as major figures in Jerusalem. The stress on Galilee makes clear that their move from Galilee was no loss. It was in Galilee, says this reminder, that all of them, even Jesus' brothers, came to see and know him as their resurrected Lord.

The Gospel of Mark ends awkwardly. "The women fled from the tomb; for trembling and astonishment had come upon them; and they said nothing to anyone, for they were afraid." Some early manuscripts supply more satisfactory endings. Scholars debate whether a once fuller ending may have been lost early on, but if it were original, what Mark might have intended by it. The explanation is simple. The Gospels were formed from fragment-libraries of random Jesus-memory. This was the only resurrection-fragment Mark found in his library-source. He saved it to the end. When he had entered it, his task was finished.

The Disciples

Preserved memories acknowledge that the women's news did not get through to the disciples easily. "These words seemed to them an idle tale, and they did not believe them." Lk 24:11 On the mountain in Galilee "some doubted." Mt 28:17 A memory in Mark, linked to the transfiguration, is notable. "As they were coming down from the mountain, Jesus charged them to tell no one what they had seen, until the son of man should have risen from the dead." So they kept the matter to themselves, *"questioning what the rising from the dead meant."* Mk 9:9-10 An era of questioning is explicitly acknowledged.

What *did* it mean? The prevailing piety assumed it meant corpses restored to the bodily life they had had before. A "resurrection at the last day," when the kingdom of God arrived, would gather the faithful dead into full participation with those who were alive on that day. But if the disciples were "questioning what the rising from the dead meant," some other possibility must have arisen to challenge that assumption.

They had believed the illusion of a futurist physiological kingdom and glory, encouraged each other in it, acted on it, imposed it on Jesus. Surely the living God would not leave his temple uncleansed, not let so awful an injustice happen, not allow his beloved son to be disgraced and die! When that hope crashed to a bitter end, however, they were not only at a loss, but torn by guilt. Their very zeal for him had gotten Jesus "numbered with the transgressors" as an insurrectionist and delivered up to the Romans to be crucified. Lk 22:37; Is 53:12 He had interceded for them, "If you seek me, let these men go," and the temple police had let them escape. Jn 18:8 But their shame was as deep as that of Judas. To live on at such cost was no comfort at all.

Others who had part in the awful event could readily justify themselves. The chief priests and Pharisees had dissipated a very real zealotic threat and averted what could have developed into a disastrous war. They had also kept their tradition intact. If God had wanted "his son," he could have saved him, they could argue, but he did not. As for Pilate, he could rationalize a greater good at the price of a lesser evil, wash his hands and hold the Judeans responsible. But for the disciples, no rationalization was possible. The women's story on the morning of that third day haunted them at first, like Jesus' ghost returning to judge them in their dark night. Mt 14:25; Jn 6:19 Mercy and light undreamed must dawn on them from the outside.

And it did. "The Lord has been raised indeed and has appeared to Simon," a brief memory says. Lk 24:34 There were two "Simons." One was the "rock" which God's word like a hammer had broken in pieces. Jer 23:29; 5:3 The other was "the Zealot" or "Iscariot," responsible for the disaster that had consumed his son Judas, as well as Jesus. For either or both, "The Lord has been raised indeed" must mean Jesus as they had known him all along, yet truly only now, whose resurrection appearance raised *them* up with himself. "This my son was dead and is alive again; he was lost and is found," a parable has it. Lk 15:24 With that revelatory appearing, any "questioning what rising from the dead meant" ceased.

The fragment in Luke of Jesus' coming to all the disciples would have been found in Judea, that in John among his memoirs in Bethsaida. Lk 24:36; Jn 20:19 The location of these entries on their respective scrolls would yield the inference that it happened in Jerusalem after the sunset of that literal third day. The location is more likely Galilee, after the disciples and the women had gone home. John's "on the evening of that day, the first day of the week" became a liturgical introduction, the time of the young church's own gatherings apart from sabbath-worship in the synagogue. His introduction, "Jesus came and stood among them," suggests that his appearing was not corporeal. ("The doors being shut, where the disciples were, for fear of the Judeans" is a copyist's enhancement, designed to accent the miracle of his bodily-appearing.)

John reports Jesus as saying, "Peace be with you!" A related memory amplifies this: "Peace I bequeath to you, my peace I give to you! Let not your hearts be troubled, neither let them be afraid." Jn 20:19; 14:27 "Then the disciples were glad when they *saw* the Lord" is a "seeing" like that of John's prologue. They "saw his glory," saw him as "the word made body and dwelling among them," saw him as "the only son of the Father" and "full of grace and truth," filling their utter emptiness. Jn 1:14 (A copyist took their "seeing" to be physiological, however. The interpolation, "He showed them his hands and his side," was suggested by Jesus' "hands" and "side" in the Thomas fragment which follows.)

With that, Jesus exhaled his breath (spirit) for them to inhale. Spirit and covenant-word are one, as when Jesus said, "The words that I have spoken to you, they are Spirit and they are life." Jn 6:63 Breathing his own resurrection-life, they were ready now to carry on his mission and the Father's of gathering and forgiving. "If you forgive the sins of any, they are forgiven; if you retain the sins of any, they are retained." They could not force this gospel on anyone, no more than Jesus himself could, but only set forth God's promising but uncompromising covenant-truth. Grace and forgiveness are received freely, but can be rejected in like freedom.

The parallel in Luke reads, "While they were saying this, Jesus stood among them. Then he said to them, 'These are my words which I spoke to you while

I was still with you, that everything written about me in the law of Moses and in the prophets and in the psalms must be filled full.' Then he opened their minds to understand the scriptures"—showing by these what it meant for him to be "the christ." A high expectation follows, "that repentance and forgiveness of sins should be preached in his name among all nations, beginning from Jerusalem. You are witnesses of these things." Lk 24:36,44-48

Copyist Corruptions. A copyist, however, fashioned an elaborate interpolation to show that the resurrection of Jesus was of *body*. Lk 24:37-43 "They were startled and frightened, and supposed that they saw a spirit," it began. "Why are you troubled and why do questionings arise in your hearts?" Jesus asks. To the copyist "in your hearts" meant "in your minds." "Believing" meant being intellectually convinced by the miraculous. Jesus overcame their disbelief and questionings by offering visible proofs. "See my hands and my feet," the copyist has him say, hands out of sleeves and feet beneath his robe. "Handle me and see" is a next level of proof, "for a ghost does not have flesh and bones as you see me have." The ultimate proof is eating. "While they still disbelieved for joy and wondered, he said to them, 'Have you anything here to eat?' They gave him a piece of boiled fish, and he took it and ate before them."

Thomas

This fragment, preserved among John's memoirs in Bethsaida, is Thomas' own succinct confession. Jn 20:24-29 It plays on the word "believe." Thomas' "believing" had been of zealotic piety, focused on a Jesus who did visible signs and wonders and looking for more. Zealotic leaders had summoned a great crowd to sing "Hosanna to the son of David" while escorting Jesus into Jerusalem. The chief priests, scribes, and elders had mocked such believing. "He is the king of Israel! Let him come down now from the cross, and *we will believe* in him, too!" Mt 27:41-42

John's memoir recalls a doubt on Thomas' part, however. When Jesus resolved to return to Judea at the call of Martha and Mary, it was Thomas who said cynically, "Let us also go, that we may die with him." Jn 11:16 A similar distress of his appears in a dialogue associated with the upper room: "Lord, we do not know where you are going; how can we know the way?" Jn 14:5 Other disciples would likely have reproved Thomas' doubts and encouraged him to "believe" as they did. He apparently tried. When the dream reached its dead-end, however, he could say bitterly, "Didn't I tell you?" or "I should never have let you talk me into this!" The memory has it that he was not with the others to hear of the resurrection. I picture him as having set out for Galilee, grimly determined to have nothing more to do with Jesus or any of them.

The other disciples would have found Thomas when they too returned home to Bethsaida. "We have seen the Lord," they told him. He taunted their "seeing" as one more fantasy. "Unless I see in his hands the print of the nails, and place my finger in the mark of the nails, and place my hand in his side, I will not believe." Testimony to the wound in Jesus' side is preserved only in John. Jn 19:34 Yet somehow Thomas was with the others in the event he relates. "Eight days later" frames his story in what became the pattern of gathering in the young church.

Copyist Corruptions. A copyist corrupted his testimony, however. Enhancements like "his disciples were again in the house" and "the doors were shut" are incidental, but a saying ascribed to Jesus utterly distorts Thomas' testimony. It assumes that Jesus, being "deity," knew what Thomas had demanded and supplied the evidence he needed: "Put your finger here and see my hands; and put out your hand and place it in my side; and be not faithless but believing."

Thomas' own testimony, told concisely for the sake of memorizing, said simply, "Eight days later, Thomas was with them. Jesus came and stood among them and said, 'Peace be with you.' Thomas answered him, 'My Lord and my God!' Jesus said to him, 'Have you believed because you have seen me? Blessed are those who have not seen and yet believe.'"

His confession, "My Lord and my God," is of the righteousness that carried Jesus through death into resurrection. By calling him "my Lord" (parallel to Mary Magdalene's "Rabboni," or "my teacher"), Thomas put himself downstream as a receiver willing and eager to learn, looking at an upstream-Jesus as his "Teacher" and "Lord." Jn 13:13 "My God" has him looking upstream beyond Jesus to God his Father, ultimate source of the covenant-revelation. "*My* Lord and *my* God" makes that ever-flowing stream personal for him. The Lord had identified himself so to Moses: "I am *the God of* your father, *the God of* Abraham, *the God of* Isaac, and *the God of* Jacob." Jesus, speaking to the Sadducees, had added, "He is not *the God of* the dead but of the living, for all live to him." Ex 3:6; Lk 20:37-38 Thomas is now of "the living."

Jesus' sowing, a grain of wheat fallen into the ground and dying, had prevailed in Thomas after all. Jn 12:24 "Have you believed because you have seen me?" No, that is not how Thomas believed him. Any "believing" that depends on visual proofs and logical calculations is self-assertive illusion. "Blessed are those who have believed without seeing," without "eyes-opened" logic. Thomas had believed what natural sight cannot see—Jesus in the flow of life from his God and Father. Jesus had believed the sonship-word at his baptism without *seeing* how it could be so. He had believed and lived Hosea's resurrection-word, too, without *seeing* how it could be so.

John ended his memoir fittingly with a note still preserved. "Jesus did many other signs in the presence of the disciples, but these are written that you may believe that Jesus is the Christ, the son of God, and that believing you may have life in his name." Jn 20:30-31 Signs are indeed *seen*. What they signal, however, is not the zealotic illusion, but the covenant-gospel.

Caiaphas, the Prophet

"It is expedient for you that one man should die for the people, and that the whole nation should not perish," Caiaphas said, facing the grim reality. If the death of just one man can stop the revolt and save the nation from destruction, that's how it must be. John's memoir, looking back on the event from the new testament side, comments, "He did not say this of his own accord, but being high priest that year he prophesied that Jesus should die for the nation, and not for that nation only, but to gather into one the children of God who are scattered abroad." Jn 11:50-52 It was like Thomas' climactic, "my God!" The hand and purpose of *God*, so long hidden, was being seen everywhere!

The history could now be told from the mind of God! "*God* so loved the world, that *he gave his only son....*" Jn 3:16 "Call his name Jesus (meaning 'Savior') for *he will save his people from their sins.*" Mt 1:21 Jesus had "saved his people" by putting himself between and averting the awful bloodbath. What "sins" were these, from which he "saved his people"? The conceit that chosenness meant superiority. The conceit that God should love them for their racial purity and law. The conceit that God should one day exalt them over the nations! "Their sins" were manifest in the "either-or" of every parable. Jesus, by his warfare to the death, had saved not only *his disciples* from their sins, but *his people*—yet not his people only, but "the world." Jn 1:29 To see this was *revelation* of *the Holy Spirit*.

CHAPTER TWENTY

Starting Over

> *"When the Counselor comes, whom I shall send to*
> *you from the Father, even the Spirit of truth, who*
> *proceeds from the Father, he will bear witness to*
> *me; and you also are witnesses, because you have*
> *been with me from the beginning."*
>
> *John 15:26-27*

Hosea's covenant-gospel did not stay dead in Jesus' dying, but raised him up as promised. By it God started the world over, like a new creation. The disciples knew its wonder. No guilt or shame or judgment hung over them any more. Forgiveness was complete and liberating. It exposed to the light also the idolatrous corruption which had held God's people in unwitting bondage for so long, from which they urgently needed to be freed.

Prophets had envisioned such a hope. "Come now and let us reason together, says the LORD; though your sins are like scarlet, they shall be white as snow; though they are red like crimson, they shall become like wool." Is 1:18 "For behold, I create new heavens and a new earth; and the former things shall not be remembered or come to mind." Is 65:17 "Behold, the days are coming, says the LORD, when I will make a new covenant with the house of Israel and the house of Judah...; and I will be their God, and they shall be my people.... for they shall all know me, from the least of them to the greatest, says the LORD; for I will forgive their iniquity and remember their sin no more." Jer 31:31-34

John

Among John's memoirs was one which perceived the revelatory "word" of God (and the God who spoke it) to have caused this entire history. Jn 1:1-18 The compiler who translated each item into Greek chose this one to begin his scroll. "In the beginning was the word," it said. Copyists, not knowing "the word" in its covenant sense, took it to mean the pre-incarnate deity of Jesus. They interpolated clarifications then which supported their misconception.

"Word" in Hebrew-Aramaic would have been *dabar*. The Septuagint (Greek translation of the Hebrew scriptures) renders it 763 times by *ho logos*, grammatically masculine, and 372 times by *to rhema*, grammatically neuter. The compiler who translated John's fragment used the masculine. Even so, in English "word" is neuter. Pronominal references should say "*it*," not "*him*." Jesus as "the word made body" does not enter John's text until verse 14. Any shift from *it to him* prior to this must have been from copyists. Let me venture a translation of John's original, excluding alterations motivated by the notion of Jesus' deity. I shall examine these later.

"In the beginning was the (covenant) word, and the word was with God.... All things were made by *it*, and without *it* nothing was made that was made. In *it* was life, and the life was the light of men. The light shines in the darkness, and the darkness has not extinguished *it*.

"There was a man sent by God whose name was John. He came as a witness, to bear witness to the light, so that all might believe through *it*.... The true light, which enlightens every man, was coming into the world. *It* was in the world..., and the world did not know *it*. *It* came to its own place and its own people did not receive *it*. But as many as did receive *it*, to them *it* gave authority to become children of God— to those who believe in *its* name. These were not born from blood or from the desire of the body or from the desire of man, but from God.

"And the word was made body and dwelled among us, and we saw *its* glory, glory as of the only (son) from the Father, (glory) full of grace and truth...; so that from *its* fullness we have all received (fullness), and grace upon grace; so that, as the law was given through Moses, grace and truth came through Jesus Christ. No one has ever seen God. The only (son), who is in the bosom of the Father, he has made him known."

The issue is God's word and the God who speaks it. From the very beginning God *by his word* created everything that exists. By his word he created John, and Jesus, and the apostles, and the young church. The resistant authorities arrested John and then killed him but they did not escape God's word. They condemned Jesus and sent him to the cross, but they did not escape God's word. They will not escape God's word by persecuting the apostles and young church.

What does this word of God *say*? It said, "Let there be light!" And there was light—not just of our eyes, but the covenant-light which is our very life— the revelation by which we know God and ourselves and our world in truth. The light shines in what is otherwise only darkness. The darkness has not shut it out.

This "Jochanan," whom your darkness resisted and killed, did not come on his own. He "was sent by God." There is no other way to account for him. His name, "Johwah is gracious," proclaims God as he defined himself to Moses on the mountain: "Johwah, Johwah, a God merciful and gracious, slow to anger and abounding in steadfast love... forgiving iniquity and transgression and sin." If you want him to be something else than this, the guilt is yours, not his. "He will by no means clear the guilty." Ex 34:6-7 He will not change to suit you.

John was not an insurrectionist plotting to take over. His offense was only that he spoke God's word. "He came for witness, to witness about the light, so that *all* might believe through *it*"—even rulers and priests, even a Herod who put him to death. By his witness God's true light was coming into the world. *It* was in the world, a light of revelation which the world did not and could not know. *It* came where *it* properly belonged, to the temple and synagogues which keep the sacred scrolls. Yet *its* own people did not receive *it*. But to those who did receive *it* (there were such), God's word and light gave author- ity to be "children of God" (defying a tradition which considers *saying this* to be arrogance). They receive and believe the *name* their God spoke by Moses, "Israel is *my son, my first-born*; let my son go that he may serve me." Believing this *covenant-name*, they are born and have life, not from the natural blood of childbirth, not from sexual impulse, not from determination to keep the ge- nealogy pure, but from God.

What about Jesus then, and the young church's testimony to him? Jesus did not invent himself or act on his own any more than John did. Blame the word of God! "And the word was made body and dwelled among us, and we saw *its* glory, glory as of the only son from the Father, glory full of grace and truth." The glory of the word of God was that it made Jesus what he was! He heard it himself, believed its light, lived its life to the full in his own body against every temptation known to man, even into death. "We," the apostles and the young church, saw how he persisted in his covenant-name and promise and calling, even while we ourselves, like you and Pilate and the whole world, loved our darkness rather than light. We saw the glory of God's covenant-word shine bright in him as "the only son from the Father full of grace and truth." We saw it come down to him alone, when there was no other. We saw how the covenant-word was not a failure after all. It won! Shall we be ashamed of it? Shall we not tell it?

"From his fullness we have all received, even grace upon grace. For the law was given through Moses; the grace and the truth came through Jesus Christ." You of synagogue and temple claim "the law given through Moses," yet your law leaves you empty of "grace and truth." Hear its revelatory wisdom again—that everything we are and have is pure gift, that we are first and always only receivers. To know this and build on it as servants of God in our own "giving" is freedom and life for us. We have seen his "grace upon grace" in all fullness, the son of God who would not abandon us to our lostness or give up on us even to his death, who will not give up on you, either. None of this is our imagination or will or doing. Every bit of it happened by the covenant-word of God, with which the world itself began.

"No one has ever seen God. The 'only (son),' who is in the bosom of the Father, he has made him known." In the dark hour when you judged him to death, when we fled in fear for our lives and left him alone—what covenant-son did God have left except Jesus only? You heaped shame on him. We did too. Yet he "finished" all alone the servanthood to which his Father called him in his body on this earth. He rests now "in the bosom of his Father" from whom he came and to whom he returned, not defeated but alive and vindicated. "No one has ever seen God. The only son, in the bosom of the Father, he has made him known." Do you want to know your God? Know him by knowing his son!

John's stress on Jesus as the "only" pervades his memoirs. "The *only* from the Father." Jn 1:14 "The *only,* who is in the bosom of the Father." Jn 1:18 "He gave *his son, his only.*" Jn 3:16 "The name of *the only son of God.*" Jn 3:18 "God sent *his son, his only* into the world, so that we might live through him." 1Jn 4:9 "Only" was another (though rare) covenant-name for Israel. "They shall mourn for him as one mourns for an *only,* and weep bitterly over him as one weeps over a *first-born.*" Zech 12:10 "I will make it like the mourning for an *only.*"

Amos 8:10 "Your *son*, your *only*, whom you *love*," the LORD said to Abraham of Isaac. Gen 22:2

"Only" for Jesus derived from the event, however. He went to his death all alone, the disciples in flight, the authorities denouncing him. "Yet I am not alone, for my Father is with me," he said. Jn 16:32 He "loved his own to the end." Jn 13:1 He chose to die alone rather than be in his Father's house alone. Jn 14:2 Even in crucifixion he prayed his Father to forgive those who did it, "for they do not know what they are doing," not wanting to lose them. Lk 23:34

There lay the embodied secret to which John's memoirs testify. The "only" of Jesus, like his sonship, did not originate with himself but with his Father's covenant-word. His love, his decision, his giving himself to death was ultimately his Father's doing. "Your will be done," the son-servant prayed, trusting the promises. "*You have not known him; I know him*," Jesus told his Judean critics. Jn 8:55 By him they can know the God they ought to know, but do not. By him they can receive their own sonship and "only" and chosenness.

John's "only" accords with the young church's confession of Jesus by the definite article, "*the* son of God." Earlier, as when the tempter said, "If you are God's son," Jesus made Israel's convenant-sonship his own. Mt 4:3,6 Now, however, there is no other. "I have seen and borne witness that this is *the* son of God." Jn 1:34 "Rabbi, you are *the* son of God." Jn 1:49 "Yes, Lord, I believe that you are the Christ, *the* son of God." Jn 11:27 "That you may believe that Jesus is the Christ, *the* son of God." Jn 20:31 "*The* son of the living God." Mt 16:16

Other images in John use the definite article with like effect. "I am *the* light of the world." Jn 8:12 "I am *the* door of the sheep," "*the* good shepherd." Jn 10:7,11 "I am *the* way, *the* truth, and *the* life." Jn 14:6 "I am *the* vine, you are the branches. He who stays in me and I in him, he it is that bears much fruit; for without me you can do nothing." Jn 15:5

Yet Jesus' sonship, his "only," was not exclusive but inclusive, the very premise of his gathering. "Whoever does the will of my Father in heaven is my brother, and sister, and mother," he said, acknowledging no barriers. Mt 12:50 "Go and say to *my brothers*, 'I am ascending to my Father *and your* Father,'" he told Mary. Jn 20:17 "To all who received him, who believed in his name, he gave authority to become children of God, born ... of God," John put it in his prologue. Jn 1:12 "The glory which you gave me I have given them, that they may be one as we are one, I in them and you in me, that the world may know that you sent me, and have loved them even as you have loved me." Jn 17:22-23 In such a people the eternal covenant-word is embodied still.

Copyist Corruptions. Copyists corrupted John's prologue very early. Not knowing "the word" as God's covenant-revelation to Israel, driven also by the assumption that "son of God" for Jesus meant deity-incarnate, they mysticized "the word" into a pre-existent deity. Thus a copyist felt it necessary to explain, "and God was the word; he was in the beginning with God." "Light" and "life" were not of the covenant-word but of the mysticized pre-existent Jesus. That made a reminder of John's inferiority necessary: "He was not the light, but came to bear witness to the light." Since "word" and "light" were synonymous with Jesus' pre-existent deity, another reminder was in order: "and the world was made through him." Ignorance and unbelief were perceived as directed not to "the word," but to Jesus. "The world knew *him* not." "His own people received *him* not." "As many as received *him*."

This misunderstanding detached "the word made body" from "the glory of grace and truth" in Jesus' serving to death, then attached it instead to the glory of his deity-incarnate as told in the birth narratives. On that assumption a copyist, intent again on rankings, paraphrased a later testimony of John, "He must increase but I must decrease," into "John bore witness to him and cried out, saying, 'This was he of whom I said, the one coming after me ranks before me, for he was before me.'" Jesus came *after* John in time but was *before* him as "deity." Jn 3:30;1:15 Another copyist entered this "of whom I said" saying into John's actual preaching. Jn 1:30

It could hardly have happened otherwise, for Greek scholarship had no way of knowing covenant-meanings. Yet the loss was grievous. John's memoir contrasted the fullness of "the word made body" with the *emptiness* of temple tradition and law. Christianity, not knowing the fullness either, suffered a deprivation and emptiness no less grievous.

The New Day

The name "son of God" for Jesus, judged blasphemous in the court of Caiaphas, emerged triumphant in Jesus' resurrection. A forgiven and liberated Peter could return to the episode at Caesarea Philippi and do it over. As "*that* rock," he had stubbornly pressed Jesus to be "the christ" of zealotic fantasy. Jesus' awful death had crushed that illusion. "Is not my word like a hammer that breaks the rock in pieces?" the LORD had declared, and it was so. Jer 23:29 As "*this* rock," Peter confessed what "the Father in heaven" had revealed" Jesus to be—"the Christ" indeed, but defined now as "the son of the living God."

The reference to "sons of the living God" is from Hosea. Hos 1:6-10 The LORD had named a recalcitrant Israel "Scattered" and "Not Pitied" and "Not my people"— but in the end his covenant-promise broke through still: "Yet the number of the people of Israel shall be like the sand of the sea...; and in the place where it was said to them, 'You are not my people,' it shall be said to them, '*sons of the living God.*'" The God who seemed "dead" had proved to be "the living God" after all. He had exalted Jesus, his steadfastly serving "son," to be Israel's "christ." By him his people would become "like the sand of the sea." "The place" for this name to "be said" was Gentile territory, like Caesarea Philippi—but also temple and synagogue, where it had not been said, either.

"Body and blood has not revealed this to you, but my Father who is in heaven," Jesus told Peter, and it was so. "And on this rock I will build my church," he added, "and the gates of Hades shall not hold out against it." Hades (Hebrew *she-ol*) is as deep down as heaven is high up. "Gates" suggests a strong fortress, defended by the wisdom of "body and blood," holding God's people as unwitting prisoners of falsities they took to be true. Priests and council did not know what they were doing. The piety of zealotic ambition did not know what it was doing, either.

Jesus, armed with his Father's covenant-word, had known how the gates of Hades would repel the word by killing its messenger. Once the authorities of synagogue and temple had spent that ultimate weapon, however, no other remained. "On this rock I will build my church," the risen Lord said, "and the gates of Hades will not hold out against it." His church would storm those gates by the word of sonship and life until the gates broke down and Hades' prisoners were freed.

Metaphors tumble on—"keys," "kingdom of heaven," "bind and loose." Peter and the disciples had been liberated. The covenant-gospel was their key to free those still imprisoned. Freedom could be forced on no one, of course, but only offered. "Whatever you bind on earth shall be bound in heaven" decrees continuing imprisonment for those who insist on it. "Whatever you loose" invokes the covenant-gospel to forgive and liberate even the most shamed of sinners.

The account of the royal procession escorting Jesus into Jerusalem at the Passover is another instance of pre-death distortion overlaid by post-resurrection celebration. Mt 21:1-9 For all the perversity of that doomed entry, the young church could look on it now in amazement. Jesus had turned out to be king after all! For whom else should garments and palm branches be spread and the refrain chanted, "Blessed is he who comes in the name of the LORD"?

"Blessed" indeed! "In the name of the LORD" indeed! This christ-king had swallowed up their shame and death in his dying. He had loved his disciples and people to the very end! He had not been a defeated victim after all, but raised in glory! Never a king like this, never again!

Never a shepherd like this! "Shepherd" is a language of kingship or priesthood. Jer 23:1-4; Ezek 34; Zech 13:7 John's memoir of Jesus as "the door" and "the good shepherd" contrasts him with a priesthood fallen prey to the self-serving wisdom of "knowing good and evil." Jn 10:1-16 Jesus enters the fold of God's people by the door, that is, by the word of sonship and life from Israel's God. The gatekeeper, his Father, has granted him access to the flock. The sheep know their true shepherd, for he calls them by their authentic name, "my son, my first-born." Ex 4:22-23 "I am the door," Jesus says, by whom "the sheep go in and out and find pasture." They flee from and do not heed the voice of strangers.

The ruling priests and elders entered by a way other than the door. They are in reality thieves and robbers. "The thief comes only to kill and sacrifice and destroy the flock. I came that they might have life and have it abundantly. I am the good shepherd. The good shepherd lays down his life for the sheep." A hired hand flees to save himself when he sees a "wolf" of danger coming, not caring what happens to the sheep. Jesus knows his sheep and they know him, as the Father knows him and he the Father. He lays down his life for the sheep. Hence the young church gathers other sheep not of this fold. And there will be one flock, one shepherd.

Never would there be a "kingdom" of Israel's superiority over the nations, never a "christ" of zealotic fantasy who would harness for them the power of God and angels. The "christ" of "the living God" was uncompromisingly anti-zealotic and anti-futurist. Thus "the Christ" became a name for Jesus—"Jesus Christ" or simply "Christ." But it always subsumed the covenant-name he had filled full to the finish, "the son of God."

Simon the Zealot

"The path of the righteous is like the light of dawn, which shines more and more until full day," a proverb says. Prov 4:18 The dawning became an era of wonder and prayer, thinking and imagining. The scriptures opened as never before, and Jesus in them. The memory in Luke has him saying so: "'These are my words which I spoke to you while I was still with you, that everything written about me in the law of Moses and the prophets and the psalms must be filled full.' Then *he opened their minds to understand the scriptures*, and said to them, 'Thus it is written, that the christ should suffer and on the third day rise from the dead.'" This yielded their mission, "that repentance and forgiveness of sins should be preached in his name to all nations, beginning from Jerusalem. You are witnesses of these things." Lk 24:44-48

The scriptures were accessible in synagogues to any who had learned to read. Mere reading is not enough, however. A reader looks down on a text from above. What his mind already knows will control his understanding. When Jesus *opened their minds to understand the scriptures*, the covenant-gospel that enlivened the disciples' hearts out of his resurrection "like showers that water the earth" took control. Hos 6:3 They believed that gospel and the Jesus who spoke and lived it. Their minds came at texts from below, from the sonship-gospel and Spirit that had made Israel God's people in the first place, that had made Jesus what he was.

I see such a mind in Simon "the Zealot," whom I have equated with the "Simon Iscariot" of John's memoir, Judas' father. He would have been a generation older than the rest. That every list of the "twelve apostles" includes him suggests that he was widely and appreciatively known. Formerly his brilliance had misled many. Now Jesus' spirit equipped his mind for reading and searching the scriptures in a new way. The many scriptural citations in Matthew had to be the harvest of somebody's searching. Let me propose Simon.

The Gospel of Matthew, I suggested, was formed from a fragment-library of Jesus-memory in Matthew's home town, Capernaum. Capernaum was on the lake. Not far off was Bethsaida, home of Simon and Andrew, James and John, and Philip, where John's memoirs were found. Later these towns came under judgment for their determined resistance. Listed with them is Chorazin to the north. Mt 11:20-24; Lk 10:13-15 No other memory of it is preserved. That Jesus' "mighty works" were abundantly manifest also there suggests that Chorazin had a notable apostle. I infer it was Simon, and that he and his son Judas had come to Jesus from Chorazin.

Viewed from below, every text of messianic hope and promise, to which Simon had once appealed in zealotic expectation, confirmed what Jesus had understood. Israel's name "my first-born son" from Moses and the exodus was the root of Jesus' sonship. The history of David, a king who had embodied God to his people and his people to God like no other, was of that covenant, too. "I have found David, my servant; with my holy oil I have anointed him.... He shall cry to me, 'You are my Father, my God, and the rock of my salvation.' And I will make him the first-born, the highest of the kings of the earth." Ps 89:20,26-27 "I have set my king on Zion, my holy hill. I will tell of the decree of the LORD: he said to me, 'You are my son, today I have begotten you. Ask of me, and I will make the nations your heritage.'" Ps 2:6-8 "I shall be his father, and he shall be my son," the LORD had promised, concerning David's son. 2 Sam 7:14

All this was covenant-language. Jesus had believed and filled it full. He was God's beloved son, blood-line descendant of David, anointed not for glory but for burial, drinking a cup of sufferings, robed in mockery, crowned with thorns, lifted up in crucifixion, heralded by a Roman governor's sign, confessed by his Roman executioner. Jesus would not rally supporters to serve him. He would not curse those who cursed him or conspire against those who fought him. He suffered abuse in love, prayed his Father to forgive those who turned deceit and violence against him, fought an enemy they did not know. He did this alone and to the very end.

Yet Jesus proved to be exactly the king for whom the prophets had longed, the king of hope even for the nations! "Give the king your justice, O God, and your righteousness to your royal son.... May he defend the cause of the poor of the people, give deliverance to the needy, and crush the oppressor!... May all kings fall down before him, all nations serve him!.... May men bless themselves by him, all nations call him blessed." Ps 72:1,17 "Behold my servant, whom I uphold, my chosen, in whom my soul delights; I have put my spirit upon him, he will bring forth justice to the nations. He will not cry or lift up his voice, or make it heard in the street; a bruised reed he will not break, and a dimly burning wick he will not quench; he will faithfully bring forth justice. He will not fail or be discouraged till he has established justice in the earth; and the coastlands wait for his law." Is 42:1-4; Mt 12:18-21

No wonder Jesus had chosen to ride that donkey! "Rejoice greatly, O daughter of Zion! Shout aloud, O daughter of Jerusalem!" Zechariah said. "Lo, your king comes to you; triumphant and victorious is he, humble and riding on an ass, on a colt, the foal of an ass.... The battle bow shall be cut off, and he shall command peace to the nations; his dominion will be from sea to sea, and from the River to the ends of the earth." Zech 9:9-10; Mt 21:5 Clearly, the hand of the Father had been on Jesus throughout, ruling this drama and overruling its rulers. He was a king not of war, but of an end to war! "He makes wars to cease to the end of the earth.... 'Be still and know that I am God. I will be exalted among the nations, I will be exalted in the earth!'" Ps 46:9-10 "The stone which the builders rejected has become the head of the corner. This is the Lord's doing; it is marvelous in our eyes." Ps 118:22-23; Mt 21:42

Never a christ like this, never again—a christ not of zealotic illusion and machinations but of Johwah himself. "I am the LORD, I have called you in righteousness. I have taken you by the hand and kept you; I have given you as a covenant to the people, a light to the nations, to open the eyes that are blind, to bring out the prisoners from the dungeon, from those who sit in darkness." Is 42:6-7 "And you are my witnesses! Is there a God besides me? There is no Rock; I know not any." Is 44:8 Simon and all the apostles were proclaiming Jesus out of the scriptures by the mind of God himself.

Birth Metaphor in Matthew

The "birth narratives" in Matthew (and Luke) open depth-perspective windows into such preaching and the history that gave rise to it. Four principles contribute toward reconstructing their origin and meaning. *First,* they need to be read "from below," that is, from within the covenant-gospel which Jesus preached and lived, and by which the young church testified to him. *Second,* they perceive and proclaim in Jesus the revelatory intervention of God. *Third,* the "birth" they visualize, by prophesies perceived as filled full, is of Jesus in the young church. *Finally,* for all their variety of imagery, these prophecies express a single theme. God's patient effort to repair or reform his relationship with his people, priests, and kings has proved futile. The only hope of recovery is to wipe out the old and start over new.

Jesus spoke of such starting-over himself. The gospel he preached and lived faced his people with an ultimate choice: either stay with the failed old, or "repent" and come into the new. When an old garment is beyond patching, it must be replaced. Old wineskin-bottles will split under pressure of new wine. New bottles are a necessity. Mt 9:16-17

These narratives incorporate bits of direct memory. John, son of Zechariah and Elizabeth, was pure of blood and born to the priesthood. He was six months older than Jesus. Jesus' parents were Mary and Joseph of Nazareth in Galilee. Joseph could trace his descent to David. The history that brought these narratives into being, however, was not of Jesus as a literal baby, but of God's starting his people over and of the scriptures filled full.

To visualize the birth narratives of Matthew, imagine the preaching of Simon the Zealot. Mt 1:18-2:23 Six metaphor texts from the prophets, each having to do with cutting off and starting over, yielded at some point a sermon. In each case, Simon appealed to those who were still resisting the covenant-gospel. Though tightly condensed, the thrust of each can be recovered.

Joseph and the Virgin Birth. Mt 1:18-25 Simon understood the "virgin" prophecy from Isaiah as a metaphor of "cutting off and starting over." Isaiah confronted King Ahaz, called "house of David." Is 7-8 Ahaz invoked the slogan "Immanuel" or "God is with us" on himself and his people confidently, thinking to be God's favorite. It was a time of tension. The northern kingdom, Ephraim (Israel) under Pekah, had allied with Syria under Rezin, to resist the giant Assyria theatening them from the north. 2 Kgs 16:1-9 Ahaz of Judah refused to join their alliance. Pekah, fearing that Judah might attack him from the south while he was occupied with Assyria, resolved with Syria to attack and control Judah first. Ahaz's counter-strategy was to bribe Assyria into attacking Syria and Ephraim from the north.

Isaiah tried to dissuade him. Ahaz's clever device would fail. The mighty River (the Euphrates, metaphor for Assyria) would not stop with Syria and Ephraim but overflow its banks to swallow up Judah, too! Let Ahaz ask for a sign by which to trust the LORD alone. Ahaz would not listen, would not believe.

Simon the Zealot perceived a like unbelief in his own people. They considered themselves "Immanuel," God's favorites, too. He and his fellow zealots had believed that deception. They had tried to "bribe" Jesus to their cause, summoning God's help on their own devices. Priests, Pharisees, and scribes had likewise believed God to be on their side. They had demanded a sign from Jesus, yet when the sign of his death and resurrection was given, they would not see it.

"Hear then, O house of David!" Isaiah cried to Ahaz in judgment. "Is it too little for you to weary men, that you weary my God also?" God's patience had run out. He did not need Ahaz, would not be "Immanuel" for him, could not use him to "father" his authentic people, either. He would cut the "house of David" off and start over with a woman, as in the garden of old. Gen 3:15 By a virgin and a son she bore, he would revive his people's "enmity" against their real enemy, the lying snake. "Therefore the LORD himself will give you a sign. Behold, a virgin shall conceive and bear a son, and shall call his name Immanuel." Is 7:14; Mt 1:23

What is preserved of the sermon is simply this imagery. By it Simon summoned the current version of "Ahaz" to repentance, however. God scorned the Judean claim of racial purity and law. They were not his "God with us" people and could not be. In no way could Judea have "fathered" the "son" he sent to them, whom they despised as a "Galilean," then slandered as a "blasphemer" for cherishing the covenant-sonship which their boast of superiority suppressed.

Jesus was God's miracle in spite of them, God's intervention, the virgin-born "starting-over" Isaiah had proclaimed. Would they receive him as such? By him they could be God's people in spirit and in truth again. Otherwise, Jesus would bear that "Immanuel" name, as would the young church that believed and proclaimed him. The very name "Jesus" was a sign also—not their enemy but their "savior," yet not from a superficial enemy and oppressor like Rome, but from the very sins that were destroying their nation and subjecting them to judgment and exclusion.

In Simon's metaphor-sermon, "Mary," the known name of Jesus' mother, depicted the virgin of Isaiah's prophecy, the unexpected instrument of God's starting-over. "Joseph, son of David," the known name of Jesus' father, depicted those who claimed superiority by racial descent. God had "betrothed" Galileans to his people ever since they had been conquered, after all. Galileans worshiped God in synagogues and made pilgimages to feasts.

Will Judeans limit what God can do by his Holy Spirit? Joseph's hesitation depicts their dilemma. Being "a just man and unwilling to put her to shame," he might simply wish the Galilean mother away so as not to have part in her and her son. However attractive this option might seem, it is not possible. God's voice speaks by an angel as in a dream: "Fear not, take her fully your wife. What is conceived in her is of God's Holy Spirit. He is indeed the 'God with us' son of the covenant! Do not fear to receive him. He has not come to condemn you either, but as his name indicates, to save you, his people, from your sins, so that in him you can truly start over!"

The "Joseph" who listens humbly is the young church within racially pure Judea. This Joseph listens to the word of God. He lets it happen as God says. He does not "know her," does not force his genealogy on the son she bears. "He calls his name Jesus," receives him as "savior" indeed. Thus the "cutting off" is not of wrath after all, but a wonder of "starting over" new!

The virgin-born "Immanuel" of Isaiah's prophecy depicts Jesus exactly. "He shall eat curds and honey, when he knows how to refuse the evil and choose the good." Is 7:15 Such is the nobility of a son who serves his Father in willing trust and hope. The devil tempted Jesus to "refuse the evil" (trouble) and "choose the good" (personal advantage) according to his own desire and fear. Jesus, however, like a little child, was not "wise" enough to abhor the "curds and honey" of the wilderness or to covet the fare of kings. Trusting his Father and loving his people to the end, he in fact chose what seemed stupid—"the evil" of rejection, cross, death—and refused what seemed "good"— a kingdom such as the zealots tried to thrust on him. He did not lose. He was

"Immanuel" indeed, God with him all the way. The young church bore his name.

The Nations. Is 60:1-7; Mt 2:1-11 In another sermon, Simon told of God's "starting over" by Isaiah's prophecy of the gathered nations. That foreigners were actually coming, not as invading enemies, but to get in on Israel's covenant-glory, was amazing! "Nations shall come to your light, and kings to the brightness of your rising.... Then you shall see and be radiant, your heart shall thrill and burst.... They shall bring gold and frankincense, and shall proclaim the praise of the LORD.... They shall come with acceptance on my altar, and I will glorify my glorious house." God's altar and house would be glorious for its covenant-truth. To see the LORD's covenant with Israel become the light of honor and hope to hearts of every nation was exciting, yet also humbling.

Simon's metaphor-sermon calls those who came "wise men," not "kings." That they came to worship the new-born king of Israel and have part in his kingdom is a wisdom his own people still resist. "From the east," the direction of sunrise, suggests a new day. The star in metaphor is the word of God shining in their night. The signal is tiny, yet it induces them to leave behind all they have possessed to bow before and have part in the young church's king. They come not to take booty but to bring gifts—"gold and frankincense," Isaiah says, to which Simon by associations of his own adds "myrrh."

"Yes, I am a king," Jesus told Pilate, not by war and power but "born" to it! Jn 18:37 Not even crucifixion and death could deny him that to which he was born. His very cross labeled him "the king of the Judeans" in Greek and Latin too, languages of the Gentiles. Will his own people read that sign? Will they see what nations far off are eager to see, if only by glimmer? Will they look to a star in their own dark night, a light of wisdom which was their heritage first and can be so still? Will they abandon their illusion of superiority and control? Will they come to their own rightful king and worship him too?

Bethlehem. Mic 3:9-12; 5:1-4; Mt 2:3-12 Micah's prophecy generated yet another sermon, applicable again to the young church. Simon the preacher longed to heal the division between Jerusalem and "Bethlehem," not aggravate or perpetuate it. In the background, however, was a cutting off. "Yet they lean upon the LORD and say, 'Is not the LORD in the midst of us?' Therefore because of you Zion shall be plowed as a field. Jerusalem shall become a heap of ruins and the mountain of the house a wooded height." Simon's sermon applied that judgment to the present "Jerusalem," ruled in metaphor by a "Herod" with whom "all the chief priests and scribes" live in comfortable complicity.

"Herod" depicts the authority of external rankings and power, demonstrated memorably not only by "Herod" called "the Great," but also by the Herod who put John to death. He stands ultimately for a priesthood which, rather than serve God, allied itself with Rome to crucify "Jesus of Nazareth"—named by Pilate's sign "the king of the Judeans."

The birth of a new king, signaled in the young church and gathering even the nations, causes "Herod the king" to be "troubled and all Jerusalem with him." Micah's imagery of "Bethlehem" derived from the history of David. When the LORD cut off Saul, he sent Samuel to Jesse of Bethlehem to anoint his youngest son, the shepherd lad David. 1 Sam 15:23; 16:1,12 Here lay Israel's hope again. "But you, O Bethlehem in the land of Judah, from you shall come forth for me one who is to be ruler in Israel. Therefore he shall give them up until the time when she who is in travail has brought forth"—a woman giving birth, as in Isaiah. This shepherd "shall stand and feed his flock in the strength of the LORD, in the majesty of the name of the LORD his God. And they shall dwell secure, for now he shall be great *to the ends of the earth.*" Mic 5:2-4

The birth narrative of Matthew weaves the compact summation of two sermons into one story—"the nations" from Isaiah and "Bethlehem" from Micah. Where will the nations find "the king of the Judeans" they seek, newborn and "great to the ends of the earth"? The priests and scribes have the scriptures. They can, if they will, direct the nations by Micah to "Bethlehem"—in metaphor to the young church where Jesus is honored and God's starting-over celebrated.

The "star" of metaphor, uninhibited by laws of astronomy, leads the wise men by day as well as by night, straight on from Jerusalem to Bethlehem. There it stops, stands still, directs them exactly to where the child is. Mt 2:9 The gathering nations do not denigrate Jesus or oppress him. Led by God's covenant-word and promises, they offer gifts of honor and thanksgiving. Will not his own people start over likewise, and so be truly free?

Egypt. Mt 2:15 Another sermon of Simon drew on Israel's deliverance from Egypt, as in Hosea. Hos 11:1-9 "When Israel was a child I loved him, and out of Egypt I called my son." The people who heard him knew also the larger context. "The more I called them, the more they went from me," the LORD grieved. A cut-off must come: "They shall return to Egypt." Yet the LORD struggles within himself, "How can I give you up, O Ephraim? ... my compassion grows warm and tender ... for I am God and not man, the Holy One in your midst, and I will not come to destroy."

Simon preached how Jesus relived the covenant-history of Moses and the exodus. The God of Israel did not forget his word to Pharaoh, "Israel is my son, my first-born; let my son go that he may serve me!" Ex 4:22-23 Jesus' "coming out of Egypt" was his Jordan crossing, the baptism at which he heard the voice from heaven name him "my son, my beloved." Mt 3:17 He had lived out that noble name faithfully. Trusting his Father's care and promises, he had filled full Israel's calling in steadfast love, through death, into resurrection and triumph. What greater honor and hope can there be? Let God's child-Israel whom he loves still, even the authorities, not be cut off in judgment but receive what Jesus did and come out of bondage into freedom with him!

Rachel Weeping. Mt 2:18 Another metaphor-sermon of cutting off and starting over drew on Jeremiah. "Thus says the LORD: 'A voice is heard in Ramah, lamentation and bitter weeping. Rachel is weeping for her children; she refuses to be comforted for her children, because they are not.'" But the promise followed. "Thus says the LORD: 'Keep your voice from weeping, and your eyes from tears; for your work shall be rewarded, says the LORD, and they shall come back from the land of the enemy. There is hope for your future, says the LORD.'" Jer 31:15-17

Ramah was a hill on the border between the two sons Rachel bore to Jacob—Joseph of the northern kingdom (Ephraim and Manasseh), and Benjamin (with Judah) of the southern. Both had been wiped out and deported, Israel by the Assyrians and Judah-Benjamin by Babylon. In Jeremiah's imagery, this was the occasion of Rachel's bitter weeping.

Simon's sermon perceived in this the situation of the young church. "Herod" in metaphor stands for the rulers of temple and synagogue, an authority fearful for its survival. Bethlehem, the young church, cherishes the gospel which they, however, fear and seek to suppress. No longer able to get at Jesus himself, they turn in wrath against all who, by confessing Jesus to be "the son of God," take this name as their own. The time-frame, "two years and under," recalls the virgin's young son in Isaiah, an age "before the child knows how to refuse the evil and choose the good." Is 7:16 "Babes" before God are too young to calculate advantage against disadvantage by the open-eyed wisdom of lust and fear. "You have hidden these things from the wise and understanding and revealed them to babes," Jesus thanked his Father. Mt 11:25; 18:3 Being too foolish to save themselves, they endure persecution and even death for Jesus' name. Rachel weeps for them, but finds comfort and courage to go on. "'They shall come back from the land of the enemy. There is hope for your future,' says the LORD."

Nazareth. Mt 2:23 In this sermon Simon associated a prophecy of Isaiah with the name "Nazareth" or "Nazarene." Jesus was often called "of Nazareth," perhaps in contempt for his Galilean ancestry. I find an old interpretation persuasive, that this was a conscious word-play on Isaiah's promise of "a branch (*netzer*)" growing from "the root" of Jesse. Mt 2:23; Is 10:33-34; 11:1-10 It is yet another dramatic instance of "cutting off and starting over."[1] The genealogical line of Davidic kings, the tree of Jesse, has been cut down to a stump. Nevertheless, a branch will sprout fresh from its root. Let "*Nazarene*" call Jesus to mind as the "*netzer*"!

That single word opens Isaiah's entire context. What sort of branch will this be? "The Spirit of the LORD shall rest upon him, the spirit of wisdom and understanding, the spirit of counsel and might, the spirit of knowledge and the fear of the LORD. He shall not judge by what his eyes see, or decide by what his ears hear; but with righteousness he shall judge the poor, and decide with equity for the meek of the earth; and he shall smite the earth with the rod of his mouth, and with the breath of his lips he shall slay the wicked. Righteousness shall be the girdle of his waist, and faithfulness the girdle of his loins." Such was the warfare Jesus actually fought and which the young church was carrying on, not with swords or conspiracies, but by the righteousness of God himself, spoken and lived!

Metaphors of peace follow. "The wolf shall dwell with the lamb," not to devour the lamb but to care for and protect it. "The sucking child shall play over the hole of the asp, and the weaned child shall put his hand on the adder's den. They shall not hurt or destroy in all my holy mountain; for the earth shall be full of the knowledge of the LORD as the waters cover the sea. In that day the root of Jesse shall stand as an ensign to the peoples; him shall the nations seek, and his dwellings will be glorious." In Jesus that day had surely come!

No brighter string of ornaments is possible than the covenant-gospel as it shines through in this series of texts, each picturing a sermon once preached. The question remains, how these six compacted sermon images, once separate, came to be strung together into a continuing narrative and so preserved. Someone must have valued them, noticed their common theme, then had the idea of fitting them together into a memorizable story sequence, so as not to lose any. To do this required constructing additional narrative to bridge gaps. A conspiracy of "Herod" would get Israel (pictured in Jesus) back to Egypt so

---

[1] So Franz Delitzsch, *The Prophecies of Isaiah*, 1877, translated from the German by James Martin. Grand Rapids, Michigan: Wm. B. Eerdmans, 1950. Vol. 1, p. 281.

that he could be called out of it (metaphoric journeys are no problem). A further conspiracy would set up the slaughter for which Rachel weeps. Another device would get Jesus from Bethlehem to Nazareth.

The composite must have been formed and written down quite early. The translator-arranger of Matthew found it in the fragment-library at Capernaum. He began his scroll with a genealogy of Jesus, then entered what appeared to be a direct memory of events at his birth.

Birth Metaphor in Luke

Luke's purpose, he explained to "Theophilus" (any God-loving reader), was to "compile a narrative of the things that have been accomplished among us," as others had done before him. His source was materials which "those who from the beginning were eyewitnesses and servants of the word handed down to us." "Eyewitnesses" were of Jesus' own generation who knew him. "Servants of the word" were those who had preached his story, framing it often in metaphor. The fragment-library Luke found in Judea preserved such materials in writing. He translated these one by one, so that his readers might have "a sure record of them." He also "studied them closely for some time," so as to enter them on his scroll in "an orderly account," a narrative sequence that made reasonable sense. Lk 1:1-4 This required grouping materials which had been random and unorganized. One grouping appeared to be birth stories, of John as well as of Jesus.

A depth-perspective reading of Luke will take account of these levels. First are the memories of the young church, memorized and retold orally, each with its own history. Next is the preservation of such memories in writing, then a process of "library exchange" by which Luke found some items already grouped. His own mind went to work then. He translated each of his findings accurately, then grouped them into a reasonable sequence for copying on his scroll. He entered first what appeared to be "birth narratives," but supplied imaginative links of his own in the interest of "an orderly account." Copyists are a final level. They dictated into Luke's work helpful emendations of their own.

Zechariah and Elizabeth. Lk 1:5-25 Among the fragments which Luke took to be "birth-stories" were testimonies of John's disciples to their master. The period of tension between Jesus' disciples and John's (the "Elijah" suggested in Peter's proposal of three tents on the transfiguration mountain) was over. Jesus and John are one. This fragment knows John's priestly origin, even his parents, Zechariah and Elizabeth. In metaphor they depict the priesthood—aged, sterile, past bearing children, but praying still and doing the worship well, like entering the holy place to burn incense. An angel of the Lord announces God's miracle, that Zechariah and his wife should be blessed to bring forth John! "Do not fear it!" the angel tells the priesthood, or see it as a threat. "Many will rejoice at his birth." John's birth and ministry happened by God's intention, as Gabriel put it. He would "turn the disobedient to the wisdom of the righteous," thus "make ready for the Lord a people prepared."

The priesthood depicted in Zechariah cannot believe this or welcome such "good news" as good. Very well, it will be dumb, without a voice to speak God's word of blessing on the people, until God's purpose is filled full. The account of John's birth focuses on Zechariah's *saying* his name, "Jochanan," meaning "Johwah is gracious." God defined himself so to Moses on the mountain, in the face of an unbelieving and idolatrous Israel. Ex 34:6-7 Once Zechariah has spoken this name, however, he (the priesthood) can perceive and sing gladly what "the Lord God of Israel" has done in Jesus and John. "He has visited and redeemed his people," as when he came to them in Egypt. He has "remembered *his holy covenant*, the oath which he swore to our father Abraham, to grant us that we, being delivered from the hand of our enemies, might serve him without fear in holiness and righteousness all the days of our life." Lk 1:67-79

Luke took this fragment to be a literal account of John's miraculous birth. In the interest of an "orderly account," he prefaced it with a time-reference, "in the days of Herod, king of Judea." Knowing that John and Jesus were near the same age (John just six months older), Luke divided his "John" fragment so as to enter a parallel announcement concerning Jesus.

The Virgin. This fragment, likewise metaphor, featured the virgin and her son from Isaiah's prophecy of cutting off and starting over. Lk 1:26-38: Is 7:1-17 Names for Jesus, which the young church celebrated, appear here—"the son of the Most High... the throne of his father David... holy, the son of God." He had not usurped any of this, neither had the young church invented it. All this was of God's word and Spirit, his purposeful intention before Jesus was even conceived in the womb. The virgin's awed question, "How can this be?" conveyed the young church's awe at the miracle which "the power of the Most High" had accomplished through Jesus—a recovery of Israel's covenant-heritage such as no one could ever have dreamed. "With God nothing will be impossible," the angel affirmed. The virgin's response, "I am the handmaid of the Lord; let it be to me according to your word," contrasts starkly with the unbelief of a self-reliant and manipulative Ahaz, on whom Isaiah pronounced judgment, "If you will not believe, surely you will not be established." No one can possess the heritage of Israel by right of genealogical descent, but only "according to your word," that is, by trusting what God says.

Luke took this fragment to announce a miraculous physiological virgin-birth, however. In the interest of his "orderly account," he located it in Nazareth, dated it "in the sixth month" of Elizabeth's pregnancy, identified the virgin as Jesus' mother, supplied her known name Mary, but had her only "betrothed" to "Joseph of the house of David," his father. When the virgin asked, "How can this be?" Luke saw the answer, "With God nothing will be impossible," as heralding the physiological miracle. Mary's "since I have no husband" is a copyist's interpolation, likewise the superfluous saying concerning "the sixth month" of her "kinswoman." Lk 1:34-37

Mary and Elizabeth. Among the metaphor-fragments in Luke's initial grouping was one which linked Elizabeth and Mary. It reflects the resolution, without competitive envy, of a post-resurrection tension between the disciples respectively of John and of Jesus. "He must increase, but I must decrease," John told his disciples. Jn 3:30 This signals their relationship as ordained by God while both were still babes in the womb. Lk 1:39-45 John's "mother," born of the Aaronic priesthood, rejoices in the nondescript Galilean mother, heralding her as "the mother of my Lord." Let the priesthood likewise acknowledge the Galilean Jesus without fear or envy! A hymn was appended, sung by the lowly mother in praise of the covenant-God who does not measure his people by pride or power or wealth, but "in remembrance of his mercy." Lk 1:46-55

Luke adjusted this imagery to fit his "orderly account," however. Assuming that the expectant mothers were literal kin, and with no concept of geographical distance, he had Mary from Nazareth visit Elizabeth in the hill country of Judea, stay with her during the three months of their overlapping pregnancies, then return home. That done, he finished entering the birth and naming of John, then a covenant-hymn ascribed to Zechariah.

Bethlehem. Now Luke could return to his fragment of the trusting virgin. The "annunciation" metaphor drew on Isaiah's prophecy of a virgin. The birth itself drew on Micah's imagery of a woman "in travail," who bears a son in Bethlehem, the town where Samuel had found and anointed the shepherd David. 1 Sam 16:11-13; Mic 5:2-5 Both prophecies proclaimed God's cutting off. Both start over by a woman as mother. Micah has her giving birth to a David-like shepherd-ruler of Israel, adding the promise, "Then the rest of his brethren shall return to the people of Israel; and he shall stand and feed his flock in the strength of Johwah, in the majesty of Johwah his God, and they shall dwell secure... to the ends of the earth. And this shall be peace!"

The fragment Luke had in hand celebrated in metaphor what had actually happened. "The time came for her to be delivered" is God's own time. "And she gave birth to her first-born son, and wrapped him in swaddling cloths and laid him in a manger, because there was no room for them in the inn." Jesus, and in him the young church, is that "first-born son"—not just of Micah's metaphoric "woman in travail," but of God. Ex 4:22 "Swaddling cloths" signal dependence, an unabashed but confident receiving, as when Jesus thanked his Father, who had "hidden these things from the wise and understanding and revealed them to babes." Mt 11:25 The manger was a feeding-trough for animals out in the open. In metaphor it signaled Jesus and the young church forced to improvise by temple and synagogue which had "no room" for him.

Yet God would not allow his covenant-son to be shamed and unknown, the amazing story went on. "The glory of Johwah" broke through into Israel's dark night. Angels heralded the new-born whom the authorities tried to exclude. Shepherds as lowly as David of old saw the glory, were delivered from fear, heard the "good news of a great joy" intended not for them only, but for "all the people." "For to you is born this day in the city of David a savior who is Christ the Lord." Their sign would be his swaddling cloths (simple dependence) and manger (exclusion). A chorus of angels sang what temple choirs could not and would not sing, "Glory to God in the highest, and on earth peace among men of his pleasure"—covenant-language for his chosen of the young church, regardless of what accusers and detractors might think. The shepherds (young church) heard this "gospel," saw it in Jesus, proclaimed it joyfully, and returned "glorifying God for all that they had heard and seen."

Luke's need for "an orderly account" posed a problem, however. He had written that Mary and Joseph were of Nazareth in Galilee. How could Jesus have been born in Bethlehem, then? They must have journeyed there. But why? To keep his narrative flowing, Luke invoked a census-edict of Caesar Augustus in the era of Quirinius, governor of Syria. "Everyone to his own city," as he told it, required Joseph, descended from David, to go to Bethlehem and Mary with him—she only "betrothed" to him. Everywhere else in the Bible "the city of David" is Jerusalem, but for Luke it is Bethlehem. Thus his patched account—no room, manger, angels, shepherds—obscures all sense of metaphor. A Greek copyist wondered who might have remembered and re-ported all this. Borrowing from the incident of Jesus as a twelve-year-old, he attributed it to Mary's memory. "But Mary *kept all these things*, pondering them *in her heart.*" Lk 2:19,51

Simeon and Anna. Lk 2:22-38 The next fragments Luke needed to enter were of Simeon, then Anna. The young church knew them both, how they had embraced the wonder of Jesus and testified to him in the temple itself, while the authorities still excluded him. Simeon, possibly of the priesthood, had served the temple tradition all his life. He let it all go now, freely and joyfully, so as to possess what had been Israel's covenant-gospel all along—long lost but newborn in Jesus and the young church. "Lord, now let your servant depart in peace *according to your word*," he sang in wonder—"your word" meaning the sonship Jesus had heard from heaven and filled full to the end. "For my eyes have seen your salvation, which you have prepared before the face of all peoples." Jesus, this lone Galilean out of nowhere, was in reality "a light for revelation to the nations and the glory of God's people Israel." Lk 2:22-38 What was this glory of Israel? Not to be exalted over the nations, but to repossess what had been its heritage all along—the covenant-love and wisdom embodied in Jesus, which all nations would crave, if they could only hear it!

But Simeon sang the conflict, too: "This child is set for the fall and rising again of many in Israel... a sign that is spoken against... that the thoughts of many hearts may be revealed." Malachi perceived this heart-choice: "They shall be mine, says the LORD of hosts, my special possession on the day when I act, and I will spare them as a man spares his son who serves him. Then once more you will distinguish between the righteous and the wicked, between one who serves God and one who does not serve him." Mal 3:17-18 Those who judge Jesus to be the son who serves his Father will be righteous with him. "The thoughts of hearts will be revealed" in a way that no outward perfor-mance or theological reasoning can hide.

In transcribing this, Luke understood Simeon to have taken up in his arms the literal baby, however. In that case, his parents must have brought him to the temple. To keep his "orderly account" flowing, Luke told of Jesus' cir-cumcision and naming on the eighth day (parallel to what had been written of John), then had his parents observe the law of purification in the temple thirty-three days later. Lev 12:2-4 His memory-fragment on the long-widowed Anna could follow. The young church in Judea cherished her as an enthusiastic "prophetess" for Jesus within the temple.

Having completed this group of entries in a sequence that seemed reasonable, Luke had the holy family return home to Nazareth.

Copyist Interpolations. A copyist misread Simeon's song, "Lord, now let your servant depart in peace *according to your word.*" Not knowing "the covenant-word" and its recovery, he supplied what God had said to the aging Simeon: "It had been revealed to him by the Holy Spirit that he should not see death before he had seen the Lord's Christ." To get Jesus' parents back into the scene, he divided the song and interpolated, "And his father and his mother marveled at what was said about him; and Simeon blessed them and said to Mary his mother, 'and a sword will pierce your own soul also.'" This "piercing" predicted her grief at the cross. Jn 19:37; Zech 12:10

The birth narratives in both Matthew and Luke, being metaphor, provide no evidence for dating Jesus' birth. A direct memory in John has him in his upper forties soon before his death. "You are not yet fifty years old," his accusers say. Jn 8:57 If Jesus died in 29 or 30 A.D., he would have been born about 18 B.C.

Jesus in the Temple. Lk 2:41-51 The next fragment Luke entered told of Jesus' Passover visit to Jerusalem at age twelve. This can only be direct memory, told by his mother in the era when memories of him were being eagerly gathered and cherished. She and Joseph had left for home and journeyed a full day. Realizing then that Jesus was not with them, they returned the next day. On the third day "they found him in the temple, sitting among the teachers, listening to them and asking them questions." "Son, why have you treated us so? Your father and I have looked for you anxiously," his mother exclaimed, when they found him. "How is it that you had to look for me?" he replied memorably. Then comes the line for which the story is preserved: "Didn't you know that I must be about my Father's business?"

The piety of the time, concerned for humility, suppressed the name of covenant-sonship and of God as "Father." Yet, appointed readings from Moses and the prophets in the synagogue every sabbath, as well as psalms, conveyed such ideas still. Acts 13:27 Jesus must have heard it recently in some form and been struck by it—like the text, "Israel is my first-born son, let my son go that he may serve me," or a hymn from Moses, "Is not he (Johwah) your father who created you, who made you and established you?" Ex 4:22-23; Dt 32:6 Perhaps he had asked some teacher about it, or mentioned it to his parents on their way to the feast. When his mother found him in the temple and said, "Your father and I," what came to Jesus' mind was his covenant-sonship beyond their human parenthood. After the resurrection, his mother understood how "my Father's business," spoken at so young an age, had actually characterized Jesus' whole life.

Corruptions appear here also. The transition, "Now his parents went to Jerusalem every year for the feast of the Passover," may have been entered by Luke in the interest of his "orderly account," rather than as remembered history. A pilgrimage to Jerusalem from Galilee was no light undertaking. For many, it was once in a lifetime. Matthew and Mark name four brothers of Jesus. They mention also sisters. How many children did his parents have by the time Jesus was twelve? To take him to the Passover at that age would likely have been very special.

The report that they found Jesus "sitting among the teachers, listening to them and asking them questions," would derive from his mother's telling. I cited earlier an inversion of this in the next verse: "All who heard him were amazed at his understanding and answers." A copyist, under the assumption that his name "son of God" (implied in calling God his "Father") meant deity, inferred that Jesus would not have needed to listen to teachers and ask questions. Even at twelve, he already knew more than any of them! Thus he exalted Jesus as the teacher and reduced the temple theologians to his astonished pupils.

Genealogy. Luke found among his fragments the David-genealogy of Jesus—which Simon had copied from the archives in Jerusalem, then secretly shared as a sign that Jesus was indeed the messiah. Someone with fresh insight had extended his sonship back to Abraham, then to Noah and even Adam, identifying him ultimately "of God." Lk 3:23-38 The location on the scroll is curious, however, as though Luke had misplaced it, then entered it at a next opportune moment.

Given the assumption that the virgin-birth was a physiological miracle, that the virgin was Jesus' mother Mary, and that Joseph was not actually her "husband" but only "betrothed" to her, a genealogy dependent on Joseph presented a problem. Someone, likely a copyist, resolved this by entering a parenthetical "supposed." "Jesus, being the son (as was supposed) of Joseph..." Lk 3:23

CHAPTER TWENTY ONE

The Peacemakers

"Blessed are the peacemakers, for they shall be called sons of God. Blessed are those persecuted for the sake of righteousness, for theirs is the kingdom of heaven."
Matthew 5:9-10

"Would that even today you knew the things that make for peace!"
Luke 19:42

The history of the young church in Galilee can be reconstructed. The disciples became gatherers with the Jesus who said, "He who is not with me is against me, and whoever does not gather with me scatters." Mt 12:30 A natural impulse would be to revisit towns in Galilee on their once-assigned routes, so that people who had known Jesus before his death might know also this amazing reversal. Some had gone to the Passover themselves, even participated in the procession that escorted him into Jerusalem. They needed to hear of the resurrection, how he had triumphed after all! Thus, quite informally, like a seed sown and growing, the young church was born.

Those who heard and believed continued to worship with their brothers in the synagogues, but they came together with one another, too, Jesus "in the midst of them." Their gatherings fell on the day after the sabbath, called "the eighth day," or "the first day of the week," like Hosea's post-sabbath "third day." They would remember and recite again sayings which Jesus had once preached and taught. Readings heard sabbath upon sabbath in the synagogue yielded covenant-sense as never before. Some began to *write* fragments of Jesus' teachings once memorized, collected these, then added memories found in neighboring towns. Spontaneous gatherings developed also in Jerusalem and towns of Judea, like the Bethany of Mary and Martha, or the Emmaus of Cleopas and Mary. The disciples and others, who had been close to Jesus, began to tell the wonder of him by fresh metaphor. Their testimonies were eagerly heard.

The symbolic "twelve" emerged to identify the young church with old Israel. Then came the impulse to fill out that holy number with actual names. Four lists are preserved. Mt 10:2-4; Mk 3:16-19; Lk 6:14-16; Acts 1:13 All have Simon Peter, Andrew, James and John, also Philip, Bartholomew, Matthew, and Thomas, then James (son) of Alphaeus. In Matthew and Mark, the tenth is Thaddaeus, followed by Simon the Cananaean (Aramaic) or "Zealot" (Greek), ending with Judas, the "deceiver" or "Iscariot." Lists in Luke and Acts have Simon the Zealot as tenth, then another Judas (called "of James"), and last, Judas Iscariot (omitted in Acts).

The beatitude, "Blessed are the *peacemakers*, for they shall be called *sons of God*," linked the young church with Jesus' own sonship and character as God's authentic chosen people. Israel's covenant-name from of old was its glory and freedom, the very heart of its faith and witness. A memoir from John has Jesus embodying it: "I am the way, and the truth, and the life. No one comes to the Father but by me. If you had known me, you would have known my Father also." Jn 14:6-7 This testimony could not be compromised. The claim of Judeans to be "chosen" by right of genealogy and law was worse than empty, it was idolatrous. Yet the young church as "peacemakers" would endure persecution and death with Jesus, rather than be cut off from or give up on their lost but still resistant brothers.

When Peter proposed "three tents, one for you, one for Moses, and one for Elijah," the voice from the cloud had answered, "This is my beloved son, with whom I am well pleased; listen to him." Mt 17:4-5 Peace by division is not possible. The gospel of sonship gathers, it does not allow scattering. Barriers that divided Jesus and the young church (the Jesus-people) from the disciples of John and their followers (the Elijah-people), or from the authorities of synagogue and temple who claimed Moses (the Moses-people), must come down. The covenant-word Jesus spoke and died for has authority to bring them down. To escape into comfortable division is to deny the covenant-sonship and to forsake the voice of the living God.

Elijah: The Disciples of John

"Elijah" signals John the Baptist. Mt 11:14; Jn 1:21; Mal 4:5 His disciples were understandably troubled by the notion that Jesus' crucifixion and death was more than just another tyrannical injustice (as when their master was beheaded), and by his disciples' testimony to his resurrection. Several indications of the conflict and of its resolution are preserved.

The Christ. Mt 11:2-6; Lk 7:18-23 A post-resurrection dialogue between "John" and "Jesus" concerned the testimony of Jesus' disciples, that he was indeed "the Christ." This succinct memory may have been framed for the sake of winning the Elijah-people. "John" (embodying the Elijah-people), having heard "about the deeds of the Christ," sent his disciples to ask, "Are you he who is to come or do we look for another?" (A copyist of Matthew, not realizing that this episode is post-resurrection, assumed that John would have heard this while he was "in prison.")

"Jesus" (embodying the Jesus-people), answered, "Go and tell John what you see and hear." What the Elijah-people "see and hear" is first, that Jesus is not a warrior-christ. The notable "deeds" they observe in Jesus testify to the power of his covenant-word, as his disciples are now proclaiming him. How that word effects healings from the heart out is visualized in familiar metaphor from the prophets. Is 35:5-6; 61:1 "The blind receive their sight and the lame walk, lepers are cleansed and the deaf hear, the dead are raised up, and the poor have the sonship-gospel preached to them. And blessed is he who takes no offense at me." The Jesus of that word is indeed the promised Christ. There will never be another.

Fasting. Conflict between "Jesus" and "John" arose also over fasting. Mt 9:14-15 John had fasted and taught his disciples so. The birth narrative confirms this of him: "He will drink no wine or strong drink." Lk 1:15 The Elijah-people continued this practice. Jesus, however, and the young church, did not practice fasting. Both John and Jesus fell under the arbitrary judgment of Pharisaic critics, however. "Like children sitting in the market places," they wanted to dictate the tune for everybody else. "We piped to you, and you did not dance; we wailed, and you did not mourn," they complained. "For John came neither eating nor drinking, and they say, 'He has a demon.' The son of man came eating and drinking and they say, 'Behold, a glutton and a drunkard, a friend of tax collectors and sinners.'" Mt 11:16-19

With respect to Jesus and John, the situation initially determined the practice. John invited the people of Judea to come out to him through the Jordan into the wilderness. His fasting, taught also to his disciples, was a sign of waiting for "the mightier one" to come, as Israel in the wilderness waited for the land. Jesus' ministry was in fertile Galilee. To eat and drink was to receive and give thanks for his Father's gifts. To eat and drink with "tax collectors and sinners," when they invited him into their homes, signaled the fellowship of a common thanksgiving.

But there was more. "Can the wedding guests mourn, as long as the bridegroom is with them?" The "wedding" is the kingdom "at hand," here and now. The people need only take possession. When "Moses and the chief men of Israel beheld God," they "ate and drank." Ex 24:11 When Israel entered the land and began eating its produce, their era of "fasting" or "manna" ceased. Josh 5:12 "You shall know that the living God is among you," Joshua said in celebration. Josh 3:10 So it is now. God's people of the resurrection era are no longer in the wilderness. The wedding is hardly an occasion to mourn and fast!

The fasting of the Pharisees ("twice a week," Jesus said in a parable) was of law. Lk 18:12 By it, they signaled their special identity and their claim on Israel's futurist kingdom. "Truly I say to you, they have their reward," Jesus said, meaning the admiration of people who noticed. Mt 6:16 "The days will come, when the bridegroom is taken away from them, and then they will fast in that day," he warned. Mk 2:20 When his own kingdom "at hand" is lost, and passion revives for a kingdom that establishes Israel's glory, then their fasting will be not ritual, but hard reality.

Baptism. Jn 3:22-30; 4:2 Another issue between Jesus' disciples and John's concerned "baptism." That term is a problem, for it misses what John actually did and taught. Baptism in Judean law and piety had do with "washings," as a note in Mark indicates. "The Pharisees, and all the Judeans, do not eat at all unless they wash their hands, observing the tradition of the elders; and when they come from the market place, they do not eat unless they purify (Greek: *baptize*) themselves, and there are many other traditions they observe, the washing (Greek: *baptizing*) of cups and pots and vessels of bronze and tables." Mk 7:3-4 John's "baptism" had to do with passing through a water-boundary, however. It was not a washing.

The account of the "transfiguration" in Luke preserves a significant indication of this authentic meaning. "And behold, two men talked with him, Moses and Elijah, who appeared with him in glory and spoke of his departure (Greek: *exodus*), which he was to fill full in Jerusalem." Lk 9:30-31 Moses had an *exodus* of his own! He brought old Israel out of Egypt through the sea—out of slavery to Pharaoh into freedom as son-servants of the LORD their God.

Elijah (referring to John the Baptist) had an *exodus* also. His, through the Jordan, brought him and those who crossed to him from Judea, out of bondage to an empty and corrupted law, into Israel's original and authentic covenant-identity as son-servants of the living God. Paul afterwards understood "baptism" to have been rooted in Israel's exodus-crossing. "Our fathers were all under the cloud (of covenant-revelation), and all passed *through the sea*, and all were *baptized into Moses in the cloud and in the sea.*" 1 Cor 10:1-2 "Baptized into Moses" means to have part by that *exodus* in Moses' word of covenant-sonship, to be a people with whom God was "well pleased."

Jesus, in his ministry in Galilee, had no "Jordan" for people to pass through, hence he did not "baptize." His transfiguration-conversation with Moses and Elijah recognizes, however, that he completed, "in Jerusalem," an *exodus* of his own. The *passing through* he made there was not of water but of death into life. It filled full the sonship and servanthood to which his Father had called him at his Jordan-baptism. Two "baptism" sayings indicate that Jesus was aware of this. "Are you able to be *baptized* with the *baptism* with which I am *baptized?*" he asked James and John, when they wanted to sit at his right hand and left in his kingdom. Mk 10:38 "I have a *baptism* to be *baptized* with; and how stressed I am until it is finished," he said, as he faced the final crisis. Lk 12:50 By his *exodus*, his Father cut off the corrupted old and started his people over new. Once his guilty and dead disciples perceived it so, it was their *exodus* also. It raised them from death to life with him. To be "baptized" with Jesus into his death was to have part in his *exodus*—take on his sonship and life, and have no part in the lying tradition that had condemned him.

It appears that John's disciples continued his mission after his death, not at his location on the wilderness side of the Jordan, however, but throughout Judea, as when they had served as John's emissaries. Their activity extended also far beyond. A memory in Acts indicates that John's word and "baptism" reached Alexandria in Egypt. Apollos then brought it to Ephesus. There John's "baptism" merged into that of Jesus. Acts 18:24-25; 19:3-6

That the term "baptism" came to be applied to *exodus*-crossings is a puzzle, however. It appears that John's disciples, though no longer at the Jordan, continued to enact by water, in some way, the "repentance" (leaving the old behind and coming into the new) implicit in "passing through" "the sea" or the Jordan. If the form of that enactment was perceived as analogous to "washings" familiar to Pharisaic and Judean piety, that could account for the term "baptism" in the history of John and of Jesus. People spoke of "John's baptism," in distinction from baptisms of the common piety. They called

John "the Baptist," as preserved in the Gospels. With that, the *exodus* sense of crossing a boundary was obscured and diffused.

A memoir of John tells of a conflict between "John's baptism" and that of Jesus. John's disciples were baptizing at "Aenon near Salim." Jn 3:22-30 (The explanation, "because water was plentiful there," is likely a copyist's enhancement.) "Jesus and his disciples went into the land of Judea," and "he remained with them and baptized," the memoir says. A clarification follows, that "Jesus himself did not baptize, but only his disciples." Jn 4:2 John, who wrote this, had himself been a disciple of the Baptist. He would have known these fellow-disciples personally.

"The Pharisees heard that Jesus was making and baptizing more disciples than John," the memoir reports, suggesting competition. Jn 4:1 "A discussion arose between John's disciples and a Judean over purifying. And they came to John and said to him, 'Rabbi, he who was with you beyond the Jordan, to whom you bore witness, here he is, baptizing, and all are going to him.'" Apparently, this "Judean," after discussing baptism with John's disciples, decided to seek it from Jesus and not from them.

John rejected any notion of competition between himself and Jesus. "You yourselves bear me witness that I said, 'I am not the Christ, but I have been sent before him.' He who has the bride (the people) is the bridegroom (God, in Jesus his son). The friend of the bridegroom (John and his disciples), who stands and hears him, rejoices greatly at the bridegroom's voice. Therefore this joy of mine is full. He must increase, but I must decrease." Jn 3:28-30

Further testimony to the merging appears in a two-fold reference to Jesus as "the lamb of God." When John introduced Jesus to Andrew and John, saying, "Behold, the lamb of God," he pictured God as shepherd and his people as his flock. Jn 1:35-36; Is 40:11 When he said, "Behold the lamb of God, *who takes away the sin of the world*," this was a post-resurrection witness to Jesus' sacrificial death, drawing on Isaiah's imagery of a lamb led to the slaughter. Jn 1:29; Is 53:6-7

Significantly, the memoir has John acknowledge also, "I myself did not know him" (that is, Jesus as the apostles were now preaching him). But John *did* know the premise on which the issue turned! "He who sent me to baptize with water said to me, 'He on whom you see the Holy Spirit descend and remain, this is he who baptizes with the Holy Spirit.' And I have seen and borne witness that *this is the son of God*." Jn 1:33-34

Jesus and John converge also in the Lucan birth narrative, as I showed earlier. Jesus' eulogy to John offers yet another testimony to their oneness. Mt 11:7-11

"What did you go out into the wilderness to see? A reed shaken by the wind? Why then did you go out? To see a man clothed in soft raiment?... Why then did you go out? To see a prophet? Yes, I tell you, and more than a prophet. This is he of whom it is written, 'Behold, I send my messenger before your face, who shall prepare your way before you.' Mal 3:1 Truly, I say to you, among those born of women there has risen no one greater than John the Baptist; yet he that is least in the kingdom of heaven is greater than he." Let comparisons cease! The only greatness that matters is to be "in the kingdom of heaven." The least of those who heard John will be there too, ahead of even the preacher. "For all the prophets and the law prophesied until John," Jesus added. All were of the stream to which John also belonged. "And if you are willing to receive it, he is Elijah who is to come." Mt 11:13-14; Mal 4:5-6 John and Jesus proclaimed the same covenant-word.

The lowliest of valley-people, even sinners and outsiders, had heard John and believed him! These were the "Elijah-people!" There were many of them. They believed "that John was a prophet." Mt 21:26 Let the mountain-critics learn from them! "Truly I say to you, the tax collectors and the harlots go into the kingdom of God before you. For John came to you in the way of righteousness, and you did not believe him, but the tax collectors and the harlots believed him; and even when you saw it, you did not afterwards repent and believe him." Mt 21:31-32

Moses: The Persecutors

To rulers of temple and synagogue, the revival of Jesus' covenant-gospel through the proclamation of his resurrection became increasingly disconcerting. The disciples heralded it with conviction, but by what authority? They were all Galileans as Jesus had been, lacking in birthright. They were untrained in the law of Moses, by which Jesus had been properly judged to death. Yet people were believing them! Initial hopes that such preaching was merely a final convulsion of stubborn zealotic fantasy proved mistaken. It did not die away. By divine irony, "the last fraud" was indeed becoming "worse than the first." Mt 27:64 Even leaders were succumbing to the message! At some point the Moses-people began to denounce the Jesus-aberration openly. They warned their people about it. They turned disciplinary pressures against it.

Anticipations in the preserved record testify to what became real. "They will deliver you up to councils and flog you in their synagogues," Jesus said.

"Brother will deliver up brother to death, and the father his child, and children will rise up against parents and have them put to death, and you will be hated by all for my name's sake.... If they have called the master of the house Beelzebul, how much more will they malign those of his household!... Do not think that I have come to bring peace on earth; I have not come to bring peace, but a sword. For I have come to set a man against his father, and a daughter against her mother, and a daughter-in-law against her mother-in-law; and a man's foes shall be those of his own household. He who loves father or mother more than me is not worthy of me, and he who loves son or daughter more than me is not worthy of me.... He who finds his life will lose it, and he who loses his life for my sake will find it." Mt 10:17,21-22,25,34-39 "They will put you out of their synagogues; indeed, the hour is coming when whoever kills you will think he is offering service to God." Jn 16:2

Let the disciples and young church walk the way of the Lord nevertheless, upright and straight, trusting the Father's promises. "When they deliver you up, do not be anxious how you are to speak or what you are to say; for what you are to say will be given to you in that hour; for it is not you who speak, but the Spirit of your Father speaking through you.... So have no fear of them; for nothing is covered that will not be revealed, or hidden that will not be known. What I tell you in the dark, utter in the light; and what you hear whispered, proclaim upon the housetops. And do not fear those who kill the body but cannot kill the soul; rather fear him who can destroy both soul and body in the valley of Hinnom. Are not two sparrows sold for a penny? And not one of them shall fall to the ground without your Father. But even the hairs of your head are all numbered. Fear not, therefore; you are of more value than many sparrows." Mt 10:26-31

Threats are the backdrop of promise. "Anyone who opens his home to a prophet, because he is a prophet, shall receive a prophet's reward, and anyone who receives a righteous man (one in 'the way of righteousness' as proclaimed by John and Jesus) will receive a righteous man's reward. And whoever gives to one of these little ones (the ordinary folk) even a cup of cold water because he is a disciple, truly, I say to you, he shall not lose his reward." Mt 10:40-42 Let the strong and bold honor those who are not ready as yet to confess Jesus' name openly. Receive the least indication of love and sympathy on their part as already a full confession.

"Blessed are those who are persecuted for righteousness' sake, for theirs is the kingdom of heaven. Blessed are you when men revile you and persecute you and utter all kinds of evil against you falsely on my account. Rejoice and be glad, for your reward is great in heaven, for so men persecuted the prophets who were before you. You are the salt of the earth." Salt burns like fire the festering wounds of those who resist you; but it is for their healing, so don't lose your saltness. "You are the the light of the world." Expose the falsity of their way. It is for their deliverance, so don't hide your light timidly under a bushel. Mt 5:11-14

The judgment on Chorazin, Bethsaida and Capernaum, mentioned earlier, suggests that this triangle of towns was the heart-center of the young church's ministry in Galilee, as it had been of Jesus. Here it was that resistance and persecution became particularly intense. Seeing their tradition threatened, the rulers did everything in their power to suppress the name of Jesus. Yet voices like Simon's in Chorazin, John's in Bethsaida, and Matthew's in Capernaum, did not waver. For all the abuse the young church endured against bodies and livelihoods, they could not give up on their "brothers" any more than Jesus could. "Father, forgive them, for they do not know what they are doing," he had prayed in his dying. The young church pressed that plea to the very end.

Yet they could not compromise the great "either-or," for it was of the covenant-God. "Woe to you, Chorazin! Woe to you, Bethsaida! For if the mighty works done in you had been done in Tyre and Sidon (or Sodom), they would have repented long ago in sackcloth and ashes.... And you, Capernaum, will you be exalted to highest heaven? You shall be brought down to the lowest Hades." Mt 11:20-24; Is 14:14-15

"Your Brother"

For all the persecution and exclusion the young church suffered, the real trouble was of "brothers" who reacted so bitterly and defensively against Jesus. "Love your enemies," he said, "and pray for those who persecute you, that you may be sons of your Father who is in heaven.... For if you love those who love you, what do you gain?" Mt 5:44-46 Sayings concerning "your brother," preserved in Matthew, were likely taught compactly by the apostle Matthew himself. ("Brother" in this usage, like "sons," though grammatically male, is a language of common humanness, not of sexual distinction.)

A disciple ruthlessly slandered will not give up on the slanderer. What might he say in Jesus' name? "You have heard that it was said to the men of old, 'You shall not kill....' But I say to you that everyone who is angry with his brother (as you are with Jesus and me) shall be liable to judgment. Whoever insults his brother (as you insult Jesus and me) shall be liable to the council. And whoever says, 'You fool!' (as you disparage Jesus and me) shall be liable to Hinnom and its fire." How you and your courts judge me is not what matters, but how God judges you!

Suppose a "brother" participates in synagogue worship faithfully, makes pilgrimages to Jerusalem in season, offers right sacrifices. Suppose he brushes aside your witness as though it means nothing to him, then treats your concern for him with contempt. What might you say? "If you are offering your gift at the altar, and there remember that I and Jesus, your brother, have something against you, leave your gift before the altar (for it is pretense and mockery) and go; first be reconciled to me and Jesus, your brother. Then come and offer your gift." Mt 5:23-24

Suppose you and a stubbornly resistant persecutor, brothers still in the same holy people, are walking together toward the consummation God has in store. If Jesus did not cut him off to be rid of him, neither can you. He resents you for pointing out insistently the dead-end fallacy of race and law and authority, which he invokes against Jesus and all who confess his name. What can you say to him? "Time is not forever! Settle things quickly with your accuser (Jesus and me) while we are on the way together, lest the accuser hand you over to the judge, and the judge to the guard, and you be cast into prison. Truly, I say to you, there will be no mercy and patience for you then, but only the law and rights on which you insist and which you so trust! By that law, you will not get out until you pay in full every last cent you owe." Mt 5:25-26

A classic text offers further wisdom. Mt 18:15-18 "If your brother goes astray, go and warn him of it between you and him alone." Your brother has been taught from childhood that the synagogue and its tradition is of Moses and the LORD, but he cannot see the deception into which his people have fallen. Talk to him alone, not where he will be fearful of and pressured by others. He has a "self" just like your own "self." Talk from your heart to his heart. Show the trap you see him in, and how the sonship-gospel Jesus taught and lived would free him of it. If he listens to you, you will have gained your brother!

But if he does not listen, don't give up! Look for a chance to talk again! Take someone with you, maybe two. Let them add their vision of covenant-honor and freedom to yours, as they have experienced it. "In the mouth of two or three witnesses, every word shall be established." Perhaps something they say will establish what you have been trying to tell him.

But if he will not hear them either, what then? Time and energy are limited.

Jesus had instructed his disciples on their earlier missions, "If no one will receive you hospitably in a town, shake off its dust from your feet as you leave and go on." Mt 10:14 Here too a point may come where you need to go on. If your love is getting you nowhere, don't let that weigh you down. God himself does not win everybody. Your brother, obsessed with law, invokes Moses to cut you off just as he cuts tax collectors and sinners off. Yet in truth, he is cutting himself off, making himself the very "Gentile and tax collector" outsider he so despises.

You are speaking and acting by the call and authority of your God. Your voice is his voice! Whatever you bind in its sin on earth, your God is binding in heaven; but whatever you loose and forgive on earth, he is loosing in heaven. So when you see a "brother" loosed and free, rejoice! Your Father and the angels will be rejoicing with you.

Assurances follow. "Again I say to you, if two of you agree on earth about anything you ask, it will be done for them by my Father in heaven. For where two or three of you are gathered in my name, there am I in the midst of them." Mt 18:19-20 The "two" of you can still pray in hope for the "brother" who has rejected you. If the church is reduced even to two or three "gathered in Jesus' name," it will still be not defeated, still be not alone.

A copyist corrupted this, however, with a third level of prescription. "Tell it to the church, and if he will not hear the church" violates the singular with which the text concludes, "let him be *to you*" (singular, still brother to brother). "The church" is now an authority structure equivalent to "the synagogue." "Tell it to the synagogue" was a formula of exclusion and persecution in the name of faithfulness. Its tactic creates "peace" by judgment and separation. Whoever the offender may be—your own father or mother, son or daughter, brother or sister—"tell it to the synagogue," so that the synagogue may call the "sinner" to account and as necessary, exclude him. Mt 10:35 A memoir of John recalls that "many even of the authorities believed in him," yet "for fear of the Pharisees did not confess it, lest they should be put out of the synagogue; for they loved the praise of men more than the praise of God." Jn 12:42-43

Peter's proposal of peace by way of three separate "tents" did not stand. Here he offers peace by setting a limit: "Lord, how often shall my brother sin against me and I forgive him? As many as seven times?" Mt 18:21-22 Let the "six" of unhappy abuse culminate in a "seven" of rest! "Against me" personalizes what Peter and others were enduring at the hand of their "brother." Yet this is not the "peace" of sonship, either. "Not seven, but seventy time seven,"

Jesus answered. The square of Peter's "seven," multiplied tenfold, implies infinity. "Rest" is not to be found in self-pity or in keeping score or in retaliating or in building walls of safety. "Take my yoke upon you and learn from me, for I am meek and lowly of heart, and you shall find rest for your souls." Mt 11:28-30 Peter wrote this of Jesus in a letter: "When he was reviled, he did not revile in return; when he suffered he did not threaten, but he trusted him who judges justly." 1 Pet 2:23

The "brother" fragments in Matthew climax in the parable of a servant who, rather than pass on the flow of God's mercy, cut it off. Mt 18:23-35 Jesus may have directed this originally to the Pharisees, but as preserved, it addresses a question like Peter's in the young church. Faced with an infinite debt, "ten thousand talents" (heaviest unit of weight multiplied by highest number), this servant remembered not mercy and thanksgiving, but only law and rights. He could not dispute God's right to retrieve his loss by selling him into slavery with his wife and children and all he had, but proposed a contract: "Have patience with me, and I will pay you everything." The king had a better idea. Out of mercy "he released him and forgave him the debt." That was peace. It revealed "Johwah" as he truly was, "a God merciful and gracious, slow to anger and abounding in steadfast love and faithfulness, forgiving his iniquity and transgression and sin."

The servant did not catch the wonder. A fellow-servant, who owed him a pittance, pleaded likewise for a restructured contract. But no, he invoked his rights under law, demanded instant repayment, and threw him into prison until he paid in full. Other servants reported the incongruity to their master. Now came a second call to account. "Should you not have had mercy on your fellow-servant, even as I had mercy on you?" Forgiveness would have kept the flow of mercy going! But if the servant reverted to law and rights, so be it also for him!

Mercy in flow is the covenant-wisdom of Moses. Its contrary, obsession with law and rights, debases "the name of the LORD your God." It contradicts Israel's call as God's "first-born son" to "love your neighbor as yourself." To live by calculating "good" or "evil" *for me* is to subject "*me*" to that same calculation, a judgment without mercy. Jesus built it into his prayer, "Forgive us what we owe you, as we forgive those who owe us." A commentary cites the great "either-or": "If you forgive others their sins, your heavenly Father also will forgive yours; but if you do not forgive others their trespasses, neither will your Father forgive yours." Mt 6:12-15

The young church understood this even when it failed. Peter told how he began to walk those waves at Jesus' command and promise, yet at some point he "saw the wind, was afraid, began to sink, and cried out, 'Lord, save me!'" Mt 14:30 Failures were frequent, no doubt, but the young church, knowing the snare in which their "brothers" were caught, could not give up on them. The persecuting "brother" needed to be loved still. To withdraw by ceasing to worship with him in synagogue and temple would be to abandon him. The walls must come down, the gates of Hades give way. "I was in prison and you came to me," Jesus said. Mt 25:34 Such was the guileless character of those he called "blessed by his Father."

Zealotry Revived

Warnings against "false christs" signal a revival of the zealotic fantasy that got Jesus crucified as an insurrectionist. Mt 24:4-28: Mk 13:5-6,13-23; Lk 17:22-37; 21:5-36

Caiaphas' prophetic strategy succeeded, "that one man should die for the people and the whole nation not perish." Jn 11:48-50 War and violence, precipitated by a zealotic revolt, did not break out. The Romans did not come in vengeful force to destroy the holy place and the nation.

Jesus was that "one man," not by Caiaphas' choice only, but by "choosing life" on his own. Named God's "beloved" or "only son," he became the peacemaker. He loved his wayward people to the end, fought all alone the enemy who had so deceived them. His Father raised him up and exalted him as king indeed—not of a futurist zealotic kingdom and glory, but of his kingdom-*now*. The shamed and despairing disciples were raised to life by his Spirit. They confessed his name, preached his covenant-gospel, brought the young church to birth in his image. Their peace transcended, refuted, and redirected the long-pervasive zealotic ambition.

As persecution suppressed the kingdom Jesus lived and died for, however, the piety of Israel's superiority and the corresponding fantasy of a futurist kingdom and conquest revived, unchecked. Hatred of Rome, the alien "enemy," stirred again and with it, contempt for a conniving and self-serving priesthood. Newly aggressive leaders offered themselves as "christs" of insurrection. If they remembered Jesus at all, they judged their past effort to thrust the kingship on him an unfortunate mistake. He had not been up to it. They would do better. They would be faithful to God's laws as Jesus had not been. They understood what needed to be done. With full courage against all odds, counting on help from heaven, they would press the warfare of Israel's glory through to the triumphant end.

The apostles in Judea and Galilee understood the illusion. They warned their people in Jesus' name of its catastrophic end. "Lo, I have told you beforehand," recalls how he had tried to dissuade them. Mt 24:25; Mk 13:23 If the spirit of revolt broke out again, Jesus would not be there as peacemaker to put himself between. The Romans might suffer momentary defeat, but they would return with ruthless force to do exactly what Caiaphas had feared, "destroy our holy place and our nation." Jerusalem and its people would be devastated, the temple perish, its sacrifices cease. A "desolating sacrilege" of the sort Daniel had seen would be erected in its place. Dan 11:31 It would be a time of "great tribulation such as has not been from the beginning of the world until now, no, and never will be." What should helpless bystanders do then? "Let those in Judea flee to the mountains." "Alas for women with child or for nursing mothers in those days. Pray that your flight may not be in winter or on a sabbath."

The people needed to hear such warnings. "See that no one leads you astray. For many will come in my name saying, 'I am the christ,' and they will lead many astray." "If anyone says to you, 'Lo, here is the christ,' or 'there,' do not believe it. For false christs and false prophets will arise and show great signs and wonders, so as to deceive, if possible, even the chosen.... So if they say to you, 'Lo, he is in the wilderness,' do not go out; if they say, 'He is in the inner rooms,' do not believe it." There will be no "christ" other than "the son of man," as Jesus called himself.

How does God's true kingdom come? A heaven-borne lightning flashes in the east of a dark sky but shines even to the west. The bright flash out of Jesus' cross and resurrection, originating in Judea, was penetrating the world's night westward to Greece and beyond even now, as far as Rome! But if God's people despise this sign, let them notice the vultures circling high, watching for the body of a dying Israel to drop, ready to swoop down and greedily devour.

Are they God's honored "chosen"? Then let them follow their living Lord and trust his promises. "Heaven and earth will pass away, but my words will not pass away." Their calling is not to judge who belongs or does not belong, not to guess who will be taken and who will be left, but to simply do what the Father in heaven grants and enables each to do day by day in his kingdom-*now*. Keep doing it freely and steadfastly, whatever may happen, trusting the Father to make even sufferings good and to gather the scattered safely home. "Blessed is that servant whom the master, when he comes, will find so doing."

A fragment in Paul corroborates this. 2 Thess 2:1-12 Rumors and "letters purporting to be from us," anticipating "the day of the Lord," were rallying Jews everywhere. They invoked the apostles too, even Jesus. But it is deception. "That day will not come, unless the rebellion comes first, and the man of lawlessness ... takes his seat in the temple of God, proclaiming himself to be God," revealed "with all power and with pretended signs and wonders and with all deception for those who are to perish, because they refused to love the truth and so be saved." It happened. A zealotic revolt under self-anointed leaders took over the temple in 66 A.D. and led to the destruction of Jerusalem by the Romans four years later.

What is "restraining him until he is out of the way"? The young church, proclaiming the kingdom in truth, warned against the lies and delusions which "God sends" on those who "refuse to love the truth and so be saved." That restraining voice was indeed silenced, thus "out of the way." A well planned persecution suddenly and systematically destroyed every written memory-fragment concerning Jesus throughout Judea and Galilee, so that not a piece of it has ever been found. The effect of that loss can hardly be imagined. The young church would have come to depend on this resource. Its treasure of oral memory was no longer recoverable. Any sustained impact its witness might have had on zealotry at home or on the church abroad was effectively silenced. The Lord Jesus, who had put himself between to save "holy place and nation" once, was not there to do it again. Jn 11:48

In 66 A.D. self-anointed leaders took over the temple. Four years later Jerusalem fell to the Romans. Flames consumed also the genealogical archives, names written on earth to certify pure descent from Abraham. Jesus and the young church heralded by contrast "names written in heaven," in God's "book of life," to certify the sons of God. Lk 10:20; Phil 4:3

Memory of it was written later into the parable of the wedding feast. "The rest seized his servants, treated them shamefully, and killed them. The king was angry, and he sent his troops and destroyed those murderers and burned their city." Mt 22:6-7 The Lucan parable of the ten pounds has it, too. "A man of noble birth went into a far country to receive kingly power and then return. But his citizens hated him, and sent an embassy after him, saying, 'We do not want this man to rule over us.'" Judgment falls at the end. "As for those enemies of mine, who did not want me to rule over them, bring them here and slay them before me." Lk 19:14,27 The God of grace will not change his kingdom to suit critics who do not want his son.

Luke's account of Jesus' entry into Jerusalem includes a fragment which may likewise have anticipated this later crisis. "Pray for the peace of Jerusalem," pilgrims would sing. Ps 122:6 But Jesus wept and said, "Would that even today you knew the things that make for peace! But now they are hid from your eyes. For the days shall come upon you when your enemies will cast up a bank about you and surround you and hem you in on every side, and dash you to the ground, you and your children within you, and they will not leave one stone upon another in you; because you did not know the time of your visitation." Lk 19:42-44 "They have made their ways crooked; no one who goes in them knows peace," Isaiah grieved. Is 59:8

Nathanael

"Philip found Nathanael and said to him, 'We have found him of whom Moses in the law and also the prophets wrote, Jesus of Nazareth, the son of Joseph.'" Jn 1:44-51 Philip's saying captures the enthusiasm of all the disciples, once they saw Jesus as he really was and had been all along. Nathanael's cynical response, "Can anything good come out of Nazareth?" suggests hurt and disappointment. "Son of Joseph" for Jesus had been a code for "son of David," implying messiah-king. He had refused such a role. Worse, the zealotic effort had succeeded only in getting him crucified. What "good" had come out of Nazareth? Nothing! "Come and see," Philip replied. Somehow Nathanael came, perhaps toward Bethsaida, Philip's home town.

The fishing narrative in John identifies him as "of Cana." Jn 21:2 I infer that Nathanael was one of the youths on Philip's assigned route, to whom he had taught messages from Jesus. After the resurrection the disciples renewed these contacts, so as to tell the whole land of Jesus as they now knew him. This compact testimony is Nathanael's own. The evangelist-compiler found it among John's memoirs in Bethsaida, but the Cana-library would likely have had it first.

Jesus met Nathanael and Philip on their way. The point is not by what kind of sight they saw him but the revelation. As Nathanael told it, Jesus said to him, "Behold, an Israelite indeed, in whom is no guile." "Guile" had characterized the zealotic conspiracy around Jesus, but his death had purged it. Nathanael had returned from the Passover bitter and shamed, but now he was at least honest. "How do you know me?" he asked. Jesus replied, "Before Philip called you, when you were under the fig tree, I saw you." "Under the fig tree" was a metaphor of peace. "They shall sit every man under his vine and under his fig tree, and none shall make them afraid." 1 Kgs 4:25; Mic 4:4; Zech 3:10

"Peace," yes, but in Nathanael's case, defeat. He would put the collapse of his fantasy out of his mind and devote himself numbly to the family business.

But Philip's "Come and see," and his meeting Jesus, transformed everything. Whatever else may have entered the conversation, it yielded Nathanael's confession: "Rabbi, you are the son of God, you are the king of Israel." "Rabbi" honors Jesus as the teacher from whom Nathanael is now humbly willing to learn. As "the son of God," he is the one of whom "Moses and the prophets wrote," so Philip put it. Jesus not only had this name, he filled it full in service to his Father and people even through death, vindicated in his resurrection by God himself. "You are the king of Israel" acknowledges Jesus as Israel's "king" in truth—not zealotic, but "the son of God" who fought Israel's battle against the true enemy all alone and won. To realize this was for Nathanael a wondrous moment. His confession is that of the young church.

But there was more. Jesus had come to the "Israelite" Nathanael as the LORD had come to the patriarch Jacob of old, from whom "Israel" had its name. On the first night of his lonely flight, Jacob had seen in a dream a ladder linking him to heaven, with the angels of God ascending and descending on it. The LORD had affirmed to him what he had promised his fathers— to give him and his descendants this land. They would be "like the dust of the earth." In them he would "spread abroad to the west and to the east and to the north and to the south." Climactically, "by you and by your descendants shall all the families of the earth be blessed." Gen 28:11-15

That promise had been frustrated for ages, but Nathanael would see it realized through "the son of man (of God)" whose name he now confessed. "Truly, truly, I say to you, you will see heavens opened, and the angels of God ascending and descending on the son of man." The blessing of nations promised to the patriarchs was happening in Jesus.

(A copyist's corruption suggested that Nathanael should "believe" Jesus for his all-knowing deity, with greater visions still to come. "Because I said to you, I saw you under the fig tree, do you believe? You shall see greater things than these." Jn 1:50)

The Good Wine

I surmise that Nathanael became a leading voice for Jesus in Cana, and that the extended metaphor of the wedding at Cana condenses a message he once preached. Jn 2:1-11

"On the third day" signals Jesus' resurrection. "Marriage" is familiar language for the joy of the kingdom. "At Cana in Galilee" pictures this wonder as it reached Nathanael's own town. "The mother of Jesus" embodies the common folk of Galilee from whom he had sprung, in distinction from pure-blooded genealogy or the authority structure of synagogue and temple. "Jesus also was invited to the marriage with his disciples," among them Nathanael and his hearers. The longed-for day of God's kingdom is here. They enjoy its new wine in abundance!

But there is a grief. "*They* have no wine" refers to the others, those of synagogue and temple who plod on in their tradition, convinced of their rightness under the law, resisting and condemning Jesus still, waiting for a futurist kingdom that will never come. Who would notice what they are lacking? Who would call it to Jesus' attention? His mother—the common folk who have heard him with joy, who have eaten his bread of life and drunk his wine! His teaching reached their hearts in a way the tradition did not. The young church is celebrating the wedding, but the synagogue, the "bridegroom" for whom it was first intended, is missing out.

"They have no wine," she tells him, grieving.

Nathanael's picture story has Jesus responding, "Woman, what is it to me and to you?" Our God-appointed leaders have been given that responsibility. Shall we interfere with their ministry? Let them supply what is lacking! "My hour has not yet come." The metaphor glimpses Jesus on the old testament side of the cross. He had spoken his message in hope and without fear, yet he had not pushed himself on the leaders or tried to usurp their office. Nathanael's hearers understood his "hour," of course. It came when Jesus by his Father's will delivered himself to death, as many testimonies make clear. Jn 8:20; 12:27; 13:1 Mt 26:45

Now his hour has come, however, and the wedding is fulfilled. "Do whatever he tells you," his mother (the common folk) instructs the servants, among them Nathanael himself. There is hope still. By doing what Jesus tells them, they will supply the wine that is lacking, so that the bridegroom and all of God's people can be in on it.

The metaphor shifts to "six stone jars standing there, for the purifying of the Judeans." They are huge, "each holding twenty or thirty gallons." They patrol the entrance. Their size and strength depicts a demanding rock-like tradition. The authority and hope of Judeans is in them.

Two deficiencies appear, however. Fullness is needed for emptiness. A seventh of "rest" is needed for the six of labor. Matthew preserves a saying of Jesus: "I came not to destroy the law and the prophets but to *fill them full*. For truly I say to you, till heaven and earth pass away not a jot, not a dot, will pass from the law until all is accomplished. Whoever then relaxes one of the least of these commandments and teaches men so, shall be called the least in the kingdom of heaven.... For I tell you, unless your righteousness exceeds that of the scribes and Pharisees, you will never enter the kingdom of heaven." Mt 5:17-20

"Fill the jars with water," Jesus said. Fill the name of your "God Most High" with the name "Johwah, a God merciful and gracious." Ex 34:6 Fill your bloodline descent from Abraham with Johwah's word to Pharaoh, "Israel is my son, my first-born; let my son go that he may serve me." Ex 4:22-23 Fill your craving for a futurist kingdom and glory with the kingdom and glory that "rules over all" *now*. Ps 103:19; Mt 4:17 Fill your chosenness with the great commandment, "You shall love Johwah your God with all your heart, and with all your soul, and with all your strength," and a second like it, "You shall love your neighbor as yourself." Dt 6:4; Lev 19:18 Fill your "hunger and thirst for righteousness" with the "wine" and "milk" and "bread," which Isaiah said are bought "without money and without price." Mt 5:6; Is 55:1-2 Fill your temple and synagogue with the covenant-gospel and the Spirit of God. Is 61:1 "And they filled them to the brim."

He said to them, "Draw some out and take it to the steward of the feast," so they took it. The steward, "not knowing where this wine came from," will judge simply by the taste. Servants like Nathanael knew their water. They knew how Jesus had lived by that fullness as son and servant even to the cross, and how the Father turned his son's shame to glory by raising him from the dead. They knew his Spirit of life, "full of grace and truth," poured out on themselves and on any who would receive it. Jn 1:16-17 Fullness is the secret of the wine and thus of the marriage. The cup drawn from the "six" conveyed the "seven" of rest.

"The steward tasted the water now become wine." Then he rendered his verdict, not to the servants who brought him this sample, though, but to the bridegroom, the synagogue authority of Nathanael's Cana. It had been his wine all along, after all. "Every man serves the good wine first, and when people have drunk freely, then the poor wine; but you have kept the good wine until now!" the steward says.

He hands the bridegroom the cup, then waits expectantly for him to sip it. The bridegroom, trusting his stone jars, has upheld the tradition against Jesus, has even joined in condemning him. Yet if he will only taste Jesus' hour to its end, he will lose nothing! Shame will not destroy him, any more than it destroyed those who now confess Jesus' name. One taste, and he too will know the glory of this "first of all signs"—not the sort which zealots promoted and grievously misconstrued, not the sort which the Pharisees demanded as proof of Jesus' authority, but of simply tasting the joy of the wedding! "He manifested his glory, and his disciples believed in him!" Let the bridegroom taste for himself and so believe in him too!

The bridegroom holds the cup in hand, wondering whether he dare try even one sip. There the metaphor-sermon ends.

Epilogue

"Jesus said to the servants, 'Fill the jars with water.'
And they filled them to the brim."   John 2:7

"In the beginning was the word"—God's idea, his message. The young church called it "the gospel," meaning a joyful, liberating, transforming glad news. Prophets called it "the covenant of peace." Is 54:10; Ezek 34:25; 37:26 I call it the "covenant-gospel." This word created Israel as God's people in the first place. Its implications are epitomized in Jesus' covenant-Prayer. Since the natural human psyche cannot even imagine this wisdom, it is never self-generated but always revealed from outside the self. Moses told of hearing it at the burning bush. Jesus told of hearing a voice from heaven. The women told of angels. Resurrection witnesses reported how Jesus came to them, not how they found him. St. Paul told of "a man in Christ lifted up to the third heaven." Always this message comes from beyond human imagination.

At its core, the "gospel-word" reveals to human self-awareness (or heart) what ought to be obvious but is not—that everything is gift and that we are pure receivers, joyfully and freely dependent. To know this word is to know the God who speaks it. Awareness of gift yields knowledge of the Giver-Creator. This is the God whom no eye can see or imagination invent, but whose word and giving reveals him. That word created Israel, its worship and its scriptures. That word created Jesus. By him it created the young church and its scriptures.

Yet the word God speaks can be lost, rejected, emptied of meaning, fouled, compromised, counterfeited. The prophets saw it happen. So did Jesus and the young church. His command, "Fill the jars with water," deals with both emptiness and fouling. The "water" to fill them is his covenant-gospel. When filled, the jars yield the wine of joy for the wedding—for life and love and freedom to serve God in the kingdom-*now*. "Repenting," letting go whatever has fouled the truth of the gospel, is the glad side-effect of believing that truth.

"Christianity" (across a great divide from "the young church") has sacred forms or jars patrolling its entrance. So does Judaism. So does Islam. The jars are fouled, their content stale, thin, meager, futile and divisive. The task of the servants is not to accuse the emptiness or argue the fouling, not to clean the jars out or replace them either, but only to "fill them with water"—Jesus' own covenant-gospel. I see myself as such a servant and this book as "water" toward the filling. For me to preach or teach in worship is to dip out a bit of "wine" and offer it to my hearers. "The beginning of signs" Jesus did was his recovery of the gospel-wine. He filled the emptiness full even in his dying. This sign is the standard of any other.

His mother, metaphor of the Galilee from which Jesus had sprung, had tasted his wine. That is how she noticed the lack and could tell him so. Symptoms of lack abound in Christianity, also in Judaism and Islam—divisions, poverty of message, stress on the "seen" to compensate for loss of "the unseen," wars waged with zealotic weaponries against mistaken enemies. The young church, rejected by synagogue and temple as Jesus had been, wondered how this could have happened. "Who sinned, this man or his parents, that he was born blind?" Jn 9:2 Who was at fault? Such a question is futile, however. What matters is to bring "light" to those for whom the light has been obscured, or wine to those who have none. The covenant-gospel does this wonder. It can work healing and joy still, not for Christianity only, but for Judaism and Islam as well.

I have told how the disjunction happened between the young church and the Christianity in which I was brought up. Jesus' prescription works still. Pour the gospel in. Fill the old and familiar jars with the cleansing "gospel" so long lost. Fill the name "son of God" with covenant-meaning. Fill the scriptures with the authority of the gospel that brought them into being. Fill liturgies and hymnody, creeds and doctrines, with covenant-meanings. Fill scholarly study with the word that harnesses mind to heart. Fill painful divisions with cheerful patience to forgive and start over, to gather and heal. Trust the gospel to work blessings in its own way. Let anything perverse and distracting wither away unneeded, "repented" wholesomely and gladly.

I mention Islam out of a yearning that it may "start over," too. The story is painful. Muhammed (A.D. 570-632), a searching youth from Arabia, looked for wisdom first from the Jews, but felt rebuffed for his racial inferiority. He looked to Christianity but was repelled by the need to believe in "God the

Father, God the Son, and God the Holy Ghost"—"three gods," as he perceived it. He defied the Jews by declaring his own people the true covenant-descendants of Abraham through Ishmael. He defied Christianity by insisting on a piety of "one God." He defied both by writing his own inspired and authoritative scriptures. His successor, Omar, captured Jerusalem in A.D. 638. An early caliph, Abd al-Malik, built the Dome of the Rock on the temple mountain as a sanctuary of Islam. It was finished in A.D. 691, the interior unchanged since. Around the top of its inner octagon, 240 meters long, he inscribed in Arabic a legend including the words, "O you people of the Book, overstep not bounds in your religion, and of God speak only the truth. The Messiah, Jesus, son of Mary, is only an apostle of God and his Word, which he conveyed into Mary, and a Spirit proceeding from him. Believe therefore in God and his apostles, and say not Three. It will be better for you. God is only one God. Far be it from his glory that he should have a son."[1]

"Fill Islam's jars, too, with water." Fill them with Israel's election out of Egypt, "my son, my first-born"—not a mark of divine favoritism but a covenant-gospel whose honor and blessing was meant from the beginning to lift up valley-people and lower mountain-people of all nations to one straight and level way. Fill Islam's jars with Jesus' name from heaven, "my beloved son"—not deity, but the covenant-sonship intended for them as well. By this he knew his Father, prayed the prayer he taught us, fought temptation, gathered the lost, loved his people to the death, overthrew the real enemy, triumphed in resurrection, liberated the captives, poured out his Spirit, raised up the young church, and gathered the nations.

"Fill the jars with water." That directive images the text from Mark with which I began, "Repent, and believe the gospel." Taste its joy! Don't fear what its healing may do to you! Tell it and live it as Jesus did himself. See it work wonders from the heart out in those who hear it today, just as it did then. "The blind receive their sight and the lame walk, lepers are cleansed and the deaf hear, and the dead are raised up, and the poor have the gospel preached to them. And blessed is he who takes no offense at me!" Mt 11:5-6

---

[1] Jerome Murphy-O'Connor, *The Holy Land* (Oxford University Press, 1980), p. 61.

Glossary

Italics indicate cross-references

Aramaic. From **Aram** (Syria). Language related to Hebrew, widely prevalent in the Near East, spoken by Jesus, his *disciples* and the *young church*.

Atonement. Priestly corruption, written into scrolls ascribed to Moses—that *Johwah* does not forgive sins simply out of his own name and character, but must be appeased by blood sacrifices administered by priests. Basis for *Christianity's doctrine*.

Authority, hierarchy. Exercise of control over others by the right and power of office, with rankings from the top down.

Authority, sequence. Jesus' kind of authority. Filling one's place in a flow of *gifts*, received in *thanksgiving*, used in *servanthood*, passed on to others in *love* and *freedom*, trusting outcomes to God.

Baptism. The crossing of a boundary from an old life to a new. In Moses, through the sea. In John, through the Jordan. In Jesus, through death into resurrection and life with him. In Judean law, however, a name for various washings, with which these crossings came to be equated.

Believe. Grasp God's joyous and liberating *gospel* in *heart*, spontaneously, on simply hearing it. Trust it and want to live by it. In *Christianity*, learn and assent to the *doctrine* outlined by *theologians*, summarized in the creedal "I *believe.*"

Beloved son. See **First-born son.** Jesus' *name* beyond human parentage—the honored identity and relationship spoken by *Johwah* as *Father* and first-Giver to his people, *promising* his continuing gifts and care, *calling* them to a *servanthood* of free conformity to his *wisdom* and will—*believed* as glad news or *gospel*.

Bible. Collection of written documents, identified by *Christianity* as the inspired *word of God* and his infallible *truth*.

Bible-believing. Conviction that the *Bible*, by virtue of its divine inspiration, is to be believed without question in everything it says or is understood to say about anything.

Biblical authority. In *Christianity*, the *Bible* as the source and secure authority of all *doctrine*. True *biblical authority* rests in the *covenant-gospel*, however, which God spoke and his people *believed* long before stories and testimonies to it were written down and so preserved. This *gospel*, when simply heard, breaks through to *hearts* as *revelation* still—no other authority needed.

Blasphemy. Talk considered arrogant, disrespectful of God, punishable by stoning.

Calling. A theme of the *covenant-word*. God's people have their *name* of worth and honor from him, hence they do not need to make a *name* for themselves. They have the *promise* of care and blessing from him, hence they trust outcomes to him without needing to know and control the future. Their privileged *calling*, then, is to be in on his work day by day. Doing his will and walking his *way* freely, they invest the *gifts* he gives in every creative opportunity he opens to them, and in every *neighbor*.

Chosen (chosenness). *Covenant-language*, parallel to *beloved son*. Persons or people, called by the *covenant-word* to know *Johwah* as *Father*, receiving *life* and the *calling* of noble *servanthood* from him.

Christ. Hebrew, **Messiah.** Originally, one anointed by oil poured on the head, marking him as *chosen* by God for a particular service, like

David. In *zealotic* hope, a leader who would bring in the ultimate kingdom for God's people by defeating those they regarded as *enemy*. In the *young church*, Jesus, the *Christ* who did indeed save his people and give them the *kingdom*, not by dominating and conquering other people, but by living out his *covenant-name*, *son of God*, in love, all alone, even to death, raised up to reveal God's true *glory*.

Christianity. The religion inferred from the study of Greek documents about Jesus (the *Gospels* and others), by scholars (*theologians*) who could read and write, taught to folk who could not.

Coherence, principle of. Expectation that every memory, written down and then preserved in the *Gospels,* originated in and will make sense in relation to the *gospel* Jesus himself believed and taught.

Compiler. Scholar sent to find and access a library of written memories of Jesus in a Judean or Galilean church, translate each item accurately from *Aramaic* into Greek, arrange his findings in sequence, copy them on a scroll, then bring this treasure back to the church which had commissioned him.

Conscience. A *self-conscious* need to be approved and accepted by one's society. A force for conformity—whether to a moral sense of right and wrong, or to a prevailing cause, or to a dominating correctness, or even to the anti-society of a gang.

Copyist. Reproducer of a handwritten scroll, by reading the original text to skilled *scribes*, who wrote it neatly on fresh scrolls.

Covenant. Word of *revelation*, by which God invites one to know and serve him—the relationship of *oneness* closed and sealed when the hearer *believes* it, knows himself and God by it, and lives it. See **Word of God**.

Covenant-gospel. The revelatory *covenant* Jesus himself heard from *heaven, believed,* taught, and lived by. The *young church* titled this the "glad news" (from Isaiah); in old English, the *gospel*. See **Gospel**.

Covenant-language. Linguistic imageries used to express the *covenant* relationship—like *Father* and son, *Johwah* and his *chosen* people, husband and bride, mother and child, shepherd and flock, vinedresser and vineyard. Whatever the imagery, the meaning is the same.

Covenant-praying. The *heart*-response, verbalized in the Lord's Prayer, of children of the *Father* in *heaven*, who believe and live by his *covenant-word*, as Jesus did. By honoring his *name* they honor their own. They serve his *kingdom* by doing his will on earth. They pass on his giving and forgiving by a *love* learned from him. They follow his lead even in *temptations*, trusting him to deliver them from the *evil*.

Contrast the praying of people for whom *wisdom* consists in *knowing good and evil* by their own *eyesopened* desires and fears. They want a God who will pity them as they pity themselves, thus serve them rather than they him. His power should help them get what they want and save them from what they don't want. Their status, vows, and performances should impress him— also the quantity and quality of their sacrifices. If such a God does not do what they expect, they dismiss him, even deny that he exists.

Covenant-sonship. Rooted in Moses and the exodus history, the noble *name "son of God"* is epitomized in *Johwah's* word by Moses to Pharaoh, "Israel is *my first-born son*," and in the *voice-from-heaven* word to Jesus at his baptism, "*my beloved son.*" Incompatible with *Christianity's* illusion that "*son of God*" for Jesus means *deity*.

Covenant-word. "The *word of God*" (or of *the* LORD) is his *covenant-word*, not the *Bible* as book. *Believing* the *Bible* is incompatible with *believing* the *covenant-word* of God, just as *believing* the *Gospels* is incompatible with *believing* the *gospel*.

Death. Physiological dying is as natural for humans as it is for flowers and animals. The issue in *covenant* terms is not bodily dying, but the *death* of personhood, evident in self-centered lust and fear which yield rot and division— thereby the loss of the *eternal life* and *spirit* (breath) of God, for which he made human bodies in the first place.

Deity-believing. In *Christianity*, the object of *believing* is Jesus' presumed deity and the *doctrine* which *theologians* have inferred from it— not the *covenant-gospel* Jesus believed and taught, spoken by God to Israel first, but intended from the beginning for all nations, all peoples.

Deity-enhancement. *Copyists* assumed that Jesus, as the *deity-incarnate son of God*, had divine knowledge and power. They dictated signals of this into the copies their scribes were preparing, so that readers might see it in action, and so *believe* in him.

Deity-incarnate. A familiar notion in Greek, Roman, and Near-Eastern cultures. Scholars in the Greek world, reading the *Gospels* and Paul with no awareness of Israel's *covenant-sonship*, assumed that the name "my *beloved son*" or "*son of God*" for Jesus meant incarnate-deity, and that to *believe* in Jesus was to *believe* this of him. The birth narratives, and the testimony to Jesus in John's prologue as "the *word made flesh*," were misread in that light.

Demon. See **Spirit, unclean.**

Depth perspective. Viewing texts with an awareness of levels in the origin of the *Gospels*. Jesus' own *gospel* is the first level, from which every preserved memory must in some way have derived (*principle of coherence*). Events or sayings, originally communicated orally (second level), were remembered and recited again (third level) in the era of the *young church*. Then came the impulse to preserve these in writing (fourth level), gather them, then search and add items from other known collections. A *compiler* (fifth level) found such a library, translated each item from *Aramaic* into Greek, arranged his *fragments* in a sequence that seemed reasonable to him, then entered them on his scroll. A *copyist* dictating to his scribes (sixth level), could modify his original as he saw fit. Evidences of misperception at any later level, testify that meanings at the level of Jesus' original *gospel* were no longer known.

Devil. In *temptation* stories, the *devil* (*snake* or Satan*)* serves God by verbalizing to his *covenant-sons* the enticement of a *life* seemingly better than that of knowing and serving God, asserting and serving instead their individualistic desires and fears. Such testing is *Johwah's* own purposeful doing. For all the risk of losing them, he leaves his children free and independent, not animals, puppets or slaves. If they choose to cling to him, then, as Jesus did, they do so of their own free will, in glad *oneness* with him.

Direct memory. Term for memories preserved in the *Gospels*, which tell some outward detail of an event (most notably the Passion), recalled by someone who was there to observe it. *Metaphor*, by contrast, pictures the inside character of an event or conflict, which gives it enduring meaning.

Disciples. Also called "sons of *prophets*." In an age of *oral literacy*, young men, gathered by a *prophet*, would commit a concise message from him to memory, also its background meaning—then set out on assigned routes to recite and teach it to others, until it quickly became the talk of the whole land.

Doctrine. A teaching—specifically, the *gospel* Jesus taught, and the apostles after him. In *Christianity*, however, *doctrine* became first the teaching which *theologians* inferred from their study of the authoritative *Bible*—then the *doctrinal* systems adopted by majority vote at conventions, enforced by discipline and schism. Taught at seminaries, approved *doctrines* explain what a church believes and why, thus what the faithful must *believe* to be saved. See **Salvation.**

Enemy. The enemy is not persons or circumstances that appear *evil* to the *eyes-opened* judgment of a *sinner*. It is not *the devil*, *snake* or *temptation*, either. The *enemy* is the tyrannical illusion of *knowing good and evil* by nothing more than individualistic desire and fear. *Hearts* so snared cannot know and serve God, the Giver-Creator-Father, trusting outcomes to him.

Either-Or. The choice between two *wisdoms*, which the *covenant-word* poses to every one who hears it—illustrated by the two trees of Eden. Believe and live by the Tree of *Life (the word of God)*, or else by individualistic desires and fears. To live by both, or by neither, is not possible.

Eternal life. The breath (*spirit*) or character of *Johwah* (God as *Father*) in his people, ruling and hallowing their bodily aliveness here and now. Not a bodily afterlife tacked on to the first.

Evil. See **Knowing good and evil.** In the *wisdom* of covenant-truth, the only real *evil* is to not know and not serve *Johwah*.

Eyes-opened. The default *wisdom* that rules anyone who rejects or does not know the *covenant-word*. Judge *good* and *evil* by how things look. Direct mind and body toward taking the one and evading the other.

Father. Jesus' substitute name for *Johwah*, who had named Israel "my *first-born*" or "*beloved son.*" The prevailing piety, by a false humility, prohibited uttering the name *Johwah*, which God himself had given his people to know and call him.

Fear Johwah. A call to humility and *repentance*. God's *covenant-sons* are not to fear what looks *evil* to merely their *eyes-opened* judgment. When so *tempted*, let them fear him instead. Then they will not try to manipulate or bribe him into being what they want him to be and doing what they want him to do—thereby distrusting as *evil* the very *name* and grace by which he *named* Israel his people in the first place, and by which he patiently forgives their sins. For this *sin* there can be no forgiveness.

First-born son, my. *Johwah*'s name of honor and hope for an Israel enslaved in Egypt. By contrast, the ruling Pharaoh, to whom Moses declared this, was the first-born son of a mere Pharaoh, now dead.

Flesh and blood, also **body and blood.** "Flesh" and "body" are two translations of the same Hebrew-Aramaic word. It means physiological humanness, blood as its life, "shed" blood as death. Also, the impulses and *wisdom* of a bodily life ruled by *knowing good and evil*, distinct from bodily life when ruled by the *word and breath (spirit)* of God.

Fragments. "Gather up the fragments left over, that nothing may be lost," Jesus said—not crumbs of bread, but sayings of his once memorized, also testimonies of his disciples afterwards. People of the *young church,* raised by his resurrection, began to recite these from memory—then write them down, so that none would be lost.

Fragment-libraries. Independent sources of all four Gospels. "Twelve baskets" of *fragments* refer to random memories of Jesus, written down, gathered and treasured in towns of Judea and Galilee, then to some extent copied and exchanged.

Freedom. The privileged *sons of God*, heirs already of everything their *Father* in *heaven* owns, desire no *wisdom* or *kingdom* other than to do his will and imitate his character all the days of their *life* on earth. This is their *freedom*. Contrast *slavery*.

Fulfill. See **Prophet.**

Galileans. Mixed-race residue of Israel's deported ten tribes. The Galilee of Jesus and his disciples, once part of Ephraim (its capital Samaria), was conquered by Judea in 80 B.C. Its people worshiped in synagogue and temple, as *Judeans* did, but were viewed as inferior.

Gift, **Given**, and **Giver.** *Wisdom* to realize the obvious, that the world was here before you. Everything in it, including your own self and the self of every other human person, comes to you as pure *gift*, to be received in humble *thanksgiving*. Honor the *givens* you see, use them freely, thereby honor the *Giver*, whom you cannot see.

Good. See **Knowing good and evil.** In the *wisdom* of covenant-truth, the decisive *good* is to know, trust, thank, and serve *Johwah* alone, "for he is *good*, and his steadfast love endures forever."

Glory. In the *psyche* of *eyes-opened*, *glory* means the weight and worth of superior rank, recognition, and domination. The *glory* of God is viewed then as his rank and power above all *heavens*. To *praise* him is to humbly recognize his utter superiority. The *glory* his *chosen* people desire in turn, is to be ranked visibly above all nations.

In the *psyche* of *covenant-sonship*, *glory* is the weight and worth of receiving a place in the flow of *righteousness* from the *Father*. The *glory* of God is the *oneness* he initiates and fills full with his people in steadfast love. They *praise* him by filling full their place in *love*, and serving him in glad *freedom*. Jesus' weight of *glory* is the *righteousness* of the *sonship* he filled full in *love* for his *Father* and people even to death—not his *deity.*

Gospel. "Glad news" of *covenant-sonship*, which Jesus believed and taught, yet *unknown* to scribal and priestly tradition. People who heard Jesus believed his *gospel* joyfully and spontaneously. It opened a new world of *truth* and understanding, with power to honor and heal, liberate and gather. See **Covenant-gospel.**

Gospels. Visible scrolls, assembled very early from *fragments* of Jesus-memory. Cherished in the Greek world, and studied by scholars, they were titled *Gospels* when the invisible *gospel,* God's *covenant-word* to *hearts,* had become *unknown.*

Healing. Viewed through Jesus' *covenant-sonship,* healing stories are likely to be *metaphor* (blind, deaf, dumb, lame, leprous, demon-possessed, prisoner, dead, poor). His *covenant-gospel* effects a wholeness of personhood from the *heart* out in those who hear and *believe* it.

Viewed through Jesus' supposed *deity-incarnate,* the disabilities are literal-physiological. A command of divine power effects a visibly *miraculous* healing of body, summoning *belief* in Jesus as God.

Heart. In biblical usage, the inmost point of self-aware humanness— hidden beneath (and so determining) emotion, will, mind, body and behavior. Place within each personal "self" of a hunger for worth and meaning that must be fed. Pivot of *believing* or not *believing* the *gospel,* of knowing or not knowing the God who speaks it.

Heaven. Dwelling place of God, above and beyond human sight and thought, as in Jesus' prayer to "Our Father, who is in heaven." In his day, also a supposedly humble substitute-name for God, as in oaths sworn *by heaven,* or in phrases like *kingdom of heaven* and *voice-from-heaven.*

Hebrew. The language of the Hebrews, specifically Israel.

Historical-critical method. Search for the meaning of any biblical text, on the assumption that the words so preserved were framed by a human mind like our own and within a history like our own. To those who know Jesus by his *covenant-word,* such inquiry is a noble *gift* and *calling.* "Ask, and it will be given you," Jesus promised. Rejected by *Bible-believers,* however, as a rationalistic repudiation of biblical authority, undermining the historicity of events on which the faith and *doctrine* of *Christianity* is founded.

Historical evidence. Any visible residue of human minds and bodies at work in the past, including writings, which an inquirer may regard as relevant to his quest for meanings.

Historical imagination. The capacity of a human mind today (the manner of its working not different from that of minds past) to think again the thoughts that prompted actions and testimonies long ago, and thereby comprehend the history. Analogous to a detective's mind at work in solving a crime.

Historical Jesus. Jesus, as people of his own time and place knew him personally, and to whom they responded in conflicting ways—prior to the *glory* ascribed to him in the *Gospels* and Epistles, prior to the *doctrine* and *believing* of *Christianity.* Jesus, as scholars have been trying to know him for more than two centuries.

Historical reconstruction. When separate items of *historical evidence* relate to the same event, the mind of an historian works to fill in gaps, so as to perceive, without prejudice or force, what the event would likely have been which left these remnants behind, each in its place.

Hope. Confidence that enables children of God, in the *way* of Jesus, to fill full their glad and free *servanthood* each day, leaving tomorrow to the *Father* whose *promises* will not fail—noticing his *signs and wonders* with *thanksgiving,* trusting him to fit it all together beyond sight and mind. One day he will finish what he began when he sent them into the world—then take them home to himself as he did Jesus, in the *eternal life* and *glory* which has been theirs all along. Like Jesus, they need and ask for nothing more.

Hypocrite. Literally "under judgment." See **Self-conscious.** A *metaphoric* imagery, intended by Jesus as diagnosis, not insult. The law and tradition of synagogue and temple yielded a *psyche,* not of knowing and serving God in love and glad *freedom,* but of play-acting performances designed to impress an audience, gain approval and avoid disapproval, directed by (but disguising) a self-serving *heart.*

Interpolation. Comment preserved in the *Bible,* but inserted by a *copyist,* as he read to his scribes from a scroll—toward clarifying what he felt readers might find confusing, or supplying an insight he thought they should not miss. Detectable as violating the *principle of coherence* or out of place.

Jesus stories. Memorizable testimonies to the wonder of Jesus from after the resurrection, framed in *metaphor,* taught and circulated orally with commentary. When these were gathered and written down on scrolls, person-to-person comments were lost and *heart* meanings *unknown.* Scholars studied in private by the mind of their own culture. *Christianity* took form from their mistaken impressions—not from the *covenant-gospel* of Jesus and the young church, source of such memories and testimonies.

Johwah. The *name* God gave Moses and Israel to know him by. Viewed in Jesus' day as too holy to be uttered, it was hidden under a pious "the *Lord.*" English Bibles signal *Johwah* by capitalizing, "*the* LORD" (or GOD). Silencing the *name* testifies to the loss of its meaning, however: "*Johwah, Johwah,* a God merciful and gracious, slow to anger and abounding in steadfast love,... forgiving iniquity and transgression and sin, but who will not clear the guilty." This *Johwah* will not change to suit kings, priests, or people, who *praise* him above the heavens, but will not hear and know him on earth by his *covenant-word.*

Judeans. Descended from the exiles who returned to Judea from Babylon, they took their special *chosenness* to imply favoritism in God's sight. They thought to please him (as their pre-Exilic fathers had not), by keeping their blood-descent from Abraham pure from the nations. In their own minds, they ranked superior also to mixed-race *Galileans*, Idumeans and the like. They observed laws that marked their special identity and kept them distinct. Thus they would qualify for God's futurist *kingdom.*

Kingdom-now. The kingdom of God, as Jesus taught it, is not future but here and now, entered without special qualifications by children who, upon simply hearing and believing the *covenant-word*, belong to and honor God as their *Father*. His kingdom comes when they, *repenting* and letting go falsities that have snared them, do his will in their bodies on this earth in every today, as angels do it in *heaven*, trusting tomorrow and its outcomes to him.

Knowing good and evil. The deceptive alternative to knowing God by his *covenant-word* and will. Be *wise* on your own, without God or anybody else, as though the world began with and centers on you. Whatever looks *good* to your eyes, act to take it. Whatever looks *evil*, act to avoid it. See **Temptation** and **Eyes-opened.**

Law. See **Torah.** Synonym for God's *covenant* made known by Moses, cherished by a people who hear and believe his *word*, thus know and serve him freely. In the age of writing, perverted into rules attributed to Moses, designed to demonstrate the special status of God's people—anticipating a day of reward for the faithful and judgment against the disobedient and outsiders.

Life. See **Eternal life.**

Lord. *Name* of respect, indicating a realistic, thankful and trusting dependency—receiver to giver, learner to teacher, servant to master. Often addressed to God.

Lord, the. In capitals. See **Johwah.**

Love. The character of *Johwah* in his people. In *oneness* with him and trusting his care, they pass on his giving and forgiving freely by their own love—without lust or fear, pride or envy, rights or rankings, concern to make a *good* impression or avoid an *evil* one. Such love transcends *eyes-opened* romance, friendships and alliances. It perceives a common human *heart* beneath evident diversities (righteous or sinner, rich or poor, young or old, black or white, male or female, friend or enemy). See **Neighbor.**

Love Johwah. God's covenant-sons or people do not *love* what looks *good* to merely their *eyes-opened* judgment. The *good* they *love* is their *Giver*-Creator-*Father*—to receive his *gifts*, trust his *promises*, serve him in *oneness* and walk his *way.*

Metaphor. Artful picture-image or story, common in *oral literacy*, analogous to a cartoon, designed to reveal and address a *heart*-conflict in the actual history. Hearers, for whom such a story was intended, could not miss the *either-or* they needed to face. Such stories, crisply framed for memorizing, were spread widely, person-to-person, with explanation. Writing preserved the words, but meanings (why they were told so) need to be searched by the *principle of coherence.*

Miracle. Frequent mistranslation of "signs." See **Signs and wonders. Healing.**

Name. A theme of the *covenant-word.* God's people receive their name, worth, and world from him. To know and honor God by the name *Johwah* or *Father,* is to know and honor their own name in relation to him—thus to *love* and *fear* him, as receivers, who depend on him humbly and gladly for everything they purpose and do. This is the rock-foundation of *servanthood* in *freedom.*

Neighbor. Another human person whose life touches yours. To "love your neighbor as yourself" is to see in that other, beneath external diversities, a "self" equal to and like your own. *Love* will not measure this other as *good* or *evil,* superior or inferior, desirable or undesirable, friend or *enemy,* to be exploited or avoided. It will create *oneness* instead, by passing on the flow of God's giving and forgiving as a high and noble *calling,* regardless of risk or cost.

New covenant. God's *covenant* with Israel, falsified by temple and synagogue, retrieved in Jesus. He filled it full in his own *sonship* and *servanthood,* even to death. In his resurrection and by his *gospel,* God's people can start over new, *sins* forgiven, *demons* expelled, born from above, liberated from emptiness and futility, raised from death to *eternal life.* (See **Testament**).

Oneness. The vision and *promise* of God's *covenant-word,* its circle closed by simply hearing and *believing* it. *Johwah's* non-partiality—the hidden commonality and equality of human personhood and worth everywhere and in every age—liberates diversities for the work of each, without value-judgments of pride or envy, in a flow of *righteousness* from the "one God and Father of all, who is above all and through all and in all." The circle of *oneness* between *Johwah* and his people closes also between each other, in *love* and honor. Man and woman are one in marriage and family. Nations, races and languages find peace and mutual honor in the God who "makes wars cease to the end of the earth."

Oral literacy. The literacy of an age when writing was unknown or reserved to scholars. Song, story, rhythmic wisdom, and *prophecy* were framed precisely, word-for-word in the mind of a *prophet* or poet, then spread to others by reciting and memorizing. Parents taught sacred memory with meanings to their children. Young men, called *disciples* or sons of *prophets,* taught their messages, with background comment, systematically and quickly to the whole land.

Overlay. Every memory of Jesus preserved in the *Gospels* was written down only after and in light of his death and *resurrection*—turning point of old *covenant* into new. The location of each *fragment* on a scroll was decided by a *compiler* from the

Greek world. Since his knowledge of actual events was limited, and his understanding of texts often mistaken, he placed items or wordings before Jesus' death, which were actually knowable only by way of and after his resurrection. These must be held apart as "overlay." The history they reveal is of the *young church* which produced them, not of Jesus within his ministry.

Parable. See **Metaphor.** A story imagery, memorizable and communicated originally mouth-to-ear, designed to make graphic a distortion which had snared God's people, so that they might *repent* of it, know and trust *Johwah* by his authentic *covenant-word*, and start over new.

Pharisees. Party of exemplary leaders, men and their families, committed to obey the *law* as taught by the *scribes.*

Praise. The response of *hearts* who know and belong to *Johwah*, freed from the tyranny of *knowing good and evil.*

Promise. A theme of the *covenant-word.* God invites the people he has *named* his own to simply do his will (their *calling*), trust his *promises*, thus leave outcomes to him. "You shall walk in all the *way* which *Johwah* your God (source of your *name*) has commanded you (your *calling*), that you may live, and it may go well with you (his *promise*)." "Seek first (your *calling*) his *kingdom* and his *righteousness,* and all these things shall be yours as well (*promise*)."

Prophet. Also **Prophecy.** One whom *Johwah* called and equipped to renew his *covenant-word* and *calling* to a people who had lost and compromised it. "False prophets" claimed to speak for *Johwah*, but conformed his word to their desires and fears— laws of sacrifice to gain his favor, or favorable predictions of future events.

Christianity erred similarly. Not knowing *covenant* meanings, it mistook "scriptures fulfilled" to mean "predictions come true"—missing the wonder that in Jesus and the *young church*, *covenant-words* of the prophets, long empty, were being filled full of meaning again, their *revelatory truth* heard, with power to liberate and heal.

Psyche. Human behavior is driven by two possible *psyches.* A *heart* secure in the honor and *hope* of *covenant-sonship* from outside the self yields a life of *servanthood* in noble *freedom,* trust and *love.* A *heart* that must satisfy its innate hunger for worth and rightness on its own is anxious and insecure. It summons mind and body *self-consciously* toward proving itself worthy and defending its rightness in any way it can.

Repent. Give up a distortion for the sake of *truth.* Hear the noble *way* *of Johwah. Believe,* and keep it. Rest secure in his love and forgiveness, trust his care and *promises,* and so love and serve him alone. For such a treasure, "sell everything you have" and start over new. *Christianity,* however, takes "repent" to mean confess your sins, feel sorry for them, want to do better, believe the doctrine, and so qualify to be forgiven.

Resurrection. The miracle that those who *repent* are raised from *death* to *life*—not future, but in the bodily life that is theirs here and now. The *promise*, "on the third day he will raise us up, that we may live before him," realized in Jesus, enables those named *sons of God* with him to persist in doing the *Father*'s will on earth to the finish, as he did, at the risk and cost even of bodily death, confident that, delivered from the real *evil*, they will "live before him."

Pharisees and priests (Sadducees) took *resurrection* to mean a futurist resuscitation of the corpses of the faithful who died before the "last day"—so that, when the kingdom of glory came, they would have part in it still. *Pharisees* and common piety believed this, *Sadducees* did not. *Christianity*, too, not knowing the *covenant-gospel* and its promises, assumes likewise that resurrection must mean resuscitated corpses—Jesus' resuscitated body the visible proof.

Revelation. The people of God come to know him, not by sight, reason or imagination, but by hearing from outside themselves his *gospel* of *name*, *promise*, and *calling*. This comes always as *revelation* from God. *Eyes-opened* to *know good and evil* could never imagine it. *Hearts* that hear this *covenant-word* believe it spontaneously and live by it freely. It satisfies their hunger for worth, purpose, and *hope*, in a way that no human striving can ever achieve.

Righteousness. "Righteousness like an ever-flowing stream," as Amos envisioned it, means to be given a place and to fill it, in the flow that originates in *Johwah*. It is to receive everything from upstream as gift, then pass the flow downstream and around in a *love* like *Johwah*'s own. The secret hunger of every human *heart* for *righteousness* is filled by Jesus' *covenant-gospel*—to know my worth as secure from the beginning, who I am and to whom I belong, where I came from and where I am going, how I fit in and what I am doing here. To do it and so be at peace. See **Authority, sequence.**

Sadducees. Party associated with priestly understanding and authority in Jerusalem and Judea.

Salvation. To be delivered by God from *sin* and *death* here and now, thus restored to the *way of Johwah* in the *kingdom-now*. Not a futurist kingdom or escape from *evil*, like dying and going to a supposedly better world or *life* in *heaven*.

Scribes. Men trained to read and write documents, a requirement for teachers in synagogue and temple. Respected by the common folk (whose *literacy* was merely *oral)* for their knowledge and teaching of the sacred writings, scribes came to be called Rabbi, literally Great One or Master.

Self-awareness. Capacity inherent in humans (distinct from animals), to be aware not only of the world outside but of oneself within that world—thus to be both subject and object of the same sentence (like, "I think about myself"). Capacity to be aware also of one's own self-awareness, to think about one's own thinking, to probe one's own *heart.*

Self-consciousness. *Self-awareness* turned inward. Sense of being judged, fear of being viewed as guilty or inadequate. Need to make a *good* impression (by dress, performance, personality) and to avoid an *evil* one (lies, excuses, cover-ups, seduction of others, bluff, accusing accusers, silencing witnesses). See **Conscience.**

The stability of being out from under judgment altogether, without need for compliments or fear of criticisms, does not occur. It is knowable only by *revelation* from outside the self—the *gospel* of *covenant-sonship.*

Servant. The *calling* of sons in their *Father's* house. "Let my son go, that he may serve me," *Johwah* told Pharaoh by Moses. Sons already possess everything that is their Father's. Working with and for him is the honor and purpose of *life* itself—glad and free, trusted and trusting, needing no supervision, looking for no reward.

Signs and wonders. Indications of the hand and presence of God, noticed with awe and *thanksgiving*—how *Johwah* pours out his promised care and blessings beyond expectation on sons who trust and serve him even through hard testings.

Popular piety looked for "signs and wonders" as hinting grander wonders about to come—like the long-desired kingdom and *glory* of Israel as God's favored people. By whispering stories of these, self-anointed *zealotic christs* rallied bold and courageous men to their cause, ready to fight for God, counting on his miraculous intervention to give them the victory.

Sin and **sinner.** See **Ungodly. Wicked.** The *psyche* and status of those for whom *wisdom* consists in *knowing good and evil* by their own *eyes-opened* desire and fear. Every choice is dictated, then, by what will work for personal advantage at the moment.

Slavery. The lot and lostness of people driven by no *wisdom* other than to have their own way, doing their own self-assertive will, thinking that God (if there is a God) should help them and that nothing and nobody hinder them. Contrast *freedom.*

Snake. Image of corrupted humanness. Snakes, unable to stand upright, see no horizon beyond self. Low in the dirt, they slither cleverly right and left to take any immediate good and evade any immediate evil. Humans, made to stand upright, can see horizons beyond self, yet they readily descend to "snakehood."

Son of God. *Covenant* meaning: God's people (gender-inclusive) deriving from him as *Father*, dependent on him, belonging to him and he to them, formed in his image and character, serving him in their bodies on earth. Jesus heard this *name* of himself at his baptism and lived it even to death. Greek, Roman and Near Eastern minds missed this, however. By their own culture, they took "son of God," in documents of *Christianity,* to herald Jesus as *deity-incarnate.*

Son of man. A piously humble opposite of *son of God* (though hinting at it still), with precedent in the scriptures. By referring to himself so, Jesus conformed to the prevailing piety. People understood the device, however, and did not miss his point, the *covenant-gospel*.

A culture that took *son of God* for Jesus to mean *deity-incarnate*, inferred that *son of man* meant his human nature, then imposed this falsity on text after text of the scriptures.

Spirit, holy. The breath of God as the life and character of his son or people, by which they believe his *covenant-word* even against sight, and live in glad oneness with him. *Christianity* obscured this. It made the *Holy Spirit* a "person" alongside *Father* and *Son*, thus completing a "Trinity."

Spirit, unclean. See **Demon.** Alien breath and character, which possesses people who do not know the Giver-Creator-God or give him thanks. They feed their hunger for worth by strategies of self-centered and self-assertive desire or fear. The behavior that results is not of honor and peace but of rot and division, often horrifying. Only the *covenant-word* can drive out such demons.

Temptation. See **Devil.** A testing. Situations of *eyes-opened* attraction (lust) or threat (fear), verbalized in some cases by *snake* or *devil*, put every *son of God* (like Jesus) to the test—alone, without supervision or prompting. A choice is inescapable. *Either*

live by the *Father's covenant-word* and *promise, or die* by the devices of self-assertion or self-salvation.

Here is a wonder of *Johwah* and the humanness he made. To face this choice with the possibility of choosing even against God, is the ultimate *freedom*. To walk through straight and upright, as Jesus did, rather than descend to slithering like a *snake*, is the *life* and nobility of the *sons of God*. Yet only from him is this even known.

Testament. A variant translation of *covenant*. The invisible *gospel* Jesus heard, believed and taught, rooted in Moses. *Christianity*, not knowing this, took *testament* as title for two parts of its visible documents. Those that derived from temple and synagogue it called "old," and those that testified to Jesus "new." This shift obscured the *new covenant* (or *testament*) of which Jeremiah spoke, perceived by the *young church* (Paul and Hebrews) as filled full by Jesus' "blood" (death) and resurrection.

Thanksgiving. The response of *hearts* who discover the wonder that everything is *gift*, and thereby know the *Giver*.

Theology. A science in *Christianity*—the study of God, based on the *authority* of the *Bible*. Scholars engaged in it were called "theologians," and their findings *doctrines*.

Torah. When treasures of *covenant*-wisdom and story, originally of *oral literacy*, were preserved in writing, temple scholars came to revere their scrolls as sacred. At some point they took the term "Torah of Moses" (the invisible *covenant-word* which Moses taught orally), as title for five visible scrolls, Genesis to Deuteronomy. This change of meaning shifted Moses' authority from what he had spoken to documents he had supposedly written. It also shifted authority from the word of *prophets* who preached to that of scholars who could read and write. See **Law.**

Truth. God's *covenant-gospel* of *name, promise,* and *calling,* heard from outside the self, embodied in Jesus. Also true is the *freedom* of humans, when given the choice, to prefer its seductive but deadly obverse—the "like God" *wisdom* of self-assertive *eyes-opened knowledge of good and evil.*

Two-document hypothesis. The long-prevailing theory of scholars regarding the origin of the *Gospels.* Mark, the first Gospel, derived his view of Jesus' deity-sonship from Paul—hence must have written late, perhaps 70 A.D. Matthew and Luke both had Mark as a source. A second source ("Q," from the German *Quelle)* provided other materials they have in common. Each had a further source of his own. John, near the turn of the century, culminated the view of Jesus as *deity.*

Ungodly. See **Sin and sinner.**

Unknown. For God's people then or Christianity, "unknown" diagnoses darkness in need of light, not willful sin. "Father forgive them, for they know not what they do," Jesus prayed. "I know you acted in ignorance, as did your rulers," Peter preached. "I received mercy because I had acted ignorantly in unbelief," Paul said. This book calls attention to an unknown darkness so that light may come, emptiness be filled, and ignorance *repented.*

Voice-from-heaven. A *revelation*—the *word of God* breaking in from outside natural *self-awareness,* to make known a *wisdom* of *truth,* honor and purpose, basic to all humanness, which no mind or imagination can discover on its own.

Way (of Johwah). The integrity of *life* and understanding, governed by the *covenant-word* to the *heart,* forming his people in his image, so that they walk his straight and level *way* of *life* freely in *love,* trust and *hope.*

Wicked. See **Sin** and **Sinner.**

Wisdom. "The *fear* of *Johwah* (rather than of *eyes-opened evil)* is the beginning of wisdom." "I thank you, my Father, Lord of heaven and earth, that you have hidden these things from the wise and understanding and revealed them to babes." "Whoever hears these sayings of mine and does them is like a wise man, who built his house upon a rock."

Word of God, or **Word of Johwah.** *Revelation* from God, its substance the *covenant-gospel,* or *voice-from-heaven,* making known to human *hearts* what a corrupted *psyche* cannot imagine. Framed in words by *prophets* and communicated by *disciples* to the people.

Christianity fell into the snare of naming its visible documents "the *word of God,*" however. From this initial fallacy, it deduced logically the inspiration and inerrancy of the *Bible.* "The Holy *Spirit* cannot deceive," it was said, and "*The word of God* cannot err." Such *authority* made the *Bible* itself an object of *believing*—thus rendering the *authority* and *believing* of Jesus' own *gospel unknown.* See **Covenant.**

Word made flesh. Summary testimony of John's Prologue concerning Jesus—that he not only heard, believed and taught Israel's ancient *covenant-word*, but filled full the work of *servant* to which it called him in his body, even to *death.* Thus he was the only *son* of the *Father,* full of grace and *truth*, now returned to the bosom of the *Father* who sent him. To see and *believe* Jesus is to know and believe the word God spoke from the beginning, by which he created heaven and earth, and gave light to the world. To reject or deny him is to reject and deny the very *covenant-word* that made Israel God's people in the first place.

Young church. *Disciples* and people who knew Jesus personally and had part in his ministry and death. Raised from *death* by his *resurrection*, they are the source of every memory and testimony preserved in the *Gospels.*

Zealotry. The piety of common folk, zealous for the *law*, who cherished hero-stories of *Johwah's* past interventions, and looked for *signs and wonders* to indicate his ultimate deliverance about to come. As God had enabled those who called on him to defeat their enemies against unspeakable odds, so he would one day send an anointed one (Greek *Christ*), like David, to establish the kingdom of his *chosen* people forever, if only they were faithful to him and ready to fight for his cause.

Appendix B

Index of Biblical Citations

About the Author

Paul G. Bretscher, a pastor of the Lutheran Church—Missouri Synod, served Redeemer Lutheran Church, New Orleans, during the 1950s, taught religion at Valparaiso University (Indiana) in the 1960s, received his doctorate from Concordia Seminary St. Louis in 1966. In 1969 he became pastor of Immanuel Lutheran Church, Valparaiso. He has done much lecturing and writing, including seven books. Upon retiring in 1992 at age 70, he undertook this work.

Membership in the Synod's Commission on Theology, 1967 to 1975, involved him in its controversy over biblical authority — caused, in his mind, by a fatal misunderstanding of *the word of God* and the *gospel*. As often in Christianity, the end was not healing but division.

Paul and Marguerite, his wife of 52 years, were blessed with ten children, twenty-three grandchildren. She died in 1998. In September 2000 he married Constance Felten, retired teacher in Immanuel School, widowed in 1998 after a marriage of 55 years.

About the Dove Group

Realizing that no church or scholarly house can publish a work so out of step with orthodox doctrine, and yet of faith, a number of people who have known and trusted Pastor Bretscher's ministry through the years took on the mission in January 2000 of making known and preserving "Christianity's unknown gospel" by publishing and disseminating this book. They derived the name "Dove" from the author's street at the time.

"Dove Group, Inc." is registered in the State of Indiana as a non-profit corporation.

Dove Group, Inc.
P.O. Box 1035
Valparaiso, IN 46384-1035